COURSEBOOK to accompany

MICROECONOMICS
PRIVATE AND PUBLIC CHOICE

SEVENTH EDITION

A. H. STUDENMUND
Occidental College

JAMES D. GWARTNEY
Florida State University

RICHARD L. STROUP
Montana State University

THE DRYDEN PRESS
Harcourt Brace College Publishers

Fort Worth   Philadelphia   San Diego   New York   Orlando   Austin   San Antonio
Toronto   Montreal   London   Sydney   Tokyo

Address for Editorial Correspondence
The Dryden Press, 301 Commerce Street, Suite 3700, Fort Worth, TX 76102

Address for Orders
The Dryden Press, 6277 Sea Harbor Drive, Orlando, FL 32887
1-800-782-4479, or 1-800-433-0001 (in Florida)

ISBN: 0-03-094847-9

Printed in the United States of America

4 5 6 7 8 9 0 1 2 3   0 9 5   9 8 7 6 5 4 3

The Dryden Press
Harcourt Brace College Publishers

PREFACE

We are often asked why we call this book a *Coursebook* rather than a "study guide." We use the title *Coursebook* because we feel that this volume goes well beyond the typical study guide in at least three ways:

1. *Critical Analysis*   We stress questions that require in-depth economic reasoning. Most of these more analytical questions force students to come up with their *own* answers rather than passively choosing between a group of prepared alternatives.
2. *Readings and Debates*   We include short and interesting readings by a broad spectrum of economists. For example, we have paired opposing viewpoints on given topics into a series of debates. These debates not only provide material for classroom discussion, they also allow students to develop their own opinions on the issues. We also include some interesting crossword puzzles.
3. *Explained Answers*   For more than half the questions, we include explanations of *why* a particular answer is correct. We also provide some references to sections in the text that explain topics in more detail.

In writing this *Coursebook,* we have attempted to strike a balance between economic reasoning and mechanics. Often, a supplementary workbook is little more than a set of mechanical exercises. Such exercises lack substance and meaning for the student who has not yet acquired a firm foundation in the economic way of thinking. Our teaching experience has shown that stressing real-world situations, presenting actual data, providing selected short readings, and explaining why particular answers are correct—as we have done in the *Coursebook*—illuminate the power and utility of economic reasoning.

The *Coursebook* has been structured to maximize the student's comprehension of the concepts presented in each chapter of *Macroeconomics: Private and Public Choice,* Seventh Edition. Each chapter is divided into several sections that combine the instruction of economic principles, as covered in the text, with mechanical exercises.

The first section of each chapter is composed of approximately 14 true-false questions. Although this section has a realistic flavor, mechanics are emphasized. "Problems and Projects," the second section, emphasizes both mechanics and economic reasoning. This section contains some case-study-type problems as well as some questions that ask students to review basic concepts. The third section, "Learning the Mechanics—Multiple Choice," contains multiple-choice questions of the type familiar to most students. Many questions are sufficiently difficult to challenge even knowledgeable students. Questions posed in the fourth section, "The Economic Way of Thinking—Multiple Choice," often utilize actual data to emphasize economic reasoning. Some items test the student's ability to distinguish between sound logic and economic nonsense; others ask the student to devise the proper policy for reaching a given set of economic goals. To answer these "complex application"-type questions, the student must be able to apply principles to realistic situations. For students unaccustomed to critical thinking, these questions will be difficult; yet they present a challenge far more stimulating than exercises that test rote learning. Finally, each chapter contains discussion questions that are intended to provoke further speculation on economic issues.

More than merely a workbook, the *Coursebook* serves as a reader, presenting a "Perspectives in Economics" section in almost every chapter. These articles are readable and engaging, will reinforce the classroom presentation of economic lessons, and will expand on important concepts discussed in the text. Some articles offer an historical perspective, clearly stating the views of such renowned economists as Milton Friedman or Walter Heller. Other readings give students the opportunity to read firsthand the ideas of newer voices such as Sam Bowles or Robert Crandall. Following each selection are questions asking the student to evaluate the position of the author. Is the reasoning sound? Is it opinionated? Does empirical evidence support the author's contention? This feature of the *Coursebook* again highlights the usefulness of economics in our everyday lives.

A popular item for students is a series of "Current Debates in Economics," paired readings that express opposing viewpoints on such topics as "Should We Raise the Minimum Wage?" and "Should We Have a Market Economy?" These debates will force students to come to grips with differences in opinion among economists and to form their own views on the issues. In addition, classes can stage formal "debates," allowing some or all of the students to develop their argumentation and oral presentation skills.

We also include some crossword puzzles in the *Coursebook*. These puzzles, which originally appeared in *The Margin*, provide a relaxing and interesting way for students to review economic definitions and concepts.

Answers to virtually every question are provided in the "Answer Key" at the back of the *Coursebook*. The Answer Key also contains two unique features that will make the questions significantly more useful for student learning. First, all the multiple-choice answers are followed by an explanation of why that particular answer is correct. In addition, we often refer the student to the section where the subject of the question is discussed in *Macroeconomics: Private and Public Choice*. In this way, a student who does not get the correct answer the first time can get an explanation of the correct answer. If that explanation is not convincing, then the student can refer to the corresponding section in the text. Students who take the time to master these questions—and who understand the rationale behind each answer—should do very well in introductory economics classes.

The Seventh Edition of the *Coursebook* has been blessed by the contributions of two talented individuals who were not previously involved with this project. Professor Mary Hirschfeld of Occidental College gave us excellent chapter by chapter suggestions for revising and upgrading the old edition. Rebecca Kopchik, a senior economics major at Occidental, provided feedback on the book from a student's point of view and helped with the task of updating questions and preparing copy for publication. Others to whom we owe a debt of gratitude include Phil Jerome, John Pike, and Betty Tracy of Occidental, Jeanie Anirudhan, Sheryl Nelson and Carlyn Hauser of The Dryden Press, and Jaynie, Scott, and Connell Studenmund. To these folks and everyone else involved in the Seventh Edition, we offer our heartfelt thanks.

A. H. Studenmund
Richard L. Stroup
James D. Gwart-

ney

CONTENTS

Economics *Microeconomics*

C H A P T E R   O N E

THE ECONOMIC APPROACH

TRUE OR FALSE

T   F

☐ ☐   1. According to economic theory, if there is an increase in the benefit derived from an activity, individuals will be more likely to choose that activity.

☐ ☐   2. The opportunity cost of going to a movie is the cost of tickets, popcorn, and drinks *plus* any money spent on transportation or babysitters.

☐ ☐   3. If human action were not influenced by changes in cost and benefits, economics would not have any predictive value.

☐ ☐   4. Only the actions of selfish men are influenced by economic incentives.

☐ ☐   5. Economic activity often has secondary effects that are not initially observable.

☐ ☐   6. Economic theory cannot be tested because it involves human decision-makers.

☐ ☐   7. One's use of time involves economic choice.

☐ ☐   8. Economists utilize empirical evidence from the real world in order to test the validity of economic theory.

☐ ☐   9. Positive economic statements involve value judgments about how the world "should be."

☐ ☐   10. Scientific methodology can be used to test normative economic statements.

☐ ☐   11. The following is a positive economic statement: "An increase in the price of butter will lead to a reduction in the quantity of butter purchased by consumers. (All else constant.)

☐ ☐   12. If public education is freely provided to the consumer, it will not qualify as a scarce or economic good.

☐ ☐   13. Economics is based on the principle that changes in economic incentives cause human decision-makers to alter their courses of action.

☐ ☐   14. Economic analysis applies only to those choices that relate to the production or consumption of physical goods.

☐ ☐   15. A person's well-being is dependent only on the consumption of material goods.

PROBLEMS AND PROJECTS

1. For each question below, use the indicated guidepost from the text to help you answer the question and explain your answer:

   a. Guidepost 1: Do "full scholarships" make education free?

   b. Guidepost 2: According to federal and state laws, Exxon was responsible for a complete cleanup of its 1989 Alaskan oil spill. Should economizing behavior have played a role in the cleanup?

   c. Guidepost 3: Suppose a sudden increase in the quality of television increased the value of leisure time to the average citizen. Would this be likely to cause a decline in the proportion of citizens who vote?

   d. Guidepost 4: Halfway through your economics course, you consider dropping the course because of its heavy workload. What should you base your decision on, the total workload of the course or the remaining workload?

   e. Guidepost 5: Should the Food and Drug Administration require that all new drugs for AIDS be exhaustively tested for safety and effectiveness before approving their use?

   f. Guidepost 6: When the United States signed a deal to sell a large volume of grain to the Soviet Union in 1973, do you think the initial impact was to raise or lower the price of U.S. beef?

   g. Guidepost 7: Many Superbowl ticketholders end up reselling their tickets, sometimes for over $1,000 each. Who benefits from this "scalping," the ticket buyers, the ticket sellers, both or neither?

   h. Guidepost 8: Does it make sense to assume that firms try to maximize their profits even though firm owners often deny that profit maximizing is their primary goal?

2. Exhibit 1 shows the relationship between gas consumption of a new Chevrolet and the number of miles traveled.

EXHIBIT 1

Total distance traveled (miles)	Amount of gasoline consumed (gallons)
0	0
75	5
150	10
225	15
300	20
375	25
450	30

a. Graph the relationship between miles traveled and gas consumption in the space provided. Measure miles traveled on the horizontal axis (x axis) and gasoline consumption on the vertical axis (y axis). Label the graph clearly.
b. Is gasoline consumption related positively or negatively to distance traveled?
c. How many miles can be traveled on a gallon of gas? What is the slope of the distance traveled-gasoline consumption line ("curve")?

(graph for question 2)

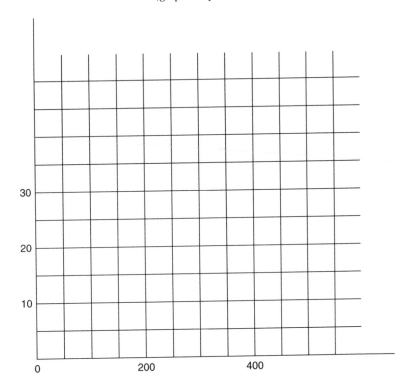

3. Height and weight are usually related. Exhibit 2 presents data for a sample of men. The average weight for men of different heights is shown.

EXHIBIT 2

Number of men in class	Height of individual (inches)	Mean weight (pounds)
20	70	160
23	71	168
17	72	176
18	73	182
14	74	186

a. Graph the height-weight relationship, plotting height on the horizontal axis and weight on the vertical axis. Be sure to label both axes.

b. What is the slope of the line ("curve") between 70 and 71 inches? Between 73 and 74 inches?

(graph for question 3)

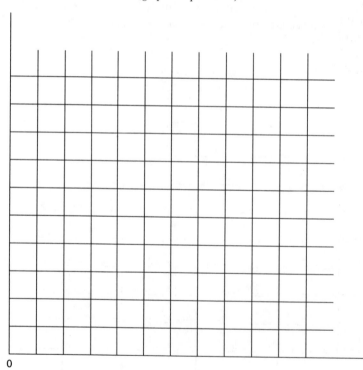

0

4. Exhibit 3 presents data on national income and personal consumption expenditures for the period from 1988 to 1993.

EXHIBIT 3

Year	Disposable personal income (in billions)	Personal consumption expenditures (in billions)
1988	3548	3296
1989	3787	3523
1990	4051	3761
1991	4231	3906
1992	4500	4140
1993	4706	4391

Source: Economic Report of the President, 1993, p. 300.

a. Graph the relationship in the space provided. Plot disposable income on the horizontal axis and consumption expenditures on the vertical axis. Be sure to label both axes.
b. Is the relationship between disposable income and consumption expenditures positive or negative?
c. Between 1988 and 1989, by how much did income increase? By how much did consumption increase? What was the slope of the consumption-income relationship during this time period?
d. Calculate the slope of the consumption-income relationship between 1989 and 1990. Is the slope of the relationship constant from year to year?

(graph for question 4)

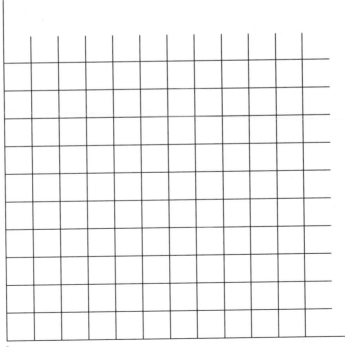

0

5. Each of the following statements ignores or violates one of the eight guideposts to economic thinking discussed in the text. In each case, identify the guidepost and explain how it has been violated.
   a. Before voting in an important election, each voter should learn as much as possible about the issues involved.
   b. Reducing the prices of necessities would clearly benefit the poor. Therefore, the government should pass laws (price controls) requiring producers of necessities to sell at low prices.
   c. One way to lower the costs associated with the armed services would be to have a military draft with low pay for those who are required to serve.
   d. Since I get the same satisfaction from reading a book, seeing a movie, or hearing a concert, it makes no difference to me which one I do.
   e. Since criminal activity is associated more with the poor than with the rich, the poor must have lower moral standards than the rich.
   f. I recently heard that some people are hiring others to do their shopping for them. It sure is silly to hire someone to do something you can clearly do for yourself.
   g. If hamburgers and pizza-by-the-slice cost the same and you like pizza more than you like hamburgers, you would always rather have another slice of pizza than another hamburger.

6. Exhibit 4 shows how the quantity of melons bought by consumers depends on the price of melons and on average consumer income.

EXHIBIT 4

Price (cents per pound)	Quantity bought (thousands of tons per year) for average income of	
	$10,000/year	$15,000/year
1.5	1500	1690
1.6	1420	1600
1.7	1350	1510
1.8	1280	1430
1.9	1210	1370
2.0	1170	1310

   a. On a piece of graph paper (if you do not have a piece of graph paper, draw your own) graph the relationship between price and quantity bought if income is $10,000. Label this curve D_1.
   b. Graph the relationship between price and quantity bought if income is $15,000. Label this curve D_2.
   c. Are price and quantity bought positively or negatively related?
   d. If price is fixed at 1.7 cents per pound and consumer income rises from $10,000 to $15,000 per year, how much will quantity bought change?

7. The text discusses three common pitfalls to avoid in the economic way of thinking:
   (1) Violation of the *ceteris paribus* condition
   (2) Association is not causation
   (3) Fallacy of composition

Indicate which pitfall applies to each of the following statements. Briefly explain each case.
a. Since everyone who buys a lottery ticket hopes to win the lottery prize, the perfect lottery would make everyone a winner.
b. Since low-income families tend to be larger than average, low-income parents must be particularly fond of children compared to the average parent.
c. In recent years, drug abuse has increased despite increased drug enforcement efforts, so it is pretty clear that drug enforcement efforts have been ineffective.

LEARNING THE MECHANICS—MULTIPLE CHOICE

1. In economics, the term "scarcity" refers to the fact that
   a. everything really worthwhile costs money.
   b. even in wealthy countries like the United States, some people are poor.
   c. no society is able to produce enough to satisfy fully the desires of people for goods and services.
   d. sometimes shortages of a good arise when its price is set below the market equilibrium.

2. Opportunity cost is
   a. the cost incurred when one fails to take advantage of an opportunity.
   b. the cost incurred in order to increase the availability of attractive opportunities.
   c. the cost of the highest valued option forgone as the result of choosing an alternative.
   d. the drudgery and undesirable aspects of an option.

3. When an economist states that a good is scarce, she means that
   a. production cannot expand the availability of the good.
   b. there is a shortage or insufficient amount of the good at the existing price.
   c. desire for the good exceeds the amount that is freely available from nature.
   d. people would want to purchase more of the good at any price.

4. When economists say that an individual displays economizing behavior, they simply mean that the individual is
   a. making a lot of money.
   b. purchasing only those products that are cheap and of low quality.
   c. learning how to run a business more effectively.
   d. making choices so as to gain specific benefits at the least possible cost.

5. "The national debt is too large. The government must stop spending so much and start thinking about the resources they are depleting." This statement is
   a. a normative statement about economic policy.
   b. an objective statement about economic policy.
   c. a testable hypothesis.
   d. a conclusion supported by economic theory.

6. Which of the following is *not* a guidepost to clear economic thinking?
   a. The value of a good is subjective.
   b. Scarce goods have a cost.
   c. Incentives matter.
   d. Goods are scarce for the poor but not for the rich.

7. A production possibilities curve indicates that when resources are being used efficiently
   a. you can produce more of one good only if you lower its price.
   b. you can produce more of one good only if you produce more of another good.
   c. you can produce more of one good only if you produce less of another good.
   d. It will be impossible to expand total output in the future.

8. Within the context of economics, the statement "There are no free lunches" refers to which of the following?
   a. Individuals must always pay for the lunch that they consume.
   b. Production of a good requires the use of scarce resources regardless of whether it is supplied free to the consumers.
   c. Restaurant owners act in their own interest.
   d. Economic maximizers are selfish and will not provide anything free for others.

9. A good economist will
   a. think much like an ecologist, recognizing the secondary effects of an action as well as the direct effects.
   b. ignore secondary effects, since in an economy such effects seldom matter.
   c. recognize that, almost always, secondary effects just reinforce the direct effects of a policy action.
   d. analyze the secondary effects of an action, so long as they occur at about the same time as the direct effects.

10. Which of the following is *not* an example of an economic resource?
   a. Human skills
   b. A water buffalo
   c. An atomic reactor
   d. All of the above *are* (or can be) economic resources.

11. If you were deciding whether to purchase a second car, the economic way of thinking would lead you to compare
   a. the total benefits expected from two cars with the cost of the two cars.
   b. the additional benefits expected from a second car with the total cost of the two cars.
   c. the dollar cost of the two cars with the potential income that the two cars will generate.
   d. the additional benefits of the second car with its cost.

Questions 12 through 14 refer to the following data:

Function Y		Function Z	
Q	P	Q	P
5	$10	5	$120
10	20	10	95
15	30	15	75
20	40	20	60
25	50	25	50
30	60	30	41
35	70	35	35

12. From the data above, we know that
   a. function Y is linear but function Z is not.
   b. function Z is linear but function Y is not.
   c. both function Y and function Z are linear.
   d. neither function Y nor function Z are linear.

13. From the data above, we know that the slope of function Y between Q = 20 and Q = 25 is
   a. −0.5.
   b. −2.0.
   c. 0.5.
   d. 2.0.

14. From the data above, we know that function Y and function Z intersect (cross each other) at
   a. Q = 35.
   b. Q = 25.
   c. an indeterminate point.
   d. the two functions do not intersect.

THE ECONOMIC WAY OF THINKING—MULTIPLE CHOICE

1. The basic difference between macroeconomics and microeconomics is that
   a. macroeconomics looks at how people make choices, and microeconomics looks at why they make those choices.
   b. macroeconomics is concerned with economic policy, and microeconomics is concerned with economic theory.
   c. macroeconomics focuses on the aggregate economy, whereas microeconomics focuses on small components of that economy.
   d. macroeconomics is associated with the fallacy of composition, whereas microeconomics has little to do with the fallacy of composition.

2. Which of the following is the best example of "economizing behavior" on the part of a student whose only objective in economics is to get an A in the course?
   a. Taking the optional final exam to improve her grade even though an A in economics is already a certainty
   b. Spending the economics lecture hour studying for an exam in another class because she is already assured of an A in economics
   c. Doing outside readings in economics which will not be beneficial for the examination
   d. Spending time reading the text and attending classes even though the teacher informed the student that her present grade, a B, could not possibly change

3. Which of the following actions is consistent with the basic economic postulate (the guidepost that incentives matter)?
   a. Consumers buy fewer potatoes because the price of potatoes declines.
   b. A politician votes against a proposal because most of her constituents are strongly in favor of it.
   c. Fewer students attend lectures in the introductory economics courses because class participation counts 40 percent of their grade.
   d. Farmers produce less barley because barley prices have declined.

4. Whenever the word "should" is included in an economist's analysis, we know that
   a. the economist is more likely to be engaged in positive economic reasoning than in normative.
   b. the economist knows what is best for us.
   c. the economist is more likely to be engaged in normative economics than in positive.
   d. the economist knows more about economics and is in a position to tell us what to do.

5. Positive economics differs from normative economics in that
   a. positive economics deals with how people react to changes in benefits, whereas normative economics deals with how people react to changes in costs.
   b. positive economic statements are, in principle, empirically testable; normative statements are not.
   c. positive economic statements tell us what we should be doing; normative economics tells us what we should have done.
   d. normative economic statements are theoretical, whereas positive statements focus on the application of the theory.

6. The basic postulate concerns human decisions about the allocation of
   a. leisure and work.
   b. food and clothing.
   c. studying and dating time.
   d. all of the above.

7. The economic way of thinking stresses that
   a. changes in the personal costs and benefits will exert a predictable influence on the choices of human decision-makers.
   b. if one individual gains from an economic activity, then someone else must lose, and in the same proportion.
   c. if a good is provided free to an individual, its production will not consume valuable scarce resources.
   d. good intentions lead to sound economic policy.

8. "The price of food usually rises when there is an increase in the general level of prices. High food prices cause inflation." This statement best illustrates fallacious reasoning stemming from
   a. the fallacy of composition.
   b. failure to recognize that association is not causation.
   c. failure to consider the secondary effects of an action.
   d. wishful thinking on the part of the spokesperson.

9. With time, which one of the following strategies would be most likely to result in an outward shift in the production possibilities curve of an economy?
   a. Passage of legislation reducing the length of the workweek to 30 hours
   b. Institution of a tax policy encouraging capital investment at the expense of current consumption
   c. Institution of a tax policy encouraging current consumption at the expense of capital investment
   d. An increase in the marginal income tax rate, which would reduce the work effort of individuals

10. If the best test of a theory is its ability to predict, and if economics deals with human beings who can think and respond in a variety of ways, can economic theories really be tested?
    a. Yes, since, on the average, human beings will respond in a predictable way to changes in personal costs and benefits.
    b. Yes, since all individuals usually respond in the same way.
    c. No, since individuals will seldom respond in a predictable way.
    d. No, since the general behavior of a large number of individuals cannot be predicted.

11. Economics assumes that decision-makers
    a. always act rationally and act only when they have full information.
    b. base their evaluations on psychic factors, leaving out the utility derived from economic goods.
    c. maximize their utility, insofar as utility indicates the pleasure derived from material goods.
    d. seek to choose those options that will best advance their objectives.

12. The central message of Adam Smith was that the production and wealth of a nation would be magnified if
    a. individuals were left free to act in their own interest.
    b. a central planning agency were established to ensure that labor and capital were allocated efficiently.
    c. the central government provided free education and training to workers.
    d. employers were more humanitarian toward workers and employees more concerned about the importance of efficiency in production.

13. Suppose that the Clinton administration cancelled a highway building project after $3 billion already had been spent on it. If the administration expected that the total value of the highways to society would be $25 billion, then:
    a. the cancellation would have made economic sense only if the remaining cost of the project exceeded $25 billion.
    b. the cancellation would have made economic sense only if the remaining cost of the project exceeded $22 billion.
    c. the cancellation would have made economic sense only if the remaining cost of the project exceeded $28 billion.
    d. the cancellation could not possibly make sense since $3 billion had already been spent on the project.

14. Positive economics is most useful in addressing which of the following pollution issues?
    a. How much pollution people ought to be willing to tolerate.
    b. The most cost-effective methods for achieving a targeted amount of pollution reduction.
    c. Who ought to be charged to finance a targeted amount of pollution reduction.
    d. None of the above; they are all normative issues.

THE ECONOMIC WAY OF THINKING—DISCUSSION QUESTIONS

1. What is scientific methodology? How does the methodology differ for economics compared to a laboratory science? For a laboratory science, experimental results must be replicable before they are accepted. How, if at all, can this standard be applied to research in economics?

2. List three things that you appreciate having and that are not scarce. List three things that are commonplace but still scarce. How did you decide whether an item was scarce or not?

3. "Economics is of limited relevance. Most people will not be directly involved in management or the production of material goods. Neither will they put much money in the stock market. Understanding the economic approach will be of limited value to the typical student." Do you agree or disagree with this view? Be honest. Explain your reasoning.

4. "A tax increase is necessary if we want inflation to subside. Higher taxes will reduce the amount of money available to the consumer, causing his spending to decline. A tax increase is the most reasonable policy alternative at this time." Indicate the positive and normative aspects of these three statements.

5. "Under our plan, health care in the United States will now be free. No citizen will be denied medical care because of inability to pay. The program will be funded by increasing the employer's tax on the wages of his employees."
    a. Will health care be free? If so, why? If not, who do you think will end up paying for it?
    b. Will the total amount of health care consumption rise or fall? Do you consider this change in health care consumption desirable or not? Explain.

6. Consider the following scenario: Mark and Janet get married; Janet acquires medical training while Mark supports the family and pays Janet's educational expenses; Mark and Janet get divorced with no physical assets to divide up. Consider the following reaction: "Janet leaves with the only jewels of the marriage. Mark deserves compensation." What are the positive and normative aspects of this reaction? Do you agree or not? Why?

PERSPECTIVES IN ECONOMICS

On Economic Ignorance
By Irving Kristol

[Reprinted with permission from
NYU Business, Spring 1986.]

As one looks back at the history of the human race, one is appalled at the human misery that can be attributed to sheer economic ignorance. It would be no exaggeration to say that, if it could be given a quantitative measure, this misery might outrank that caused by warfare. Whole populations have been devastated by the economic ignorance of their rulers; whole civilizations have deteriorated and crumbled. To take an easy and relatively modern example: Spain in the 16th century was one of the richest and most powerful nations in Europe. For the next three centuries, it slid ineluctably downhill, becoming one of Europe's most impoverished countries. The only reason for its decline was that Spain's ruling elites were possessed of an invincible ignorance of elementary economics.

Today, whole continents—Africa and Latin America, most notably—are being pushed to ruination by that same seemingly invincible ignorance. There is no reason why the people of Argentina should not be as affluent as the people of Canada—the two countries are almost twins from an economic standpoint. Nor is there a reason why the people who live in Nigeria should be so much poorer than the people (white *and* black) who live in South Africa.

There is a puzzle here. Economic activity has been around almost as long as the human race itself, and one would have thought ruling elites would have benefitted from accumulated experience and wisdom. Moreover, while these elites, being human, are likely to make occasional egregious errors in policy, they are rarely self-destructive in the sense of wishing to persist over long periods in policies that are clearly counterproductive. Except in economics, that is, where such persistence is quite common.

The puzzle is especially exasperating at this time. After all, Adam Smith's *Wealth of Nations*, which distills the economic experience of mankind into plain, readable English, was published over two centuries ago. A 20-page précis of the book would suffice for anyone interested in grasping the fundamentals of an economic policy that leads to growth. Watching the downright economic silliness that prevails in so many countries, one finds oneself wondering: Since we really do know better, why does such silliness persist?

The answer, I suggest, is in two parts. First, it turns out to be less easy to grasp the fundamentals of elementary economics than one might think. Second, while no government likes the idea of presiding over a declining economy, there are many governments that have other priorities. And these two issues are closely related.

Anyone who has tried to teach elementary economics knows that students are quick to grasp the principles—and almost as quick to forget them. This is because those principles, though clear and simple, are often counterintuitive. It's like trying to understand Einstein's Special Theory of Relativity. It's not hard—I myself have learned to understand it at least a dozen times. The trouble is that, having learned it, I then forget it.

Any economics teacher who touches on the topic of rent control or wage and price controls can attest that something of the same sort happens. Students promptly perceive that the adverse, unanticipated consequences—unanticipated by the economically ignorant, that is—of such controls soon overwhelm the immediate benefits. But for them to remember the essence of what they have learned, they have to have developed the intellectual habit of looking for second-order and third-order consequences. And such a habit is not easily acquired. It involves intellectual formation—a cast of mind—not just learning a few principles by rote. One has to learn to "think economically."

To think economically with any degree of consistency, one has to be motivated. There is rarely an immediate "payoff" to an individual in thinking economically about a matter of public policy—indeed, the benefits to an individual may be most tangible when the policy makes no economic sense. (Just think of all the people who do benefit from rent control!) In short, the habit of thinking economically must be an integral part of the national culture, the sort of thing one does almost instinctively.

In most Western democracies, this process of integration has occurred, at least to some extent. No democratic government can proceed with a policy of economic nonsense without also provoking controversy—and that's about as much as one can reasonably hope for. But in large areas of the world, the national cultures have little but contempt for the "economic way of thinking" even while the people are promised the fruits (affluence, mobility and modern conveniences) that only respect for such an intellectual formation can, in fact, deliver.

In a way, this is easily explained. Historically, most national cultures have regarded money-making, the pursuit of wealth, and the market arrangements that make both possible, as necessary evils at best. They distract from the "higher things" in life—religious piety, military valor, ideological rectitude, imperial aspirations. Any civilized person would have to agree that there is indeed something "higher" (most of the time, anyhow) than the pursuit of wealth. Still, most people, practically everywhere and at every time, do wish to participate in economic growth. Their problem is that they don't know how to think and act to achieve it and their governments either share their ignorance or are willing to impose their own priorities.

To put it another way: for any national culture to be economically rational, it must have a large "bourgeois" component, i.e., it must be sympathetic (or at least not antipathetic) to the mundane aspirations of ordinary men and women, as distinct from "higher" aspirations. Unfortunately, such a culture then incites hostility among its intellectual elites. But that is another story.

Discussion

1. What is Kristol's main point? Do you agree with him? Why or why not?

2. Do you really believe that to "think economically" is different from any other kind of thinking? Why or why not? In particular, how would you characterize the economic way of thinking? [*Hint:* refer to the eight guideposts to economic thinking.]

3. Kristol suggests it is "less easy to grasp the fundamentals of elementary economics than one might think." Such an opinion is similar to a common complaint from beginning students that runs something like "Economics seems so logical when I read it in the book, but when it comes time to apply it myself, I have more trouble." What reasons can you give for economics seeming easier to learn than it actually is? What can *you* do in your studies of economics to make sure that you *do* learn the material?

CHAPTER TWO

SOME TOOLS OF THE ECONOMIST

TRUE OR FALSE

T F

☐ ☐   1. The opportunity cost of washing your car is the discomfort and drudgery associated with the task.

☐ ☐   2. Time is not a component of opportunity cost.

☐ ☐   3. If you are an avid football fan, the opportunity cost of going for a drive while the Super Bowl is on television would probably be high.

☐ ☐   4. The law of comparative advantage helps explain why fathers often have their 12-year-old sons mow the lawn even though the fathers could do it more rapidly.

☐ ☐   5. It would usually be economical for a lawyer to do her own typing if she could type better than her secretary.

☐ ☐   6. The economic way of thinking suggests that an individual should consider only monetary cost when making consumption decisions.

☐ ☐   7. A rainy day often reduces the opportunity cost of a farmer's going to town.

☐ ☐   8. A country such as the United States, which has an abundance of fertile grain-growing land but little land available for raising sugarcane, can gain by exporting wheat to other countries and buying sugar from them.

☐ ☐   9. The principle of comparative advantage causes both individuals and nations to specialize in the production of those things for which they have the greatest relative advantage.

☐ ☐   10. According to the principle of comparative advantage, it would never make economic sense for a young doctor to be a professional ice skater.

☐ ☐   11. All economies must make decisions about what to produce, how to produce it, and to whom to distribute the goods produced.

PROBLEMS AND PROJECTS

1. Sam and Larry jointly operate a shop. They specialize in the production of tables and chairs. Their respective production possibilities schedules are presented in Exhibit 1.

EXHIBIT 1

Sam's weekly production possibilities		Larry's weekly production possibilities	
Tables	*Chairs*	*Tables*	*Chairs*
5	0	4	0
4	2	3	1
3	4	2	2
2	6	1	3
1	8	0	4
0	10		

a. In terms of chairs, what is Sam's opportunity cost of producing a table? What is Larry's?
b. On average, they sell three times as many chairs as tables. Thus, Sam currently produces two tables and six chairs, while Larry produces one table and three chairs. Total production is three tables and nine chairs. Is this the maximum joint output that Sam and Larry could produce? If not, how could total output be expanded?

2. Exhibit 2 presents the annual production possibilities schedules for two typical farmers—one in California, the other in Kansas. Currently, the California farmer is producing 200 bushels of oranges and 600 bushels of wheat. The Kansas farmer is producing 100 and 400 bushels of oranges and wheat, respectively. Thus, the total output of the two farmers is 300 bushels of oranges and 1000 bushels of wheat.

EXHIBIT 2

California Farmer		Kansas Farmer	
Oranges (bushels)	*Wheat (bushels)*	*Oranges (bushels)*	*Wheat (bushels)*
0	1000	0	800
100	800	50	600
200	600	100	400
300	400	150	200
400	200	200	0
500	0		

a. The California farmer is able to produce more oranges and wheat than his Kansas counterpart, so he has an absolute advantage in the production of both goods. Does this mean that gains from trade are impossible? (*Hint:* Ignore transportation costs throughout this question.)
b. Suppose both want to consume their initial amounts of wheat—600 bushels for the Californian and 400 for the Kansan. The Kansan decides to specialize in wheat production (800 bushels). Setting aside 400 bushels of wheat for herself, she offers to trade 400 bushels of wheat to the Californian for 150 bushels of oranges. Would the Kansan gain from this transaction? What consumption combination would she end up with?

   c. Could the Californian gain if he increased his orange production to 400 and then traded the 150 bushels to the Kansan for the 400 bushels of wheat? If so, by how much (be specific) would the Californian gain compared to his original situation? What will happen to the total output of this two-farmer economy if these production changes and trades take a place? (Be specific)

   d. Are *both* farmers made better off by the specialization and trade described in parts b and c? Explain why such gains from trade are or are not possible. (*Hint:* Begin by calculating opportunity costs.)

3. The following questions relate to the constant hours of work required for production specified in Exhibit 3.
   a. Calculate each country's opportunity cost of producing one ton of coffee (in terms of tobacco) and one ton of tobacco (in terms in coffee).
   b. Which country has a comparative advantage in (is the relatively efficient producer of) coffee? Why? Which country has a comparative advantage in tobacco? Why?
   c. Which country should specialize in coffee production? Why?
   d. Which country, if either, has an absolute advantage in the production of both goods? Explain your answer.

EXHIBIT 3

	Hours of work required per ton of	
	Coffee	*Tobacco*
United States	15	45
Brazil	25	50

4. Exhibit 4 shows the production possibilities curve for growing wheat and corn.

EXHIBIT 4

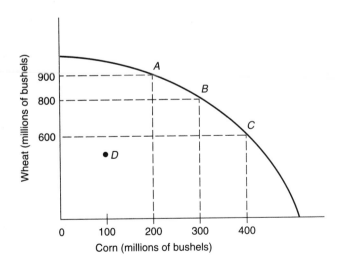

Corn (millions of bushels)

   a. Are resources efficiently employed at point A? At point B? At point D?

   b. At point A, how much wheat is being produced? How much corn?

   c. To increase corn production from A to B, how much wheat must be sacrificed? What is the opportunity cost of one bushel of corn when production moves from point A to B?

   d. What is the opportunity cost of one bushel of corn when production moves from point B to C?

5. Exhibit 5 presents information regarding expenses for childbirth and the first year of child care for the Pastor family. The primary-care parent quits his/her job for the first year of the child's life. As a fringe benefit, the employer of the spouse of the primary-care parent covers all of the child's medical expenses.

EXHIBIT 5

Medical expenses	$ 2,000
Direct expenses (food and clothing, for example)	
50 percent purchased by family, 50 percent gifts	2,000
Before-tax income of primary-care parent	15,600
After-tax income of primary-care parent	12,000

a. What is the cost to the family of the child for the first year?
b. What is the cost to society (which includes the family) of the child for the first year?
c. If this were the case for the typical American family, what do you think would happen to the U.S. birthrate if the cost to the family became equal to society's cost?

6. The division of labor enhances the value that citizens contribute to an economy. Each of the five statements below is a potential answer to a question about the division of labor; read them before going on.
   (1) According to the laws of physics, matter is never created or destroyed, it is only rearranged. Manufacturing reshapes matter; distribution relocates it. Both activities, done wisely, rearrange matter in a way that increases its value.
   (2) Deciding which activities to undertake and how to undertake them are risky and costly activities.
   (3) "You measure the worth of a ballplayer by how many fannies he puts in the seats." (George Steinbrenner, baseball team owner).
   (4) For jobs which are not inherently pleasant, groups of workers left on their own may not accomplish much.
   (5) Lots of activities generate value without being exchanged in the marketplace.

Now read each of the questions below and indicate in the blank space to the left of the question the number of the statement above that best answers the question:
___ a. How can a baseball player like Barry Bonds ever be worth over $6 million a year?
___ b. Why not buy direct more often and cut out the wasteful middleman?
___ c. Why do so many house spouses just "sit at home" instead of going out and getting a "real" job?
___ d. Why don't we encourage more labor-managed firms so we can eliminate unproductive jobs, like shift leaders and supervisors?
___ e. Why does the compensation of presidents and owners of corporations often rise and fall with the profitability of their firms instead of being fixed like most salaries?

7. Exhibit 6 contains a production possibility curve for consumption (C) and investment (I) goods for a country. Output is measured in millions.

EXHIBIT 6

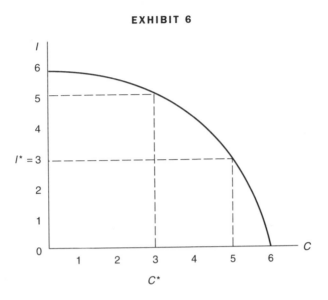

C* indicates the economy's subsistence level of consumption good C.
I* indicates the amount of the investment good I necessary to replace capital equipment that wears out each year. If investment falls short of I*, the economy's production possibilities curve will shrink from its present position. If investment exceeds I*, the economy's production possibilities curve will expand.
  a. What will be the consumption/investment good production point(s) if
    (1) it wants to grow as rapidly as possible without starving its citizens?
    (2) it wants to enjoy as much consumption as possible without reducing its future production capabilities?
    (3) it wants to produce at least C* and I* simultaneously?
  b. Suppose that a severe long-term drought forces the country's production possibilities curve to shift inward until the point (C = 3, I = 3) is on that curve. How does this shift change your answer to part a of this question?

LEARNING THE MECHANICS—MULTIPLE CHOICE

1. The opportunity cost to the United States of placing a man on the moon was
  a. the loss of government revenues that were allocated to the moon shot.
  b. the money prices paid to all factors of production involved in the space program.
  c. the loss of utility from the highest valued bundle of products that had to be foregone because of the moon shot.
  d. less than zero, since the long-run benefits of the project will be greater than the cost.

2. When Benjamin Franklin wrote, "Remember that time is money!" he understood
  a. the principle of substitution.
  b. the law of comparative advantage.
  c. the concept of opportunity cost.
  d. the Protestant ethic.

3. The opportunity cost of building a new civic auditorium in your town would be
   a. the money cost of the structure.
   b. the necessary increase in tax revenues to finance the building.
   c. the highest valued bundle of other goods and services that must be foregone because of the auditorium construction.
   d. the enjoyment that must be foregone because the capacity of the current structure prevents many people from attending athletic and community events.

4. Which of the following best describes the implications of the law of comparative advantage? If each person sells goods for which he or she has the greatest comparative advantage in production and buys those for which his or her comparative advantage is least, then the
   a. total output available to each person can be expanded by specialization and exchange.
   b. total output can be expanded, although some individuals will be net "losers."
   c. buyers of goods will gain at the expense of sellers.
   d. total output will increase if, and only if, persons with a comparative advantage also have an absolute advantage, relative to their trading partners.

5. When comparative advantage exists, then
   a. voluntary exchange is likely to occur independent of government action.
   b. economists must inform the public that exchange will improve the general welfare before trade will occur.
   c. trade will occur until the weakest of the parties finds it impossible to continue trading.
   d. exchange can make one trader better off, but only at the expense of the other.

6. Which of the following is *not* one of the basic economic questions that all economies must answer?
   a. What will be produced?
   b. To whom will the goods produced be allocated?
   c. What is the highest opportunity cost method of producing each good?
   d. How will goods be produced?

7. Private property rights give owners a chance to act selfishly, but they also make owners responsible and accountable for their actions. As a result, when deciding on the wisest use of their resources, property owners are likely to
   a. always disregard the wishes of others.
   b. disregard the wishes of others to the extent that accountability for misuse of the property is not enforced.
   c. be concerned about the wishes of others whether or not accountability is enforced.
   d. lose revenue when the wishes of others are taken into consideration.

Use the following information to answer questions 8–10. Exhibit 7 outlines the production possibilities of Italia and Slavia for food and clothing.

EXHIBIT 7

Italia		Slavia	
Food	*Clothing*	*Food*	*Clothing*
0	8	0	32
2	6	2	24
4	4	4	16
6	2	6	8
8	0	8	0

8. What is the opportunity cost of producing one unit of clothing in Slavia?
   a. One unit of food.
   b. Two units of food.
   c. One-twelfth unit of food.
   d. One-fourth unit of food.

9. Which of the following is true?
   a. Italia has a comparative advantage in the production of both goods.
   b. Slavia is the high-opportunity cost producer of clothing.
   c. Slavia has a comparative advantage in the production of food.
   d. Italia is the low-opportunity cost producer of food.

10. The law of comparative advantage suggests that
    a. both countries would gain if Slavia traded food for Italia clothing.
    b. neither country would gain from trade even if the transportation costs for the products were zero.
    c. both countries would gain if Italia traded food for Slavia clothing.
    d. Slavia would not gain from trade because it has an absolute advantage in the production of both goods.

11. When resources are being used wastefully
    a. the production possibilities curve shifts inward.
    b. the production possibilities curve shifts outward.
    c. the economy is operating at a point inside its production possibilities constraint.
    d. the economy is operating at a point outside its production possibilities constraint.

12. The production possibilities curve
    a. assumes that technology is increasing at a constant, long-run rate.
    b. assumes that all individuals have equal incomes.
    c. is normally convex (bowed in) to the origin over its entire range.
    d. assumes that the level of technology is constant.

13. Which of the following is a transaction cost?
    a. The price of a ticket to a concert
    b. The price of food eaten before a concert
    c. Time spent buying the ticket
    d. Time spent driving to the concert

14. Transaction costs
    a. can be reduced by gathering more information about many possible alternative exchanges.
    b. can be reduced by consulting people who specialize in providing information about alternative exchanges.
    c. cannot be reduced by forming consumer cooperatives.
    d. cannot be reduced at all; they are fixed by law.

15. Private property rights exist when property rights are
    a. exclusively controlled by one owner.
    b. transferable to others.
    c. both a and b.
    d. neither a nor b.

THE ECONOMIC WAY OF THINKING—MULTIPLE CHOICE

1. Any economy that fails to realize all its potential gains stemming from the domestic division of labor (specialization) is
   a. operating outside its production possibilities curve.
   b. operating inside its production possibilities curve.
   c. operating on its production possibilities curve but in an inefficient manner.
   d. operating on its production possibilities curve and therefore need not be concerned about comparative advantage.

2. Suppose that the production possibilities of Robinson Crusoe and Friday are as follows:

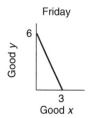 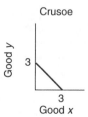

   Which of the following would maximize the consumption alternatives available to Crusoe and Friday?
   a. Crusoe should specialize in the production of good *x* and Friday should specialize in the production of good *y*, but there should be no trade allowed.
   b. Crusoe should specialize in the production of good *x* and Friday should specialize in the production of good *y* and trade should occur.
   c. Crusoe should specialize in the production of good *y* and Friday should specialize in the production of good *x*, and trade should occur.
   d. This is a special case. Both individuals should strive for self-sufficiency, since this maximizes output.

3. When an economy is operating efficiently, the production of more of one commodity will result in the production of less of some other commodity because
   a. all resources are specialized and only imperfectly mobile.
   b. resources are limited (i.e., scarce) and efficiency implies that all are in use.
   c. the structure of demand is fixed at any given time.
   d. material wants are insatiable.

4. "Since I am going to start school soon, I will have to quit my current job." This statement most clearly reflects
   a. the law of comparative advantage.
   b. the principle of opportunity cost.
   c. gains for technology.
   d. a decision that is inconsistent with economizing behavior.

5. "Now that John washes all the dishes and I mow the lawn, we can finish in two-thirds the time it took when we shared both functions." This statement most clearly reflects
   a. the law of comparative advantage.
   b. gains from capital formation.
   c. gains from technology.
   d. choices that are inconsistent with economizing behavior.

6. "If I didn't have a date tonight, I would save $10 and spend the evening playing tennis." The opportunity cost of the date is
   a. $10.
   b. $10 plus the foregoing of a night of tennis.
   c. dependent upon how pleasant a time one has on the date.
   d. the foregoing of a night of tennis.

7. Use the diagram below to answer the following questions.

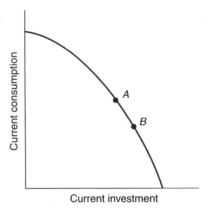

   Points *A* and *B* indicate the current levels of consumption and investment for two different economies. Other things constant, which of the two economies is likely to grow more rapidly?
   a. *A*
   b. *B*
   c. They can be expected to grow at the same rate.
   d. Uncertain, since the growth rate is not influenced by the factors indicated in this hypothetical example.

8. Dr. Jones, a dentist, is choosing between driving and flying from Florida to Montana for her vacation. If Jones drove, she would have to close her office three days earlier than if she flew. Her expected income (after taxes) from her practice is $80 per day. Jones's preferences are such that she would rather drive: She would stand to gain $50 worth of nonpecuniary (non-monetary) benefits if she drove and saw the beautiful countryside. If Jones was a rational decision-maker, she would drive if the price differential (air cost minus driving) was greater than
   a. $50.
   b. $80.
   c. $130.
   d. $190.

9. According to the law of comparative advantage
   a. each producer should strive toward self-sufficiency in order to maximize the total production of the economy.
   b. each product should be produced by the lowest opportunity cost producer in order to maximize output.
   c. one should never compare one's abilities with those of another; in doing so production time is lost.
   d. each product should be produced by the individual who can produce more of that product than any other individual.

10. "The economic wealth of this country was built primarily by some individuals profiting from a transaction, whereas others were harmed by that transaction." This statement indicates the spokesman
    a. fails to comprehend the mutual gains resulting from specialization and exchange.
    b. fails to comprehend the fallacy of composition.
    c. fails to understand the significance of the production possibilities constraint.
    d. utilizes the economic way of thinking. The statement is essentially correct.

11. Which of the following is most likely to occur under a system of clearly defined and enforced private property rights?
    a. Resource owners will tend to abuse resources and use them selfishly.
    b. Resource owners will fail to conserve vital resources for the future even if they expect their scarcity to increase.
    c. Resource owners will ignore the wishes of others, including others who would like to use the resource that is privately owned.
    d. Resource owners will consider the wishes of others, including potential future purchasers, when they decide how to employ privately owned resources.

12. Which of the following is a disadvantage that may arise when individuals specialize in the production of those things for which they are the low opportunity cost producer?
    a. When individuals specialize in production, they have little incentive to trade for other commodities that they may also enjoy.
    b. Specialization does not allow individuals to enjoy the benefits of learning by doing; that is, repetition prevents individuals from developing more efficient methods of production.
    c. A worker may become bored with performing the same monotonous task over a period of time.
    d. Individuals have little incentive to utilize their particular talents.

Questions 13–15 refer to Exhibit 8 below:

EXHIBIT 8

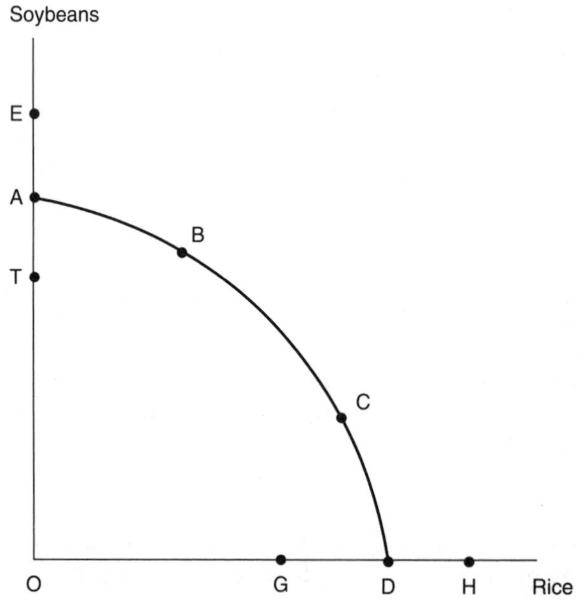

13. The diagram in Exhibit 8 indicates Japan's production possibilities for rice and soybeans. Given the exhibit, Japan's opportunity cost of producing more soybeans, in terms of rice
    a. increases from D to A.
    b. decreases from D to A.
    c. does not change from D to A.
    d. is impossible to determine from the information given.

14. Suppose Japan experiences a long-term water drought that reduces its ability to produce all agricultural goods. The new Japanese production possibilities frontier will most closely resemble a curve connecting
    a. T and G.
    b. T and D.
    c. E and H.
    d. A and H.

15. Suppose Japan invents new improved soybean seeds that cost the same as the old ones but allow more beans to be grown with the same amount of other inputs as the older seeds. If nothing else has changed, the new Japanese production possibilities frontier will most closely resemble a curve connecting
    a. E and G.
    b. A and G.
    c. E and D.
    d. A and H.

THE ECONOMIC WAY OF THINKING—DISCUSSION QUESTIONS

1. As an individual, you will ultimately take part in determining how your economy answers its three basic economic decisions. What will help you choose what *you* should produce, how *you* should produce it, and *for whom* you should produce it? Are these answers at all interrelated?

2. "In the progress of the division of labor, the employment to the . . . great body of the people comes to be confined to a few very simple operations, frequently to one or two . . . The man whose whole life is spent in performing a few simple operations . . . becomes as stupid and ignorant as it is possible for a human creature to become."—Adam Smith, *The Wealth of Nations.*
    a. Smith seems to be saying that specialization carries with it a loss in utility due to monotony and alienation. Do you agree? Why or why not?
    b. If it is true that specialization increases productivity but also increases worker boredom, how do we decide the extent to which we should specialize?
    c. Smith's comments were made in the context of the production specialization as it was known in the 18th century. How applicable is his analysis to today's "high-tech" world? Why?
    d. Smith felt that education was the best remedy for this problem associated with the division of labor. Do you agree? Why or why not?

3. Consider the cost to you of this economics course.
    a. About how much money did you spend on tuition and books for this course? When did you incur these costs?
    b. What is the cost of actually attending the class once you've paid your tuition and purchased your books?
    c. Use your answer to part b to comment on the following quote (heard at a Southern California liberal arts college with fairly high tuition): "I could earn $15 if I worked during today's economics class, but tuition averages out to $20 per lecture, so I can't afford to go. If only I went to UCLA, where tuition is lower, I could skip class and earn the money." Do you agree or disagree? Explain your answer.

4. Explain why it is often efficient for faculty members with training in computer programming to hire student programmers to do their computer work.

5. Consider the following quote by a lawyer who knows something about economics: "It doesn't make sense for me to care for my own lawn when my opportunity cost is $80 per hour."
   a. Do you agree with the lawyer's view? Explain.
   b. Would you be surprised to find this lawyer's lawn exquisitely maintained? Explain.

6. After a class discussion of how Capitalist and Socialist nations approach their three economizing decisions, your friend says: "I'm a capitalist on questions one and two but a socialist on question three." What does your friend mean? Why do you think she feels that way? Could such a system ever work? Why or why not?

Unfair Competition With The Sun
By Frédéric Bastiat

[From Frédéric Bastiat, "Petition of the Manufacturers of Candles, Wax-Lights, Lamps, Candlesticks, Street Lamps, Snuffers, Extinguishers, and of the Producers of Oil, Tallow, Resin, Alcohol, and Generally, of Everything Connected with Lighting." To messieurs the members of the Chamber of Deputies.]

Gentlemen,—You are on the right road. You reject abstract theories, and have little consideration for cheapness and plenty. Your chief care is the interest of the producer. You desire to protect him from foreign competition, and reserve the *national market for national industry.*

We are suffering from the intolerable competition of a foreign rival, placed, it would seem, in a condition so far superior to ours for the production of light that he absolutely *inundates* our *national market* with it at a price fabulously reduced. The moment he shows himself our trade leaves us—all consumers apply to him; and a branch of native industry, having countless ramifications, is all at once rendered completely stagnant. This rival, who is no other than the sun, wages war to the knife against us, and we suspect that he has been raised up by *perfidious Albion* (a good policy as times go); inasmuch as he displays towards that haughty island a circumspection with which he dispenses in our case.

What we pray for is, that it may please you to pass a law ordering the shutting up of all windows, skylights, dormer-windows, outside and inside shutters, curtains, blinds, bull's-eyes, in a word, of all openings, holes, chinks, clefts, and fissures, by or through which the light of the sun has been in use to enter houses, to the prejudice of the meritorious manufactures with which we flatter ourselves we have accommodated our country—a country, which, in gratitude, ought not abandon us now to a strife so unequal.

We trust, Gentlemen, that you will not regard this our request as a satire, or refuse it without at least previously hearing the reasons which we have to urge in its support.

And, first, if you shut up as much as possible all access to natural light, and create a demand for artificial light, which of our French manufacturers will not be encouraged by it?

We foresee your objections, Gentlemen, but we know that you can oppose to us none but such as you have picked up from the effete works of the partisans of Free Trade. We defy you to utter a single word against us which will not instantly rebound against yourselves and your entire policy.

You will tell us that, if we gain by the protection which we seek, the country will lose by it, because the consumer must bear the loss.

We answer:

You have ceased to have any right to invoke the interest of the consumer for, whenever his interest is found opposed to that of the producer, you sacrifice the latter. You have done so for the purpose of encouraging workers and those who seek employment. For the same reason you should do so again.

You have yourselves obviated this objection. When you are told that the consumer is interested in the free importation of iron, coal, corn, textile fabrics—yes, you reply, but the producer is interested in their exclusion. Well, be it so; if consumers are interested in the free admission of natural light, the producers of artificial light are equally interested in its prohibition.

If you urge that the light of the sun is a gratuitous gift of nature, and that to reject such gifts is to reject wealth itself under pretense of encouraging the means of acquiring it, we would caution you against giving a death-blow to your own policy. Remember that hitherto you have always repelled foreign products, *because* they approximate more nearly than home products to the character of gratuitous gifts.

Nature and human labor co-operate in various proportions (depending on countries and climates) in the production of commodities. The part which nature executes is very gratuitous; it is the part executed by human labor which constitutes value, and is paid for.

If a Lisbon orange sells for half the price of a Paris orange, it is because natural, and consequently gratuitous, heat does for the one what artificial, and therefore expensive, heat must do for the other.

When an orange comes to us from Portugal we may conclude that it is furnished in part gratuitously, in part for an onerous consideration; in other words, it comes to us at *half-price* as compared with those of Paris.

Now, it is precisely the *gratuitous half* (pardon the word) which we contend should be excluded. You say, How can national labour sustain competition with foreign labour, when the former has all the work to do, and the latter only does one-half, the sun supplying the remainder. But if this *half*, being *gratuitous*, determines you to exclude competition, how should the *whole*, being *gratuitous*, induce you to admit competition? If you were consistent, you would, while excluding as hurtful to native industry what is half gratuitous, exclude *a fortiori* and with double zeal, that which is altogether gratuitous.

One more, when products such as coal, iron, corn, or textile fabrics are sent us from abroad, and we can acquire them with less labour than if we made them ourselves, the difference is a free gift conferred upon us. The gift is more or less considerable in proportion as the difference is more or less great. It amounts to a quarter, a half, or three-quarters of the value of the product, when the foreigner only asks us for three-fourths, a half or a quarter of the price we should otherwise pay. It is as perfect and complete as it can be, when the donor (like the sun is furnishing us with light) asks us for nothing. The question, and we ask it formally, is this: Do you desire for our country the benefit of gratuitous consumption, or the pretended advantages of onerous production?

Make your choice, but be logical; for as long as you exclude as you do, coal, iron, corn, foreign fabrics, in proportion as their price approximates to zero what inconsistency it would be to admit the light of the sun, the price of which is already at zero during the entire day!

Discussion

1. What does the Bastiat reading have to do with this chapter? (*Hint:* the text states that the law of comparative advantage applies to nations as well as to individuals.) Does comparative advantage mean that *all* trade is good? Explain your answer.

2. Do you think that individuals or industries ever need protection from competition? If so, how would we decide whether an industry (like the lighting industry or the automobile industry) deserves to be protected from competition?

3. What arguments would you, as an economist, use before a congressional hearing on a bill to accomplish what Bastiat suggests? How would you deal with the political problems involved?

CHAPTER THREE

SUPPLY, DEMAND,
AND THE MARKET PROCESS

TRUE OR FALSE

T F

☐ ☐   1. Consumers will purchase less beef at higher prices than at lower prices if other factors remain the same.

☐ ☐   2. If the price of bananas increased, many consumers would substitute oranges, apples, ice cream, and other related commodities for bananas.

☐ ☐   3. The law of supply reflects the willingness of producers to expand output in response to an increase in the price of a product.

☐ ☐   4. Excess demand in the market will cause the price of a product to decline.

☐ ☐   5. An increase in demand for wheat would cause price to rise and producers to expand output.

☐ ☐   6. A reduction in the supply of fertilizer relative to its demand would cause the price of fertilizer to decline.

☐ ☐   7. Payments to input suppliers provide them with an incentive to acquire skills that that are valuable in the production process.

☐ ☐   8. The market price is in short-run equilibrium when suppliers are willing to supply only the amount demanded by consumers at the current price.

☐ ☐   9. When a market is in long-run equilibrium, the opportunity cost of supplying the product will be equal to the product's market price.

☐ ☐   10. Three factors that will each cause the supply curve for Napa county wine to shift to the left include a drought in Napa county, higher wages for Napa county grape pickers, and higher prices for Napa county wine.

☐ ☐   11. If the government fixed the price of farm products above the competitive equilibrium, consumer demand would increase.

☐ ☐   12. An increase in the price of inputs used in the construction industry would cause housing prices to rise and the demand for housing to decline.

PROBLEMS AND PROJECTS

1. Exhibit 1 presents hypothetical supply-and-demand schedules for shoes in a local market area.

EXHIBIT 1

Price (1)	Initial quantity demanded (2)	Quantity supplied (3)	New quantity demanded (4)
$ 6	270	120	320
9	230	170	280
12	200	200	250
15	170	220	220
18	130	250	180
21	90	300	140

a. Graph the initial demand (column 2) on the chart below.
b. What is the initial equilibrium price (*Hint:* Graph supplied.)?
c. The region experiences a boom and consumer income increases, causing an increase in demand. The new demand schedule is indicated in column 4. Graph the new schedule.
d. What is the new equilibrium price?
e. Suppose the price of shoes is fixed by law at $9; draw in this fixed price on your diagram. Describe the market for shoes at the initial demand level. Describe the market for shoes at the increased demand level. What has happened?

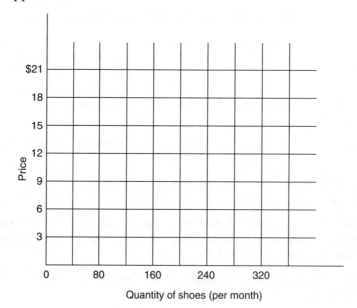

2. As indicated by Exhibit 2, the initial demand for soybeans was D_1. The supply was S.
    a. What was the initial market-clearing price? Quantity sold?
    b. Soybeans have a protein content and are a substitute for meat. Higher meat prices caused the demand for soybeans to increase to D_2. What is the new equilibrium price? Quantity sold?
    c. Wheat is also a substitute for soybeans. What will happen in the wheat market if the price of soybeans changes, as in part b? Illustrate your answer with a graph.

EXHIBIT 2

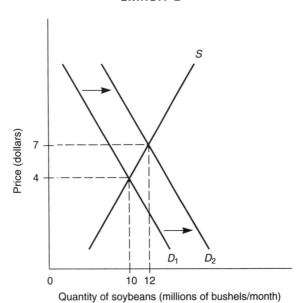

Quantity of soybeans (millions of bushels/month)

3. The pricing system sends out signals that influence the decisions of producers and consumers. Under-standing the secondary effects of a change in market conditions is essential if one is to understand how a market system works. For example, what impact did the substantially higher fuel (e.g., gasoline, fuel oil) prices of the mid-1970s have on
    a. the demand for large cars? small cars?
    b. the relative demand for steel and aluminum by the auto industry?
    c. the demand for home swimming pools, relative to cross-country driving vacations?
    d. employment conditions in the automobile industry?
    e. the farmer's cost of producing wheat?
    f. the demand for solar heating units and the incentive to produce them?
    g. the demand for home insulation?
    h. the incentive to speed up the development of the Alaskan pipeline during the mid-1970s?
    i. the incentive to undertake research on the development of low-pollution, coal-generated electricity?
    j. the supply of petroleum-derived fertilizers?
    k. the supply of non-petroleum-derived fertilizers?
    l. the short-run price of firewood?

4. Use the diagrams below to indicate the changes in demand (D), supply (S), equilibrium price (P) and equilibrium quantity (Q) in response to the events described to the left of the diagrams. First show in the diagrams how supply and/or demand shift in response to the event, and then fill in the table to the right of the diagrams using + to indicate increase, – to indicate decrease and 0 to indicate no change. If an effect cannot be determined show this by using "?". As an example, the first question has been answered.

Market	Events	Diagrams	D	S	P	Q
a. Automobiles	Price of gasoline rises; cost of producing autos rises.		–	–	?	–
b. Oranges	Frost destroys half the Florida orange crop.					
c. Butter	There is an increase in the supply of margarine.					
d. Lumber	Lower interest rates cause a housing construction boom; lumberjacks' wages fall significantly.					
e. Wine	The cost of growing grapes falls; consumer income decreases.					

5. Exhibit 3 below shows the market for rental housing in Limitville, a small, fictitious town on the California coast. The curve labeled D is the demand for rental housing, S_{sp} is the *short-run* supply curve, and S_{lr} is the *long-run* supply curve.

EXHIBIT 3

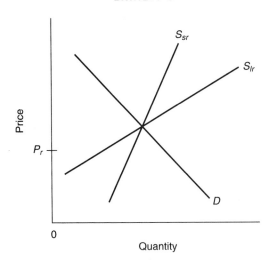

a. Indicate in the diagram the equilibrium price and quantity for rental housing in Limitville.
b. If the Limitville Municipal Council decided to limit rentals charged by landlords to P_r, what would happen to the quantity of rental housing demanded?
c. In the short run, what is the quantity of rental housing supplied in Limitville at the price P_r? In the diagram, indicate the excess demand ("shortage") of rentals in the short run.
d. Now indicate the excess demand in the long run. Suggest reasons why the reduction in quantity supplied would be greater in the long run than in the short run.
e. At the controlled price of rentals, P_r, is price fully performing its rationing function? What sorts of *non*-price rationing mechanisms might be used to ration rentals?

6. Consider the information about the market for corn contained in Exhibit 4. (Quantities are in billions of bushels.)

EXHIBIT 4

Quantity demanded	Price per bushel	Quantity supplied
3.0	2.65	3.9
3.1	2.50	3.7
3.2	2.35	3.5
3.3	2.20	3.3
3.4	2.05	3.1
3.5	1.90	2.9
3.6	1.75	2.7
3.7	1.60	2.5

a. Diagram an initial equilibrium in the market for corn. What is the equilibrium price and quantity?

Now suppose that the U.S. government imposes a price floor for corn at a price of $2.50 per bushel. The government buys up and stockpiles the corn surplus that results from the price floor.

b. Depict the price floor in your diagram from part a. What are quantities produced, consumed, and stockpiled?

c. What is the value of the total dollar receipts of corn farmers? The total spending on corn products by consumers? By taxpayers?

Some have proposed that a better way of supporting corn prices would be to replace the price floor with a target price at the same price level. Farmers would base their production decisions on the target price but would dump their entire output on the market for whatever price consumers would pay for it. The government would then give farmers a "deficiency payment" equal to the difference between the target price and the market price.

d. Indicate in your diagram the market price and the size of the deficiency payment under this target price policy. What would be the market price? The size of the deficiency payment?

e. Comparing the target price option to the price floor policy:
   (1) Do the total receipts of farmers (and therefore the total spending of consumers and taxpayers combined) rise, fall, or remain the same?
   (2) Does the quantity of corn consumed by the public rise, fall, or remain the same? Which policy do you prefer? Explain briefly.

7. Consider the following passage from *Business Week* magazine:

"Says Irvin Elkin, president of the Associated Milk Producers Inc. 'Major cuts in [dairy] support prices run the risk of driving many dairy farm families out of business, which would mean higher milk prices.'" What is probably correct about Elkin's assertion? What is incorrect? Support both answers.

LEARNING THE MECHANICS—MULTIPLE CHOICE

1. If the price of tickets to the World Series were below the competitive equilibrium price, then
   a. the quantity supplied would be greater than the quantity demanded.
   b. the demand for World Series tickets must be elastic.
   c. there would be no transactions between buyers and sellers of the tickets.
   d. the number of persons seeking to obtain tickets to World Series games would be greater than the number of available tickets.

2. Which of the following would cause the price of wheat to rise?
   a. A decrease in the price of corn, a substitute for wheat
   b. An increase in the price of soybeans, a substitute for wheat
   c. A decrease in the price of fertilizer
   d. A diet craze among Americans that decreases their demand for bread products

3. A demand curve gives the relationship between price and quantity demanded, *other things constant*. These "other things" include all of the following except
   a. consumer preferences.
   b. income.
   c. the price of the commodity.
   d. the price of substitute goods.

4. If cigars and cigarettes are substitute goods, an increase in the price of cigars would result in
   a. an increase in the sales of cigarettes.
   b. a decrease in the price of cigarettes.
   c. a decrease in the sales of cigarettes.
   d. an increase in the sales of cigars.

5. If the price of a bushel of wheat is fixed (say, by government price regulations) *above* its market equilibrium price, the most likely result would be
   a. an increase in the quantity of wheat demanded.
   b. a decrease in the quantity of wheat supplied in the short run.
   c. a decrease in the incentive to expand the future supply of wheat.
   d. a surplus of wheat.

6. Which of the following would be most likely to cause the demand for Miller beer to increase?
   a. An increase in the price of Budweiser beer
   b. A decrease in consumer income
   c. A decrease in the price of barley used to make Miller beer
   d. An increase in the price of pretzels, eaten with beer

7. The demand curve for a commodity indicates the maximum amount the consumer would be willing to pay for each unit of the good. What will be the effect of an increase in the price the consumer must pay for the product?
   a. There will be a decrease in the quantity demanded.
   b. The entire demand curve will shift to the right.
   c. There will be no effect, since the maximum amount the consumer would be willing to pay stays the same.
   d. The consumer's demand will decrease.

8. All things constant, a decrease in bus, train, and airplane fares will
   a. shift the demand curve for automobiles to the left.
   b. cause a movement along the demand curve for automobiles.
   c. shift the demand curve for automobiles to the right.
   d. have no impact on the demand curve for automobiles.

9. In the absence of government intervention, the pricing system would ration gasoline to those individuals and firms
   a. who were able and willing to pay the highest price.
   b. who had the highest income.
   c. who lived the farthest from their place of work.
   d. who owned automobiles that used the most gas.

10. If the market price is above the equilibrium price, there will be a tendency for price to fall, causing
    a. quantity demanded to fall and quantity supplied to rise.
    b. quantity demanded to rise and quantity supplied to fall.
    c. both quantity demanded and quantity supplied to fall.
    d. both quantity demanded and quantity supplied to rise.

11. Quotas restricting imports of Japanese automobiles will have what effects on the supply of and demand for *domestically* made automobiles?
    a. Cause demand and supply to increase
    b. Cause demand and quantity supplied to increase
    c. Cause supply and quantity demanded to increase
    d. Cause demand to increase and supply to decrease

12. Alfred Marshall helped develop the concepts of "long run" and "short run." Which of the following is the most accurate description of the distinction between the two?
    a. The short run is a time period of less than three months, whereas the long run covers time periods of more than seven months.
    b. The long run is a time period of sufficient length for decision-makers to make adjustments that are too costly (or impossible) to make in the short run.
    c. The long run is a time period of sufficient length for producers to develop new technologies, whereas in the short run, technology is constant.
    d. The long run is a marathon, whereas the short run is more like the hundred-yard dash.

13. The tendency for capital investment in each market to move toward a uniform or normal rate of return is called the
    a. uniform market law of supply
    b. uniform market law of demand.
    c. capital investment equilibrium principle.
    d. rate-of-return equalization principle.

14. Under competitive conditions, market prices
    a. are always in long-run equilibrium.
    b. can be determined only after a detailed study of supply and demand conditions has been made.
    c. are incapable of coordinating the actions of buyers and sellers.
    d. generally bring the self-interest of individual consumers and producers into harmony with the general welfare, resulting in economic efficiency.

THE ECONOMIC WAY OF THINKING—MULTIPLE CHOICE

1. If the quantity demanded is greater than the quantity supplied, the pricing system (through the invisible hand) will respond by
   a. lowering the product price and therefore the profits of the firms responsible for not producing enough.
   b. raising the product price and producer profits.
   c. lowering product price, but increasing producer profits.
   d. raising product price, but lowering producer profits.

2. "If gasoline were taxed, the price of gasoline would rise. Consequently, the demand for gasoline would fall, causing the price to fall to the original level. Therefore the tax would not be effective." This statement
   a. is essentially correct.
   b. is incorrect—after the demand falls, the price would fall, but to some level higher than the original level.
   c. is incorrect—demand and quantity demanded are confused.
   d. is incorrect—the tax would be effective even if the price fell to the original level, since the demand for gasoline dropped (which was the primary purpose of the tax).

3. Which of the following was a result of the increased prices of gasoline and petroleum-related products in early 1979?
   a. The demand for small cars expanded.
   b. The incentive to use more oil for heating increased.
   c. Tourism in south Florida increased relative to 1977–1978.
   d. The demand for used Cadillacs and Lincoln Continentals increased.

4. About two-thirds of the private rental housing in New York City is subject to rent control. The rent control price is usually set below the market equilibrium price. Economic theory suggests that this rent control price would
   a. increase landlords' profits.
   b. cause many rental units to be abandoned or poorly kept up by landlords.
   c. result in a surplus of rental units in the near future.
   d. reduce housing discrimination against minorities.

5. With a price ceiling *above* the equilibrium price,
   a. quantity demanded would exceed quantity supplied.
   b. quantity supplied would exceed quantity demanded.
   c. the market would be in equilibrium.
   d. the equilibrium price would be expected to fall over time.

6. "The price of wheat rose sharply because (a) the drought reduced the yield per acre, and (b) millers sought to stockpile wheat to protect themselves from future price increases that would occur if the drought were to continue." This quotation suggests that the price rise was caused by
   a. an increase in demand and a movement along the supply curve.
   b. an increase in supply and a movement along the demand curve.
   c. an increase in both supply and demand.
   d. a reduction in supply and a short-run increase in demand.

7. "The winds of the recent hurricanes in Florida are bringing financial gain to California citrus growers. Because of the extensive damage to the Florida citrus crop, California citrus products are commanding their highest prices ever." Which of the following statements best explains the economics of this quotation?
   a. The supply of Florida oranges has decreased, causing their price to increase and the demand for the substitute California oranges also to increase.
   b. The supply of Florida oranges has decreased, causing the supply of California oranges to increase and their prices to rise.
   c. The demand for Florida oranges has been reduced by the hurricane, causing a greater demand for the California oranges and an increase in their price.
   d. The demand for Florida oranges has been reduced, causing their prices to fall and thereby increasing the demand for the substitute California oranges.

8. Which of the following is an example of one of the basic questions being solved with the price mechanism?
   a. What to produce is decided by a central planning board, and the decisions on what prices to charge are passed down to the retailers.
   b. How to produce is decided only after negotiation with union leaders.
   c. What to produce is decided when consumers who want more of a good bid up the price of that good, attracting more production.
   d. For whom to produce is decided by setting up a rationing program and charging a fair price to all consumers.

9. All of the following would affect the supply of automobiles except one. What would *not* effect the supply of automobiles?
   a. Higher prices for steel and other resources used in the production costs of automobiles
   b. A successful physical fitness plan encouraging all Americans to walk to their destinations
   c. A technological improvement reducing the production costs of automobiles
   d. Increased wages for the members of the United Auto Workers

10. Per capita expenditures for physicians' services increased from $31.45 in 1960 and $47.70 in 1966, an increase of 35 percent in dollars of constant purchasing power. Most of this change occurred in price, rather than in quantity of services delivered. Economic theory would suggest that the observed data could best be explained as
    a. an increase in supply, but little change in demand.
    b. a decrease in both supply and demand.
    c. an increase in demand, while supply remained relatively constant.
    d. a sharp increase in both supply and demand.

The following background will help answer questions 11–14.

In the United States today, it's difficult to find affordable, dependable, and responsible day care for children of working parents. For simplicity, let's assume that the day-care market has two halves. One half is made up of day-care centers, both privately and publicly funded. The other half is made up of "at home providers," principally nannies. Some of the nannies are illegal immigrants who have no other job opportunities, while others have special visa status with the INS (Immigration and Naturalization Service). Further assume that equilibrium in the day-care center market is at $140 a week and that equilibrium in the nanny market is $120 a week. Finally, suppose that the INS cracks down on illegal aliens and restricts the number of special "nanny visas."

11. After the crackdown, you'd expect the equilibrium price in the nanny market could most easily be confused with price and quantity changes resulting from
    a. less than $120 a week.
    b. still $120 a week.
    c. more than $120 a week.
    d. equal to the equilibrium price in the day-care market.

12. The price and quantity changes caused by the crackdown in the nanny market could most easily be confused with price and quantity changes resulting from
    a. the establishment of free, national day care.
    b. a marked increase in the desire and ability of parents to stay at home with their children.
    c. the closing of all federally funded day-care centers.
    d. an increase in the legal job opportunities available in the United States for people with local experience as nannies.

13. After the crackdown, you'd expect the new equilibrium price in the day-care market to be
    a. unchanged.
    b. less than $140 a week.
    c. greater than $140 a week.
    d. equal to the equilibrium price in the nanny market.

14. Suppose that Congress passes a law that fixes prices at $140 per week for the day-care centers and $120 per week for nannies. If the INS does not change its crackdown policy, the Congressional act would
    a. restore the nanny market to its original equilibrium.
    b. cause a shortage (excess demand) in the nanny market.
    c. cause a surplus (excess supply) in the nanny market.
    d. have an indeterminate effect on the nanny market.

THE ECONOMIC WAY OF THINKING—DISCUSSION QUESTIONS

1. Air traffic congestion is a major problem at the municipal airports of many major cities. Some economists have suggested that charging a higher usage price, particularly during peak traffic periods (8–10 A.M. and 5–10 P.M.), would improve the situation. What impact would the higher fees have on the
   a. scheduling of flights?
   b. number of landings and takeoffs during heavy traffic periods?
   c. fuel wastage and other costs of circling the airport?
   d. number of small private planes using major airports?

2. Consider the following statement: "Campus parking permits and meters are inefficient and unfair. Campus parking should be free, with parking spaces allocated on a first-come, first-served basis."
   a. Is "free" parking more efficient than permit or meter parking?
   b. With "free" parking, who, if anyone, gains? Who loses?
   c. Would you favor "free" parking on your campus? Why or why not?

3. Consider the choice between "rationing by price" (with prices flexible) and "rationing by waiting" (with prices fixed) in the health care industry.
   a. What type of waste occurs with rationing by waiting?
   b. Suppose that there is a surge in demand for health care services. Which rationing system provides health care providers with better information and incentives? Explain.

4. Explain what is wrong with the following reasoning: "When meat prices rise due to a decrease in the supply of meat, the demand for meat decreases, so meat prices end up falling."
   a. Suppose a price is temporarily above its equilibrium level. How do you think producers figure out that the price is in fact "too high"? Explain how a lower price causes both production and consumption adjustments that help to correct the situation.
   b. Suppose a price is temporarily below its equilibrium level. How do you think producers figure out that the price is in fact "too low"? Explain how a higher price causes both production and consumption adjustments that help to correct the situation.

5. People often use the term "demand" when they actually mean "quantity demanded"; the same is true of "supply" and "quantity supplied."
   a. What causes a change in quantity demanded but not a change in demand?
   b. What absurd condition is implied by the following statement: "The supply of oil is expected to exceed demand by 1995."
   c. How can you rephrase the statement of part b so that it makes economic sense?

6. In an effort to control rising prices during the 1970s, many governments adopted price controls, fixing prices (and wages) for extended periods of time and thereby causing shortages of some goods and surpluses of others. Respond to the following statement: "Shortages are a disadvantage of price controls, but surpluses are an offsetting advantage."

7. How would a prolonged drought in the Midwest affect each of the following?
   a. Water prices in the Midwest
   b. Farmland prices in the Midwest
   c. Farmland prices in other parts of the country
   d. Fertilizer prices
   e. Manufacturing wages in the Midwest

CURRENT DEBATES IN ECONOMICS

Debate Number One: Should We Raise the Minimum Wage?

Yes, We Should Raise the Minimum Wage:

A Living Wage
A *Los Angeles Times* editorial

[Reprinted with permission from the *Los Angeles Times*, October 14, 1986, page 4, Part II.]

It used to be that the minimum wage provided more than just gas money for middle-class teenagers. Back when it was $1.60 an hour, in 1967, a 40-hour work week at minimum wage brought home enough to support a family of three. Now, at $3.35, it is scarcely enough to keep one worker out of poverty. The working poor will keep working themselves deeper into poverty as long as the minimum wage is stagnant.

Congress established the minimum wage in 1935 to prevent workers from savagely undercutting each other during the Depression. In doing so, it sought to guarantee a decent—a minimum—standard of living for all workers. Until this decade the minimum wage did that, equaling about half of the average private industry wage. But the wage floor that Congress built has sunk into the depths of neglect. Today's minimum wage is only 38% of the average private industry wage, its lowest point by that measure since 1949. Its buying power has dropped 25% since 1981, when Congress last raised it. It was inadequate then, a cruel joke now.

About 8 million individuals now work at or near the minimum wage. A worker clocking a 40-hour week 50 weeks a year at minimum wage earns $6,964. For an individual not heading a family, that's just above the official poverty line, generously drawn at $5,600. Try living on it. Worse, try supporting a family. The minimum wage is dismally deficient for any worker who has to support someone else. The income, for example, of a family of three headed by a minimum wage worker is $1,700 under the poverty line—20% less than it takes to live decently. Mini-

mum wage earners are not just well-to-do teens; indeed employers in some cities and suburbs cannot find anyone to work at that wage. Almost half of minimum wage workers are 25 years or older, and one of every four is a head of household. In 1984, 2.1 million people worked full-time year round, but they and their families remained in poverty, including 1.2 million heads of households.

Most states, like California, prop up the working poor with programs such as Medicaid, food stamps and AFDC. These usually do not, nor were they designed to, lift a family out of poverty. They just make poverty less miserable.

In some states, workers forfeit their benefits once they take a job. That, of course, destroys the incentive for welfare recipients to take a job that pays less than welfare, as in most circumstances minimum wage jobs do. Thus it is expensive and self-defeating to keep the minimum wage so low. Taxpayers are subsidizing the wages of the working poor, making up for what employers ought to be paying.

After five years of inaction, Congress should lift the minimum wage to at least $4.35 an hour, which would be equivalent to its traditional level of half the average private industry wage. If raised gradually, it wouldn't squeeze employers who have to pay more. A better minimum wage won't stoke inflation; there are simply too few who work at it. It might result in fewer jobs, but any loss should be more than offset by higher earnings. And those stung would most likely be youths, not adults. Raising the minimum wage would cut welfare expenses, restore the purchasing power of the working poor, and most important, lift many of them from the throes of poverty.

Economics aside, the decision to raise the minimum wage is a moral one. It is unnecessary and unconscionable for persons to work and be poor. The term, *working poor*, should be an oxymoron. Right now, it's not. Congress can change that.

No, We Should Not Raise the Minimum Wage:

Minimum-Wage Politicking
By Robert J. Samuelson

[Reprinted with permission from *Newsweek*, July 11, 1988. Abridged.]

Some of you may think that raising the minimum wage is a long-overdue way of helping the poor. Please discard this outdated idea. Increasing the minimum wage is misguided social policy, even if it seems the fair thing to do.

Popular wisdom is understandable and well meaning. The current minimum—$3.35 an hour—hasn't been raised since 1981. By 1987 it stood at only 37% percent of average

hourly earnings. It hasn't been that far below the average wage rate since 1949. This seems monstrously indecent. Workers stuck in minimum-wage jobs are being progressively impoverished. Their pay is about $7,000 a year. That's less than two-thirds of the government's official poverty floor for a family of four. It's a dismaying picture. It's also thoroughly misleading.

The profile of minimum-wage workers simply doesn't fit the popular stereotype. Consider:

• Most aren't from poor families. About 70 percent come from families with incomes at least 50 percent above the poverty line, according to a study by the Congressional

Budget Office. Only 19 percent come from families below the poverty line.

- Most minimum-wage jobs aren't held by heads of families. About two-thirds are held by young (24 and under) and single workers. About a third are teenagers. The typical minimum-wage worker is a teenager from a non-poor family working as a waiter or waitress. A third of all minimum-wage jobs are in restaurants.

- Most workers don't get stuck in full-time minimum-wage jobs; indeed, two-thirds of minimum-wage jobs are part time. Some jobs permanently pay the minimum, but they have high turnover. Other jobs may start at the minimum, but companies quickly give raises to employees they want to keep. Since 1980 the proportion of workers receiving the minimum has fallen from 11 to 4 percent.

Government policies shouldn't be based on stereotypes that are demonstrably false. Legislation passed by the House Education and Labor Committee would raise the minimum wage about 51 percent, to $5.05, by 1992. Enacting this sort of increase to help the minority of workers who fit the stereotype—heads of families with full-time jobs—is self-defeating. It would raise unemployment and inflation in return for, at most, a tiny reduction in poverty.

When government mandates higher labor costs, someone has to pay for them. Companies are likely to raise prices and fire (or not hire) the least productive workers. After reviewing the available studies, economists Frederick Furlong and Marc Charney of the Federal Reserve Bank of San Francisco concluded that the present proposal would raise inflation at least a quarter of a percentage point and result in the loss of 100,000 to 300,000 jobs. "The increase in unemployment would be among lower-wage workers, the group that the minimum-wage law is supposed to help," they write.

Supporters of a higher minimum dismiss these side effects as trivial. For instance, they point out that the extra joblessness would add only 0.1 to 0.3 percentage points to the unemployment rate. This argument is absurd. It justifies bad legislation as long as the bad effects are small, as Rep. Richard Armey, Republican of Texas, says. "Why not raise [the minimum] to $10 or $20 an hour?" he asks. "The adverse effect of the minimum wage is perfectly obvious when we imagine it inflated to $10 an hour . . . At $5.05 the effects on employment are not quite so blindingly apparent. Instead of millions of workers being laid off, there will be only a mere few hundred thousand."

Tough choices: There are better ways of helping the working poor. Rep. Thomas E. Petri, Republican of Wisconsin, suggests improving the earned-income tax credit, which goes to working parents with low incomes. The maximum credit is now $874. Because most of these workers don't owe income taxes, the credit is refundable. It's a direct payment that covers their social security taxes and a bit more. But today's credit doesn't vary according to family size. Petri would provide bigger credits for larger families, up to $2,500 for four children. This approach wouldn't raise prices, wouldn't deter hiring and would direct benefits to those in need.

It's not a partisan idea. An early advocate was economist Robert Reischauer of the Brookings Institute, a Democrat. Privately, some Democratic congressmen concede it's a good concept. But the Democratic congressional leadership clings to the minimum wage out of habit and expediency. It's superficially popular. One recent Gallop poll showed 77 percent of Americans support a higher minimum. It's also heavily favored by organized labor, a major Democratic constituency. Finally, it doesn't add to the budget deficit. By contrast, Petri's proposal would cut tax revenues about $2 billion. Doing it right would mean raising someone else's taxes or cutting some spending.

There's no taste for such tough choices. Even raising the minimum wage is harder than it seems. The dilemma is basic: the larger the increase, the greater the economic damage; the smaller the increase, the more it's a gesture.

A lot of intricate legislative maneuvering lies ahead. It should be fascinating. But be assured that it doesn't have much to do with the poor. It's over political symbolism. Raising the minimum wage involves the worst kind of backdoor spending and feel-good politics: people can say they're helping the poor when they're really not.

Holding a Debate

Many students will benefit from and will enjoy participating in a debate on this topic either in class or in an informal study group. After completing both readings and possibly doing some additional research (for example, see your textbook), get three or four volunteers for each side of the debate, choose a moderator if your instructor is not available, and devote about a half an hour to opening statements, rebuttals and summaries. Good luck!

Discussion

1. If you read both articles, see if you can explain the following paradox. Most politicians, including both major party candidates in the 1988 presidential campaign, are in favor of increasing the minimum wage,

and yet most economists, including economists from almost every political and cultural background, think that the minimum wage hurts many of those it is intended to help. How can you explain this difference in opinion?

2. If you read the *Los Angeles Times* editorial, do you agree with the normative judgment in the last paragraph? Explain. Is the phrase "working poor" an oxymoron? (What *is* an oxymoron?)

3. If you read the Samuelson article, do you see any potential problems with his suggestion that we improve the earned-income tax credit instead of increasing the minimum wage? Which do you think will cost more? Which do you think will help the poor more? Explain.

CHAPTER FOUR

SUPPLY AND DEMAND
FOR THE PUBLIC SECTOR

TRUE OR FALSE

T F

1. When production of a good results in externalities that impose a cost on secondary parties, the output level of the good often exceeds the socially ideal amount.

2. The total social cost of an action includes the costs to the voluntary participants and any costs imposed on secondary parties.

3. Any commodity provided by the public sector is defined as a public good.

4. It is often difficult to exclude nonpaying citizens from receiving the benefits of a public good.

5. When an activity imposes spillover costs on secondary parties, a government tax policy that would reduce the level of the activity could improve economic efficiency.

6. Well-organized special interest groups may be able to use the political process for their own gain even though the action results in a net social loss.

7. A policy that provides immediate, readily identified benefits at the expense of a cost that is in the future and difficult to identify tends to be very attractive to a legislator seeking to enhance his or her chances of winning an election.

8. Spillover costs often result from the production of steel when the air is used for purposes of waste disposal.

9. The public sector produces nothing and therefore contributes nothing to the improvement of resource allocation.

10. Although income distribution may not be ideal, the voluntary exchange mechanism will always lead to the socially efficient allocation of resources.

11. National defense is an example of a public good.

PROBLEMS AND PROJECTS

1. Indicate which of the following goods is a private good (P), a public good (PG), or has characteristics of both (B). Explain your answer in each case.

   a. A measles shot _____

   _____

   b. A fireworks display _____

   _____

   c. National defense _____

   _____

   d. Neckties _____

   _____

   e. A television program _____

   _____

   f. A filet mignon steak _____

   _____

   g. A taxicab _____

   _____

   h. A rose garden _____

   _____

   i. A flood control project _____

   _____

   j. A poem _____

   _____

2. Consider the supply and demand for public-sector action, and decide whether each of the following illustrates
   (1) rent-seeking behavior by private parties,
   (2) vote-seeking behavior by elected officials, or
   (3) the rational ignorance effect.
   ___ a. Members of Congress have resisted curbing lobbying activities of political action coalitions (PACs).
   ___ b. Election results are often distorted by poorly informed voters and low voter turnouts.
   ___ c. Liquor wholesalers in most states have lobbied for state laws that compel retailers to buy their liquor supplies only from the nearest available wholesaler, instead of shopping around.
   ___ d. A majority of voters support protectionism against imports even though such protectionism cost consumers over $80 billion in 1988.

3. Exhibit 1 illustrates what the world demand for petroleum might look like in the short run. The supply curve (S) represents the world supply of petroleum if petroleum suppliers behave competitively.

EXHIBIT 1

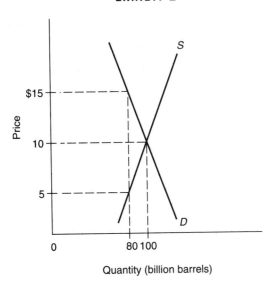

Quantity (billion barrels)

a. What would be the long-run, competitive equilibrium price and quantity of petroleum? Show these in the diagram.
b. At competitive equilibrium, calculate the total revenues earned by petroleum suppliers. (Remember that total revenue is price times quantity sold.)
c. Suppose now that petroleum suppliers agree to restrict the quantity they sell to 80 billion barrels. Draw in the supply curve. What price would they charge? What would total revenue be?
d. If only 80 billion barrels were sold, what is the value (in dollars) of the consumers' valuation of the last barrel produced and sold? Is this consumer valuation of the last unit larger or smaller than the producers' opportunity cost of producing that last unit? Is this an efficient or an inefficient outcome for society?
e. Could government policy have helped avoid this problem? How?

4. Exhibit 2 shows the supply and demand schedules for pulp paper in Academia, a hypothetical country.

EXHIBIT 2

Price (per ton)	Quantity (ton/year)	
	Demanded	Supplied
$150	1000	7000
140	2000	6000
130	3000	5000
120	4000	4000
110	5000	3000
100	6000	2000

a. On a piece of graph paper, plot the demand and supply curves and show the equilibrium price and quantity for pulp paper in Academia.
b. Suppose that the production of pulp paper results in external pollution costs of $20 per ton produced. In your diagram, show a supply curve that would include these external costs. What are the "ideal" (efficient) price and output for pulp paper? Show these in your diagram.

5. Exhibit 3 below depicts the market for baseball teams, with the total number of teams on the horizontal axis and the price of each team (in millions of dollars) on the vertical axis.

EXHIBIT 3

Quantity demanded	Price	Quantity supplied
17	68	35
20	62	32
23	56	29
26	50	26
29	44	23
32	38	20
35	32	17

a. Diagram the supply and demand curves and determine the values of the free market equilibrium price and quantity.

Some have argued that a baseball team generates external benefits for a city by increasing the city's morale and pride and bringing in extra tourist revenue.

b. Suppose the value of these external benefits turns out to be $24 million per team. Use your diagram from part a to depict these externalities. What is the efficient total number of baseball teams?
c. What type of policy could a city government use to attract a baseball team?
d. Suppose that there really are no external benefits associated with baseball teams. What theory described in the text suggests that the policies you described in part c might get adopted anyway?

LEARNING THE MECHANICS — MULTIPLE CHOICE

1. All but one of the following public sector actions will help to provide an economic environment that can facilitate the attainment of gains from market exchange. Which one *reduces* the efficiency of the market process?
   a. Promoting competitive markets
   b. Protecting persons from fraud
   c. Providing a stable monetary framework
   d. Protecting consumers by fixing prices below equilibrium

2. Competition among producers is important because it
   a. serves to protect the consumer by providing him with alternatives to the prices offered by any single seller.
   b. serves to protect the producer, assuring her of at least a fair rate of return.
   c. means that the market will always meet the social conditions of ideal economic efficiency.
   d. always leads to prices that reflect the total social cost of producing each good.

3. Ideal public sector action can potentially improve economic efficiency
   a. because political decision-makers are generally concerned with problems associated with income distribution.
   b. if the government sets prices above equilibrium for commodities in a competitive market and below equilibrium for commodities in monopolistic markets.
   c. when spillover or external effects cause market inefficiency.
   d. because of the rational ignorance effect.

4. An action that imposes spillover costs on a secondary party results in
   a. voluntary exchange.
   b. public sector action.
   c. involuntary exchange.
   d. market adjustments that lead to the ideal social outcome.

5. It is difficult for the market process to provide public goods because
   a. they must be produced by government.
   b. it will be difficult to get potential consumers to pay for such goods since there is not a direct link between payment for and receipt of the good.
   c. consumers do not really want public goods, even though such goods are best for them.
   d. individual consumers will fail to gain from the production of goods that benefit the general public.

6. When there is no interference with the market mechanism
   a. the market will under-allocate resources to the production of goods with external costs.
   b. the market will over-allocate resources to the production of goods with external benefits.
   c. the cost to society from production will be greater than the private cost to producers when external costs are present.
   d. the output of public goods will generally exceed the optimal level of output.

7. Public sector action
   a. promotes economic efficiency except when self-interest leads to political corruption.
   b. sometimes improves efficiency and sometimes generates inefficiency, since proposals that help win elections are not necessarily efficient.
   c. generally leads to economic inefficiency because the public sector is bureaucratic in nature, and bureaucrats are lazy.
   d. promotes economic efficiency when collective decisions are made democratically.

8. All of the following are true about the market and public sectors *except*
   a. competitive behavior is present in both sectors.
   b. the public sector utilizes the price mechanism more than the private sector.
   c. the public sector can break the individual consumption-payment link more easily than can the private sector.
   d. there is more free choice for individual consumers in the private sector than in the public sector.

9. Which of the following is *not* true of the concept of economic efficiency?
   a. Economic efficiency defines the ideal income distribution.
   b. An economically efficient solution occurs when all exchanges that will lead to an improvement in the well-being of individuals have been undertaken.
   c. The largest possible benefit is obtained from a given level of cost.
   d. Each good is produced at the lowest possible cost.

10. Simply stated, the rational ignorance effect explains why
    a. consumers are rational but not very intelligent.
    b. voters are rational but not very intelligent.
    c. voters are intelligent to remain rational.
    d. rational voters remain ignorant.

11. Despite many differences, the market and public sectors are *similar* in which one of the following respects?
    a. In both sectors, income (or power) is distributed on the basis of the same criterion.
    b. Consumers in the market sector and voters in the public sector are equally well informed.
    c. Voluntary exchange, rather than compulsion, is characteristic of both sectors.
    d. It will be costly to use scarce goods, whether through the private or the public sector.

12. Which of the following activities is *least* likely to give rise to external costs or benefits?
    a. Spraying to control mosquitos in your backyard
    b. Driving one's car during rush hour
    c. Inoculating your children during a flu epidemic
    d. Watching fewer movies on television

13. Which of the following is the best example of rent-seeking?
    a. A lobbying organization that has no position on rent control makes contributions to politicians who favor rent control.
    b. A steel company makes contributions to politicians who favor lowering taxes on steel.
    c. A politician convinces colleagues of the advantages of renting an apartment rather than buying a home while in Washington, D.C.
    d. A diaper manufacturer hires only those employees who favor lower taxes on diapers.

THE ECONOMIC WAY OF THINKING—MULTIPLE CHOICE

1. Driving your automobile in Los Angeles during the rush hour causes externalities because
    a. it adds congestion and pollution from auto exhaust, reducing the welfare of others.
    b. gasoline is scarce and you must pay for it.
    c. gasoline is a public good.
    d. your actions will benefit others even though you will be unable to charge them for the service.

2. In the absence of government action, the private market would not produce as much national defense as citizens desire because
    a. individual citizens do not receive personal benefits from national defense.
    b. private firms do not like to produce goods with public good characteristics.
    c. it would be difficult for private firms to charge for national defense since it cannot usually be withheld from nonpaying customers.
    d. national defense benefits a country but not its citizens.

3. If economic efficiency is the criterion, which of the following is the most important justification for the government, rather than private enterprise, providing certain economic goods and services?
    a. The government can provide political goods free of charge.
    b. The government can redistribute incomes such that the poverty problem is mitigated.
    c. A private market cannot eliminate the misallocation that results from the rational ignorance of consumers.
    d. A private market does not provide a way to sell certain "public goods" because the benefits derived cannot be limited to those persons who pay for them.

4. Apart from income distribution, criteria of ideal economic efficiency require that (I) all trading in which both buyers and sellers can gain take place; (II) no trading take place for which the social cost (including any cost imposed on nonconsenting parties) exceeds the social benefit derived from the exchange.
   a. Both I and II are true.
   b. Neither I nor II is true.
   c. I is true, II is false.
   d. II is true, I is false.

5. Under a market system, individuals normally pay for a particular good; when goods are allocated through the public sector,
   a. an individual "pays" the approximate value of the government service through taxes.
   b. the individual does not pay—nor does anyone else—since the government simply prints money to finance the service.
   c. although the individual consumer often does not pay, costs are incurred that must be covered by someone (or some group).
   d. payment is avoided since the production of the services is not for profit.

   The following quotation relates to questions 6 and 7.
   "The ideal policy, from the viewpoint of the state, is one with identifiable beneficiaries, each of whom is helped appreciably, at the cost of many unidentifiable persons, none of whom is hurt very much"— George Stigler, *A Dialogue on the Proper Economic Role of the State.*

6. This statement is probably
   a. incorrect, because voters are well informed on a wide range of political issues.
   b. incorrect, because the political process dilutes the influence of special interest groups, since like other citizens, their members have only one vote.
   c. correct, because the well-informed voter will favor policies that cater to the views of small groups of people.
   d. correct, because voters who have a strong personal interest in an issue will tend to support candidates who cater to their views, whereas most other voters ignore the issue.

7. Which of the following groups does the above quotation suggest would have the most influence on public sector action?
   a. Taxpayers
   b. Nonunion laborers
   c. Special interest groups
   d. Consumers

8. Which of the following "goods" is the best example of a pure public good?
   a. Interstate highways
   b. Clean air
   c. Cultural centers
   d. Public education

9. An action that improves economic efficiency is one
   a. that does not involve any discrimination.
   b. for which the sum of the net benefits to those who favor the action is less than the sum of the net costs imposed on those who oppose the action.
   c. for which the sum of the net benefits to those who gain from the action is greater than the sum of the net costs to those who lose.
   d. that results in a majority of the people benefiting from the action.

10. If there are no spillover effects, voluntary exchange results in (**I**) an expected net gain for all participants in the transaction, (**II**) a social benefit that exceeds the social cost.
    a. Both I and II are true.
    b. Neither I nor II is true.
    c. I is true, II is false.
    d. II is true, I is false.

11. Special interest issues may lead to economic inefficiency since
    a. special interest groups consist, in general, of individuals who are less worthy than the general populace.
    b. politicians are members of special interest groups.
    c. individual voters are irrational in not obtaining information on special interest issues.
    d. the political process is likely to give undue weight to special interest groups, even though contrary action may be more efficient.

12. Economists use the term *short-sightedness effect* to describe which one of the following phenomena?
    a. Politicians tend to support actions that have immediate and easily recognized current benefits.
    b. Individuals are apt to spend their income on goods that bring immediate personal benefits.
    c. Voters elect politicians on the basis of campaign promises, regardless of what they may do once they are in office.
    d. Politicians support the programs of special interest groups in order to get elected; however, special interest support may be detrimental later, costing politicians popularity after the programs are implemented.

13. In the absence of government intervention, goods with external costs tend to be
    a. overproduced and overconsumed.
    b. overproduced and underconsumed.
    c. underproduced and overconsumed.
    d. underproduced and underconsumed.

THE ECONOMIC WAY OF THINKING—DISCUSSION QUESTIONS

1. What are two conditions for economic efficiency? Provide a specific example for each of four reasons why unregulated markets might fail to be efficient. Give three reasons why government intervention might promote inefficiency.

2. Respond to the following statement: "In the private sector, it's one vote per dollar. In the public sector it's one vote per citizen. Lobbying can be useful in bridging this gap between dollar votes and ballot votes: it can promote efficiency by offsetting the tendency of the political process toward a tyranny of the majority."

3. For some public goods it is feasible to withhold the benefits from those who don't contribute to the costs of production; for other public goods it is not feasible. List some examples of both types of public goods. Which type is more commonly provided by the private sector? Why?

4. Do you find the public choice theory of political behavior convincing? What do you see as its strengths? Its weaknesses? Do you think most politicians are motivated by personal self-interest? Cite evidence in support of your answer.

5. Why are well-organized special interest groups likely to be politically powerful? Why will vote-seeking political entrepreneurs have an incentive to cater to their views?

6. List as many goods as you can think of that have substantial public good characteristics that are provided by the private sector. Try weather forecasts and television signals for starters.

7. Chapter 2 introduced the concept of transaction costs. How do transaction costs help to explain why there is more (and more effective) lobbying by special interest groups than by the general public?

PERSPECTIVES IN ECONOMICS

New Buzzword, Old Philosophy
A Mobil advertisement

[From the *Los Angeles Times*, February 18, 1986, p. 4. Reprinted with the permission of the Mobil Corporation. ©1986 Mobil Corporation.]

The "mixed economy," that mixed marriage of public and private enterprise so widely hailed in the 1960s, has lost some of its pizzazz these days. The buzzword of the '80s is privatization, and it's firing the imagination of countries the world over—Capitalist, Socialist and Communist alike.

In Europe, for example, the British government has sold more than a dozen state-owned companies—some of the giants of its aerospace, communications, energy, tourism and trucking industries—and shifted more than 400,000 workers from public to private payrolls. Similar moves are taking place in France, Germany, Italy, Spain and Sweden.

In Asia, Japan is divesting the government railway, airline and telephone systems. South Korea is selling off banks and heavy industry. Less developed nations like Bangladesh and Pakistan are returning nationalized jute, textile, rice and flour mills to their former owners.

The economic momentum has even spread to the communist world. The Cuban government is selling state-owned houses to tenants. More than 10 million self-employed capitalists operate restaurants, street stalls, repair shops and other small enterprises in China. And in rural areas, farmers are prospering by selling surplus produce in the cities, and keeping the proceeds. Entrepreneurs in Hungary bid for the right to run their own businesses, and the system is catching on in other Eastern European nations.

Why the interest in privatization? Mostly because it works. Especially in the Communist lands, privatization has tended to raise the standard of living.

Not surprisingly, privatization is becoming popular in America, too. Prompted by the need to cut the deficit, the Reagan administration is seeking to cut costs by turning over to private operators such traditional loss leaders as Amtrak and the Federal Housing Administration, which insures private mortgages. Other possible initiatives: selling airport landing slots to individual carriers, for example, or letting private companies sort and deliver first-class mail.

Actually, in this country municipal governments have gotten the jump on the feds—contracting out for everything from hospital care to airport management. The town of La Mirada, California, has been one of the leaders, using the private sector for almost all key services—including police and fire protection, social welfare, and public works. Phoenix, Arizona, has saved millions of dollars by having its municipal agencies bid against outside companies for city contracts. A money-losing teaching hospital that the city of Louisville, Kentucky, turned over to a private company in 1983 is not only making money now, but also providing better patient care.

Privatization, in short, has meant more efficiency and lower costs—and, usually, better service. And if it involves the sale of an asset, the government gets a whopping one-time capital gain as well. So why has privatization been so long in coming? Fact is, it's been around for some time. Privatization is just a modern-day buzzword for an old, old philosophy. Adam Smith called it the free market. We call it a pretty good deal all around.

Discussion

1. What exactly *is* privatization? Why should a citizen who is not involved in a given industry care whether or not that industry's product is provided to the government by privately owned or publicly owned producers?

2. This article was published as an advertisement paid for by the Mobil Corporation. How could publishing such an ad possibly help to sell gasoline? Does Mobil's decision to publish the ad mean that they are a special interest group? Explain your answers.

3. The advertisement cites a hospital in Louisville, Kentucky. Why do you think that the private hospital was making money while the public hospital was losing money? What sorts of generalizations can you draw from such an example?

GOVERNMENT SPENDING AND TAXATION

TRUE OR FALSE

T F

□ □ 1. As one's marginal tax rate increases, the percentage of each additional dollar earned that the tax-payer is permitted to keep for personal expenditures will decline.

□ □ 2. If the supply curve of labor were perfectly vertical, the burden of an earnings (or payroll) tax would fall entirely on the employee in the form of a lower after-tax wage rate.

□ □ 3. A tax that takes more dollars from a low-income recipient than it takes from an high-income recipient must be regressive.

□ □ 4. A tax that takes more dollars from a high-income recipient than it takes from a low-income recipient must be progressive.

□ □ 5. One problem with the corporate income tax is that income generated by corporations is taxed twice—first by the sales tax and then by corporate income tax on the net income of the business firm.

□ □ 6. Federal expenditures on cash income maintenance constitute a larger share of the federal budget than do expenditures for national defense.

□ □ 7. A tax that is equitable is sure to be economically inefficient because the concepts of equity and efficiency are inherently opposed.

□ □ 8. If the percentage of income that is taxed away increases as an individual's income increases, the tax must be regressive.

□ □ 9. Borrowing and user charges are two alternatives to taxes as sources for government revenue.

□ □ 10. According to the benefit principle of taxation, the benefits of taxes should be levied according to the ability of the taxpayer to pay.

□ □ 11. Since the mid-1950s, the purchases of goods and services of the Federal government have declined as a share of GDP.

□ □ 12. Under the proportional income tax, the dollar tax liability of a high-income taxpayer will exceed the dollar tax liability for a low-income taxpayer. (*Hint:* Assume all income is taxable.)

PROBLEMS AND PROJECTS

1. Assume that a massive tax reform bill changes the current federal income tax rate schedule to the following simple tax schedule:

Income (dollars)	Marginal tax rate
Under 20,000	10%
20,000–50,000	20%
Over 50,000	30%

   a. If your income is $30,00, what is your total tax? (*Hint:* it is not $6,000; that would be correct if 20% were the average tax rate.)
   b. If your income is $60,000, what is your total tax?
   c. Is this tax schedule progressive or regressive?
   d. Assume that the tax bill included indexed marginal tax rates and that inflation last year was 10%. Calculate what the new (indexed) tax schedule would be.

2. Exhibit 1 summarizes a portion of the U.S. federal income tax schedule for married couples filing jointly in 1983.

EXHIBIT 1

Bracket number	Taxable income	Total tax
1	$12,000	$ 1,166
2	24,000	3,518
3	36,000	6,904
4	48,000	11,214
5	60,000	16,014
6	72,000	21,294
7	84,000	26,574

   a. Calculate the average tax rate for brackets 2 and 6. Is your tax rate structure proportional, regressive, or progressive?
   b. Calculate the marginal tax rate for a married couple whose income increases from bracket 1 to bracket 2. From bracket 5 to bracket 6. Are these marginal rates greater or smaller than the corresponding average you calculated in part a?
   c. Suppose that the tax structure in 1982 was the same as that in Exhibit 1. Suppose also that you had the money income of $48,000 in 1982 and that your money income rose to $60,000 in 1983. If the rate of inflation between 1982 and 1983 had been 25 percent, would you have had an increase in your *constant purchasing power* (real) income? Would you have been required to pay a higher percentage of your income in income taxes? What phenomenon does this represent?

3. Exhibit 2 shows average income tax rates and the aggregate amount of taxable income that would be generated by economic activity at each rate.

EXHIBIT 2

Average tax rate (percent)	Aggregate taxable income (billions)	Tax revenue (billions)
20	$600	$120
30	500	_____
40	450	_____
50	400	_____
60	350	_____
70	300	_____
80	250	_____

a. Fill in the remaining entries in the tax revenue column.
b. On a piece of graph paper, plot the relationship between the tax rate (on the vertical axis) and tax revenues (on the horizontal axis). What is this relationship called?

4. Use the diagrams in Exhibit 3 to help you answer the questions below:

EXHIBIT 3

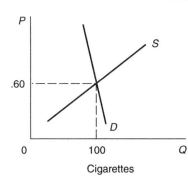 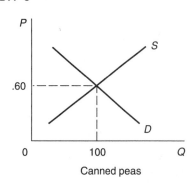

a. Suppose the government imposes a tax of $.40 per unit on cigarettes and on canned peas. Diagram the results. For which good does the incidence of the tax fall more heavily on sellers? On buyers? (*Note:* You do not have to determine actual numerical values.)
b. If the government could tax only one of these products and wanted to generate as much tax revenue as possible, which product should it tax? Why does the product you chose generate more tax revenue?
c. Some have argued that a tax on cigarettes promotes greater efficiency. Why do you think that might be true?

5. Each of the three tax options in Exhibit 4 generates about $40,000 of revenue to finance government spending by taxing three equal-sized families.

EXHIBIT 4

	Taxable income	Income taxes					
		Option 1	ATR	Option 2	ATR	Option 3	ATR
Family 1	$ 20,000	$13,333	_____	$ 4,444	_____	$ 3,000	_____
Family 2	60,000	13,333	_____	13,333	_____	12,000	_____
Family 3	100,000	13,333	_____	22,222	_____	25,000	_____

a. Fill in the average tax rate (ATR) for each family under each option.
b. Classify each tax option as either progressive, proportional or regressive.
c. Consider the following statement: "Government programs such as education, fire protection, and defense are equally available to all taxpayers, so it makes economic sense for all taxpayers to contribute an equal amount to finance these programs." Do you agree? If so, explain why. If not, explain why not and then indicate which tax option you prefer and briefly explain why.

LEARNING THE MECHANICS—MULTIPLE CHOICE

1. In the United States, the total tax revenues of the federal, state, and local governments constitute
   a. approximately one-tenth of the gross domestic product.
   b. approximately one-fifth of the gross domestic product.
   c. approximately one-third of the gross domestic product.
   d. approximately one-half of the gross domestic product.

2. The size of the public sector relative to total output is smaller in one of the following countries than for the United States. Which one?
   a. Japan
   b. France
   c. United Kingdom
   d. Sweden

3. The "incidence" of a tax is the term that indicates
   a. the person who is responsible for paying the tax to the Federal Treasury.
   b. the person who actually bears the burden of the tax.
   c. whether the tax is progressive.
   d. whether the tax results in greater benefits than costs.

4. If we assume that the demand for and supply of Big Jim's Sour Mash Whiskey is described by typically sloped demand and supply curves, which of the following would be the most likely impact of a tax placed on Big Jim's whiskey?
   a. Consumers would pay more, and Big Jim would receive more.
   b. Consumers would pay more, and Big Jim would receive less.
   c. Consumers would pay the same amount, and Big Jim would receive less.
   d. Consumers would pay more, and Big Jim would receive the same amount.

5. A progressive tax
   a. takes a similar percentage from all income brackets.
   b. takes a higher percentage from higher income brackets.
   c. takes a lower percentage from higher income brackets.
   d. is one that does not impede progress.

6. If the tax liability of a couple increases from $1000 to $1200 as their income increases from $10,000 to $11,000, the couple's marginal tax rate is
   a. 10 percent
   b. 11 percent
   c. 12 percent
   d. 20 percent

7. Inflation is likely to increase the actual tax rates paid by most households if tax rates are progressive and if tax brackets are held constant. One method of avoiding this tax increase is tax rate indexing, which consists of
   a. decreasing (narrowing) nominal income tax brackets in proportion to the general increase in prices.
   b. increasing (widening) nominal income tax brackets in proportion to the general increase in prices.
   c. pushing taxpayers into higher and higher tax brackets even if the growth of their income is just keeping up with the price increases.
   d. none of the above.

8. The largest single source of revenue for local, state, and federal governments (combined) is
   a. the personal income tax.
   b. the sales tax.
   c. the property tax.
   d. the corporate income tax.

9. Which of the following categories represents the largest percentage of total federal expenditures in the early 1990s?
   a. Interest on the national debt
   b. Revenue sharing
   c. National defense expenditures
   d. Cash income maintenance—including such expenditures as social security, Medicare, and veterans' benefits

10. In general, the relative size of the government sector in the United States
    a. is smaller than in countries that are just beginning to develop.
    b. is less than western European nations (such as France, West Germany, and the United Kingdom).
    c. is of no economic significance.
    d. falls primarily on the upper class.

11. Which of the following is clearly an example of a regressive tax?
    a. One that takes more from the rich than the poor
    b. One that is forward looking and leads to future economic growth
    c. One that takes a larger percentage of income as income rises
    d. One that taxes each individual the same number of dollars no matter what his income

12. If families at most income levels consume approximately the same amount of gasoline per year, then gasoline excise taxes are
    a. progressive.
    b. proportional.
    c. regressive.
    d. impossible to classify.

THE ECONOMIC WAY OF THINKING — MULTIPLE CHOICE

1. Assuming that individuals are primarily concerned with their own welfare, which of the following taxes are high-income families *least* likely to prefer?
   a. A progressive tax
   b. A regressive tax
   c. A proportional tax
   d. Any type of sales tax

2. A major problem with the current U.S. method of taxing capital gains is that the capital gains tax:
   a. combines with the corporate income tax to double-tax income.
   b. is unintentionally indexed in times of inflation.
   c. often taxes nominal gains (caused by inflation) instead of real gains (caused by real capital appreciation).
   d. fails to index nominal interest income.

3. According to positive economic analysis, the corporate income tax
   a. is bad, compared to other taxes.
   b. is good, compared to other taxes.
   c. is, in the end, paid by individuals, since only individuals can bear the burden of taxes.
   d. is not a burden on consumers.

4. In 1986, Congress approved a new tax bill that decreased marginal tax rates and increased the tax base by eliminating a number of deductions (or tax "loopholes"). Which of the following groups would be most likely to oppose such a tax revision?
   a. Low-income taxpayers with few if any deductions
   b. Middle-income taxpayers with few if any deductions
   c. High-income taxpayers with few if any deductions
   d. Employees of an industry whose product's status as a deduction is in danger of being eliminated

5. A 2-cents-per-gallon increase in the gasoline tax caused the price of gasoline to rise by two cents with no change in quantity. The incidence of the gasoline tax fell on
   a. the producers of gasoline.
   b. gasoline station operators.
   c. gasoline station employees.
   d. the consumers of gasoline.

6. Which of the following is *most* likely to be correct?
   a. An increase in tax rates will lead to a proportional increase in tax revenues.
   b. An increase in tax rates will lead to a more than proportional increase in tax revenues.
   c. An increase in tax rates will lead to a less than proportional increase in tax revenues.
   d. An increase in tax rates will always lead to a decrease in tax revenues.

7. The excess burden of a tax refers to
    a. the loss of private purchasing power due to the revenues transferred to the public sector.
    b. the additional tax that must be levied because some taxpayers engage in tax avoidance activities.
    c. the excess tax levied on high-income taxpayers relative to a taxpayer with an average income.
    d. the additional burden imposed on taxpayers because taxes distort prices and eliminate some mutually advantageous exchanges.

8. Which of the following would occur if a nation's tax structure were fully indexed?
    a. If one's money income rose at the same rate as the nation's inflation rate, one's tax liability would be unchanged.
    b. If one's money income rose more rapidly than the inflation rate, one's average tax rate would be unchanged.
    c. If one's money income rose less rapidly than the inflation rate, one's average tax rate would increase.
    d. If one's money income rose at the same rate as the nation's inflation rate, one's average and marginal tax rates would be unchanged.

9. In order to decide whether it is worthwhile to take a second job, a smart taxpayer would consider the
    a. marginal tax rate.
    b. average tax rate.
    c. before-tax income.
    d. wage rate, independent of taxes.

10. Under which conditions below would the incidence of a tax on a product fall entirely on buyers?
    a. Upward-sloping supply curve and downward-sloping demand curve
    b. Horizontal supply curve and vertical demand curve
    c. Vertical supply curve and horizontal demand curve
    d. The incidence of a tax is always shared between buyers and sellers

11. George Washington is said to have cautioned his colleagues, during the American Revolution, not to increase a particular tax rate too much for fear of raising less, and not more, revenues for the war effort. If this statement is true, which of the following does it imply about the Laffer curve?
    a. George Washington knew about the Laffer curve.
    b. Laffer stole the idea of his curve from Washington.
    c. The principle behind the Laffer curve has been understood, at least at some levels, for many years.
    d. Nothing at all; the Laffer curve has nothing to do with the relationship between tax rates and total tax revenues.

Questions 12–14 refer to Exhibit 5:

EXHIBIT 5

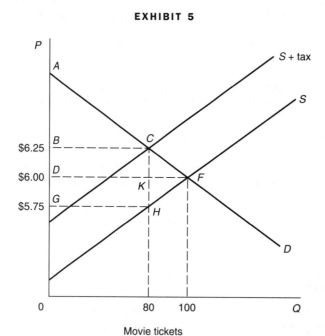

12. Suppose the government imposes a tax on movie tickets, causing the supply curve to shift from S to "S + tax." How much was the tax per ticket?
    a. $6.25
    b. $6.00
    c. $0.50
    d. $0.25

13. As a result of the tax, the government collected additional tax revenues of
    a. $50
    b. $40
    c. $25
    d. $20

14. The deadweight loss associated with this tax is best represented by the area
    a. CFK
    b. CFH
    c. BCKD
    d. BCHG

THE ECONOMIC WAY OF THINKING — DISCUSSION QUESTIONS

1. What are the major sources of federal tax revenues? State revenues? Local revenues? Which revenue source do you think is most likely to be progressive? Regressive? Explain your reasoning.

2. By law, Social Security taxes are split 50-50 between employees and employers.
   a. Respond to the following statement: "By the laws of economics, there is no guarantee that the incidence of the Social Security tax is shared evenly by employees and employers."
   b. Evidence suggests that the supply curve for labor is much steeper than the demand curve. Use a labor market supply and demand curve to indicate who absorbs most of the cost of payroll taxes.

3. According to the economic way of thinking, "businesses don't pay taxes, people do." How do you think people end up paying the taxes imposed on business?

4. Consider the following statement: "If we just raised the tax rates of the rich—taxpayers whose incomes are in excess of $50,000—we could cut the tax rates of the average American." What might be wrong with the logic of this statement?

5. Income taxes are set up in a way that keeps the marginal tax rate higher than the average tax rate for most taxpayers. Social Security taxes are levied at a constant rate until an income ceiling is reached; beyond that income ceiling, no further Social Security taxes are paid. As income rises, what happens to the average income tax rate? The average Social Security tax rate? Support both answers with numerical examples.

6. Suppose that you were running for Congress:
   a. Write a short campaign position paper outlining your platform on government spending and taxation policy. If you advocate any new programs, what would you say about their tax cost?
   b. Do you think your positions will help you raise campaign finances? Will they help you get elected? Why or why not? Address these questions in a letter to your finance chairman.

7. When governments provide electricity and garbage collection services, these services are usually financed with user charges, prices charged to the customers who use the services. Do you think this is a good idea? Why or why not? Would resource use be different if these services were financed by taxation and provided "free" to customers?

8. What is the tax base? Why is it important? More specifically, why is the size of the tax base generally inversely related to the rate of taxation? Would you favor increasing or decreasing the tax base? Why?

PERSPECTIVES IN ECONOMICS

A Government Health Plan for Free-Marketeers
By Laurence S. Seidman

[From *The Wall Street Journal,* July 23, 1991.
Reprinted with permission from the Wall Street Journal
©Dow Jones & Co., Inc. All Rights Reserved Worldwide.]

In 1971, Harvard economist Martin Feldstein, chairman of the Council of Economic Advisers in the mid-1980s, set out a simple, elegant plan for the health sector: universal major-risk insurance provided by the federal government. Recently Cornell economist Alfred Kahn, an architect of transportation deregulation in the late 1970s, said he believes major-risk insurance provided by the federal government is the best approach in 1991. What is MRI, and why have these two distinguished economists supported it?

Under MRI, financed by general tax revenue, coverage would be automatic and universal. Every household would have an income-related ceiling on its annual medical financial burden; MRI would thus achieve universal income-related catastrophic protection. At the same time, prior to reaching its out-of-pocket ceiling, every household would pay a share of any medical bill, so each consumer of medical care would have an incentive to be cost-conscious.

For example, a household with $60,000 of income might pay 30% (its "cost-sharing rate") of any medical bill until its annual burden reached 8% of its income, $4,800 (its "out-of-pocket ceiling"). Note that this would occur when its annual medical bill reached $16,000. MRI would then pay 100% of any additional medical bill. The lower a household's income, the lower would be its cost-sharing rate and out-of-pocket ceiling.

Each year, based on its tax return, each household would receive an MRI credit card and be told two numbers: its cost-sharing rate and its out-of-pocket ceiling. For example, the $60,000 household would be told 30% and $4,800. Each household would use its MRI credit card to buy medical care. Households with little or no income would file a short-form tax return in order to obtain an MRI credit card. The government would pay the doctor or hospital and then bill the household for its cost-share (in practice, the government would contract with private insurance companies to process bills). If a household's income dropped sharply, it could file to amend its cost-sharing rate.

MRI is designed to strike a compromise between two conflicting objectives: giving each household an incentive to be cost-conscious, and reducing its financial risk from a medical problem. MRI concentrates on the incentive when the household's financial burden is tolerable but switches to risk reduction when the household's burden threatens to become intolerable.

To protect patient cost-sharing, MRI should not pay any bill for which the household obtains any assistance from a private insurer; nor should employer contributions to health insurance premiums continue to be excluded from employee taxable income. If MRI were enacted with these provisions, many employees would ask their employers to cancel their private insurance and convert the employer's annual premium contribution of several thousand dollars to cash compensation. Employers would welcome an escape from escalating health costs and premiums. Instead of our current mix of myriad private insurance, Medicare, Medicaid, and no insurance, all households (except a minority who bought private insurance) would be covered by MRI.

Why do Messrs. Feldstein and Kahn, economists who generally favor markets over government regulation, support MRI? Because they think it has the best chance to prevent intrusive, inefficient government regulation that tries to micro-manage the practice of medicine. No sector can remain free of government micro-regulation if its product is "free" to most consumers. When a product is "free"—when there is no consumer cost-sharing—demand escalates, costs escalates, and government must come in to try to get the sector under control. But this inevitably requires detailed micro-management of the behavior of producers and consumers. Such micro-management has already begun for Medicare patients. Like disease, it will gradually spread to all patients.

While doctors are protesting today, consumers will suffer in the end. Free medical care is not really free, for it requires every consumer to give up some control and power. If patients do not pay for the services they use, then their demands for more services are not credible. "The system" will therefore decide which patients must wait, and which must be denied. By contrast, if the patient pays some of the cost, as he would under MRI, he self-regulates. Government can move away from regulating behavior and fees, letting medical providers respond promptly to self-regulated patient demand.

Will consumer cost-sharing work better than government micro-regulation? True, doctors will continue to make most medical decisions. But with the introduction of MRI, doctors will soon recognize that their patients have a new attitude toward costs. Patients will now want their doctors to weight cost against benefit. So what will happen?

At the time of decision to enter a hospital, the average patient will probably acquiesce in his doctor's decisions. But a month later, when the recuperating patient receives his bill and estimates his cost-share, he will review his doctor's choices. Was the 10th day really necessary? Was hospital A, the most costly in the area, really best for his problem? Why did he need test Z? Doctors will begin to receive feedback from patients. Knowing this in advance, most doctors will find it in their self-interest to weight cost against benefit in hospital care decisions. The medical market will begin to self-regulate.

What happens if we instead continue down the road of micro-management by regulators? Consider Medicare hospital and physician fee schedules. Hospitals or doctors who provide a particular category of service now must be paid a designated fee regardless of quality. Because a regulator cannot assess quality from a distance, the government fee schedule must ignore it. Hence, hospitals and doctors have little financial incentive to improve the quality of their service. In the long run, the consequences for all patients will be severe.

The only way to cure this worsening regulatory disease is to restore consumer cost-sharing; the only way to make cost-sharing acceptable to the public is to relate it to incomes; and the only way to have income-related cost-sharing is to enact government MRI.

Discussion

1. What exactly *is* MRI? Does its effectiveness depend on the particular cost-sharing rate and out-of-pocket ceiling percentages chosen?
2. What do you see as the major advantages of MRI? What are its major disadvantages? Would you vote to have the federal government provide universal major-risk insurance?
3. Seidman seems to think that Professors Feldstein and Kahn are in favor of MRI because they fear complete government regulation of the health-care industry. What do you think of proposals supported by arguments that, in essence, say "this idea might have flaws but it sure is a lot better than what everyone else is thinking of."

CHAPTER SIX

DEMAND AND CONSUMER CHOICE

TRUE OR FALSE

T   F

□ □   1. The consumer's desire for goods usually exceeds what his or her income can buy; thus, choice is essential.

□ □   2. The price of diamonds exceeds that of water; therefore, consumers derive more total utility from diamonds than water, according to the law of diminishing marginal utility.

□ □   3. The law of diminishing marginal utility suggests that you would value the third milkshake on a given day higher than the fourth.

□ □   4. The market demand curve is a reflection of the law of diminishing marginal utility—thus, one would expect price to be negatively related to amount purchased.

□ □   5. When supply is more elastic, suppliers will bear a greater part of the burden of a tax.

□ □   6. A decline in the price of automobiles would almost certainly cause the demand for cars to increase.

□ □   7. An increase in the price of wheat would probably cause a decline in the demand for corn, a substitute product.

□ □   8. An increase in consumer income would cause the demand for most commodities to increase.

□ □   9. If people expected the price of General Electric stock to rise in the near future, the current demand for shares of GE would increase.

□ □   10. If consumers expected the price of automobiles to increase by 20 percent next week, the current demand for automobiles would fall.

□ □   11. Economists assume that price or money cost is the only factor that influences consumer decisions.

□ □   12. The opportunity cost of a bus trip from New York to Los Angeles includes both the money and time cost to the consumer.

□ □   13. When demand is elastic, an increase in the price of a good causes total revenue to rise.

□ □   14. The demand for hamburger is more elastic than the demand for beef.

□ □   15. The short-run demand for gasoline is less elastic than the long-run demand.

PROBLEMS AND PROJECTS

EXHIBIT 1

Price of gasoline (per gallon)	Consumption level		
	Auto tires (millions)	Yellowstone tourists (millions)	Air travel passenger miles (millions)
$0.30	40	3.5	7.500
0.50	38	3.2	8.000
0.75	36	3.0	9.000
1.00	34	2.6	12.000

1. Exhibit 1 presents data on the effect of a change in the price of gasoline on the amount demanded of automobile tires, tourism in Yellowstone National Park, and air travel. Which of the following goods are substitutes: gas and tires? gas and Yellowstone tourism? gas and air travel? Which are complementary? Explain how you could tell from the data.

EXHIBIT 2

Price	Quantity (million bushels)	Total revenue	Elasticity of demand
$1	1500	_____	
2	700	_____	_____
3	550	_____	_____

2. Exhibit 2 indicates the estimated demand schedule for wheat in the United States.
   a. Fill in the total revenue schedule. Is the demand schedule elastic or inelastic between $1 and $2? Between $2 and $3? How can you tell? (*Hint:* Look at total revenue.)
   b. Calculate the price elasticity coefficient over the $1 to $2 range, the $2 to $3 range. Use arc elasticity.

EXHIBIT 3

Food			Clothing			Housing		
Quantity	Total utility	Marginal utility	Quantity	Total utility	Marginal utility	Quantity	Total utility	Marginal utility
1	30	_____	1	10	_____	1	35	_____
2	55	_____	2	17	_____	2	65	_____
3	75	_____	3	22	_____	3	85	_____
4	90	_____	4	26	_____	4	100	_____
5	100	_____	5	28	_____	5	110	_____
6	105	_____	6	29	_____	6	118	_____

3. Exhibit 3 provides Samantha Smith's hypothetical total utility schedule for three goods—food, clothing, and housing.
   a. Fill in the marginal utility schedule for each of the goods.
   b. Assume that the price of food was $20, clothing $10, and housing $30. What is the marginal utility *per dollar* derived from consumption of the first unit of each of the three commodities? If Smith had only $20 to spend, which good(s) would she buy?
   c. Assume that Smith's income is $130 per week. If she purchased only the three commodities and faced the price structure indicated in b, how many units of each good would she demand per week?
   d. Assume that Smith's weekly income, the price of clothing, and the price of housing remain constant, but the price of food increases from $20 to $30. How much would she buy? How much food would Smith demand at $15 per unit? Indicate these points on Smith's demand schedule for food, assuming that her weekly income is $130 and the prices of clothing and housing are $10 and $30, respectively.
   e. What would happen to Smith's demand curve for food if her income rose from $130 to $250 per week? (Assume prices indicated in b.)

4. Suppose that in reviewing the material of this chapter you were sitting in your college cafeteria sipping coffee for two or three hours. Exhibit 4 shows some information about your preferences regarding coffee. The column "Marginal valuation" refers to the maximum amount you would be willing to pay for the particular unit of goods in the first column (e.g., you would be willing to pay a maximum of $0.10 for the 5th cup).

EXHIBIT 4

Quantity of cups	Marginal utility	Marginal valuation
1	200	$2.00
2	100	1.00
3	50	.50
4	25	.25
5	10	.10
6	5	.05
7	0	.00

   a. If you behave according to the theory of consumer choice developed in this chapter, how many cups of coffee will you purchase if the price of coffee is $0.25 per cup?
   b. Calculate the value of your consumer surplus at a price of $0.25 per cup.
   c. Suppose (again at a price of $0.25) you bought seven cups of coffee. Calculate the value of your consumer surplus in this case. How does it compare to the value for consumer surplus in part b above?
   d. How would your answers to this questions change if the price of a cup of coffee were $.10?

5. Fill in the missing entries in Exhibit 5.

EXHIBIT 5

Price elasticity	Change in price	Change in total revenue
0.2	down	_____
3.5	_____	down
1.0	up	_____
0.9	_____	up
_____	down	none
6.3	down	_____

6. For each of the following events, fill in the table in Exhibit 6 to indicate which curve shifts—demand (D) or supply (S)—and whether price, quantity, and total expenditure rise (+), fall (−), stay the same (0), or change in an unpredictable direction (?).
   a. Personal income in the United States rises this year.
   b. The government imposes an excise tax on all cars.
   c. New environmental standards require that all new cars be equipped with more expensive pollution control devices.
   d. The federal government passes a law requiring that all imported cars contain at least 90 percent U.S.-made parts.

EXHIBIT 6

		Event a	Event b	Event c	Event d
New U.S. cars (price elasticity less than 1)	Shift	D			
	P	+			
	Q	+			
	TE	+			
New foreign cars (price elasticity greater than 1)	Shift				
	P				
	Q				
	TE				
Used cars, an inferior good (price elasticity equal to 1)	Shift				
	P				
	Q				
	TE				
Auto repairs, a complement of used cars (price elasticity greater than 1)	Shift				
	P				
	Q				
	TE				

D = demand; S = supply; P = price; Q = quantity; TE = total expenditure
(*Hint:* Elasticities are in absolute value terms.)

7. Suppose that the demand and supply curves for denim jeans are given by the following equations:

   Demand: $Q_d = 81 - 3P$
   Supply: $Q_s = 27 + 6P$

where P is the price in dollars, and the Q's represent the quantities of denim jeans (in thousands of pairs).
   a. Complete the table in Exhibit 7:

EXHIBIT 7

P	Q_d	Total expenditure	Value of price elasticity of demand
18	____	____	
15	____	____	____
12	____	____	____
9	____	____	____

   b. Based on your computations, does price elasticity of demand rise, fall, or remain the same as we move down a linear demand curve?
   c. Choose the term "elastic," "unit elastic," or "inelastic" to fill in the blanks below:
      (1) Price and total expenditure move in the same directions when demand is

      _____

      (2) Price and total expenditure move in opposite directions when demand is

      _____

      (3) Total expenditure remains constant when price changes if demand is

      _____

   d. What are the equilibrium values for the price and quantity of denim jeans?

LEARNING THE MECHANICS—MULTIPLE CHOICE

1. A rise of 15 percent in the price of beef reduces the consumption of beef by 30 percent. As the result of the price increase, households
   a. spend more money on beef.
   b. spend less money on beef.
   c. spend the same amount on beef as before.
   d. spend more on goods that are complementary with beef.

2. Which of the following would *not* cause a shift in the demand curve for green peas?
   a. An increase in the income of consumers
   b. A decrease in the price of potatoes (a complement)
   c. A decrease in the price of green peas
   d. A decrease in the price of beans (a substitute)

3. Which of the following statements most accurately reflects the basic postulate of demand theory?
   a. Individuals act purely out of selfish motives, but they will be less likely to pursue selfish ends as these actions become more costly.
   b. Individuals act primarily out of humanitarian motives; this explains why less of a product is bought at a higher price.
   c. Individuals respond from a variety of motives, including both selfish and humanitarian impulses; however, they are less likely to follow a course of action (for example, purchase a commodity) as the cost of the action increases.
   d. Individuals' behavior has many causes, but their actions are affected by changes in the cost of activities only when they are motivated by self-interest, narrowly defined.

4. Consumer surplus (as economists use the term) is
   a. the surplus of goods owned by consumers that has not been consumed.
   b. the difference between the amount that consumers would be willing to pay and the amount they actually pay for an item.
   c. the surplus of goods produced for consumption that have not been purchased.
   d. the difference between the amount that consumers would be willing to pay and the producer's cost of an item.

5. An inferior good is distinguished by
   a. a negative price elasticity of demand.
   b. a positive price elasticity of demand.
   c. a positive income elasticity of demand.
   d. a negative income elasticity of demand.

6. If the price of grapefruit rose, the market demand curve for the substitute good (oranges) would
   a. shift to the right.
   b. shift to the left.
   c. remain stationary.
   d. become horizontal.

7. When an economist says that the demand for a product has increased, she means that
   a. the demand curve has shifted to the left.
   b. product price has fallen and, as a result, consumers are buying more of the product.
   c. the product has become particularly scarce for some reason.
   d. consumers are now willing to purchase more of this product at any given price.

8. If the money income of consumers decreased and, as a result, the demand for product A increased, it could be concluded that product A is
   a. an inferior good.
   b. a substitute good.
   c. a complementary good.
   d. a normal good.

9. An increase in the demand for milk can be explained most reasonably by which of the following?
   a. The supply of milk has increased because costs of production have declined.
   b. The price of milk has declined and, as a result, consumers want to purchase more of it.
   c. Consumers preferences have changed in favor of milk so that they now want to buy a larger quantity at the current market price.
   d. The price of milk has increased and, as a result, consumers want to purchase less of it.

10. "After listening to nothing but rock music on my vacation, I was anxious to return home and play something different." This statement most clearly reflects the law of
    a. the budget constraint.
    b. consumer irrationality.
    c. greater demand elasticity with time.
    d. diminishing marginal utility.

11. Which of the following would be most likely to cause the demand for beef to increase?
    a. A decrease in the price of pork
    b. An increase in the price of catsup, a complementary good
    c. An increase in consumer income
    d. A decrease in the price of bean curd, a substitute good

12. Demand theory implies that, for pork chops, price is negatively related to quantity demanded, all other things constant. The "all other things" include each of the following *except*
    a. the price of pork chops.
    b. consumer preferences.
    c. the price of hamburger.
    d. consumer income.

13. If a 50 percent increase in the price of hula hoops led to a 10 percent reduction in the quantity of hula hoops purchased, this would suggest that
    a. an additional 20 percent increase in price would surely cause a sharp reduction in sales.
    b. the demand for hula hoops was elastic over this range.
    c. the income elasticity for hula hoops was low.
    d. households increased their spending on hula hoops.

THE ECONOMIC WAY OF THINKING—MULTIPLE CHOICE

1. "The year 1963 was a year tobacco makers are unlikely to forget. It was a year that regular-size cigarettes received their worst publicity ever. The discussion of a possible link between cigarette smoking and cancer reached alarmist proportions. Increasingly, people were buying aids designed to reduce the smoking habit." This statement indicates that
    a. the supply of cigarettes was reduced because of the possible adverse effects of cigarette smoking.
    b. as income increases, the demand for cigarettes declines because their income elasticity is negative.
    c. the price of cigarettes had finally reached the point at which people began to turn to substitute products.
    d. the demand for cigarettes decreased because of a change in the preferences of consumers.

2. "Because of the unseasonably cold weather, Florida orange growers expect (a) fewer bushels of oranges to be harvested and (b) larger total revenues from this year's crop." Assuming that the demand for Florida oranges is constant, the statement would most likely be correct if
    a. the demand for Florida oranges were elastic.
    b. the supply of Florida oranges were highly inelastic.
    c. the demand for Florida oranges were inelastic.
    d. the supply of Florida oranges were elastic.

EXHIBIT 8

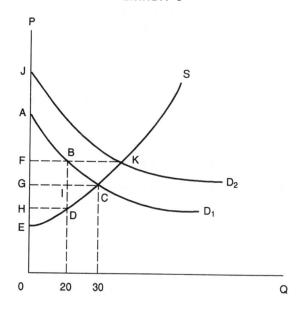

Questions 3 and 4 refer to the market for ballpoint pens depicted in Exhibit 8:

3. Consider demand curve D_1. The buyer of the twentieth good on that curve receives a consumer surplus from that purchase of
   a. ACG.
   b. ABIG.
   c. (B−I).
   d. (B−D).

4. Assume that demand shifts to D_2. As a result of this increase in demand, the total consumer surplus in the market should
   a. increase because ACG will be greater than JKF.
   b. decrease because ABF will be smaller than ACE.
   c. increase or decrease, depending on whether JKBA is greater than or less than FBCG.
   d. increase or decrease, depending on whether JKCG is greater than or less than FKE.

5. Which of the following will most likely cause a decrease in the *current* demand for fuel oil?
   a. An increase in income
   b. The expectation that the future price of fuel oil will increase
   c. A decline in the price of fuel oil
   d. A decline in the price of electricity, a substitute good

6. As the price of precious gems (diamonds, pearls, and so forth) increases, other things constant, the quantity demanded may also increase. Which of the following offers the best explanation of this phenomenon?
   a. The demand for precious gems is like the demand for other goods.
   b. Precious gems are an inferior good.
   c. The demand for precious gems is subject to a "snob" effect, in which higher prices increase their marginal utility.
   d. The demand for precious gems is inelastic.

7. "A number of mass transit systems have been experiencing declining revenues despite fare increases." This statement suggests
   a. that the automobile is a poor substitute for mass transit in urban areas.
   b. that the demand for the mass transit service was inelastic.
   c. that the demand for the mass transit service was elastic.
   d. that a profit-maximizing firm would have raised the price charged for mass transit service by a larger amount.

8. Operators of the midway at the Seattle Center reduced the price of admission to their carnival rides after Labor Day even though "for all practical purposes, once our weekly schedule is announced, all our costs are fixed costs," as one manager explained. The change in prices would increase the firm's profits if
   a. marginal costs were now zero.
   b. the elasticity of demand were now unitary.
   c. the demand for rides at the Seattle Center were now elastic.
   d. the income elasticity for carnival rides were now negative.

9. The Radio Corporation of America (RCA) is considering a 10 percent price reduction on its black-and-white television sets, whereas the firm's price for color television sets (a substitute) is held constant. With this information, what can we say about how the price reduction will affect the firm's total revenue?
   a. Revenues from black-and-white sets will fall, whereas revenues derived from color sets may either increase or decrease.
   b. Revenues from black-and-white sets will increase, whereas revenues derived from color sets will fall.
   c. Revenues from color sets will fall, whereas revenues from black-and-white sets could either increase or decrease.
   d. Revenues from color sets will increase, whereas revenues derived from black-and-white sets will fall.

10. (I) The number of fly rods owned by a fishing enthusiast will probably be limited because income necessitates choice. (II) The number of fly rods owned by an angler will probably be limited because of the law of diminishing marginal utility.
    a. Both I and II are true.
    b. Both I and II are false.
    c. I is true, but II is false.
    d. II is true, but I is false.

11. Use the diagram below to answer this question.

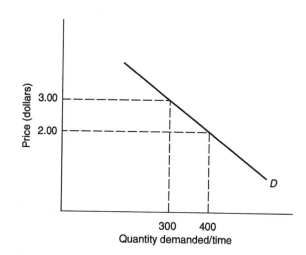

For this demand curve, the price elasticity of demand is
a. more elastic at $3 than at $2.
b. more elastic at $2 than at $3.
c. identical at $2 to that at $3.
d. equal to 1.0 over the range from $3 to $2.

12. If the owners of Pac-Kong, a video arcade game, increased the price they charged for one play of the game from 25 cents to 50 cents, what can be said about their perception of the elasticity of demand with respect to the price of a game of Pac-Kong?
a. It is impossible to say anything about the owners' perceptions without interviewing them.
b. The owners expect that the price elasticity of demand for Pac-Kong is elastic.
c. The owners expect that the price elasticity of demand for Pac-Kong is unitary (equal to one).
d. The owners expect that the price elasticity of demand for Pac-Kong is inelastic.

13. All else equal, if bus fares rise by 20 percent and bus fare receipts rise by only 10 percent, then
a. the demand for bus ride must be elastic.
b. the demand for bus rides must be inelastic.
c. the demand for bus rides must be unit elastic.
d. we can't be sure about elasticity, but we do know that the demand for bus rides will fall.

14. For a consumer who initially buys eight ice cream cones per month, if the price of an ice cream cone suddenly falls by $.25,
a. consumer surplus will rise by $2.00, and total expenditure will fall by $2.00.
b. consumer surplus will rise by at least $2.00, and total expenditure will fall.
c. consumer surplus will rise by at least $2.00, and total expenditure will change in an uncertain direction.
d. consumer surplus will rise by $2.00, and total expenditure will change in an uncertain direction.

THE ECONOMIC WAY OF THINKING—DISCUSSION QUESTIONS

1. a. What causes a change in quantity demanded? In demand?
   b. Decide whether the following is true or false: "A change in demand causes a change in quantity supplied, and vice versa."
   c. What factors should you hold constant when constructing a demand curve? A supply curve?

2. Will each of the following cause a shift of or movement along the demand curve for electricity? Will equilibrium quantity rise or fall in each case?
   a. An increase in consumer income
   b. An increase in price of natural gas, an alternative source of energy
   c. Higher electricity prices, due to increased fuel costs
   d. The expectation that electricity prices will rise sharply in the future
   e. Lower prices for electrical appliances

3. For each of the following pairs of products, indicate which you think will have the lower price elasticity of demand. Explain your reasoning.
   a. Salt or green peas
   b. Volkswagens or all automobiles
   c. Electricity (short run) or electricity (long run)
   d. Tires (short run) or tires (long run)
   e. Physician services or bus transportation

4. "Affluent customers spend much of their income on useless items. If consumers limited their purchases to those items they needed, our economic problems would be reduced to manageable proportions."
   a. What items do people spend their money on that are not necessary? Do you buy things you do not need? If so, why?
   b. "If people spent less time working to purchase more things that they do not need, they would have more leisure time." Is leisure a "useless" item that people do not need? Explain.
   c. How can you determine if an item is useful or needed? Are demand and usefulness the same thing?

5. List three goods you buy that you think of as necessities and three goods you buy that you think of as luxuries.
   a. Are the necessities you listed always used for essential purposes? Why or why not?
   b. Are the luxuries you listed entirely wasteful? Why or why not?
   c. Is leisure time a necessity or a luxury? Why would a person who is already wealthy choose work over leisure?

6. Explain in your own words why diamonds, which appear to be useless, are more expensive than water, which is life supporting? Which law of economics helps to explain why diamonds are more expensive than water?

7. What's wrong with this way of thinking? "Although economists argue that the amount demanded is negatively related to price, the evidence doesn't always support this view. For example, in 1970 the average price for the installation of a 20 x 40 home swimming pool was $4000. By 1980 price had soared to more than $8000. Yet Americans bought 50 percent more swimming pools in 1980 than 1970. The higher price did not discourage sales."

8. Suppose that the "Helpful Navy," a local charity, takes in donations of clothes and food in order to assist the needy. The Navy sells the better donated clothes at their second-hand shop, which last month had total sales of $1400, while the cost of rent, utilities, and shopkeeper salaries was $1350.
   a. Did the store earn an economic profit? Why or why not?
   b. According to economic theory, is more consumer surplus created by selling the clothes or by giving the same clothes away? Explain.

PERSPECTIVES IN ECONOMICS

Moonshiners in South Find Sales Are Down as Their Costs Go Up
by Jonathan Kwitney

Habersham County, Ga.

"There probably isn't a family around here that hasn't had at least one member involved with a still," observes Clyde Dixon, executive vice president of the Peoples Bank in Cleveland, Ga. "It hasn't been so long around here since moonshine was the only way to make money. My father made moonshine," Mr. Dixon says.

But two years ago the price of sugar—an essential ingredient in moonshine—tripled, and life in the laurel thickets changed rapidly. It takes at least 10 pounds of sugar to make a gallon of barnyard whiskey. With other inflationary factors added, moonshine that sold a few years ago for $6 a gallon at the still began pushing $15 a gallon.

At that price the moonshine market contracted severely, because for $15 plus retail markup, a customer can buy government whiskey. ("Government whiskey" is the hill country term for legal booze—stuff on which the tax has been paid. Unlike hastily made moonshine, its manufacturer relies on slowly drawing natural sugars from the grain being distilled, and therefore its price is unaffected by the sugar market.)

Revenuers Look Elsewhere The price squeeze on moonshine has forced new occupations on a lot of people who were engaged, one way or another, in what may have been, even as late as the 1950s, the largest industry in such counties as Habersham, Dawson, and Gilmer. Not all of those people whose employment depended on illegal booze were moonshiners themselves, however.

Billy Corbin is a revenue agent with the Treasury Department's Bureau of Alcohol, Tobacco and Firearms (ATF). He chased moonshiners in North Georgia for 10 years and says his team of five agents used to bust up an average of 10 stills a month. Then, in December, he was transferred to a new office with emphasis on non-whiskey violations. "When I left (the moonshine post) it was down to no more than one still a month," Mr. Corbin says.

Mr. Corbin's boss, Bill Barbary, agent in charge of ATF's Gainsville, Ga., office, says the 108 revenue agents in Georgia used to spend 75% of their time on liquor offenses, the rest on other crimes, mostly the unlicensed sale of firearms. Now, he says, agents spend only about 25% of their time on moonshine patrol. To help fill the slack, the Treasury Department this year reassigned its gambling tax enforcement to ATF from the Internal Revenue Service.

So, for the government, one beneficial by-product of the sugar inflation and moonshine depression is an increase in arrests for firearms violations and illegal wagering. Some 15 or 20 revenue agents from the countryside were reassigned to Atlanta this spring and broke up a big numbers ring there, federal officials say; they promise to follow up with the indictment of 30 to 40 gambling operators.

The Pot Shuttle On the other hand, with the whiskey business in turmoil, many former moonshine overlords—Mr. Barbary says most of them—have simply reapplied their resourcefulness to trafficking in other illicit goods that are still profitable. They are suspected of being responsible for the recent big increase in the airlifting of drugs, particularly marijuana, from South America to small airstrips in Georgia and neighboring moonshine states.

For example, two long-reputed North Georgia moonshine czars, Garland "Bud" Cochran and Ben Kade "Junior" Tatum, were indicted in federal court in South Carolina last summer for allegedly masterminding a DC-4 pot shuttle from Colombia. Mr. Tatum was convicted and is appealing. Mr. Cochran—who the ATF says was shipping 7,000 gallons of moonshine a month into Atlanta in trailer trucks during the 1960s—has been a fugitive since the smuggling indictment came down. Officials believe he is in South America directing more smuggling operations.

Radical as the change in North Georgia life has been since the price of sugar rose, it actually is the culmination of an evolutionary change that began in the early 1940s.

Revenue agents agree that the old-time, 100% corn liquor made in pure copper stills—the fabled "white lightning"—was as good as or better than bonded whiskey. But when copper became scarce at the start of World War II, moonshiners turned to sheet metal vats, and in more recent times began cooling the liquor in automobile radiators instead of copper coils. The result often is a fatal dose of lead poisoning. In probably the most famous case of this, the late Fats Hardy, a Gainesville moonshine king, was sentenced to life in prison in the late 1950s after many persons died from drinking the moonshine he shipped to Atlanta.

The people who do drink it, authorities say are almost exclusively poor, urban blacks. The biggest retail distribution centers are so-called "shot-houses," operated in private homes or stores in black neighborhoods of Atlanta, Macon, and other cities throughout the Southeast. Because the price of a shot has soared to 75 cents, almost the price of safer, stronger legal bar whiskey, the ATF estimates that there are only a few hundred shot-houses in Atlanta now, down from a few thousand before the crunch.

Assistant U.S. Attorney Owen Forrester in Atlanta—who says his grandmother had a still on her land, though she didn't drink—says he doubts that even a new rise in sugar prices could wipe out moonshine entirely. "The revenue agents who work the shothouses here tell me that there are still a lot of old-timers who like the taste of it," Mr. Forrester says. "There's a certain zang, or sizzle, going down."

How To Make It Hill folks and revenue agents have described the methods moonshiners use to get that "zang" and "sizzle" in there.

First, there's a widespread belief, often put into practice, that horse manure added to the corn mash speeds its fermentation. In addition, sanitary conditions aren't always up to FDA standards. Mr. Dixon, the country banker, says, "I've seen a hog get in (the vat) to drink some of that slop and drown. They just take the hog out and go ahead. They can't afford to lose all that money (by throwing out the contaminated mash). I'll tell you, Jack Daniel's does it a lot cleaner." Mr. Forrester, the prosecutor, recalls a moonshiner who "put in dead possums at the end to flavor it."

Later, still other foreign matter is added. Moonshine usually is 110 proof when it's sold at the still to a "tripper," who usually is either an independent truck driver or an employee of an urban distributor. To stretch the product, the distributors usually water it down as much as 50%. Then, to make it look its original strength, they add beading oil, which stimulates the swirls that alcohol makes in liquor.

"It's damn hard work to make whiskey," Mr. Dixon says. "They have to hide the stills in laurel thickets on a mountain. You have your barrels and boxes of malt—it's corn meal mostly, some barley malt. They'll carry 200 or 300 pounds of sugar up that mountain at a time on their backs. All the time (the mash) is working it has to be stirred. That corn meal has a tendency to lump up. I've seen them get stark naked and get in there and mash it. If you don't think it's hard work, try it."

Much of the hard work, high price, and poor quality is caused by the revenue agents, whose presence puts constant pressure on moonshiners to finish their work fast and get out. Moonshiners need costly sugar because they must dash off each batch of their product in about 72 hours. Bonded distillers have controlled conditions and plenty of time, so they can apply even heat as required and wait out the two weeks or so it takes to get sugar out of the natural grains.

Byron Davis of Gainesville, who retired in 1968 after 31 years as a revenue agent because "it's a young man's job," says he remembers capturing a lot of moonshiners by cruising the hills looking for smoke. In fact, he attributes the switch in still materials from copper to other metals at least in part to a switch in cooking fuels from wood to bu-

tane gas. The butane largely eliminated the telltale smoke trail, he says, but didn't work well with copper equipment.

Keeping tabs on sugar sales also has helped agents to corral a few moonshiners. "One of these little country stores starts selling 500 pounds of sugar a week, you smell a rat," Mr. Corbin says.

Nowadays, however, agents say they make most of their arrests through tips from informants. Moonshiners love to tell on each other, Mr. Corbin says. Certainly the ATF needed information 18 months ago in order to discover a fabulous 2,000-gallon-a-week underground still, which was entered by opening the trunk of an old Ford sitting in a Habersham Country junkyard, and climbing down a ladder. Agents believe that the operator obtained electric power for his still by tapping into nearby underground Tennessee Valley Authority lines.

On the whole, authorities say their problem is less in catching moonshiners than in obtaining justice afterwards. Judges and juries just "didn't consider whiskey to be a crime," Mr. Forrester recalls of his moonshine trial days. The operator of the underground still beneath the old Ford, for example, pleaded guilty and received a suspended sentence, Mr. Forrester says.

Professional So relaxed is the atmosphere at moonshine trials that one notorious moonshiner from Adairsville, Ga., used to feel comfortable attending them. Mr. Forrester recalls, "Every term he'd come to court with mash all over his pants and listen to testimony in other cases to learn new techniques."

A typical still operation is financed and overseen by a man with substantial income from legitimate business, such as a farm or store. He hires three to six still hands and one or two women who live with them while the still is in operation, to keep house and to make the group appear to be a normal family. While the still hands sometimes wind up serving a year or two in federal prison, the boss, if convicted, usually get probation, often impressing the judge and jury with letters of commendation from leaders in the community.

Discussion

1. Did the increase in the price of sugar affect the supply of or the demand for moonshine? Use the principles of supply and demand to analyze the moonshine market.
2. Use supply and demand diagrams to analyze the market for federally regulated whiskey and for federal regulatory agents. Would owners of regulated whiskey distillers be helped or hurt by the sugar price increase? Explain your answer.
3. The title of the article says that sales went down as costs went up. If by sales the author meant total revenue, and if by costs the author meant price, what can we determine about the elasticity of demand for moonshine? Explain your answer.

CHAPTER SEVEN

COSTS AND THE SUPPLY OF GOODS

TRUE OR FALSE

T F

1. Implicit costs involve the foregoing of opportunities, even though monetary costs are not incurred.

2. Rental income foregone because the Widget Manufacturing Company uses its business-owned 200,000-square-foot structure to produce widgets is an example of an implicit cost.

3. The economists's concept of costs imputes an implicit market rate of return to capital assets that are owned by a business firm.

4. Average fixed costs (AFC) will always decline as output is expanded in the short run.

5. Average per unit cost is defined as total cost divided by the number of units produced.

6. The law of diminishing returns alone implies that the long-run average total cost (ATC) curve will be U-shaped.

7. When a firm's output level is small (relative to plant size), ATC is high because of the high AFC.

8. Marginal cost (MC) represents the opportunity cost of producing an additional unit.

9. MC is equal to ATC at the point where ATC is a minimum.

10. ATC will always decline when MC is less than ATC.

11. A profit-maximizing business entrepreneur never sells a good for less than his ATC.

12. The owner of a drugstore may fail to make an economic profit even though her total revenues exceed her costs on labor, wholesale products, and equipment.

13. A firm can reduce its total fixed cost by reducing output.

14. A firm can avoid the opportunity cost of interest by using its own monetary resources in the business.

PROBLEMS AND PROJECTS

EXHIBIT 1 INCOME STATEMENT

Revenues		Costs	
Sales	$55,000	Wholesale clothing	$30,000
Inventory adjustment	2,000	Equipment	2,000
		Labor	15,000
		Utilities and insurance	1,000
Total revenues	$57,000	Total costs	$48,000

1. Exhibit 1 represents the annual income statement of Joe's Clothing Store for 1991. Joe worked full time in the store and invested $30,000 to buy the store and stock it with merchandise. He recently turned down an offer of a salaried position paying $10,000 per year to manage another store. He did not pay himself a salary during the year. According to Exhibit 1,
   a. what were Joe's accounting profits?
   b. what major items did he exclude from his costs?
   c. assuming that the market rate of interest was 10 percent recalculate Joe's total costs.
   d. what was the economic profit or loss of Joe's Clothing Store in 1991?

EXHIBIT 2 COSTS AND OUTPUT

Output (per week)	Total cost	Total fixed cost	Total variable cost	Average total cost	Average variable cost	Marginal cost
1	$100	$50				
2	140					
3	177					
4	216					
5	265					
6	324					
7	399					
8	496					

2. Jaynie owns a small shop and produces dining room sets. Exhibit 2 presents data on her expected total cost per set at various output levels.
   a. Complete Exhibit 2.
   b. At what output level is Jaynie's average total cost at a minimum?
   c. At what output level are diminishing marginal returns (given the current plant size) confronted?
   d. Graph the firm's average total cost, average variable cost, and marginal cost curves.

3. The data necessary to evaluate the cost of owning and operating two alternative automobiles are in Exhibit 3.

EXHIBIT 3

	Auto A	Auto B
Purchase price	$5000	$4000
Annual fee for insurance and license	200	100
Operating cost per mile including gas, oil, and maintenance	0.15	0.14
Resale value one year from now	4000	2800

a. Assuming that the market rate of interest is 10 percent, calculate the average cost per mile of owning the automobile one year and driving it 10,000 miles for both auto A and auto B. Which is cheaper?

b. If the automobiles were driven 20,000 miles during the year, their respective resale values would be $3700 for A and $2200 for B. Which would be cheaper to purchase, own, and drive 20,000 miles during the year? Explain.

c. What happens to the average total cost per mile as the miles driven per year increase? Explain.

4. Carl Bergstrom is harvesting some wheat that he planted in the spring. Bergstrom uses a variety of fixed inputs (land, machines, and so on), the fixed costs of which are $100 per day. The only variable input is labor. Exhibit 4 shows the relationship between the quantity of labor Bergstrom can hire at $50 per day and the total output.

EXHIBIT 4

Daily labor inputs	Total product (bushels/day)	Marginal product (bushels/day)	Marginal cost (dollars/ bushel)	Total cost (dollars/day)
1	20			150
		30	1.67	
2	50			200
		____		
3	70			
		____		
4	85			
		____		
5	95			
		____		
6	100			
		1	50.00	
7	101			

a. Fill in the missing information in the table.

b. On a piece of graph paper plot the marginal product curve and the marginal cost curve. Does marginal cost rise when marginal product falls? Explain your answer.

5. Complete the table in Exhibit 5 based on the information from the diagram in that exhibit.

EXHIBIT 5

Q	TC	TVC	TFC	MC
3	___	___	___	___
6	___	___	___	___

6. Suppose that you want to start a cable TV channel. You learn that the local cable company charges a flat fee of $1,000,000 per year to lease a channel. You figure production and broadcast costs for each 30 minutes of programming will equal $20,000. In other words, the cost equation for your operations is:

$$TC = 1,000,000 + 20,000 \cdot Q$$

where Q is the number of programs you produce and broadcast.

a. Indicate whether each of the following rises (+), falls (−), or remains constant (0) as your output rises:
  ____ i. marginal cost
  ____ ii. average variable cost
  ____ iii. average total cost

b. Is your overall production characterized by economies of scale, diseconomies of scale, or constant returns of scale? Why?

c. How large will your average total cost be if you decide to produce 20 shows? If an advertiser offers to sponsor a twenty-first show for $50,000, would you accept her offer? Why or why not?

LEARNING THE MECHANICS — MULTIPLE CHOICE

1. Economists argue that the short-run average total cost curve is U-shaped because
   a. initially the law of diminishing marginal returns is operating, but later the law of increasing returns takes effect.
   b. factor prices will be higher for both small and large firms.
   c. the average fixed costs are high when output is low, and marginal costs are high when a plant is used too intensively.
   d. large plants are usually more efficient than small ones, but eventually bureaucratic inefficiency causes costs to rise.

2. The law of diminishing marginal returns indicates why
   a. beyond some point, the extra utility derived from additional units of a product will yield the consumer larger and larger additional amounts of satisfaction.
   b. the demand curve for goods produced by purely competitive industries is downward sloping.
   c. a firm's long-run average total cost curve is U-shaped.
   d. a firm's marginal costs will eventually increase as the firm expands output in the short run.

3. Which of the following is most likely to be an implicit cost?
   a. Rental income foregone on assets owned by the firm
   b. Salaries paid to the firm's board of directors
   c. Transportation cost on raw materials
   d. Interest payments on an outstanding loan of the firm

4. Use statements I and II to answer this question. (I) The demand for a product represents the voice of consumers instructing firms to produce the good. (II) Costs of production represent the desire of consumers for other items that could be produced with the resources.
   a. I is true, II is false.
   b. I is false, II is true.
   c. Both I and II are true.
   d. Both I and II are false.

5. The short run is a time period of insufficient length for the firm to change its
   a. output.
   b. amount of labor utilized.
   c. plant size and heavy equipment.
   d. price.

6. Sunk or "historical" costs are
   a. costs associated with current operational decisions.
   b. costs that have already been incurred as the result of past decisions.
   c. costs that add to the firm's marginal costs.
   d. costs that form the major component of the firm's variable costs.

7. The corporation enables a single business firm to raise large amounts of capital because
   a. stockholders like to participate in the operation of large firms.
   b. the limited liability concept protects the stockholder from potential debts incurred by the corporation.
   c. stockholders usually participated in the daily operations of the firms in which they own shares.
   d. large firms are operated more efficiently than small firms.

8. The average variable cost curve and average total cost curve tend to converge as output rises because
   a. the marginal cost curve intersects the average total cost curve at its minimum.
   b. average fixed costs are constant as output rises.
   c. the difference between them (average fixed cost) declines.
   d. output is rising more rapidly than inputs are being increased.

9. Which of the following factors is *not* likely to have shifted the cost curve for Slaughter's Demon Rum upward?
   a. The demand for rum has increased, pushing up its price.
   b. The price of glass for bottling the rum has increased.
   c. The excise tax on alcoholic beverages has increased.
   d. A new law requiring the purchase of an extra rum filtration machine was enacted by the Federal Demon Rum Administration.

10. The firm's average total costs will be a minimum at the output level where
    a. the firm just begins to confront diminishing returns to the variable factors.
    b. the marginal costs are a minimum.
    c. the firm's profits would always be a maximum.
    d. the marginal cost curve crosses the firm's average total cost curve.

11. Economic profit is frequently
    a. greater than total revenue.
    b. defined as total revenue minus total fixed cost.
    c. irrelevant to the owner of a firm who is concerned instead with accounting profit.
    d. less than accounting profit.

12. The law of diminishing returns states that
    a. as we continually add variable factors to a fixed amount of other resources, output eventually increases at a decreasing rate.
    b. as we increase plant size, costs must diminish.
    c. old industrialists never die, they just get smaller returns on their investments.
    d. as fixed costs increase, profits diminish.

Questions 13–15 refer to the following cost curves for one very small firm in a large market:

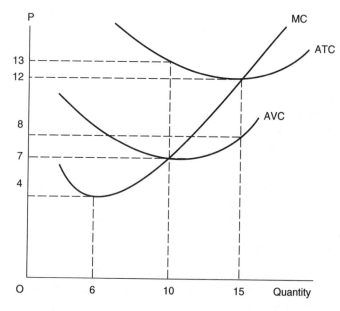

13. If the firm produces at Q = 15, the average fixed cost is:
    a. 4.
    b. 5.
    c. 6.
    d. 60.

14. Total fixed costs for the firm
    a. fall until Q = 15 and then increase.
    b. fall until Q = 10 and then increase.
    c. fall until Q = 15 and then remain constant.
    d. none of the above.

15. Diminishing marginal returns to the variable factor of production for this firm set in at
    a. Q = 6.
    b. Q = 10.
    c. Q = 15.
    d. Q > 15.

THE ECONOMIC WAY OF THINKING—MULTIPLE CHOICE

1. "During the past five years, the price of raw materials in our industry has increased, and the costs of both labor and machinery are up. Yet we have held our product price constant, and our profits have actually increased." Which of the following statements offers the best explanation for this phenomenon?
    a. Technology and/or economic efficiency has improved in the industry, making it possible to produce at low per unit cost, in spite of the increase in input prices.
    b. Economically speaking, the statement is a logical impossibility.
    c. The number of firms in this competitive industry has decreased so that the law of diminishing marginal returns decreased fixed costs.
    d. The demand for the product has increased enough to offset the higher per unit costs of output.

2. Which of the following represents a long-run adjustment?
    a. A steel manufacturer cuts back on its purchases of coke and iron ore.
    b. A farmer uses an extra dose of herbicide on his zucchini crop.
    c. The owner of a hamburger stand hires an additional carhop.
    d. A publisher builds a new plant to produce paperback books.

3. The fact that the physical constraints (size of buildings, number of operational machines, etc.) of a plant are more binding over a month's time than over a six-month period explains why
    a. it is less costly to increase output rapidly than slowly.
    b. the long-run average cost curve is U-shaped.
    c. it is less costly to product output in the present, rather than in the future.
    d. the quantity supplied is more flexible in the long run than in the short run.

4. "Actually, big businesses are generally no more and no less efficient than medium-sized businesses even when the gains wrung by monopoly power are included in efficiency. This is the one general finding in comparative cost studies and comparative profitability studies." This quotation from Professor George Stigler would most accurately reflect that
    a. the minimum long-run per unit costs of medium-size firms are similar.
    b. the short-run average costs fail to increase as medium-size and large-size firms are similar.
    c. the long-run average total cost curve is U-shaped.
    d. the law of diminishing marginal returns is the major explanation of why long-run marginal cost increases.

EXHIBIT 6

Purchase price	$2000
Gas and oil (10¢ per mile–5000 miles)	500
Depreciation	600
Insurance	800
Maintenance	400
License tag	100
Total	$3400

5. A political science major has calculated the cost of *owning and operating* a used car for one year. He included the items in Exhibit 6. Which of the following constitutes the best appraisal of his calculations?
   a. They are correct.
   b. There is only one error—depreciation should not be included.
   c. They contain only one error—omission of the interest earnings.
   d. There are two errors—the purchase price should not be included, but the interest earnings foregone because of buying the car should be.

6. A homeowner will be away from her house for six months. The monthly mortgage payment on the house is $300. The local services, *to be paid by the owner,* cost $100 per month if the house is occupied; otherwise zero. If the owner wishes to minimize her losses from the house, she should rent the house for as much as the market will bear, as long as monthly rent is greater than which of the following? (Assume wear and tear to be zero regardless of whether the house is occupied.) *Hint:* Remember the concept of opportunity cost.
   a. $0
   b. $100
   c. $200
   d. $400

7. The best way to think about marginal product is as
   a. the profit margin due to production.
   b. total product divided by average product.
   c. the change in total output associated with each additional unit of an input (like labor).
   d. total output divided by the total number of units of an input (like labor).

8. Craig inherited a pizza store and enough money to pay the inheritance tax. The store did not cost him a cent. If Craig operated it, paying himself the full opportunity cost of his time, plus interest on the money he used to buy supplies and the like, his accounting profits would apparently be
   a. equal to his economic profit.
   b. less than his economic profit by the amount of salary he could earn elsewhere.
   c. greater than his economic profit by the value of the store's rental value.
   d. greater than his economic profit by the amount of salary he could earn elsewhere.

9. Which of the following constitutes a good reason for selling a product for less than it cost to produce?
   a. The product is about to spoil and will become worthless.
   b. Market conditions have changed, and the equilibrium price is now well below what it was expected to be.
   c. Both of the above.
   d. Neither of the above; it never pays to sell a product for less than its production costs!

10. Mark owns a firm that makes waterbeds. Last year his average total cost per bed was $210 while his selling price was $195. He tells his banker that if the bank would lend him more money, he could keep his price the same, and make a profit by selling more beds. The banker knows that rent, labor, materials, and other resource costs will not decline. Mark says he is losing money on each unit, but plans to make it up by selling more and more units. Mark is
   a. clearly a con artist—he is not telling the truth.
   b. correct, if fixed costs were a small enough part of last year's costs.
   c. correct, if fixed costs were a large enough part of total costs.
   d. correct, if the law of diminishing marginal returns had already begun to affect his firm.

11. If consumers suddenly increased their demand for oranges, the average total cost curve would probably shift upward for growers of
   a. bananas, if bananas were frequently consumed with oranges.
   b. apples, which consumers often substitute for oranges.
   c. exotic hogs, which often eat discarded orange peels.
   d. grapefruit, since grapefruit growers use the same land and labor pool as orange growers.

12. Which of the following factors is most likely to shift the cost curves of an Iowa corn farmer downward?
   a. An increase in the price of fertilizer
   b. An increase in the tax on diesel fuel, which is used by the farmer
   c. The development of a new, more efficient corn harvester
   d. An increase in the demand by soybean farmers for land such as his

13. From an economics perspective, accounting methods tend to
   a. overstate profits and losses.
   b. overstate profits and understate losses.
   c. understate profits and overstate losses.
   d. understate profits and losses.

14. The shaded area in the diagram in Exhibit 7
   a. should be larger than area 0abc.
   b. should be smaller than area 0abc.
   c. should be the same size as area 0abc.
   d. could be larger, smaller, or the same size as area 0abc.

EXHIBIT 7

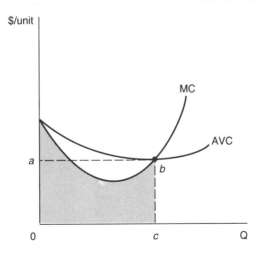

THE ECONOMIC WAY OF THINKING—DISCUSSION QUESTIONS

1 . a. What are the reasons that economic profit differs from accounting profit?
   b. In the real world, which reason do you think is the most significant?
   c. Could it make economic sense for a firm to leave an industry when the firm's accounting profits are positive? When its economic profits are positive? Explain both answers.

2. a. Suppose you compute the average weight of the students present at the start of class. Then a student weighing 175 pounds shows up late and your computed average rises. If another student weighing only 145 pounds shows up, could your computed average rise again, even though the second late student weighs less than the first?
   b. Suppose you are part way through a course, and then your course grade falls because you do poorly on an assignment. Will your course grade necessarily rise back up again if you do better on the next assignment than you did on the last one?
   c. Decide whether the following is true or false, and explain: If average cost is falling (rising), then we can conclude that marginal cost is also falling (rising).

3. What are the main reasons that per unit production costs are often lower for larger firms than for small firms in the same industry? Why don't the small firms go bankrupt because of their higher production costs?

4. How would each of the following influence the cost of producing new housing?
   a. An increase in the price of lumber
   b. The development of a new lighter brick that reduced labor requirements without increasing the costs of material
   c. A reduction in the price of cement
   d. A new "occupational safety" regulation that required all construction workers to wear safety glasses, aluminum hats, and steel-toed shoes.
   e. Passage of state legislation requiring all contractors to pay a $10,000 licensing fee.

5. a. Suppose some friends of yours buy a trailer. After some time, you ask them if they are glad they bought the trailer and they respond, "No, we wouldn't buy one again, but we spent so much on it that we do travel more now." Does their reasoning make sense? If so, why? If not, why not, and why do you think they do travel more now?
   b. Decide whether you agree or disagree with the following, and explain: "In deciding whether to produce more of an item, a firm should consider total cost in the long run, but only variable cost in the short run."

6. What are the advantages of corporations compared to proprietorships? The disadvantages?

7. Indicate why you either agree or disagree with the following statements:
   a. "I have to keep driving my old car in order to make up for the loss that I took when the transmission went out." (*Hint:* Remember the relevance of sunk costs.)
   b. "It does not make sense to keep operating an old machine when new machines can produce more efficiently."
   c. "Accounting costs yield valuable information, but they are not the relevant cost consideration when making business decisions."
   d. It does not make sense for a profit-maximizing firm to sell a product for less than it costs to produce.

8. In 1911, Thomas Edison wrote in the *Wall Street Journal:*

> Thirty years ago my balance sheet showed me that I was not making much money. My manufacturing plant was not running to its full capacity. I couldn't find a market for my products. Then I suggested that we undertake to run our plant on full capacity and sell the surplus products in foreign markets at less than the cost of production. Every one of my associates opposed me. I had my experts figure out how much it would add to the cost of operating the plant if we increased this production 25 percent. The figures showed that we could increase the production 25 percent at an increased cost of only about 2 percent. On this basis I sent a man to Europe who sold lamps there at a price less than the cost of production in Europe.

   a. When Edison suggested that he would sell in foreign markets "at less than the cost of production," of what cost was he speaking?

   b. What was happening to Edison's marginal cost as he expanded output by 25 percent?

   c. Edison's pricing idea was opposed by his associates. Assuming that he was motivated by profit, who was right—Edison or his associates? Explain.

9. What is the nature of the principle agent problem? How does the principle agent problem affect the cost-efficiency of large corporations in the market sector? Can you think of factors that limit the ability of corporate managers to follow policies that are inconsistent with economic efficiency (cost-effectiveness)?

PERSPECTIVES IN ECONOMICS

Marginal-Cost Policy Making and the Guy Next Door
by Thomas L. Wyrick

[From *The Wall Street Journal*, April 12, 1984, abridged. Reprinted with permission of Thomas L. Wyrick, Southwest Missouri State University]

Imagine yourself in a supermarket when the manager announces that for the next five minutes bottles of your favorite soft drinks will be sold two for $1 rather than the regular price of $1 each. "Buy one, get one free."

Back at home, a half-hour later, a neighbor with unexpected company calls to ask if you would sell him a bottle of the same soda. You agree, but before he gets there you must decide how much to charge him. Three possibilities come to mind—$1, 50 cents, or nothing—but there doesn't seem to be any way of knowing which is appropriate.

It doesn't take long to narrow your choices to two. Only the most altruistic would figure that the neighbor was getting the free bottle anyway, and shouldn't have to pay for it.

If you concentrate on the average price per bottle, then 50 cents will seem correct. After all, it is impossible to say which bottle was purchased and which one was "free," so it may appear reasonable to split the difference and charge your neighbor 50 cents.

But before the neighbor arrives, you have two bottles of soda. Once he leaves you will have one bottle and 50 cents, if you charge according to average cost. Since the two-for-one sale was only a one-time thing, it will be neces-

sary to spend an additional 50 cents of your own money to replace the bottle once it is gone.

So averaging costs to set a price reduces your wealth by the difference between replacement cost for soda and its average cost to you.

Now, you may charge the neighbor 50 cents just to prevent hard feelings in case he later learns about the two-for-one special. But that is the consequence of placing friendship above economic considerations. If the deal is purely an economic one, then it is proper to charge the neighbor $1. This represents the soda's replacement cost, or the marginal cost incurred by you when selling the soda.

Sound simple? That's because it is. Unfortunately, however, government officials often have difficulty translating such ideas into policy.

Our nation's energy policies have usually been based on the naive view that firms set prices according to their average costs of doing business. Instead, profit-seeking firms use marginal-cost pricing. Thus policies can (and often do) have consequences opposite to those intended.

Recall the experience with oil price controls in the 1970s. The price of domestic crude oil was held down to artificially low levels to try to lower the costs of producing gasoline. As everyone knows, though, gasoline prices have declined (rather than increased) since President Reagan abolished controls in early 1981. This is contrary to what price controllers had expected, so they generally explain the (three-year) decline as temporary.

But a different explanation emerges from the marginal-cost pricing perspective. Oil refiners produce gasoline (and other products) from crude oil purchased from both domestic and foreign sources. Controls held the price of U.S. oil to $2 or $3 a barrel while foreign suppliers charged $36 or more in 1979. Refiners rationally bought all of the U.S. crude available, and turned to OPEC members only as a last resort.

Like a person selling soda to his neighbor, however, refiners charge customers a price based on their marginal costs of selling oil. That is, because Exxon or Texaco had only a limited amount of $2 oil available, a sale of that oil meant they had to rely on OPEC sources to replenish their inventories. Since that meant an additional (marginal) outlay of $36 a barrel, then the price of gasoline had to be high enough to reflect this cost rather than the lower controlled price.

So price controls on oil allowed refiners to pay less than a market price on some of their inputs, while they charged a market price on all of their output. Thanks to Congress, refiners' profits were at an all-time high during the price-control years. Of course, U.S. landowners and others who sold crude to refiners were harmed in proportion to the latter's gain.

The 1981 removal of price controls gave domestic owners of oil reserves more incentive to find and sell crude, and they responded in kind. As new domestic supplies came into competition with foreign oil, OPEC and others were forced to lower their prices to the current range of $28 to $29. This lowered refiners' marginal costs of doing business, and allowed them to lower the price of gasoline.

Meanwhile, because of the average cost-marginal cost confusion, Congress remains unwilling to remove price controls from certain categories of natural gas. Doing so, it is thought, would result in price increases for consumers perhaps by 50% or more within a few months.

In reality, however, controls cause owners of artificially low-priced gas to hold down production, so pipeline companies must turn to more expensive (uncontrolled) sources to satisfy customer demands. That drives up the latter's utility companies, and pushes up prices to consumers.

Decontrol would allow all natural gas to sell for the same price. The owners of decontrolled gas would increase production to profit from higher prices, and the now familiar dynamic would be seen again. Lessened demand for higher-priced gas on the margin would bring down the market price of gas. And lower marginal costs for pipelines would ultimately help reduce the heating bills of consumers.

The lesson to be learned is that market participants respond to marginal costs, not average costs. If a firm's costs rise by X dollars when it produces and sells one more unit of output, then price will tend toward X dollars regardless of the firm's costs averaged over all units of output.

Policy makers intent on helping consumers, borrowers and others would do well to stop trying to control the various components of production costs. Such efforts usually end up reducing the total supply of the good or service in question, and customers pay higher retail prices as a result. Public officials should spend more effort understanding how the private economy works; then they wouldn't waste so much energy trying to fix it.

Discussion

1. How much would *you* have charged your neighbor for the bottle of soda? Why?

2. Wyrick seems to be arguing that getting rid of price controls on crude oil actually helped *reduce* the retail price of gasoline. How is this possible? Why is the role of marginal cost crucial in all of this?

3. Do you agree with Wyrick's predication that removing price controls from natural gas would decrease natural gas prices rather than increase them (even though an increase is what most people seem to expect)? Why or why not?

CHAPTER EIGHT

THE FIRM UNDER PURE COMPETITION

TRUE OR FALSE

T F

☐ ☐ 1. The model of pure competition assumes that a large number of independent firms produce a homogeneous product.

☐ ☐ 2. Competitive firms will never be able to earn economic profit.

☐ ☐ 3. A firm under pure competition faces a perfectly elastic demand curve for the product it sells.

☐ ☐ 4. A profit-maximizing competitive firm will expand output as long as the market price exceeds marginal cost.

☐ ☐ 5. An increase in market demand would cause price to rise, profit to increase, and competitive firms to expand their short-run output level.

☐ ☐ 6. Economic profits provide an incentive for competitive firms to allocate resources toward the production of goods for which the consumers' valuation exceeds the opportunity cost of production.

☐ ☐ 7. Competitive firms always produce at the level of output at which average total costs are a minimum.

☐ ☐ 8. In the competitive model, the firm's average total cost curve is also its short-run supply curve.

☐ ☐ 9. Economic losses cause firms to exit from an industry in the long run, and the market supply declines.

☐ ☐ 10. The firm's marginal cost curve indicates the opportunity cost of producing additional units of the product in the short run.

☐ ☐ 11. The minimum point of the firm's long-run average total cost curve represents the opportunity cost of producing the good in the long run.

☐ ☐ 12. In a constant cost industry, an increase in demand will cause price to rise in the long run.

☐ ☐ 13. The market supply curve usually becomes more inelastic with time.

☐ ☐ 14. The competitive model suggests that an increase in the demand for wheat would cause prices to rise, profits to increase, and consumers to buy less.

PROBLEMS AND PROJECTS

EXHIBIT 1

Monthly output	Total Cost	Average total cost	Average fixed cost	Average variable cost	Marginal cost
1	$ 25	_____	0	_____	_____
2	50	_____	_____	_____	_____
3	69	_____	_____	_____	_____
4	84	_____	_____	_____	_____
5	100	_____	_____	_____	_____
6	119	_____	_____	_____	_____
7	140	_____	_____	_____	_____
8	168	_____	_____	_____	_____

1. The student government of a major university arranges a monthly campuswide "flea market" sale where talented students can sell products they produce in their leisure time. Mary brings her handmade wallets to sell at the flea market. Since there are several other suppliers, Mary has no control over the market price. Mary's estimated cost and output data are presented in Exhibit 1.
   a. Fill in the missing cost information.
   b. If Mary was a profit maximizer, how many wallets would she produce monthly if the market price was $20? Indicate her economic profit (or loss).
   c. Indicate what Mary's monthly output and maximum profit would be if the price rose to $25.

EXHIBIT 2

Housing units per month	Total cost per month	Fixed cost (FC)	Variable cost (VC)	Average total cost (ATC)	Average fixed cost (AFC)	Average variable cost (AVC)	Marginal cost (MC)
0	$ 40,000	_____	_____	_____	_____	_____	_____
1	60,000	_____	_____	_____	_____	_____	_____
2	80,000	_____	_____	_____	_____	_____	_____
3	100,000	_____	_____	_____	_____	_____	_____
4	120,000	_____	_____	_____	_____	_____	_____
5	142,000	_____	_____	_____	_____	_____	_____
6	168,000	_____	_____	_____	_____	_____	_____
7	198,000	_____	_____	_____	_____	_____	_____
8	232,000	_____	_____	_____	_____	_____	_____
9	270,000	_____	_____	_____	_____	_____	_____
10	315,000	_____	_____	_____	_____	_____	_____

2. Joe Green operates a construction firm, Joe's Construction Company, Inc., that specializes in the production of small frame houses. Joe's expected cost schedule is presented in Exhibit 2.
   a. Complete the chart indicating Joe's FC, VC, ATC, AFC, AVC, and MC.
   b. The current market price for houses of the quality produced by Joe's Construction is $29,500. Assume Joe wants to maximize profits. How many houses should he produce per month? What is his profit (or loss)?
   c. Suppose that there is population growth in the area, causing the demand for housing to expand. The market price of houses increases to $32,000. Indicate Joe's new profit maximizing monthly output and profit (or loss).
   d. Indicate Joe's output and maximum profit (or minimum loss) if the market price were to fall to $25,000; to $21,000. Should Joe continue in business at the latter price? Explain.

EXHIBIT 3

Price	Quantity demanded (new housing)	Quantity supplied (new housing)
$21,000	850	400
25,000	700	500
29,000	600	600
31,000	500	700
35,000	450	900

3. Market conditions stabilize in the market area served by Joe's construction firm. The market demand schedule for housing of the quality produced by Joe is presented in Exhibit 3.
   a. Suppose that there are 100 competitive firms—including Joe's Construction—that supply the market area. Each firm has the cost conditions indicated in Exhibit 2. What is the market supply schedule?
   b. What is the short-run market-clearing price?
   c. What is the profit or loss of the firms? Is there any incentive for new firms to enter the market?
   d. Given competitive conditions, what will happen to the market price with time? Explain.

4. Exhibit 4 presents selected monthly information relating to a single firm in a purely competitive market.

EXHIBIT 4

Price	$ 8
Total Revenue	8000
Total Variable Cost	7000
Output	_____
Average Total Cost	8
Total Cost	_____
Marginal Revenue	_____
Marginal Cost	8
Total Profit	_____

   a. Fill in the missing information in the exhibit.
   b. Is this firm in *long-run* equilibrium?

   Suppose the government decides that firms in this market must be licensed to operate and establishes a licensing fee of $6000 payable by each firm yearly regardless of the economic circumstances of the firm.
   c. In the *short-run*, how will the firm adjust its output in response to the licensing fee?
   d. If the firm expects market conditions to remain the same in the long run, how will it adjust its output?

5. Exhibit 5 shows a situation of long-run equilibrium for both the market and a typical firm in the cheese industry. Suppose that government decides (perhaps to raise incomes for dairy "farmers") to place a price support on dairy products at the level P$_s$ and enforces this price by agreeing to purchase any quantity of dairy products produced but not sold to the private sector.

EXHIBIT 5

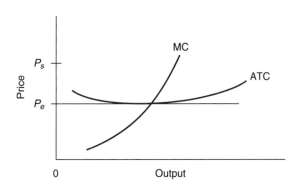 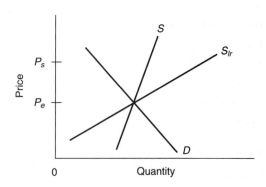

a. For the short run, indicate in the diagrams how the market and the typical firm will adjust to this price support policy. (Indicate the new quantity demanded in the market and the new quantity supplied both in the market and by the typical firm.) How much cheese will the government need to buy in the short run in order to maintain the price, P$_s$?

b. Now indicate how the market and the typical firm will adjust to the price support policy in the long run. (Remember that an upward-sloping long-run supply curve indicates that the industry is an increasing-cost industry.) Will the government be required to purchase more cheese per period in the long run than in the short run?

c. Is this policy consistent with the achievement of *productive efficiency* in the dairy products industry? Is it consistent with the achievement of *allocative efficiency*? Explain. (*Hint:* Be sure to decide how long the "long" run is.)

6. Use the diagram in Exhibit 6 to answer the following questions:

EXHIBIT 6

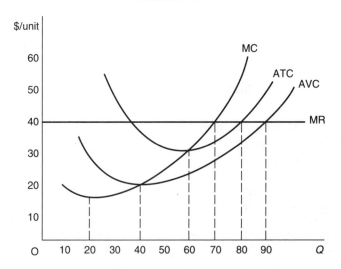

Suppose the price of output is $40 per unit. What output level is implied by each of the following statements?

____ a. Ms. A: "I work for the sales department of my employer. My annual bonus is tied to the company's sales revenue, so I push the firm to sell as much as possible—without causing overall losses, of course."

____ b. Mr. B: "My specialty is cost control. My plan for moving up in my department is maximizing the spread between price and marginal cost. Avoid diminishing returns, I always say."

____ c. Mr. C: "I am a middle level manager, and I have a strategy for reaching the top: maximizing profits as a share of sales." [*Hint*: Profits as a share of sales = $(TR - TC)/TR$, where $TR = P \cdot Q$ and $TC = ATC \cdot Q$.]

____ d. Ms. D: "I own this company, and I would like all of you to maximize the return on my capital investment, in short, my profits."

7. Suppose you own a hotel at a ski resort. The left-hand panel of Exhibit 7 depicts the market supply of rooms and the demand for rooms in the winter (W), spring (Sp), summer (Su), and fall (F). The right-hand panel depicts your unit costs per room rented; these costs are the same for each season.

EXHIBIT 7

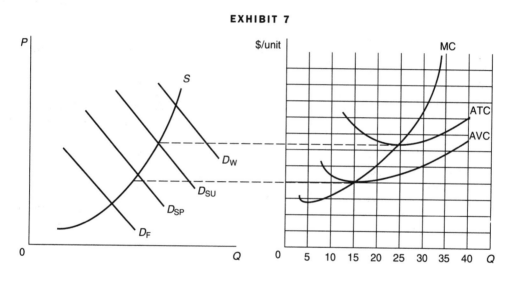

a. Use the diagrams in Exhibit 7 to help you complete the following table. For the profits column, indicate whether your profits for the season are positive (+), negative (−), or zero (0).

Season	Number of rooms rented	Profits
Winter	_____	_____
Spring	_____	_____
Summer	_____	_____
Fall	_____	_____

b. Given the fluctuations in demand and profits, how would you decide whether or not to remain in this industry?

LEARNING THE MECHANICS—MULTIPLE CHOICE

1. The reason we do not refer to long-run variable cost as distinguished from long-run cost is that
   a. all costs are fixed in the long run.
   b. all costs are constant in the long run.
   c. all costs are variable in the long run.
   d. all costs decline in the long run.

2. A decrease in demand that results in economic losses in industry A will
   a. induce new, more efficient firms to enter the industry.
   b. cause the existing firms in industry A to expand the scale of their operation.
   c. induce both new and existing firms in industry A to bid more resources away from other industries.
   d. encourage owners of resources to move their resources from industry A to other industries.

3. If the firms in a competitive industry were incurring costs that were less than the prices they were charging, the firms
   a. would enjoy short-run economic profits that would be offset by long-run economic losses.
   b. would face new competition, which would drive price down to the cost of production in the long run.
   c. would enjoy long-run economic profit.
   d. must be colluding or otherwise "rigging the market."

4. Which of the following statements is correct?
   a. In order to maximize profits in the short run, a purely competitive firm should produce at the output level where marginal cost is equal to price.
   b. In long-run equilibrium, a purely competitive firm will produce at the level of minimum average variable cost.
   c. A purely competitive firm will produce in the short run, so long as total receipts are sufficient to cover total fixed costs.
   d. A purely competitive firm will always close down in the short run, whenever price is less than average total cost.

5. Which of the following would be most likely to lead to a reduction in the price of a competitively produced product X?
   a. An increase in the price of Y, a substitute
   b. A decrease in the price of Z, a complementary product
   c. A decrease in the price of K, a factor of production that is utilized to produce X
   d. A decrease in the price of L, a factor of production utilized to produce Z, the complementary product

6. In an industry with low barriers to entry, when positive economic profits are present and expected
   a. firms will exit from the industry.
   b. the marginal cost curve will shift down.
   c. the average fixed cost curve will shift up.
   d. firms will enter the industry, forcing the price down such that only zero economic profits will be possible.

7. The long-run supply curve is more elastic than the short-run supply curve because, given sufficient time
   a. production techniques become more expensive.
   b. new firms can enter the industry and old firms can increase their plant size.
   c. producers become less competitive.
   d. consumers become more demanding.

8. In the short run, the basic relationship between an individual firm's supply curve under perfect competition and the market supply curve under perfect competition is
   a. the individual firm's supply curve is horizontal, but the market supply curve is upward sloping.
   b. the individual firm's supply curve is vertical, but the market supply curve is upward sloping.
   c. the market supply curve is the summation of all the individual firms' supply curves.
   d. the market supply curve is equal to the average of all the individual firms' supply curves.

9. The actions of a firm in a purely competitive industry have no effect on market price; therefore, the demand curve faced by the firm is
   a. unknown.
   b. a downward-sloping curve.
   c. a horizontal line at the level of market price.
   d. the firm's total revenue curve.

10. According to the text, a study of the dairy industry indicates that the long-run elasticity of supply of milk with respect to its price is
    a. much more elastic than would have been expected.
    b. much more inelastic than would have been expected.
    c. dependent on the demand for milk.
    d. none of the above.

11. The difference between the short-run and the long-run supply curves for a product is that the short-run supply curve is usually
    a. horizontal.
    b. more inelastic than the long-run curve.
    c. more elastic than the long-run curve.
    d. of unitary elasticity.

12. Laboratory experiments in economics:
    a. are part of a field called experimental economics.
    b. tend to support the concept of the competitive model.
    c. have been undertaken mainly since the 1950s.
    d. All of the above are correct.

Questions 13 and 14 refer to the following cost curves for a firm in a competitive market:

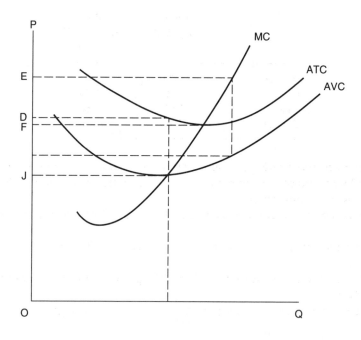

13. In order for the preceding firm to be BOTH allocatively and productively efficient, the market price P must equal
    a. OE.
    b. OD.
    c. OF.
    d. OJ.

14. For the firm to be in long-run equilibrium (given the cost curves above and a price equal to OE),
    a. other firms must leave the industry.
    b. demand for the industry's good must increase.
    c. the firm must invest in cost-cutting equipment.
    d. the market supply curve must shift out (increase supply).

THE ECONOMIC WAY OF THINKING—MULTIPLE CHOICE

1. If firms in a competitive industry were forced to install antipollution devices that increased their production costs, we should expect
   a. the demand for their product to decline.
   b. the market price of their product to increase in the short run, but not in the long run.
   c. that the firms in the industry would be saddled with long-run economic losses.
   d. that the firms in the industry would make normal economic profits in the long run, as the higher production costs were passed along to consumers.

Use the following table in answering the next two questions:

	Price, July 1972 (bushel)	Price, August 1973 (bushel)
Wheat	$1.70	$4.90
Oats	0.80	2.06
Rye	1.01	3.86
Soybeans	3.50	12.00

2. In July 1972, the Nixon administration announced it had concluded the largest agricultural commodity sale in history—selling 25 percent of the American wheat crop to the Soviet Union. Which of the following best explains the impact of this transaction?
   a. The demand for American wheat increased sharply, the short-run supply was highly inelastic and price rose sharply.
   b. The domestic production of wheat declined, and price rose sharply in spite of the highly elastic demand.
   c. The demand for American wheat increased, but the price change suggests that the short-run supply was highly elastic.
   d. The supply of American wheat fell sharply, but the price change suggests that the current demand was elastic.

3. Which of the following would *not* result from the Russian wheat deal?
   a. The income and profits of American farmers would increase.
   b. The price of agricultural land—particularly land suitable for growing grain products—would rise.
   c. The price of wheat would rise more in the short run than over a longer period of time that would allow for a supply response.
   d. The price of breakfast foods, bread, and beef to the American consumer would be unaffected by the wheat deal.

4. The agricultural sector is often said to approximate closely the competitive market structure because of the large number of firms and the low barriers to entry. Assume that the government fixes the price of wheat above the market equilibrium price and pledges to purchase quantities of wheat that cannot be sold to private purchasers. Wheat farmers will
   a. expand the output of wheat and bid up the prices of factors used in the production of wheat.
   b. expand the output of wheat and continue to make long-run economic profits.
   c. increase their sales of wheat to private consumers because of the higher price.
   d. produce less wheat because of higher factor prices and therefore increased cost.

5. If the demand for food increased drastically over the next ten years in the United States, and farmers became much more productive during the same period, then
   a. the price of food would definitely fall over the next ten years.
   b. the price of food would definitely rise over the next ten years.
   c. it is possible that the price of food would not increase over the next ten years, relative to its current level.
   d. the supply curve for food would shift to the left because of increased farm productivity and the increased demand for food.

6. The competitive market tends toward a state of long-run normal rate of return (zero economic profits) because
   a. firms will moderate their price demands under fear of government legislation.
   b. with firms able to enter and leave the industry freely, competition between rivals will drive prices down to the level of production costs.
   c. cutthroat competition will cause some firms to incur losses, but barriers to entry will result in profits for others.
   d. barriers to entry will prevent firms from earning excess profits.

7. Suppose that there is a sharp increase in the demand for small cars as drivers seek to conserve fuel during the energy crisis. The most likely long-run market adjustment would be
   a. lower short-run small car prices because of greater sales volume, but higher prices as the long-run stock of small cars is depleted.
   b. higher short-run prices, leading to an increase in long-run quantity supplied which would moderate the long-run price increase.
   c. moderate increases in short-run prices, followed by larger long-run price increases as the stock of small cars is depleted.
   d. higher short-run prices because of greater sales volume and still higher prices later, as plant sizes are adjusted.

8. During peak periods, like the middle of the day during a summer hot spell, power companies often experience brownouts because the quantity of electricity demanded exceeds the capacity of the power company. These brownouts are costly, since they reduce available electricity without regard to the need for that electricity, and they may damage sensitive machinery. These costs could be reduced if
   a. the barriers to entry in the utility industry were reduced.
   b. the long-run demand for electricity was perfectly elastic.
   c. the long-run supply of electricity was perfectly elastic.
   d. the power company had the right to charge a higher price for electricity consumed during peak periods.

9. Which portion of the marginal cost curve is used to create a firm's short-run supply curve?
   a. The entire marginal cost curve
   b. The marginal cost curve above its intersection with the average variable cost curve
   c. The marginal cost curve above its intersection with the marginal revenue (demand) curve
   d. The marginal cost curve above its intersection with the average total cost curve

10. "My fixed costs are killing me. I am only covering my variable costs plus a third of those fixed costs. I see no change coming in either my costs of production or in product prices." Economic analysis indicates that this producer will minimize her losses by
    a. shutting down immediately and selling her business as soon thereafter as possible.
    b. continuing to produce until it is possible to sell her business.
    c. continuing to produce, recognizing that true economic profits do not include fixed costs.
    d. continuing to produce as long as marginal costs are covered.

11. "I have been making furniture for 27 years. I have never heard of either marginal costs or Adam Smith. Fancy economic theories mean nothing to me. I just know how to do well in business. Common sense and watching the market are good enough for me." For producers like this, the competitive model
    a. will not usually predict their behavior accurately.
    b. indicates nothing about the behavior of such producers.
    c. will probably predict their actions fairly accurately.
    d. does not apply, because the producers do not understand the terminology.

12. "Our marginal cost exceeds our marginal revenue at current factor prices." In plain English, this means that
    a. profit would increase if one more unit were produced.
    b. producing one more unit right now would either reduce the profit or enlarge the loss of the firm.
    c. management must be operating correctly right now.
    d. the firm should shut down and cease production even in the short run.

13. Use the diagram in the left-hand panel in Exhibit 8 to answer this question. From the information in the diagram we can conclude that:
    a. Q_0 is more profitable (has smaller losses) than Q_1.
    b. Q_1 is more profitable (has smaller losses) than Q_0.
    c. Q_0 and Q_1 are equally profitable.
    d. we don't have enough information to determine which output level is more profitable.

EXHIBIT 8

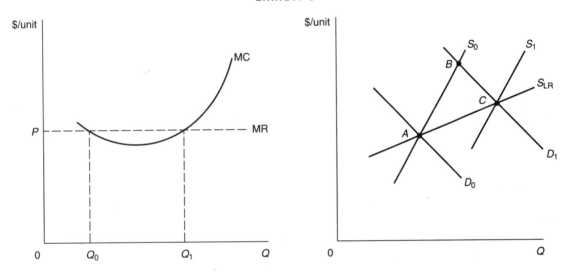

14. Use the diagram in the right-hand panel in Exhibit 8 to answer this question. Which of the following is correct ranking of profits for the firms in this industry?
    a. A is more profitable than B, which is more profitable than C.
    b. B is more profitable than A, which is more profitable than C.
    c. B is more profitable than C, which is more profitable than A.
    d. B is more profitable than A, which is just as profitable as C.

15. Suppose that the demand curve for playing cards is downward sloping and that the cards are produced in a constant cost competitive industry. If a 50 cent per deck tax is levied on playing cards, by how much will the price of a deck of cards increase in the short run and in the long run?

	Short run	Long run
a.	50 cents	more than 50 cents
b.	less than 50 cents	50 cents
c.	less than 50 cents	more than 50 cents
d.	50 cents	less than 50 cents

THE ECONOMIC WAY OF THINKING—DISCUSSION QUESTIONS

1. When price is above minimum average variable cost, why is the firm's marginal cost curve its supply curve in the short run? Why isn't the same thing true when price is below minimum average variable cost?

2. Use the competitive model to indicate how each of the following would affect the market price of green vegetables:
   a. Higher fertilizer prices
   b. Development of a hybrid bean seed that triples output per acre
   c. An increase in meat prices
   d. Increased demand for potatoes, which can be grown instead on the land used for green vegetables
   e. Passage of a general sales tax on agricultural products including vegetables.

3. a. Clearly distinguish between competition in the rivalry sense and pure competition.
   b. What type of competition applies to wheat farmer Smith and wheat farmer Smythe? To Boeing and Lockheed?
   c. From an economic perspective, how would Smith fare if misfortune befell Smythe? How would Boeing fare if misfortune befell Lockheed?

4. A winter freeze destroys 50 percent of the orange trees in Florida. What impact would the freeze have on
   a. the current supply of oranges?
   b. the price of grapefruit?
   c. the incomes of California orange growers?
   d. the incomes of Florida orange growers?

5. Use the competitive model to explain fully how a reduction in demand for shrimp would affect (a) the economic profit or loss of shrimp producers and (b) the market price and output in both the short and long run. Use diagrams relating the adjustments of the producers (firms) to the market in explaining your answer.

6. Consider the following statement: "Profits and losses are merely signals providing producers with the incentive to produce what consumers want." Do you think this is true when industries are competitively structured? When they are not competitively structured? Explain both answers.

7. Our economy is in a continuous process of change: new firms start up and many existing firms go bankrupt.
   a. Do bankruptcies increase or decrease efficiency?
   b. Who loses when a firm goes bankrupt? Who gains?
   c. If a firm is producing a good or service at a loss, how is it affecting national wealth? Explain.
   d. The government occasionally rescues bankrupt firms, such as Chrysler and many savings and loan associations. Do you approve of these bailouts? Why or why not?

8. Do you think economics ever can become a true laboratory science like chemistry or biology? Why or why not?

PERSPECTIVES IN ECONOMICS

The Economic Organization of a Prison Camp
by Richard A. Radford

[Abridged from "The Economic Organization of a Prison Camp," *Economica*, November 1945, pp. 189–201. Reprinted with permission.]

After allowance has been made for abnormal circumstances, the social institutions, ideas and habits of groups in the outside world are to be found reflected in a Prisoner of War Camp. One aspect of social organization is to be found in economic activity, and this is to be found in any P.O.W. camp. True, a prisoner is not dependent on his exertions for the provision of the necessaries, or even the luxuries of life, but through his economic activity, the exchange of goods and services, his standard of material comfort is considerably enhanced.

Everyone receives a roughly equal share of essentials: it is by trade that individual preferences are given expression and comfort increased. All at some time, and most people regularly, make exchanges of one sort of another. Our essential interest lies in the universality and spontaneity of this economic life: it came into existence not only by conscious imitation but as a response to the immediate needs and circumstances. Any similarity between prison organization and outside organization arises form similar stimuli evoking similar responses.

The Development And Organization Of The Market
We reached a transit camp in Italy and received one-quarter of a Red Cross food parcel each a week later. At once exchanges, already established, multiplied in volume. Starting with simple director barter, such as a non-smoker giving a smoker friend a cigarette issue in exchange for a chocolate ration, more complex exchanges soon became an accepted custom. Stories circulated of a padre who started off round the camp with a tin of cheese and five cigarettes and returned to his bed with a complete parcel in addition to his original cheese and cigarettes: the market was not yet perfect. Within a week or two, as the volume of trade grew, rough scales of exchange values came into existence. Sikhs, who had at first exchanged tinned beef for practically any other foodstuff, began to insist on jam and margarine. It was realized that a tin of jam was worth one-half pound of margarine plus something else; that a cigarette issue was worth several chocolate issues, and a tin of diced carrots was worth practically nothing.

By the end of the month, when we reached our permanent camp, there was a lively trade in all commodities and their relative values were well known, and expressed not in terms of one another, but in terms of cigarettes. The cigarette became the standard of value. In the permanent camp people started by wandering through the bungalows calling their offers—"cheese for seven" (cigarettes)—and the hours after parcel issue were bedlam. The inconvenience of this system soon led to its replacement by an Exchange and Mart notice board in every bungalow, where sales and wants were advertised. When a deal went through, it was crossed off the board. The public and semi-permanent records of transactions led to cigarette prices being well known and thus tending to equality throughout the camp, although there was always opportunities for an astute trader to make a profit from arbitrage. With this development everyone, including non-smokers, was willing to sell for cigarettes, using them to buy at another time and place. Cigarettes became the normal currency though, of course, barter was never extinguished.

The unity of the market and the prevalence of a single price varied directly with the general level of organization and comfort in the camp. A transit camp was always chaotic. Organization was too slender to include an Exchange and Mart board, and private advertisements were the most that appeared. Consequently a transit camp was not one market but many. The price of a tin of salmon is known to have varied by two cigarettes in 20 between one end of a hut and the other. Despite a high level of organization in Italy, the market was morcellated in this manner at the first transit we reached after our removal to Germany. In this camp there were up to 50,000 prisoners of all nationalities. French, Russian, Italian and Jugo-Slavs were free to move about within the camp: British and Americans were confined to their compounds, although a few cigarettes given to a sentry would always procure permission for one or two men to visit other compounds. The people who first visited the highly organized French trading center, with its stalls and known prices, found coffee extract—relatively cheap among the tea-drinking English—commanding a fancy price in biscuits or cigarettes, and some enterprising people made small fortunes that way.

The permanent camps in Germany saw the highest level of commercial organizations. In addition to the Exchange and Mart notice boards, a shop was organized as a public utility, controlled by representatives of the Senior British Officer, on a no-profit basis. People left their surplus clothing, toilet requirements and food there until they were sold at a fixed price in cigarettes. Only sales in cigarettes were accepted and there was no haggling. The capital was provided by a loan from the bulk store of Red Cross cigarettes and repaid by a small commission taken on the first transaction. Thus the cigarette attained its fullest currency status, and the market was almost completely united.

There was an embryo labor market. Even when cigarettes were not scarce, there was usually some unlucky person willing to perform services for them. Laundry advertised at two cigarettes a garment. A good pastel portrait cost thirty. Odd tailoring and other jobs similarly had their prices.

There were also entrepreneurial services. There was a coffee stall owner who sold tea, coffee or cocoa at two cigarettes a cup, buying his raw materials at market prices and hiring labor to gather fuel and to stoke: he actually enjoyed the services of a chartered accountant at one stage. After a period of great prosperity he overreached himself and failed disastrously for several hundred cigarettes. Such large-scale private enterprise was rare but several middlemen or professional traders existed. One man capitalized his knowledge of Urdu by buying meat from the Sikhs and selling butter and jam in return: as his operations became better known more and more people entered this trade, prices in the Indian Wing approximated more nearly to those elsewhere, though to the end a "contact" among the Indians was valuable, as linguistic difficulties prevented the trade from being quite free. Some were specialists in the Indian trade, the food, or even the watch trade. Middlemen traded on their own account or on commission. Price rings and agreements were suspected and the traders certainly cooperated. Nor did they welcome newcomers. Unfortunately the writer knows little of the workings of these people: public opinion was hostile and the professionals were usually of a retiring disposition.

One trader in food and cigarettes, operating in a period of dearth, enjoyed a high reputation. His capital was originally about 50 cigarettes, with which he bought rations on issue days and held them until the price rose just before the next issue. He also picked up a little by arbitrage; several times a day he visited every Exchange or Mart notice board and took advantage of every discrepancy between prices of good offered and wanted. His knowledge of prices, markets and names of those who had received cigarette parcels was phenomenal. By these means he kept himself smoking steadily—his profits—while his capital remained intact.

Credit entered into many transactions. Naturally prices varied according to the terms of sale. A treacle ration might be advertised for four cigarettes now or five next week. And in the future market "bread now" was a vastly different thing from "bread Thursday." Bread was issued on Thursday and Monday, and by Wednesday and Sunday night it had risen at least one cigarette per ration. One man always saved a ration to sell then at the peak price: his offer of "bread now" stood out on the board among a number of "bread Monday's" fetching one or two less, or not selling at all—and he always smoked on Sunday night.

The Cigarette Currency Although cigarettes as currency had certain peculiarities, they performed all the functions of a metallic currency as a unit of account, as a measure of value and as a store of value, and shared most of its characteristics.

Cigarettes were also subject to the working of Gresham's Law. Certain brands were more popular than others as smokes, but for currency purposes a cigarette was a cigarette. Consequently buyers used the poorer qualities and the Shop rarely saw the more popular brands: cigarettes such as Churchman's No. 1 were rarely used for trading. At one time cigarettes handrolled from pipe tobacco began to circulate. Pipe tobacco was issued in lieu of cigarettes by the Red Cross at a rate of 25 cigarettes to the ounce and this rate was standard in exchanges, but an ounce would produce 30 home-made cigarettes. Naturally people with machine-made cigarettes broke them down and re-rolled the tobacco, and the real cigarette virtually disappeared from the market. For a time we suffered all the inconveniences of debased currency.

While the Red Cross issue of 50 or 25 cigarettes per man per week came in regularly, and while there were fair stocks held, the cigarette currency suited its purpose admirably. But when the issue was interrupted, stocks soon ran out, prices fell, trading declined in volume and became increasingly a matter of barter. This deflationary tendency was periodically offset by the sudden injection of new currency. Private cigarette parcels arrived in a trickle throughout the year, but the big numbers came in quarterly when the Red Cross received its allocation of transport. Several hundred thousand cigarettes might arrive in the space of a fortnight. Prices soared, and then began to fall, slowly at first but with increasing rapidity as stocks ran out, until the next big delivery. Most of our economic troubles could be attributed to this fundamental instability.

Price Movements The general price level was affected by other factors. An influx of new prisoners, proverbially hungry, raised it. Heavy air raids in the vicinity of the camp probably increased the non-monetary demand for cigarettes and accentuated deflation. Good and bad war news certainly had its effect, and the general waves of optimism and pessimism which swept the camp were reflected in prices. Before breakfast one morning a rumor of the arrival of parcels and cigarettes was circulated. Within ten minutes I sold a treacle ration for four cigarettes (hitherto offered in vain for three). By 10 o'clock the rumor was denied, and the treacle that day found no more buyers even at two cigarettes.

Changes in the supply of a commodity, in the ration scale or in the make-up of Red Cross parcels, would raise the price of one commodity relative to others. Tins of oatmeal, once a rare and much sought after luxury in the parcels, became a commonplace in 1943, and the price fell. In hot weather the demand for cocoa fell, and that for soap rose. A new recipe would be reflected in the price level: the discovery that raisins and sugar could be turned into an alcohol liquor of remarkable potency reacted permanently on the dried fruit market. The invention of electric immersion heaters run off the power points made tea, a drug on the market in Italy, a certain seller in Germany. Any change in conditions affected both the general price level and the price structure.

Public Opinion Public opinion on the subject or trading was vocal if confused and changeable. Certain forms of trading were more generally condemned; trade with the Germans was criticized by many. At one time, when there had been several cases of malnutrition reported among the more devoted smokers, no trade in German rations was permitted, as the victims became an additional burden on the depleted food reserves of the Hospital. But while certain activities were condemned as antisocial, trade itself was practiced, and its utility appreciated, by almost everyone in the camp.

Taken as a whole, opinion was hostile to the middleman. His function, and his hard work in bringing buyer and seller together, were ignored; profits were not regarded as a reward for labour, but as a result of sharp practice. Despite the fact that his very existence was proof to the contrary, the middleman was held to be redundant in view of the existence of an Official Shop and the Exchange and Mart. Appreciation only came his way when he was willing to advance the price of a sugar ration, or to buy goods spot and carry them against a future sale. In these cases the element of risk was obvious to all, and the convenience of the service was felt to merit some reward. Particularly unpopular was the middleman with an element of monopoly, the man who contacted the ration wagon driver, or the man who utilized his knowledge of Urdu.

There was a strong feeling that everything had its "just price" in cigarettes. While the assessment of the just price, which incidentally varied between camps, was impossible of explanation, this price was nevertheless pretty closely known. It can best be defined as the price usually fetched by an article in good times when cigarettes were plentiful. The "just price" changed slowly; it was unaffected by short-term variations in supply, and while opinion might be resigned to departures from the "just price," a strong feeling of resentment persisted.

Conclusion The economic organization described was both elaborate and smooth-working in the summer of 1944. Then came the August cuts and deflation. Prices fell, rallied with deliveries of cigarette parcels in September and December, and fell again. In January 1945, supplies of Red Cross cigarettes ran out; and prices slumped still further; in February the supplies of food parcels were exhausted and the depression became a blizzard. Food, itself scarce, was almost given away in order to meet the non-monetary demand for cigarettes. Laundries ceased to operate, or worked for £'s or Reichmarks: food and cigarettes sold for fancy prices in £'s hitherto unheard of. The Shop was empty and the Exchange Mart notices were full of unaccepted offers for cigarettes. Barter increased in volume, become a large portion of a smaller value of trade.

By April, 1945, chaos had replaced order in the economic sphere: sales were difficult, prices lacked stability. Economics has been defined as the science of distributing limited means among unlimited and competing ends. On 12 April with the arrival of elements of the 30th U.S. Infantry Division, the ushering in of an age of plenty demonstrated the hypothesis that with infinite means economic organization and activity would be redundant, as every want could be satisfied without effort.

Discussion

1. The prisoners used cigarettes as their medium of exchange. Was this a good choice? What else could they have used?

2. Were the prisoners' exchanges really similar to what would take place under perfect competition? Could you diagram these exchanges on supply and demand graphs? Try it!

3. How moral is it to use the price mechanism to allocate food when life and death may be at stake? Can you think of a better method than the one that was used?

MONOPOLY AND HIGH BARRIERS TO ENTRY

TRUE OR FALSE

T F

☐ ☐   1. It is not easy to regulate a monopoly well. The cost—plus orientation—toward which pricing methods gravitate tends to weaken incentives for efficiency.

☐ ☐   2. In some industries (for example, telephone), per unit costs may decline with size of firm, generating a tendency for the industry to be monopolized.

☐ ☐   3. Like pure competition, the barriers to entry of a monopoly are fairly low.

☐ ☐   4. A profit-maximizing monopolist would expand output, as long as price exceeds her marginal cost.

☐ ☐   5. The marginal revenue curve of the monopolist will lie below the firm's demand curve.

☐ ☐   6. Since an unregulated monopolist is assured of economic profit, there is little incentive for such a firm to produce efficiently.

☐ ☐   7. Within the framework of the hypothetical model of monopoly, high barriers to entry prevent competitive pressures from driving the market price down to the level of production cost.

☐ ☐   8. In the long run, the profits of a monopolist will be eliminated.

☐ ☐   9. The price of goods produced by a monopolist may substantially exceed their opportunity cost of production.

☐ ☐ 10. Economists usually argue that the output of a monopolized industry is less than the socially ideal level of output.

☐ ☐ 11. Ideal price regulation could improve resource allocation by forcing a monopolist to charge a price equal to her average (or marginal) cost of production.

☐ ☐ 12. Practically speaking, the advantages of government regulation are greatly limited because of imperfect information about cost and demand conditions.

☐ ☐ 13. Monopolists have little incentive to influence regulatory agencies, whereas the typical consumer has a great incentive to be concerned with regulatory activities.

☐ ☐ 14. Historically, regulatory agencies have sometimes been used as vehicles to maintain high prices and limit competition.

PROBLEMS AND PROJECTS

EXHIBIT 1

Price	Quantity demanded (per week)	Marginal cost	Total revenue	Marginal revenue	Fixed cost	Total cost
$60	1	$50	_____	_____	$40	_____
55	2	20	_____	_____		_____
50	3	26	_____	_____		_____
45	4	30	_____	_____		_____
40	5	40	_____	_____		_____
35	6	50	_____	_____		_____

1. Suppose that you produce and sell dining tables in a localized market. Past experience permits you to estimate your demand and marginal cost schedules. This information is presented in Exhibit 1.
   a. Fill in the missing revenue and cost schedules.
   b. If you were currently charging $55 per dining table set, what should you do if you wanted to maximize profits?
   c. Given your demand and cost estimates, what would be the maximum weekly profit you could earn?

2. Exhibit 2 indicates the demand and long-run cost conditions in an industry.
   a. Explain why the industry is likely to be monopolized.
   b. Indicate the price that a profit-maximizing monopolist would charge and label it *P*.
   c. Indicate the monopolist's output level and label it *Q*.
   d. Indicate the maximum profits of the monopolist
   e. Will the profits attract competitors to the industry? Why or why not? Explain.

EXHIBIT 2

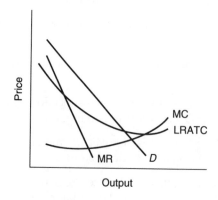

3. The food service at many university campuses is operated by a single firm. Suppose that Exhibit 3 indicates the monthly demand for meals and total operating cost for the food service firm on your campus.

EXHIBIT 3

Sales (in 1000s)	Price (per meal)	TR	MR (per 1000)	Total cost	MC (per 1000)
4	$1.60	_____	_____	$ 6000	_____
5	1.40	_____	_____	6400	_____
6	1.30	_____	_____	6800	_____
7	1.20	_____	_____	7300	_____
8	1.10	_____	_____	8000	_____
9	1.00	_____	_____	9000	_____
10	0.90	_____	_____	10200	_____

a. Fill in the firm's TR, MR, and MC schedules.
b. What price (of those shown) would a profit-maximizing monopolist choose?
c. Is the monopolist making economic profits? If so, how large per month?
d. Students often complain about the price and quality of food. Suppose that a group of economics majors was asked to regulate the monopolists by setting a price for meals that would maximize consumer welfare. What price would they choose? (Total costs must be covered or service will cease.)
e. In the absence of student regulation, suppose that the university competitively auctioned the food service rights to the highest bidder. How much would a firm pay for this property right for one year? Who would reap the monopoly profits under this arrangement?

4. Exhibit 4 indicates the demand, marginal revenue, marginal cost, and average cost curves for a monopolist.
   a. What price would an unregulated private monopolist set? Indicate with a colored pen or pencil the border of the area on the graph that represents the monopolist's profit or loss.
   b. Suppose that a regulatory agency wanted to force a normal rate of return (zero economic profit) on the monopolist. What price would the regulatory agency set? Would this price necessarily force a zero economic profit on the monopoly? Why or why not?
   c. What price would be most efficient from the viewpoint of allocative efficiency? (Assume any profit or loss would be absorbed by the government and that all else remains constant.) Indicate with another colored pen or pencil the border of the area on the graph that represents the monopolists's profit or loss. Does this area represent a profit or a loss?

EXHIBIT 4

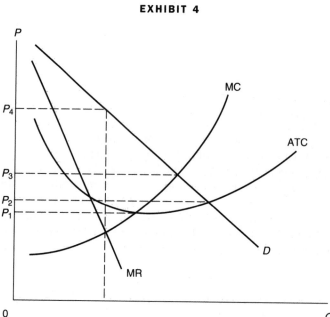

5. When a seller can effectively separate his or her total market into two segments, the theory of price discrimination indicates that a higher product price will be charged in the market segment with the lower elasticity of demand. For each of the markets below, indicate in the blank which segment, (1) or (2), you think will be charged the higher price and be ready to explain why you think that segment has a lower elasticity of demand.
   _____ a. Sales of movie tickets to (1) adults (2) children
   _____ b. Sales of airline tickets to (1) business travelers (2) spouses traveling with them
   _____ c. Sales of new cars to (1) those who presently own a car (2) those who do not
   _____ d. Sales of cosmetic surgery to (1) the poor (2) the rich

6. Suppose the diagram in Exhibit 5 depicts the situation facing the seller of a special prerecorded cassette tape. The quantity is in millions of units.

EXHIBIT 5

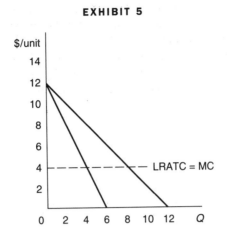

Consider each of the following alternative output strategies for the cassette seller, and complete the following table:
a. The firm produces the efficient level of output.
b. The firm produces the profit-maximizing level of output.
c. The firm produces the total revenue-maximizing level of output.

	Q	P	Total revenue	Total cost	Firm profits	Consumer surplus	Efficiency loss
a.							
b.							
c.							

7. Suppose you are a Buster's ice cream fanatic. Your demand for scoops of Buster's ice cream is given in the first two columns of Exhibit 6 (ignore the remaining columns for now):

EXHIBIT 6

Price	Scoops per day	For questions a and b:		For questions c and d:	
		Total revenue	Marginal revenue	Total revenue	Marginal revenue
$1.20	0	0	xxxx	0	xxxx
1.10	1	_____	_____	_____	_____
1.00	2	_____	_____	_____	_____
.90	3	_____	_____	_____	_____
.80	4	_____	_____	_____	_____
.70	5	_____	_____	_____	_____
.60	6	_____	_____	_____	_____
.50	7	_____	_____	_____	_____
.40	8	_____	_____	_____	_____

a. Complete the middle two columns of Exhibit 6.
b. Suppose Buster's average and marginal cost of ice cream is $.50 per scoop. If Buster's wants to maximize the profits it earns from sales to you, what price should it charge you? How many scoops will you buy? How large will Buster's profits be?

Now suppose you go into Buster's one day and see the following new pricing schedule for ice cream:
  1 scoop $1.00
  2 scoops   1.90
  3 scoops   2.70
  4 scoops   3.40
  5 scoops   4.00
  Additional scoops $.50 each
c. Complete the last two columns of Exhibit 6. (*Hint*: Recall that the price you are willing to pay for a scoop reflects the marginal value you place on that scoop.)
d. How many scoops will you buy? How large will Buster's profits be?
e. Is Buster's new pricing system a smart strategy? Why or why not?

LEARNING THE MECHANICS—MULTIPLE CHOICE

1. Which of the following best defines a monopoly?
  a. A firm that is the sole producer of a product for which there are no good substitutes?
  b. A firm that produces a differentiated product
  c. A firm that is licensed by the government
  d. A firm that has made profits over a long-run time period

2. Which of the following is a major economic criticism of monopoly as a source of economic inefficiency?
   a. Monopolists fail to expand output to the level where the consumer's valuation of the additional until is just equal to its opportunity cost.
   b. Monopolists have no incentive to produce efficiently, because even the inefficient monopolists can be assured of high economic profits.
   c. Monopolists will always make profits, and profits are an indication that prices are too high.
   d. Monopolists have an unfair advantage since they can purchase inputs, including labor, at a lower price than competitive firms in other industries.

3. If economies of scale could not be realized in an industry, imposition of the monopoly industrial structure on an otherwise purely competitive industry would result in
   a. higher prices and a smaller industry output.
   b. higher prices and a larger industry output.
   c. lower prices and a larger industry output.
   d. lower prices and a smaller industry output.

4. Use statements I and II to answer this question. (I) If a monopolist's marginal revenue exceeded marginal cost at the current price and output level, the monopolist should reduce price and expand output in order to maximize its profits. (II) A monopolist will maximize its profits by charging a price that maximizes the difference between its sale price and its average total cost.
   a. I is true, II is false.
   b. I is false, II is true.
   c. Both I and II are true.
   d. Both I and II are false.

5. When economies of scale are important, and therefore when an industry tends toward natural monopoly, breaking the industries into several firms of small size would
   a. lead to lower short-run prices.
   b. lead to higher prices or at least to a higher per unit cost for the smaller firms.
   c. cause prices to rise if demand were inelastic, but fall if it were elastic.
   d. cause prices to fall because of the decline in producer profits.

6. Which of the following best describes the supply policy of a monopolist? The monopolist will expand supply until
   a. total revenues equal total cost.
   b. per unit profits are at a maximum.
   c. average total costs are at a minimum.
   d. marginal costs equal marginal revenues.

7. All of the following except one are sometimes a source of monopoly. Which one is not a source of monopoly?
   a. Substantial economies of scale
   b. Government licensing of producers
   c. Control over an essential source
   d. Inefficiency because of bureaucratic decision-making procedures

Use the following quotation in answering questions 8 and 9.

"It is commonly argued that, for criteria of ideal economic efficiency to be met, production of a good should be expanded as long as consumers are willing to pay a price that is greater than the cost of producing one more unit."

8. How will the actions of an unregulated, profit-maximizing, *competitive* firm compare with this standard of efficiency?
   a. Output will be too small, and price will be too low.
   b. Output will be too small, and price will be too high.
   c. Output will be too large, and price will be too high.
   d. Output and price will be consistent with the ideal standard.

9. How will the actions of an unregulated, profit-maximizing *monopolist* compare with this standard?
   a. Output will be too small, and price will be too low.
   b. Output will be too small, and price will be too high.
   c. Output will be too large, and price will be too high.
   d. Output and price will be consistent with the ideal standard.

10. Which of the following factors limits the monopoly power of a firm?
   a. Competition from producers of substitute products
   b. Potential competition from entrepreneurs who may develop substitute products
   c. Competition from all other producers seeking the dollar votes of consumers
   d. All of the above

11. As the text states, an old and effective way to protect a business from competition is through
   a. legal barriers.
   b. economies of scale.
   c. natural monopoly.
   d. understocking the market.

12. Use statements I and II to answer this question. (I) Since patent rights give firms a monopoly on the production and marketing of a product, the patent system is a potential source of static economic inefficiency. (II) Since a patent system enables owners to enforce their property rights over a new product and technique, it encourages the development of new lower-cost products, essential to dynamic economic efficiency.
   a. I is true, II is false.
   b. I is false, II is true.
   c. Both I and II are true.
   d. Both I and II are false.

THE ECONOMIC WAY OF THINKING—MULTIPLE CHOICE

1. A major problem with regulatory agencies is that they
   a. have no real legal power over the industries they are supposed to regulate.
   b. tend to be too tough on the firms they are regulating.
   c. often underestimate the firm's cost of production, and consequently force regulated firms into a loss position.
   d. often become a vehicle to be used by the existing producers to limit the competition of potential rivals.

2. If a monopolist selling in the inelastic region of its demand curve raises its price, then
   a. profits will rise.
   b. profits will fall.
   c. profits will remain the same.
   d. we can't predict what will happen to profits without production cost information.

3. Suppose that all wholesale liquor distributorships in your state were brought under the control of a single firm and that government licensing was used to eliminate the potential competition of rivals. Relative to a competitive situation, economic theory suggests that the monopoly firm would
   a. charge higher prices and restrict output.
   b. charge lower prices and restrict output.
   c. charge higher prices and expand output.
   d. charge lower prices and expand output.

4. "A firm with a secure monopoly in its market and with no fear of regulation or new entrants will never want to operate at a price at which its demand curve is inelastic." Economic theory suggests that this statement is
   a. correct.
   b. correct only if the firm's costs are constant.
   c. correct only if the firm's costs are rising.
   d. correct only if the firm's costs are decreasing.

5. For which of the following reasons do regulatory agencies sometimes fail to bring the price and output of a natural monopoly to the ideal level?
   a. The regulatory agency does not have all the information concerning opportunity costs.
   b. Monopolists may conceal profits by inflating the costs of items that are in accord with their personal objectives.
   c. Regulatory agencies often come to reflect the views of the industries they are supposed to regulate.
   d. All of the above.

6. Economic theory suggests that government-operated monopolies will
   a. be highly efficient and follow policies that are in the consumers' interest.
   b. be dominated by persons who, while seeking to serve the public interest, are not hard nosed enough to run a business efficiently.
   c. be inefficient, because no small group of persons is in a position to capture the benefits from operational efficiency.
   d. favor the consumer at the expense of special interest groups in and out of government.

7. Which of the following firms best fits the description of a monopolist?
   a. General Motors
   b. Columbia Broadcasting System
   c. Your local power company
   d. Exxon Corporation

8. Suppose you invent a new product and sell your patent to a firm in exchange for a percentage of the firm's total sales receipts from making and selling your product. If both you and the firm want to make as much income as possible, then
   a. you and the firm will agree about how much output should be produced.
   b. the firm is likely to produce more than you would like.
   c. the firm is likely to produce less than you would like.
   d. the firm will go bankrupt if it produces the amount you would like.

9. In a famous antitrust case, the government charged the DuPont Company with attempting to monopolize the cellophane industry. The company argued that, while it was the major producer of cellophane, it was competing in the broader market of "flexible packaging," a very competitive industry. Waxed paper, glassine, and aluminum foil all had sizable shares of the flexible packaging market. To determine whether DuPont was, in fact, competing in the flexible wrap industry, one would be interested in determining
   a. evidence of collusion between flexible wrap producers.
   b. the per unit cost as a function of output for cellophane.
   c. the income elasticity of demand for cellophane, relative to the other flexible wraps.
   d. whether other potential flexible wraps were actually good substitutes for cellophane.

Questions 10–14 refer to Exhibit 7.

EXHIBIT 7

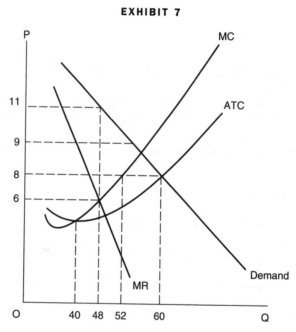

10. The maximum profits this monopolist can earn are
    a. less than $240.
    b. $240.
    c. between $240 and $528.
    d. $528.

11. If total fixed costs increased by $48, the monopolist will
    a. increase price by $1, and profit will be unchanged.
    b. increase price by $1, and profit will fall by $48.
    c. leave price unchanged, and profit will be unchanged.
    d. leave price unchanged, and profit will fall by $48.

12. Return to Exhibit 7 (without the increase in fixed costs mentioned in question #11). Now suppose that the government imposes a tax of $2.00 per unit, payable by the monopolist. What will be the profit maximizing marginal revenue per unit?
    a. $6.00
    b. between $6.00 and $8.00
    c. $8.00
    d. more than $8.00

13. Suppose that instead of imposing the tax mentioned in question #12 above, the government announces a price ceiling of $8.00. The monopolist would choose to produce
    a. 40 units.
    b. 52 units.
    c. between 52 and 60 units.
    d. 60 units.

14. In order to induce the monopolist to supply the allocatively (socially) efficient amount of output, the price ceiling in question #13 above would have to be set at
    a. P = $6.00.
    b. P = $8.00.
    c. P = $9.00.
    d. P = $11.00.

THE ECONOMIC WAY OF THINKING—DISCUSSION QUESTIONS

1. Economists have historically had a very negative view of monopoly. What are the major criticisms of monopoly? Which, if any, of the criticisms, might be a distributional issue rather than an efficiency issue? Why might it be an efficiency issue after all?

2. a. List some real-world examples of price discrimination.
   b. Why do you think price discrimination is more common in the sale of services than in the sale of physical goods?
   c. Phone prices are generally lower on weekends than on weekdays. Do you think this is price discrimination? Explain.

3. "In some industries, pure competition would result in higher prices and a greater waste of resources than monopoly." Do you agree? Can you think of any such industries? Discuss.

4. What are the advantages of regulating the activities of a monopolist? The major problems? Why does regulation, over time, tend to become a source of economic inefficiency?

5. What are the major sources of monopoly? Can a monopolized industry sometimes be transformed into a competitive industry? Why may it sometimes be costly to break up a monopoly into several smaller independent firms? Explain.

6. Use economic analysis to evaluate the government-operated firm as an alternative to monopoly. What factors will influence the price, output, and operational efficiency of the public sector firm? Explain.

7. Under Former Chairman Dennis Patrick, the Federal Communications Commission (FCC) recently replaced profit regulation with price regulation. Which do you think is easier administratively, profit regulation, or price regulation? Explain. Which seems more economically efficient? Why?

PERSPECTIVES IN ECONOMICS

The Parable of the Parking Lots
by Henry G. Manne

[From *Public Interest*, No. 23 (Spring 1971), pp. 10–15, Copyright © by National Affairs Inc. 1971. Reprinted by permission.]

In a city not far away there was a large football stadium. It was used from time to time for various events, but the principal use was for football games played Saturday afternoons by the local college team. The games were tremendously popular and people drove hundreds of miles to watch them. Parking was done in the usual way. People who arrived early were able to park free on the streets, and late comers had to pay to park in regular improvised lots.

There were, at distances ranging from 5 to 12 blocks from the stadium, approximately 25 commercial parking lots all of which received some business from Saturday afternoon football games. The lots closer to the stadium naturally received more football business than those further away, and some of the very close lots actually raised their price on Saturday afternoons. But they did not raise the price much, and most did not change prices at all. The reason was not hard to find.

For something else happened on football afternoons. A lot of people who during the week were students, lawyers, school teachers, plumbers, factory workers, and even stock brokers went into the parking lot business. It was not a difficult thing to do. Typically a young boy would put up a crude, homemade sign saying "Parking $3." He would direct a couple of cars into his parent's driveway, tell the driver to take the key, and collect the three dollars. If the driveway was larger or there was yard space to park in, an older brother, an uncle, or the head of the household would direct the operation, sometimes asking drivers to leave their keys so that shifts could be made if necessary.

Some part-time parking lot operators who lived very close to the stadium charged as much as $5.00 to park in their driveways. But as the residences-turned-parking-lots were located further from the stadium (and incidentally closer to the commercial parking lots), the price charged at game time declined. In fact houses at some distance from the stadium charged less than the adjacent commercial lots. The whole system seemed to work fairly smoothly, and though traffic just after a big game was terrible, there were no significant delays parking cars or retrieving parked cars.

But one day the owner of a chain of parking lots called a meeting of all the commercial parking lot owners in the general vicinity of the stadium. They formed an organization known as Association of Professional Parking Lot Employers, or APPLE. And they were very concerned about the Saturday parking business. One man who owned four parking lots pointed out that honest parking lot owners had heavy capital investments in their businesses, that they paid taxes, and that they employed individuals who supported families. There was no reason, he alleged, why these lots should not handle all the cars coming into the area for special events like football games. "It is unethical," he said, "to engage in cutthroat competition with irresponsible fender benders. After all, parking cars is a profession, not a business." The last remark drew loud applause.

Thus emboldened he continued, stating that commercial parking lot owners recognize their responsibility to serve the public's needs. Ethical car parkers, he said, understand their obligations not to dent fenders, to employ only trustworthy car parkers, to pay decent wages, and generally to care for the customers' automobiles as they would the corpus of a trust. His statement was hailed by others attending the meeting as being very statesmanlike.

Others at the meeting related various tales of horror about nonprofessional car parkers. One homeowner, it was said, actually allowed his fifteen-year-old son to move other peoples' cars around. Another said that he had seen an $8,000 Cadillac parked on a dirt lawn where it would have become mired in mud had it rained that day. Still another pointed out that a great deal of the problem came on the side of the stadium with the lower-priced houses, where there were more driveways per block than on the wealthier side of the stadium. He pointed out that these poor people would rarely be able to afford to pay for damage to other peoples' automobiles or to pay insurance premiums to cover such losses. He felt that a professional group such as APPLE had a duty to protect the public from their folly in using those parking spaces.

Finally another speaker reminded the audience that these "marginal, fly-by-night" parking lot operators generally parked a string of cars in the driveways so that a driver had to wait until all cars behind his had been removed before he could get out. This he pointed out, was quite unlike the situation in commercial lots where, during a normal business day, people had to be assured of ready access to their automobiles at any time. The commercial parking lots either had to hire more attendants to shift cars around, or they had to park them so that any car was always accessible, even though this meant that fewer cars could park than the total space would actually hold. "Clearly," he said, "driveway parking constitutes unfair competition."

Emotions ran high at this meeting, and every member of APPLE pledged $1 per parking space for something mysteriously called a "slush fund." It was never made clear exactly whose slush would be bought with these funds, but several months later a resolution was adopted by the city council requiring licensing for anyone in the parking lot business.

The preamble to the new ordinance read like the speeches at the earlier meeting. It said that this measure was designed to protect the public against unscrupulous, unprofessional and undercapitalized parking lot operators. It required, *inter alia*, that anyone parking cars for a fee must have a minimum capital devoted to the parking lot business of $25,000, liability insurance in an amount not less than $500,000, bonding for each car parker, and a special driving test for these parkers (which incidentally would be designed and administered by APPLE). The ordinance also required, again in the public's interest, that every lot charge a single posted price for parking and that any change in the posted price be approved in advance by the city council. Incidentally, most members were able to raise their fees about 20 percent before the first posting.

Then a funny thing happened to drivers on their way to the stadium for the next big game. They discovered city police in unusually large numbers informing them that it was illegal to pay a non-licensed parking lot operator for the right to park a car. These policemen also reminded parents that if their children were found in violation of this ordinance it could result in a misdemeanor charge being brought against the parents and possible juvenile court proceedings for the children. There were no driveway parking lots that day.

Back at the commercial parking lots, another funny thing occurred. Proceeding from the entrance of each of these parking lots within twelve blocks of the stadium were long lines of cars waiting to park. The line got larger as the lot was closer to the stadium. Many drivers had to wait so long or walk so far that they missed the entire first quarter of the big game.

At the end of the game it was even worse. The confusion was massive. The lot attendants could not cope with the jam up, and some cars were actually not retrieved until the next day. It was even rumored about town that some automobiles had been lost forever and that considerable liabilities might result for some operators. Industry spokesmen denied this, however.

Naturally there was a lot of grumbling, but there was no argument on what had caused the difficulty. At first everyone said there were merely some "bugs" in the new system that would have to be ironed out. But the only "bug" ironed out was a Volkswagen that was flattened by a careless lot attendant in a Cadillac Eldorado.

The situation did not improve at subsequent games. The members of APPLE did not hire additional employees to park cars, and operators near the stadium were not careful to follow their previous practice of parking cars in such a way as to have them immediately accessible. Employees seemed to become more surly, and a number of dented-fender claims mounted rapidly.

Little by little, too, cars began appearing in residential driveways again. For instance, one enterprising youth regularly went into the car wash business on football afternoons, promising that his wash job would take at least two hours. He charged five dollars, and got it—even on rainy days—in fact, especially on rainy days. Another homeowner offered to take cars on consignment for three hours to sell them at prices fixed by the owner. He charged $4.00 for this "service," but his subterfuge was quickly squelched by the authorities. The parking situation remained "critical."

Political pressures on the city council began to mount to "do something" about the inordinate delays in parking and retrieving cars on football afternoons. The city council sent out a stern note of warning to APPLE, and the local university's computer science department to look into the matter. This group reported that the managerial and ad-

ministrative machinery in the parking lot business was archaic. What was needed, the study group said, was less goose quills and stand-up desks and more computers and conveyor belts. It was also suggested that all members of APPLE be hooked into one computer so that cars could be really shifted to the most accessible spaces.

Spokesmen for the industry took up the cry of administrative modernization. Subtle warnings appeared in the local papers suggesting that if the industry did not get its own house in order, heavy-handed regulation could be anticipated. The city council asked for reports on failures to deliver cars and decreed that this would include any failure to put a driver in his car within five minutes of demand without a new dent.

Some of the professional operators actually installed computer equipment to handle their ticketing and parking logistics problems. And some added second stories to their parking lots. Others bought up additional space, thereby raising the value of vacant lots in the area, but many simply added a few additional car parkers and hoped that the problem would go away without a substantial investment of capital.

The commercial operators also began arguing that they needed higher parking fees because of their higher operating costs. Everyone agreed that costs for operating a parking lot were certainly higher than before the licensing ordinance. So the city council granted a request for an across-the-board ten percent hike in fees. The local newspaper editorially hoped that this would ease the problem without still higher fees being necessary. In a way, it did. A lot of people stopped driving. They began using city buses, or they chartered private buses for the game. Some stayed home and watched the game on TV. A new study group on fees was appointed.

Just about then, several other blows fell on the parking lot business. But transportation to the area near the stadium was improved with a federal subsidy to the municipal bus company. And several new suburban shopping centers caused a loss of automobile traffic in the older area of town. But most dramatic of all, the local university, under severe pressure from its students and faculty, dropped intercollegiate football altogether and converted the stadium into a park for underprivileged children.

The impact of these events on the commercial parking lots was swift. Income declined drastically. The companies that had borrowed money to finance the expansion everyone wanted earlier were hardest hit. Two declared bankruptcy, and many had to be absorbed by financially stronger companies. Layoffs among car parkers were enormous, and APPLE actually petitioned the city council to guarantee the premiums on their liability insurance policies so that people would not be afraid to park commercially. This idea was suggested to APPLE by recent congressional legislation creating an insurance program for stock brokers.

A spokesman for APPLE made the following public statement: "New organizations or arrangements may be necessary to straighten out this problem. There has been a failure in both the structure of the industry and the regulatory scheme. New and better regulation is clearly demanded. A sound parking lot business is necessary for a healthy urban economy." The statement was hailed by the industry as being very statesmanlike, though everyone speculated about what he really meant.

Others in the industry demanded that the city bus service be curtailed during the emergency. The city council granted every rate increase the lots requested. There were no requests for rate decreases, but the weaker lots began offering prizes and other subtle or covert rebates to private bus companies who would park with them. In fact, this problem became so serious and uncontrollable that one owner of a large chain proclaimed that old-fashioned price competition for this business would be desirable. This again was hailed as statesmanlike, but everyone assumed that he really meant something else. No one proposed repeal of the licensing ordinance.

One other thing happened. Under pressure from APPLE, the city council decreed that henceforth no parking would be allowed on any streets in the downtown area of town. The local merchants were extremely unhappy about this, however, and the council rescinded the ordinance at the next meeting, citing a computer error as the basis for the earlier restriction.

The ultimate resolution of the "new" parking problem is not in sight. The parking lot industry in this town not very far from here is now said to be a depressed business, even a sick one. Everyone looks to the city council for a solution, but things will probably limp along as they are for quite a while, picking up with an occasional professional football game and dropping low with bad weather.

MORAL. If you risk your lot under an apple tree, you may get hit in the head.

Discussion

1. In this fable, who was protected by the regulations? From what? At what cost?

2. Do you see similar situations in regulated businesses in your own area? In state or federally regulated industries? How are they similar? How do they differ? Who gains, and at what cost?

3. In this article, businesses that lobbied to protect themselves from competition ended up hurting themselves in the long run. Do you think that this is a typical result, or did author Manne stretch things a bit to make it come out this way? Explain your answer.

CHAPTER TEN

BETWEEN COMPETITION AND MONOPOLY: MODELS OF RIVALRY AND STRATEGY

TRUE OR FALSE

T F

☐ ☐ 1. Oligopolistic industries will be dominated by a small number of firms.

☐ ☐ 2. Economics of scale are an important reason for oligopoly in the automobile, typewriter, and steel industries.

☐ ☐ 3. There are no local restraints on collusive behavior by oligopolistic firms.

☐ ☐ 4. Firms in oligopolistic industries make profits because they are free from competitive pressures.

☐ ☐ 5. Collusion would be easier (less costly) if the barriers to entry were higher and the number of producers in the industry were smaller.

☐ ☐ 6. Inability to police the nonprice characteristics of a product offered by a competitive firm reduces the likelihood of successful collusion among oligopolists.

☐ ☐ 7. The monopolistic competitor who is better able to correctly anticipate changes in consumer demand and adjust to those changes is, *ceteris parabus*, more likely to make economic profits.

☐ ☐ 8. A monopolistically competitive firm maximizes profits by producing at a level of output at which price is equal to shortrun marginal cost.

☐ ☐ 9. In recent years, concentration has increased in almost all manufacturing industries.

☐ ☐ 10. Monopolistically competitive firms often emphasize quality, location, and advertising as competitive weapons (in addition to price competition).

☐ ☐ 11. The smart investor will purchase the stock of firms in oligopolistic industries because the high average rate of profit in these industries will mean a greater return on the investor's dollar.

☐ ☐ 12. The larger the number of competitors and the more similar the products offered by the firms of a monopolistically competitive industry, the greater will be the elasticity of the individual seller's demand curve.

PROBLEMS AND PROJECTS

EXHIBIT 1

Output (market)	Price	Total revenue (market)	Total revenue (each firm)	Average total cost (firm)
1,000	$750	_____	_____	$200
2,000	500	_____	_____	170
3,000	450	_____	_____	150
4,000	400	_____	_____	150
8,000	300	_____	_____	150
12,000	250	_____	_____	150
16,000	200	_____	_____	150
20,000	175	_____	_____	150
24,000	150	_____	_____	150
28,000	125	_____	_____	150
32,000	100	_____	_____	150

1. Currently there are four rival firms in the typewriter industry. Assume that the four firms are of identical size, produce similar products (consumers think they are homogeneous), and have identical cost schedules. The cost schedule for a *firm* along with the market demand schedule is presented in Exhibit 1.
   a. Fill in the missing information.
   b. What price would prevail if there were no collusion and each firm sought to offer the consumer a better deal than that available from rivals (as long as the firm's opportunity cost of production was covered)? How many units would be sold in the market? How many would each firm sell?
   c. If each firm produced one-fourth of the total market, what market price would prevail when *each firm* supplied 1000 units? 2000 units? 3000 units?
   d. Which of the listed prices would prevail if the firms acted cooperatively (so as to maximize their joint profit)?
   e. Given the demand and cost conditions in this oligopolistic industry, what outcome would be most likely to prevail in the real world? Explain.

2. Johnson Tricycle Manufacturers currently sells 20,000 tricycles per month at a price of $10 each. The firm's fixed costs are currently 60 percent of the sales revenues. At the current level of production, the firm's average variable cost per tricycle is $4. The firm is just covering its total cost. The sales manager argues that a reduction in the price of tricycles to $9 would enable the firm to earn a monthly profit of $5000 as the results of increased sales. Since the firm has ample capacity, the necessary expansion in output could be accomplished without any increase in the average variable cost of tricycles.
   a. Does the sales manager's argument make sense? Explain.
   b. How much would sales have to increase in order for the firm to earn a monthly profit of $5000? (*Hint:* Remember that fixed costs will not vary with output.)
   c. What price elasticity of demand is necessary for the sales manager's prediction to be realized?

3. Sociable Corporation (SC) produces and sells gizmos in an oligopolistic market comprised of only a very few firms. Exhibit 2 presents two different demand schedules for SC. The first one shows how SC's quantity demanded varies when the industry price varies, and the second one shows how SC's quantity demanded varies when only SC's price varies. Assume throughout that SC's marginal cost is constant at $10 per gizmo and that fixed costs are zero.

EXHIBIT 2

Demand when industry price varies				Demand when only SC's price varies			
Quantity	Price	Total revenue	Marginal revenue	Quantity	Price	Total revenue	Marginal revenue
1	$130	$130	$130	1	$100	$100	$100
2	110	220	90	2	90	180	80
3	90	___	___	3	80	___	___
4	70	___	___	4	70	___	___
5	50	___	___	5	60	___	___
6	30	___	___	6	50	___	___
7	10	___	___	7	40	___	___
8	0	___	___	8	30	___	___
9	0	___	___	9	20	___	___
10	0	0	0	10	10	___	___

a. Fill in the missing information. (*Hint:* Remember that marginal revenue can be negative as well as positive.)

b. Suppose the industry could engage in successful collusion. What price would SC want the industry to set? Calculate SC's profits at this price. Explain your answer.

c. Suppose the industry has established the collusively determined price of part b above and that SC believes it could "cheat" on the agreement and not be detected. Assuming that sales of gizmos must be in whole units, what quantity would SC decide to sell? What price would it charge? Compare SC's new profit level to the level it achieved in part b.

d. If each firm in the industry believes what SC believes, could each firm increase its profits the way SC believes it can? Explain.

4. International Oil, Incorporated (IOI), has come under public criticism for earning excessive profits. In its defense, IOI releases information indicating that profit constitutes only $0.01 of the firm's price of $1.00 per gallon of gasoline. Is this information useful in resolving the issue? If no, what type of profit information would you want in order to attempt a resolution?

5. Consider the following production information about the U. S. steel industry (units are in millions of tons):

Firm	Production	Firm	Production
Armco Steel	8.1	National Steel	9.4
Bethlehem Steel	16.6	Republic Steel	9.2
Inland Steel	7.8	United States Steel	28.8
Jones and Laughlin	7.0	Remaining (small) producers	33.3
Lykes Corporation	4.5		

a. Construct a four firm concentration ratio (CR4) for the U. S. steel industry.
b. A loose rule of thumb suggests the following tentative classification of industry structure:

> CR4 of 70 or more: tight oligopoly;
> CR4 between 50 and 70: loose oligopoly;
> CR4 below 50: competitive.

What category describes the steel industry? What is the minimum average market share of the top four firms in a loose oligopoly?

6. Suppose the cardboard box industry is suspected of collusion (the industry has, in fact, been accused of collusion in the past). Classify each of the following items as likely evidence in support (+) or against (–) successful collusion.

___ a. The four firm concentration ratio of cardboard box manufacturers is 19.
___ b. Members of an industry trade association exchange invoice information about the prices charged to specified customers.
___ c. The members of the trade association account for 90 percent of the cardboard box output.
___ d. Cardboard boxes are standardized (homogeneous) products and prices are pretty uniform throughout the industry.
___ e. At the current price level, demand is inelastic.
___ f. Throughout the period of trade association activity, cardboard box prices have been falling and entry has been occurring.

LEARNING THE MECHANICS—MULTIPLE CHOICE

1. Long-run economic profit requires
   a. barriers to market entry that limit potential competitors.
   b. an inelastic market demand for the product.
   c. free entry, but a small number of competitors.
   d. a differentiated product.

2. Which of the following factors will weaken the ability of an oligopolist to charge a price in excess of production cost?
   a. The existence of a small number of competitors
   b. An inelastic demand for one's product
   c. Quality competition from one's rivals
   d. Licensing procedures and other factors that limit entry into the industry

3. For the monopolistic competitor
   a. price will exceed the firm's short-run marginal cost at the profit-maximizing output level; in the long run, however, economic profit will be eliminated.
   b. price will equal marginal cost at the profit-maximizing output level; long-run profits will be positive.
   c. price will always equal average total cost in the short-run; in the long run either profits or losses may result.
   d. marginal revenue will equal average total cost in the short run; long-run economic profits will be zero.

4. Which of the following factors will make it more difficult for oligopolistic firms to collude on prices?
   a. A reduction in the number of firms
   b. A homogeneous product
   c. High barriers to entry
   d. Instability and uncertainty concerning the demand and cost conditions in the industry

5. Economic theory suggests that prices in oligopolistic industries will
   a. be above the cost of production, but less than what a monopolist would charge.
   b. be below the firms' marginal costs, but higher than their average total costs.
   c. be equal to the firms' per unit costs.
   d. rise as the number of rival firms in the industry increases.

6. Suppose you were asked to determine whether a firm was perfectly competitive or monopolistically competitive by looking at a graph of the firm's cost and revenue curves. The key is that for the monopolistically competitive firm,
   a. the firm's marginal revenue curve lies to the left and below the demand curve, not above and to the right.
   b. there are only total costs, not variable costs, on the graph.
   c. the firm's demand curve is downward sloping.
   d. all of the above.

7. Using industrial concentration ratios as the measure of competitiveness, one finds that during the last three decades, the U. S. economy has
   a. become more competitive.
   b. become less competitive.
   c. on balance, changed little in competitiveness.
   d. become fully dominated by highly concentrated, oligopolistic industries.

8. Amy is widely known among restauranteurs in Seattle as the best fast-food restaurant manager in town. Since the restaurant business is monopolistically competitive, Amy
   a. would make more money if she could establish her own restaurant.
   b. would make just as much money working for one of the many firms bidding for her services as she would with her own firm.
   c. can never be paid what she is really worth in such an industry.
   d. could make long-run economic profit if she established her own restaurant.

9. It would be difficult for a group of oligopolists to follow a price and output policy similar to that of a monopolist if
   a. there were many producers.
   b. firms could not compete on the basis of quality (of the product).
   c. supply of substitute products were highly inelastic.
   d. prices charged in some states were higher because of higher sales taxes.

10. The concentration ratio of an industry provides
    a. an excellent measure of competitiveness in the industry.
    b. an indication, albeit an imperfect one, of competitiveness in the industry.
    c. a measure of the availability for the products of the industry.
    d. no indication at all of competitiveness in the industry.

11. Which of the following is the most accurate description of the conditions that exist under the monopolistically competitive market structure?
    a. Barriers to entry are low; firms will consistently incur economic losses in the short run.
    b. Barriers to entry are low; firms will realize normal profits in the short run, but losses in the long run.
    c. Barriers to entry are low; firms may realize either profits or losses in the short run, but they will tend to realize a normal profit in the long run.
    d. Barriers to entry are high; firms will consistently realize economic profits in the short run.

12. If economic profits were present in a monopolistically competitive industry
    a. production inefficiency would develop, causing costs to increase until the profits had been eliminated.
    b. firms would operate in the short run, but they would be forced out of business in the long run as competition eliminated the economic profit.
    c. competition from new entrants would expand supply and depress prices until the economic profits had been eliminated.
    d. the firms would lower their prices, since profits would attract government regulation.

13. Comparative profitability studies between oligopolistic and competitive industries suggest that
    a. dynamic competitive forces are one important determinant of profitability in oligopolistic as well as competitive industries.
    b. collusion and monopoly profit are prevalent in almost all oligopolistic sectors.
    c. competition has little effect on the profitability of firms.
    d. large firms almost always earn a higher rate of return than their smaller counterparts.

14. If one firm produced 60 percent of an industry's output, the industry's four-firm concentration ratio would be
    a. about 15 percent.
    b. about 30 percent.
    c. between 60 and 100 percent.
    d. about 240 percent.

THE ECONOMIC WAY OF THINKING—MULTIPLE CHOICE

1. If large automobile manufacturers were to collude secretly on prices, as has often been charged, what short-run factor might tend to undermine the effectiveness of their agreements?
    a. The economies of scale in the industry
    b. The size of the firms in the industry
    c. The ease with which a new competitor could enter the industry if profitability increased
    d. The difficulty of policing style and quality competition among firms

2. Which of the following would be the most likely to happen if the firms in a monopolistically competitive industry were suffering economic losses?
    a. The firms would eliminate production inefficiencies, which must be the source of the losses.
    b. Some firms would leave the industry, and the market price would rise.
    c. Some firms would operate in the short run, but all firms would go out of business in the long run.
    d. All firms in the industry would continue producing at their current output levels, but they would charge a higher price.

3. If you were going to invest in the stock market, you would be
   a. wise to purchase the stock of an oligopolist so that you could share in the oligopoly profits.
   b. unwise to purchase only the stock of an oligopolist, because the inefficiency of oligopoly often leads to losses.
   c. wise to purchase the stock of an oligopolist if the firm had made economic profit in the long run.
   d. unwise to purchase only the stock of an oligopolist, because the expectation of future profits has already increased the current market value of the stock.

4. Neither pure nor monopolistic competitors will be able to earn long-run economic profit because
   a. with free entry and exit, competition between rivals will drive prices down to the level of production costs.
   b. high barriers to entry will prevent the firms from earning excess profits.
   c. government legislation will cause firms to moderate their price demands.
   d. cutthroat competition will cause some firms to incur losses, but barriers to entry will result in profits for others.

5. A profit-maximizing oligopolist who has invested heavily in brand-name advertising does not want adverse publicity. The owner of such a firm would pay more to avoid shoddy output and to keep its good (brand) name if
   a. it were part of an oligopolistic group of firms that looked forward to high economic profits.
   b. government price regulation were about to be imposed, ensuring low future profits.
   c. it were part of an oligopolistic group of firms in which secret competition was hindering collusion.
   d. it dealt with buyers who shopped only for the lowest available price.

6. The local plumbing contractors have called a meeting to discuss ways to improve their long-run profitability. Of the four plans being discussed seriously, which would most likely increase their long-run profits?
   a. An "off-the-record" agreement that each plumbing contractor would increase his or her prices by an average of 7 percent
   b. Passage of legislation requiring the local government to share the cost of installing all private sewage systems
   c. Passage of legislation requiring *new* contractors to pass a stiff licensing exam and to pay a $5000 fee to obtain a contractor's license
   d. Repeal of the current tax on installations of plumbing units

7. "If few firms colluded successfully and looked forward to long-run economic profits, they would lose all monetary incentive to innovate. Successful collusion eliminates any contribution to profit that innovation would otherwise make." This statement is
   a. essentially correct.
   b. correct, if quality competition had been eliminated.
   c. correct, if there were few substitutes for the product produced by the colluding firms.
   d. incorrect, because lower costs for producing the same good *or* a better product for the same cost would benefit even a group of colluding oligopolists.

8. Suppose that recent fuel shortages and rising fuel prices have raised the delivery costs for diaper services in Los Angeles. If that industry were characterized by monopolistic competition, we could expect that
   a. competition would keep the price of diaper service the same as before, until eventually some firms were forced out of business by rising costs.
   b. diaper service prices would rise quickly (by the full amount of the cost increase multiplied by the market rate of interest).
   c. diaper service prices would rise, and in the long run the full amount of increase in cost would be passed along to consumers.
   d. if the diaper service industry were in long-run equilibrium before the cost increase, its economic profits would absorb the cost increase; there would be no change in price.

9. Introducing a new process that produces widgets at half the current cost with identical product quality would be most valuable in the long run to a firm in
   a. a purely competitive industry.
   b. a monopolistically competitive industry.
   c. an oligopolistic industry with little hope of successful collusion.
   d. an oligopolistic industry with successful collusion and little fear of new entrants in the future.

10. An oligopolist's incentive to "cheat" on a secret collusive agreement increases when
    a. quality competition is more easily detected.
    b. the demand for his product at the current price is shrinking.
    c. the demand for his product at the current price is expanding.
    d. his marginal cost is closer to the oligopoly price.

The following information applies to the next two questions: The taxicab industry is basically competitive. However, taxicab operators must generally obtain licenses, and regulators in many large cities use these licenses to artificially restrict entry into the profession. (In Boston, for example, the number of licenses has not risen since 1930.) New cab drivers must then purchase a license from existing drivers.

11. A taxicab license costs $35,000 in Boston and $65,000 in New York.
    a. It is probably more profitable to become a taxicab driver in Boston than in New York.
    b. It is probably more profitable to become a taxicab driver in New York than in Boston.
    c. It is probably equally profitable to become a taxicab driver in New York and in Boston.
    d. Taxicab drivers probably lose money in both cities.

12. Suppose you decide to become a taxicab driver in New York and pay $65,000 to buy a license. Right after you start operating, the taxi industry is deregulated, and your license becomes worthless.
    a. You entered the industry just in the nick of time.
    b. You should now exit the industry.
    c. You should sell your license in Boston.
    d. You may as well stay in the industry.

13. One large motel chain uses the slogan "the best surprise is no surprise" to advertise that its motels are always about the same. Critics charge that this approach fails to take advantage of local architecture, local customs, and—in general—is just too "drab" and "plastic." The motel's profits have been high enough to attract many competitors. Since the motel industry is monopolistically competitive, our economic model
    a. is contradicted, since this firm does *not* offer much variety.
    b. is contradicted, since *economic* profits do not fit into the model.
    c. is contradicted by the fact that the firm advertises.
    d. indicates that some travelers appreciate predictability at the expense of other values.

THE ECONOMIC WAY OF THINKING—DISCUSSION QUESTIONS

1. Do firms in oligopolistic industries have an incentive to collude? What factors will reduce the likelihood of successful collusion (from the viewpoint of the firms)? Will the threat of potential new rivals in an oligopolistic industry influence the price and output policies of the existing firms in the industry? Explain.

2. Suppose the only information you have about an industry is that it is highly concentrated. Will the firms in the industry make high profits? What factors may limit their ability to do so?

3. Consider the alternatives of pure competition, monopolistic competition, oligopoly, and contestable markets.
   a. How is the structure of monopolistic competition different from pure competition? How is it similar?
   b. How is the structure of oligopoly different from pure competition? How is it similar?
   c. How is the structure of contestable markets different from oligopoly? How is it similar?
   d. Compared to pure competition, what tends to be true about the levels of price and profitability under monopolistic competition? Oligopoly? Contestable markets?

4. Does the town where you live have too many gas stations or quick-stop mini food stores? Is this duplication and competitiveness wasteful? Does it result in higher prices than those that would prevail under alternative arrangements? Explain why you think that monopolistic competition is either
   a. wasteful and inefficient, or
   b. consistent with efficiency and a consumer-directed economy.

5. Explain why economic theory predicts that collusion to rig the market against consumers will be far more prevalent under oligopoly than under monopolistic competition.

6. Do you think that the long-run profits that an oligopolist may be able to earn will make the oligopolist less concerned about holding down production costs? Why or why not?

7. Assume that the Barbers Association for Short Hair (BASH) successfully convinced the state of Florida to pass legislation increasing the price of haircuts to $15. Suppose that there are no barriers to entry into the barbering profession, but that everyone who charges a price for cutting hair must comply with this legislation (i.e., charge $15). What would you expect to happen to the
   a. sales revenues of Florida barbers?
   b. profits of Florida barbers in the short run? Long run?
   c. waiting time to get a haircut?
   d. quality of a haircut and the auxiliary services provided with it?
   e. number of black market haircuts?

8. What is meant by competition? How does the element of monopoly in monopolistic competition affect the process of competition? Why is competition important if markets are to work efficiently? Can competition protect the consumer from the market power of sellers? Is competition sometimes destructive or counterproductive? Defend or criticize competition as a method of allocating goods and resources. Be specific. Feel free to suggest and defend alternatives that you think are superior to the competitive market process.

BUSINESS STRUCTURE, REGULATION, AND DEREGULATION

TRUE OR FALSE

T F

☐ ☐   1. Bigness and lack of competition are not always synonymous.

☐ ☐   2. Predatory pricing is another term for high, monopolistic pricing.

☐ ☐   3. An exclusive contract is commonly involved in dealerships.

☐ ☐   4. One of the shortcomings of regulatory agencies is that with the passage of time they tend to represent broad groups such as consumers at the expense of labor and business interests.

☐ ☐   5. The effectiveness of the Sherman Act encouraged Congress to pass the Clayton Act.

☐ ☐   6. Most economists believe that antitrust policy has had a dramatic impact on market structure.

☐ ☐   7. While there are a number of difficulties involved in applying antitrust policy in the United States, distinguishing between competitive and anti-competitive behavior is not one of those difficulties.

☐ ☐   8. Social regulation seeks to provide a cleaner, safer, healthier environment for workers and consumers.

☐ ☐   9. The antitrust position of the Reagan administration might best be characterized as "bigness necessarily means badness."

☐ ☐   10. American cars are approximately 500 pounds heavier than they would have been without the CAFE standards.

☐ ☐   11. The merger wave of the 1980s relied on a new method of financing, called leveraged buyouts, in which the acquiring firm borrowed large amounts of money to purchase another firm.

PROBLEMS AND PROJECTS

1. Consider the problem of regulating your local water company. Originally, huge amounts of money had to be spent to install pipe, build water treatment plants, and construct aqueducts between your town and the local sources of water. The costs of building these facilities were met with a bond issue, the annual payments on which are fixed. Given the existence of these facilities, however, the marginal cost of an extra gallon of water is quite low (consisting mainly of the marginal cost of treating the water plus maintenance and billing activities). Suppose that the following chart describes the cost structure of your local water company:

EXHIBIT 1

Quality supplies (millions of gallons)	Total fixed cost (millions of dollars)	Average fixed cost (cents per gallon)	Marginal cost (cents per gallon)	Average total cost (cents per gallon)
40	$10	.25	.06	.31
50	10	.20	.06	_____
60	10	_____	.06	_____
70	10	_____	.06	_____

a. Fill in the missing information in Exhibit 1.
b. Suppose regulators set price equal to marginal cost (which will make consumers happy and increase the quantity demanded). What is the water company's profit/loss situation at each output level?
c. Suppose regulators set price equal to average total cost (which will make consumers unhappy and decrease the quantity demanded). What is the water company's profit/loss situation at each output level?
d. Is either pricing mechanism a good option in this case? How do you balance the goal of economic efficiency with that of fairness to the owners of the water company? What would you do if you were on the town's water regulation board?

2. For each of the following historical cases, indicate which antitrust law applies and which side you think won the case. (Some research may be necessary to fully answer this question.)
a. Plaintiff: United States
   Defendant: Standard Oil

   Standard Oil aggressively protected its 90 percent share of the petroleum market with practices that included receiving a rebate from railroads of the price charged for shipping oil (both its own oil and the oil shipped by competitors).

   Antitrust law: _____
   Winning side: _____

b. Plaintiff: United States
   Defendant: Vons Grocery Store

   Vons, the Los Angeles area's third largest grocery store chain, merged with Shopping Bag, the sixth largest, resulting in the second largest chain with a market share of 7.5 percent.

   Antitrust law: _____
   Winning side: _____

c. Plaintiff: Curt Flood
   Defendant: Major League Baseball

   Curt Flood accused baseball owners of a collective boycott of his services because of a player contract clause that prevented Flood from becoming a free agent and offering his services to the highest bidding team.

Antitrust law: _____
Winning side: _____

d. Plaintiff: United States
   Defendant: Alcoa

Alcoa maintained its monopoly position beyond the expiration date of its legal patents, mainly by constantly adding capacity in anticipation of future aluminum demand.

Antitrust law: _____
Winning side: _____

e. Plaintiff: United States
   Defendant: International Salt

International Salt required that firms using its patented machines for injecting salt into canned foods also purchase their salt from International Salt.

Antitrust law: _____
Winning side: _____

3. The insurance industry, whose activities are generally exempt from U. S. antitrust laws, is often suspected of collusion. California voters passed a law ("Proposition 103") requiring a twenty percent rollback in auto insurance rates. The diagrams in Exhibit 2 contrast two alternative initial situations in the California auto insurance industry, pure competition, and perfect collusion:

EXHIBIT 2

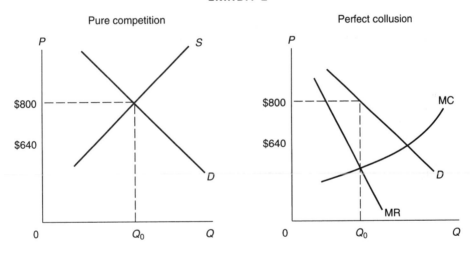

a. For the two alternative initial situations, indicate below whether quantity demanded and quantity supplied will rise (+), fall (−), remain the same (0), or change in an uncertain direction, as a result of California's price ceiling on insurance rates:

	Pure competition	Perfect collusion
Quantity demanded:	_____	_____
Quantity supplied:	_____	_____

b. Will the insurance rate rollback necessarily result in a shortage if the industry is perfectly competitive? If it is perfectly collusive?

4. Research and write a short paper on the size, power, and role of big business in the U. S. economy. [Selected references that might be helpful: Walter Adams, *The Structure of American Industry,* 4th ed. (New York: Macmillan, 1971); William N. Leonard, *Business Size, Market Power, and Public Policy* (New York: Crowell, 1969); M. A. Adelman, "Two Faces of Economic Concentration," *Public Interest,* Fall 1970; Joe Bain, *Barriers to New Competition* (Cambridge, MA: Harvard University Press, 1956); John S. McGee, *In Defense of Industrial Competition* (New York: Praeger, 1971); Yale Brozen, *The Competitive Economy: Selected Readings* (Morristown, NJ: General Learning Press, 1975); and William Shepherd, *The Economics of Industrial Organization* (Englewood Cliffs, NJ: Prentice-Hall, 1979).]

LEARNING THE MECHANICS—MULTIPLE CHOICE

1. Predatory pricing would involve charging some customers a price that is
   a. lower than the price of a competitor.
   b. lower than average total cost.
   c. lower than marginal cost.
   d. any of the above.

2. The concept of economic regulation typically involves
   a. the regulation of product price and production processes in various industries.
   b. the regulation of product price but not production processes or industrial structure in various industries.
   c. the regulation of product price and industrial structure but not production processes in various industries.
   d. the regulation of industrial structure in various industries.

3. Economists who defend the merger and acquisition wave of the 1980s point to several ways in which the recent corporate reorganizations have enhanced economic productivity. Which of the following is *not* one of their points?
   a. The new larger firm may be a more efficient size than either of the smaller ones were.
   b. The merged firms may have complementary strengths.
   c. The new managers of the firm may be more capable of making needed management/production changes than were the old ones.
   d. There are often tremendous tax benefits to merging a high-profit firm with one with substantial losses.

4. Data on national income by sector suggest that the private economy in the United States is
   a. dominated by small firms that produce in industries approximating the conditions of pure competition.
   b. dominated by large firms that produce in industries approaching monopoly conditions.
   c. increasingly dominated by an effectively competitive sector.
   d. increasingly coming to be dominated by manufacturing—a sector whose revenues are increasing more rapidly than our national income.

5. All but one of the following are clearly illegal under current antitrust laws. Which is usually *not* legal?
   a. Collusion and conspiracies to restrain trade
   b. Horizontal mergers that tend to lessen competition
   c. Serving on the board of directors of a competing firm with assets of more than $1 million
   d. Conglomerate mergers

6. An example of a government action designed to promote competition among producers is
   a. the institution of higher tariffs (import taxes) on Volkswagens.
   b. an extension of occupational licensing procedures to many additional occupations.
   c. imposition of additional regulations on small businesses.
   d. legislation prohibiting interlocking corporate directorates.

7. Use statements I and II to answer this question. (**I**) Regulation of business firms and labor interests tends to be inflexible. It often fails to adjust very rapidly to dynamic changes that affect a competitive market. (**II**) The demand for regulation often stems from organized groups seeking to profit from the regulation, rather than from forces seeking an economically efficient solution.
   a. I is true, II is false.
   b. I is false, II is true.
   c. Both I and II are true.
   d. Both I and II are false.

8. Since 1950, which of the following sectors has grown most rapidly in the United States?
   a. Agriculture
   b. Manufacturing
   c. Service and government
   d. Construction

9. Which of the following is not prohibited by current antitrust legislation?
   a. Tying contracts that substantially lessen competition
   b. Collusion to fix prices of products in competitive markets
   c. Quantity discounts that reflect cost savings stemming from a large purchase
   d. Horizontal mergers that serve to lessen competition

10. The Herfindahl index is a fairly sophisticated tool for measuring the level of
    a. market concentration in an industry.
    b. merger and acquisition activity in a given year.
    c. vigor with which a given administration is enforcing antitrust policies.
    d. deregulation in an industry.

11. Buick and Oldsmobile are divisions of General Motors. If we were to consider the incentives facing the officers of each division, we would expect
    a. complete cooperation and no rivalry between them.
    b. a good deal of rivalry, as well as cooperation, between them.
    c. no cooperation, but simply an intense rivalry between the two.
    d. no interest in what the other is doing.

12. Use statements I and II to answer this question. (**I**) The new social legislation seeks to improve the health, safety, and quality of the environment. (**II**) Whereas the older economic regulation generally increased costs of production, social regulation usually reduces the cost of production and, in turn, the price of products to the consumer.
    a. Both I and II are true.
    b. Both I and II are false.
    c. I is true, II is false.
    d. I is false, II is true.

THE ECONOMIC WAY OF THINKING—MULTIPLE CHOICE

1. When state governments use business licensing to limit the entry of potential competitors into an industry and create a situation whereby the licensed firms can earn *long-run* economic profit, profit-seeking business entrepreneurs
   a. have an incentive to use both economic and political means in attempting to obtain the valuable licenses.
   b. have little incentive to enter the licensed industry.
   c. would enter the industry only if the licenses were free.
   d. would use economic methods, but not political ones, in attempting to obtain the valuable licenses.

2. Which of the following best explains why competitive private firms seek to produce efficiently?
   a. The pressures of competition demand efficient production, which, other things constant, is rewarded with larger profits or smaller losses.
   b. Efficient production results because private decision-making is invariably less bureaucratic.
   c. Employees in the private sector know that they must produce, whereas waste and inefficiency characterize public sector production.
   d. Analysis of incentives does *not* suggest that competitive firms will produce efficiently.

Use the following quotation to answer the next question.

The world's first plant for the manufacture of gasoline from natural gas will be shut down as uneconomical, it was announced today by the Amoco Chemicals Corporation. J. H. Forrester, president of Amoco, a subsidiary of Standard Oil Company (Indiana), said, "We have determined that the plant cannot make gasoline and chemicals from natural gas at present market prices as cheaply as they can be made by other processes." [*New York Times*, September 14, 1957.]

3. If the facts in this quotation are correct, a decision by the firm to close down the plant
   a. results in economic inefficiency, because of the abandonment of a technically sound project.
   b. is consistent with economic efficiency, because lower-cost alternative production methods were available.
   c. will increase the demand for gasoline because of its lower cost.
   d. is sound from the firm's point of view, but not from the point of view of society.

4. Suppose that the Barbers' Association of Florida (BAF) was designing legislation to increase the average earnings of its members. Which of the following proposals would be most likely to lead to large and permanent net income gains for those already in the barbering profession in Florida?
   a. Legislation fixing the minimum price of haircuts at $6, and instituting the free licensing of any graduate of a U.S. barber college
   b. Establishment of strict licensing requirements that would prevent any new entrants into the barbering business without the approval of BAF
   c. Legislation requiring that all employees in the barbering profession be paid double time for any hours worked beyond the normal 40-hour week
   d. Establishment of a $6-per-hour minimum wage for barbers who are paid hourly wages

5. Which of the following is most descriptive of public policy toward competitive markets?
   a. Public policy has consistently promoted competitive markets.
   b. Public policy has tolerated big business while following a regulatory and taxation policy that favors smaller businesses.
   c. Public policy has sometimes promoted competition, but it also has used regulatory, tariff, and subsidization powers to stifle and weaken competitive markets.
   d. Public policy has attempted to promote competition, although the effort has been negated by the rapid growth of the manufacturing sector, which has been spurred on by modern technology.

6. Which of the following would increase an economist's expectations that competitive pressures were present in an industry?
   a. A high concentration ratio
   b. An increase in the availability of close substitutes made by another industry
   c. Few entrants into the industry
   d. A decrease in the availability of foreign products similar to those produced in the industry

7. Regulation that requires the producers of a product to adopt more costly production techniques will
   a. increase supply and lead to a lower market price of the product.
   b. decrease supply and lead to a higher market price of the product.
   c. increase demand and lead to a higher market price of the product.
   d. leave the market price unchanged, since producers are forced to bear the burden of regulatory costs.

Questions 8–11 refer to the following description of the market for the services of midwives (non-doctors who deliver children) in Pasadena, California. Assume that midwives are in a perfectly competitive industry with an equilibrium quantity of 100 children delivered per year at a price of $400 each.

Now suppose that local doctors convince the city council to pass a law requiring that an MD must be "on-call" for all midwife-handled births even if the midwife does all the work. The doctors establish a fixed fee of $100 (to be paid by the midwives) for being on call. After the enactment of the new law, the midwife industry experiences a decrease in the equilibrium number of children delivered per year to 80 and the price rises to $450.

8. By how much did the total annual income (after paying doctors' fees) of all the midwives in Pasadena fall due to the new law?
   a. $28,000
   b. $12,000
   c. $8,000
   d. $4,000

9. By how much did the total annual income of doctors in Pasadena rise due to the 80 midwife births covered by the new law?
   a. $28,000
   b. $12,000
   c. $8,000
   d. $4,000

10. What is the deadweight loss caused by the new law? (*Hint:* Assume that the only deadweight losses caused by the new law are in the midwife industry and that the supply and demand functions in the relevant range are straight lines.)
    a. $4,500
    b. $1,000
    c. $500
    d. Zero

11. If the Pasadena City Council is responsive to lobbying, which of the following describes the likelihood of the new law being repealed during the next few years?
    a. Very likely, because the midwives will point out the large deadweight loss due to the new law.
    b. Very likely, since the midwives lost more money than the doctors gained, and they'll spend it on lobbying.
    c. Very unlikely, because the doctors will point out the zero deadweight loss due to the new law.
    d. Very unlikely, because the doctors gained not only the fees from the 80 midwife handled births but also from the 20 births no longer handled by the midwives. Thus, they'll have more to spend on lobbying than the midwives.

THE ECONOMIC WAY OF THINKING—DISCUSSION QUESTIONS

1. Some economists have proposed that the United States repeal its antitrust laws except for Section 1 of the Sherman Act. Do you agree or not? Explain.

2. How much of the U.S. economy is competitive today? Is the economy less competitive today than three or four decades ago? What are some of the major changes in the economy in recent years that have affected its competitiveness?

3. In recent years there has been considerable dissatisfaction with regulatory policies in the airline and trucking industries. This has led to significant movements toward deregulation in these industries. Do you think deregulating these industries is a good idea? Why or why not?

4. How does social regulation differ from economic regulation? Why is social regulation more difficult to administer than economic regulation? Do the higher costs of social regulation make it less desirable than economic regulation? Explain.

5. Suppose that the government uses licensing to limit the number of firms in the retail liquor industry. Thus, ignoring the cost of a license, firms in the industry make substantial economic profit.
   a. Analyze the price, costs, and profits of firms when the limited number of licenses (good for five years) are auctioned off to the highest bidders. Assume that ownership of the licenses is widespread, so there is no problem in collusion.
   b. Analyze the price, costs, and profits of firms when the limited number of licenses are granted "free" to persons approved by a committee appointed by the legislature (or governor).
   c. When choosing between these two, state legislatures have almost exclusively chosen alternative b. Can you explain why?

6. Do you think General Motors is too big? Would you vote to have it broken up into several smaller firms? What are the major factors that influence your views on this question? Assume that the head of the Pontiac division of General Motors earns his bonuses and promotions on the basis of how Pontiac division (not GM as a whole) performs. The same applies to the heads of Chevrolet, Buick, and other GM divisions. Can you explain why rivalry and competition among divisions should be expected? Will there also be cooperation? What kinds? Will testing laboratories be shared? Will consumers gain? What might consumers lose if GM is *not* broken up? Write a short essay either defending GM or arguing for its breakup. Address the questions raised here.

7. Present your case for or against each of the following:
   a. Laws to make mergers and takeovers more difficult
   b. A "no-fault" monopoly law that breaks up large, dominant firms unless the firms can prove that major inefficiencies will result

PERSPECTIVES IN ECONOMICS

Single-Digit Oil and Auto Mileage Standards Don't Mix
by Robert W. Crandall

[From *The Wall Street Journal*, April 3, 1986, p.26. Reprinted with permission of The Wall Street Journal; ©Dow Jones & Co., Inc. (1986). All rights reserved.]

As we watch the demise of the world petroleum cartel, debate continues whether fuel-economy standards for automobiles prescribed by Congress during the heyday of OPEC should be adjusted slightly. We are even treated to the unsightly spectacle of the Big Three auto company—Chrysler—arguing for the retention of the Corporate Average Fuel Economy program just to hobble the other two companies. Surprisingly, almost no one has suggested the abolition of the entire fuel-economy program—the only sensible decision.

To understand why we have government-mandated fuel-economy standards for cars, one has to return to the 1970s and the unstable oil market of that time. In 1975, most people believed that the real price of fossil fuels would rise ad infinitum. In this environment, Congress enacted the CAFE program for all manufacturers selling new passenger cars in the U.S., requiring that their fleet averages rise from 18 to 27.5 miles per gallon between 1978 and 1985 with subsequent years' standards to be set by the secretary of transportation.

At the time, this policy seemed a not too irrational antidote to a truly irrational policy of regulating crude-oil and gasoline prices. If Congress was not going to allow gasoline prices to rise to world market clearing levels, thereby encouraging conservation, it would have to mandate conservation more directly by requiring that automobiles be produced to deliver more fuel economy than consumers would desire at artificially low prices.

Of course, we finally came to our senses and abandoned oil-price controls. After the Iranian debacle, oil prices made one last surge. By early 1981, crude-oil prices had risen to the range of $35 a barrel and gasoline prices had climbed to about $1.40 a gallon. Since that time, as we all know, oil and gasoline prices have declined dramatically. In fact, gasoline prices in February were less than 70% of their 1981 level in real terms despite an increase in the federal gasoline tax, and they will continue to drop. The cost of the crude oil in a gallon of gasoline has fallen from about 65 cents to 30 cents in the past three months. With real gasoline prices falling so rapidly, why do we want to require auto makers to direct their scarce capital and trained manpower to increasing fuel economy far beyond the level that consumers would willingly pay for? Obviously, if the price of gasoline is falling, you and I are likely to be less willing to pay more for each additional mile per gallon promised by Detroit's newest models.

Visionaries say we need CAFE to protect us against another round of OPEC price increases somewhere in the distant future. But are they better equipped to predict these price increases than today's market participants? And if they are, why do they focus only on the gasoline consumed by new cars, which are only about 8% of all cars on the road and account for less than 3% of oil consumption? Why don't they argue for conservation standards on industrial boilers, home furnaces, locomotives and plastics producers?

If the conservationists were truly interested in reducing oil consumption, they would advocate a tax on all petroleum products. If they were concerned about OPEC-led embargoes or other supply disruptions, they would press for more rapid accumulation of oil in the Strategic Petroleum Reserve, which Congress has chosen to ignore just when the reserve could be filled at low prices.

In the past year, the debate over CAFE standards has taken a number of twists that suggest fuel economy is not really the issue. The United Auto Workers union has become an ardent supporter of CAFE even though the program raises Detroit's costs and thereby leads to fewer new-car sales. The reason for this anomalous behavior is to be found in the law's curious distinction between imported and domestic cars. Manufacturers must tote up their CAFE numbers for cars they produce in the U.S. separately from those they import. Given General Motors' and Ford's success with large cars, they have fallen short of the CAFE standard the past three years. As a result, they will have to increase their production of small cars in the U.S. or make heroic progress on their larger cars if they are to comply.

Recent studies suggest that the U.S. companies are not competitive with Japan or Korea in producing small cars. Therefore, without CAFE, it would make sense for Ford and General Motors to import their small cars. Unfortunately, CAFE makes this difficult because these companies are required to pay $50 a car for every mile per gallon they fall short of CAFE. In short, CAFE serves as a nontariff trade barrier for small-car imports.

Even more curious are the strategic battles among the domestic Big Three companies. Chrysler insists that the CAFE program not be weakened because the company has complied easily while Ford and GM will owe potentially hundreds of millions of dollars of fines a year for not meeting the standard. Last year, Chrysler argued strenuously but unsuccessfully against the secretary of transportation's decision to lower the standard to 26 mpg for the current (1986) model year, saying that since Chrysler had spent the capital resources to meet the standard, GM and Ford should be forced to do so as well. In fact, Chrysler has the worst fuel economy of the Big Three for given weight of car and engine power. It has succeeded in meeting CAFE because it was forced to end its production of large cars during its brush with bankruptcy in the last 1970s. Now it wants to penalize Ford and GM for having the foresight and financial wherewithal to keep their full line of cars.

Even Ford and General Motors are not arguing for an abolition of this misguided program. They simply want the 26-mile-per-gallon standard to be extended to the 1987 and 1988 model years. Why? Could the answer be that a 26 mpg standard severely constrains the major large-car competitors in the world—Mercedes, Volvo, BMW, Peugeot, and Saab—from exporting freely to the U.S.? These European companies are forced to offer diesels or simply lower-performing cars in order to comply with the standards. Incidentally, the first company to pay CAFE penalties was not an American company, but Jaguar.

The CAFE program has become an anomaly or even an absurdity in an era of declining oil prices. If the visionaries in congress wish to protect us from unforeseen disasters, they should look to improving our ability to survive a shock, perhaps by enlarging the Strategic Petroleum Reserve. CAFE standards simply penalize U.S. consumers by offering them cars with too much fuel economy and too little performance, and a reduced choice between imported and domestically produced smaller models. Or Congress could enact an oil-consumption tax. Who knows, such a tax might even help to solve certain other pressing problems of the day.

Discussion

1. Is Crandall saying that auto mileage standards are *always* a bad idea or just a bad idea when gasoline prices are low? Explain your answer.

2. If the free-market system worked, wouldn't high gasoline prices lower the demand for gas guzzlers (and increase the demand for fuel-efficient cars) and make auto mileage standards redundant? Did this happen?

3. Crandall seems to find it "curious" that at least one of the same automobile makers who opposed the mileage standards when they were introduced is now arguing to have them retained. Would the special interest effect make this more understandable? How?

CHAPTER TWELVE

THE SUPPLY OF AND DEMAND FOR PRODUCTIVE RESOURCES

TRUE OR FALSE

T   F

☐ ☐   1. An increase in demand for wheat would cause the price of wheat-producing land to rise.

☐ ☐   2. Under pure competition, the marginal revenue product of a resource would be equal to the resource price.

☐ ☐   3. A profit-maximizing firm will continue to employ a resource as long as its marginal revenue product exceeds its marginal cost to the firm.

☐ ☐   4. The availability of good substitutes for a resource will tend to make the demand for it less elastic.

☐ ☐   5. In the short run, the supply of doctors is quite inelastic.

☐ ☐   6. In the short run, the supply of filling station attendants is quite inelastic.

☐ ☐   7. Physical capital and human capital cannot be substituted for each other.

☐ ☐   8. The marginal products—and therefore wage rates—of employees will be positively influenced by the amount of physical capital per worker in a firm.

☐ ☐   9. An increase in the price of a resource increases the incentive of producers to find a substitute for it.

☐ ☐   10. The demand for a resource will be negatively related to its price partly because producers will substitute other factors of production for the resource as it increases in price.

☐ ☐   11. A firm that purchases resources competitively must buy at the price that is determined in the market.

☐ ☐   12. An employer will hire workers as long as their marginal revenue product is positive.

☐ ☐   13. Because of the law of diminishing marginal returns, the value of a worker's marginal product eventually declines as more workers are hired in a given plant.

☐ ☐   14. The demand for a resource is strongly dependent upon its contribution to the production of a good demanded by consumers.

☐ ☐   15. A unique resource will command a high price, regardless of demand conditions.

PROBLEMS AND PROJECTS

EXHIBIT 1

Units of labor	Total output (per week)	Marginal physical product (per week)	Product price	Total revenue	Marginal revenue product (per week)
1	5	_____	100	_____	_____
2	9	_____	100	_____	_____
3	12	_____	100	_____	_____
4	14	_____	100	_____	_____
5	15	_____	100	_____	_____

1. Nichole sells building materials in a competitive industry. Her firm receives $100 for each unit of material. Given the firm's current fixed capital, Exhibit 1 shows how total output changes as additional units of labor are hired. Assume that Nichole hires labor from a competitive market in which the market-determined wage is $200 per week.

   a. Fill in the marginal physical product, total revenue, and marginal revenue product columns.

   b. How many employees should Nichole hire if she wants to maximize profits? (*Hint:* If two different labor levels maximize profits, assume Nichole will produce at the higher of the two levels.)

   c. How many units of labor should Nichole hire if the wage rate goes up to $300?

EXHIBIT 2

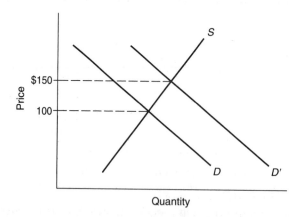

   d. The supply-and-demand conditions in the building market are represented in Exhibit 2. Suppose that the demand for building materials increases as indicated by *D'*. Given the new wage rate in part c, indicate the firm's new employment level, total revenue, and profits (refer to Exhibit 3). (*Hint:* Assume profits = TR minus TVC.)

EXHIBIT 3

Units of labor	Units of output	Product price	Total revenue	MRP	Profit
0	0	$150	_____	_____	_____
1	5	150	_____	_____	_____
2	9	150	_____	_____	_____
3	12	150	_____	_____	_____
4	14	150	_____	_____	_____
5	15	150	_____	_____	_____

e. Nichole has a weekly fixed charge of $800 in addition to her variable cost for labor. Given her *fixed costs*, would Nichole stay in business if she operated at the level of output you determined in part d?

2. Magic Carpet, Inc., produces and sells handmade oriental rugs in a competitive industry. The firm receives $100 per square meter for each rug produced. Given the firm's current fixed capital, Exhibit 4 shows how total output (in square meters) changes as additional units of skilled labor are hired.

EXHIBIT 4

Units of skilled labor	Total output (square meters per week)	MPP	Price per square meter	TR	MRP
0	0	_____	$100	_____	_____
1	5	_____	100	_____	_____
2	12	_____	100	_____	_____
3	18	_____	100	_____	_____
4	21.5	_____	100	_____	_____
5	24	_____	100	_____	_____
6	25	_____	100	_____	_____

a. Complete the table.
b. What is the firm's demand schedule for labor?
c. Given the equilibrium wage rate as $200 per week, indicate how many workers the firm would hire if it wanted to maximize profits.
d. How many workers would Magic Carpet hire if the market wage increased to $300 per week?

3. Use the diagrams below to indicate the changes in demand (D), supply (S), equilibrium price (P) and equilibrium quantity (Q) in response to the events in the resource markets. First show in the diagrams how the described event or events affect demand and/or supply of the resource, and then fill in the table to the right of the diagrams using + to indicate increase, – to indicate decrease, 0 to indicate no effect, and ? to indicate uncertain. (*Hint:* The diagrams are of the resource markets themselves; for example, the diagram in part a is of the market for high school math teachers.)

Resource market	Events	Diagrams	D	S	P	Q
a. High school math teachers	Wages for mathematicians employed in industry rise.					
b. Computers	Technological change raises the speed of computer calculations.					
c. Computer technicians	The cost of obtaining computer training falls.					
d. Welders	Technological change lowers the cost of robots used to weld auto parts on auto assembly lines.					
e. Agricultural land in Southern California	Population migration raises homesite values; a vitamin C fad raises the price of oranges.					

4. In the growing of corn a farmer uses two fertilizers, Vitacorn and Cornpower. The farmer has estimated that at the current rate of usage of the two fertilizers, the marginal (physical) product of one ton of Vitacorn is 200 bushels per acre and the marginal product of one ton of Cornpower is 400 bushels per acre. The best price quotations the farmer has been able to get are $800/ton for Vitacorn and $1200/ton for Cornpower.

   a. From the above information, does the farmer's current usage of the two fertilizers meet the "condition for cost minimization when multiple resources are employed"?

   b. Suppose the farmer used one more ton of Cornpower and two fewer tons of Vitacorn. How would total output change? How would total cost change? Would this substitution be consistent with the goal of profit maximization?

   c. If the farmer continued to substitute Cornpower for Vitacorn, assume that the marginal product of Cornpower would fall. Would these changes lead toward fulfillment of the condition for cost minimization you discussed in part a? How?

5. Suppose that the world's long-run and short-run demands for crude petroleum can be represented by the diagram in Exhibit 5.

EXHIBIT 5

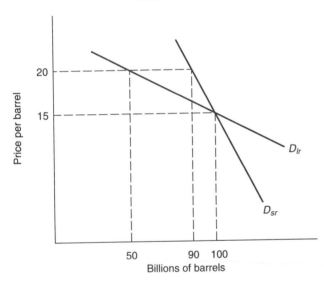

a. From the information in the diagram, calculate the arc-price elasticity of demand (between $15 and $20) for crude petroleum in the short run and in the long run.

b. Of the many possible reasons behind the demand for petroleum being more elastic in the long run than in the short run, which do you think is most important? Which is second most important? Explain your reasoning.

6. Thin Air is a monopolistic seller of breathing devices. Labor is the firm's only variable input.
   a. Complete the following table:

Units of labor	Units of output	Price of output	Total revenue	Marginal revenue product
1	10	50	_____	_____
2	19	48	_____	_____
3	27	46	_____	_____
4	34	44	_____	_____
5	40	42	_____	_____
6	45	40	_____	_____
7	49	39	_____	_____
8	52	38	_____	_____
9	54	37	_____	_____
10	55	36	_____	_____

   b. If fixed costs are $100 and labor costs $100 per unit, what are the profit-maximizing values of units of labor hired, output, profits and average cost?
   c. What is the value of the marginal product of the last worker hired? Is the worker paid the full value of his or her marginal product?

LEARNING THE MECHANICS—MULTIPLE CHOICE

1. The short-run supply of a human resource will be more elastic the
   a. more elastic the demand for the product to be produced.
   b. more inelastic the demand for the product to be produced.
   c. lower the skill level necessary to perform the job.
   d. harder it is to acquire the skill and knowledge necessary to provide the resource.

2. A decrease in the demand for a product will cause
   a. the price of resources to decrease and, therefore, output to increase.
   b. output to decrease, and demand for (and prices of) resources used to produce the product to decrease also.
   c. output to decrease, but the demand for resources to remain constant.
   d. output to decrease and resource prices to fall if, and only if, their supply is elastic.

3. Empirical evidence indicates a close relationship between quantity of schooling and income. A cost-minimizing firm would be willing to pay a highly educated person higher wages than those with less education if
   a. the marginal revenue product of the highly educated person were greater.
   b. the demand for the highly educated group was inelastic.
   c. the supply of the highly educated group was smaller.
   d. the total cost of schooling was greater for the highly educated employee.

4. The more elastic the demand for a product
   a. the more inelastic the demand for the productive resources used.
   b. the less elastic the supply of factors used in producing the product.
   c. the more elastic the demand for the productive resources used.
   d. the longer the time period before the product will be sold.

5. Which of the following expresses the correct decision-making rule for a profit-maximizing firm hiring units of labor?
   a. If the MRP were rising, less labor would be employed as time passed.
   b. The firm should continue to hire workers as long as their MRP is greater than the wage rate.
   c. The firm should continue to hire workers until the total costs of all workers equals the total revenue from the output of the workers.
   d. The firm should continue to hire workers until the wage rate equals the price of the product.

6. The demand for a productive resource
   a. is a derived demand.
   b. is independent of the selling price of the product.
   c. is dependent on the supply side of the resource at the time.
   d. shifts when the price of the resource changes.

7. Increasing the price of a natural resource will
   a. cause consumers to choose substitute goods that do not use the natural resource intensively.
   b. decrease the demand for the natural resource.
   c. increase the demand for the natural resource.
   d. increase the quantity of the resource demanded.

8. Compared to the short-run demand, the long-run demand for carpenters is
   a. less elastic.
   b. more elastic.
   c. equally elastic.
   d. either more or less elastic; we cannot predict which.

9. In a purely competitive industry, the marginal revenue derived from the sale of an additional unit of the product is equal to the market price of the product. In these circumstances, the additional revenue derived from the employment of an additional unit of a resource is referred to as the resource's
   a. marginal cost.
   b. value of marginal product.
   c. marginal physical product.
   d. marginal productivity.

10. If the cost of using skilled labor was twice the cost of using unskilled labor, and both were used by a profit-maximizing firm, the firm would adjust the quantity of each type of labor until
    a. the marginal physical product of each was the same.
    b. twice as much unskilled labor was used.
    c. half as much unskilled labor was used.
    d. the marginal physical product of unskilled labor was half that of skilled labor.

11. If a firm used only two factors of production, labor (L) and capital (K), which of the following conditions would be present if the firm were minimizing its cost of production?
    a. The $MPP_L/P_L = MPP_K/P_K$
    b. MPP_L times the price of labor = MPP_K times the price of capital
    c. $MRP_L = MRP_K$
    d. $MPP_L = MPP_K$

12. A shift in the demand for a particular resource can be caused by all the following *except*
    a. a change in the demand for the product that uses the resource as a factor of production.
    b. a change in the productivity of the resource.
    c. a change in the price of *other* resources that could be used as substitutes for the resource in question.
    d. a change in price of the resource.

Questions 13 and 14 refer to the market for midwestern law clerks. Law clerks produce materials that law firms need to provide law services to their clients. Assume that the law clerks currently work in a perfectly competitive market.

13. Suppose a major toxic waste disaster causes damages throughout the midwest, and everyone expects an increased demand for legal services to result (all else constant). Law clerks should expect
    a. an increase in wages as their marginal products increase.
    b. an increase in wages as their marginal revenue products increase.
    c. a decrease in wages as their clients no longer afford high bills.
    d. a decrease in wages as the firm hires more clerks.

14. Suppose that all the midwestern law firms consolidate, becoming a monopoly in the area. We'd expect the wages of midwestern law clerks to
    a. fall, but more clerks would be hired.
    b. fall, and fewer clerks would be hired.
    c. rise, but fewer clerks would be hired.
    d. rise, and more clerks would be hired.

15. A firm in Clinton, N.Y., currently employs 80 units of labor and 50 units of capital equipment to produce 300 hamster cages. Given the current input levels utilized, the marginal product of labor is 4 and the marginal product of capital is 10. If we assume that labor costs $20 per unit and capital costs $10 per unit, then
    a. if the firm wants to expand output, when doing so, it should use the same proportions of labor and capital it now does.
    b. the firm could increase its output with no extra costs by using more capital and less labor.
    c. the firm could lower its production costs by using more labor and less capital.
    d. the firm is maximizing profits.

THE ECONOMIC WAY OF THINKING—MULTIPLE CHOICE

1. Which of the following resources will have the most inelastic supply in the short run?
    a. Land in downtown Chicago
    b. Trucks used to transport a variety of products
    c. Elevator operators
    d. Secretaries in Eagle Rock, California

2. Suppose that the number of economists engaged in teaching positions in 1985 decreased 10 percent from the 1975 level, while the number of economists in all positions declined 5 percent. Furthermore, suppose the median salary of those teaching declined relative to the average for economists as a group. The apparent paradox of a relative decrease in economists in teaching positions concurrent with their lower salaries relative to all economists can be explained by which of the following?
    a. The demand for teachers in economics is positively sloped, as evidenced by the smaller quantity employed at the lower salary rate.
    b. The demand elasticity for teachers in economics was smaller than that of the demand for all economists.
    c. The demand for economists decreased, and the demand for teachers in economics decreased relative to the demand for all economists.
    d. The larger decrease in the demand for research economists increased the relative median salaries of all economists.

3. Given the education required to become an engineer, which of the following best describes the expected market reaction to an increase in demand for the services of engineers?
   a. A large decrease in the wages of engineers in the short run, but a small increase in wages over time.
   b. A substantial increase in the wages of engineers, followed (later) by an increase in the number of engineers, moderating the initial wage increase
   c. A substantial increase in the number of engineers and no increase in the wage level
   d. A substantial increase in the wages of engineers in the short run, and no change in the number of persons choosing to become engineers

4. In which of the following resource markets do you think supply would be most elastic in the short run?
   a. Pharmacists
   b. Physicians
   c. Unskilled labor
   d. Airplane pilots

5. During his administration, President Carter advocated a $1.46 billion aid program for college students from low- and middle-income families. The program was designed to halt the decline in college enrollments. If the program had been implemented, which of the following would have been the most likely outcome?
   a. Starting salaries for new college graduates would have risen because of an increase in the number of high-quality graduates.
   b. Starting salaries for college graduates would have been unaffected.
   c. Inflation would have decreased as more young people chose to be students instead of workers.
   d. Starting salaries of new college graduates would have fallen as the supply of graduates increased.

6. Suppose that a school board adopted a policy whereby all teachers were paid at the same wage rate. Furthermore, suppose that there was a vacancy in economics for which there were no applicants, and there was no vacancy in political science but there were 50 inquiries regarding any possible vacancy. Economic analysis implies that
   a. the nation needs to train more economists.
   b. the wage rate paid the teachers is below the market wage for economists.
   c. economists have fewer alternatives to teaching than do political scientists.
   d. the wage rate offered is below the market wage for political scientists.

7. Suppose that the United Auto Workers Union is successful in obtaining a 15 percent increase in the wages of auto workers and that the large wage increase necessitates an increase in automobile prices. Employment in the automobile manufacturing industry would be *least* likely to fall if
   a. the demand for American automobiles was relatively constant, but highly elastic.
   b. the supply of foreign-produced automobiles was highly elastic.
   c. American consumers felt that foreign automobiles were a good substitute for American automobiles.
   d. the demand for American automobiles was increasing and highly inelastic.

8. Human capital differs from physical capital in that
   a. only physical capital depreciates.
   b. the use of physical capital is affected by working conditions and monetary return; human capital is predominantly affected by monetary return.
   c. physical capital may be purchased and sold; human capital may not be sold in a non-slave society (only the services of human capital may be purchased and sold).
   d. only human capital depreciates.

9. According to marginal productivity theory, a law forcing firms to pay higher wages to HHLs (heads of households with large families) would tend to
   a. decrease the employment and marginal productivity of HHLs.
   b. decrease the employment of HHLs, but lead to a higher marginal productivity for those HHLs hired.
   c. reduce the wages of workers without families.
   d. have no impact on HHLs.

10. The cost of electricity is a large component of the cost of making aluminum. In the Pacific Northwest, federal agencies sell electricity to aluminum manufacturers at roughly one-fourth its market value. Among those eager to eliminate this implicit subsidy would be
    a. firms that make wooden bats and wooden canoes.
    b. firms that supply aluminum ore to aluminum makers, since ore would then be a smaller part of the total cost of producing aluminum.
    c. buyers of aluminum products (who gain when aluminum profits decline).
    d. employees of the aluminum makers (who would then be justified in asking for higher wages when aluminum prices go up).

11. Where human capital is concerned, nonpecuniary considerations are likely to be
    a. irrelevant, since owners' decisions are based on money prices.
    b. unimportant, since people are very mobile.
    c. important, since workers have objectives other than money.
    d. important, since human capital is not transferable.

12. If the demand for chemical engineers suddenly increased, salaries for them would be higher one year later if
    a. several other kinds of engineers became chemical engineers by enrolling in a special one-semester training course.
    b. the price of goods produced by the chemical engineers was highly sensitive to changes in price.
    c. chemical engineering was so specialized that few persons in other areas could become chemical engineers without taking at least three additional years of training.
    d. there were many unemployed chemical engineers before the increase in demand.

13. If a college education did not increase worker productivity,
    a. no one would go to college.
    b. wages would tend to be the same for workers with and without a college education.
    c. wages would still be higher for workers with college degrees because of the cost of going to college.
    d. the total lifetime earnings of workers who go to college and those who don't would tend to be the same.

THE ECONOMIC WAY OF THINKING—DISCUSSION QUESTIONS

1. In recent years, the computer industry has grown quite rapidly as a result of technological advances. Suppose that the application of computers in the workplace continues at an accelerated rate.
   a. What would happen to the supply of computer technicians in the short run? In the long run?
   b. What would happen to the earnings of computer technicians in the short run? In the long run?
   c. What would happen in the long run to the supply and earnings of workers in industries that compete for the type of workers who become computer technicians?
   d. What would happen to the demand for inputs (for example, bookkeepers and clerks) for which computers are substitutes?

2. Is human labor really a "thing" that can be bought and sold like any other productive resource? What about the feelings of the human beings involved? While we can buy a person's time, we can't buy his or her enthusiasm or loyalty so easily. What sort of advantages and disadvantages does the "human element" in purchasing labor inputs have?

3. a. Why is the amount demanded of a productive resource negatively related to the price of the resource? Why is the demand likely to be more elastic when buyers have more time to respond?
   b. If the price of unskilled labor rises, what will tend to happen to the demand for substitute resources? For complementary resources?
   c. Will the demand for unskilled labor be more or less elastic as a result of the demand change described in part b for substitute resources? For complementary resources?

4. Do individuals seek to maximize their income from supplying resources? How does the rate of return to resource suppliers influence their investment decisions? Do investors necessarily seek the highest possible pecuniary rate of return on their resources? Why or why not?

5. Suppose that the question in part e of problem and Project #1 had specified the weekly fixed cost at $1000 instead of $800. How would this have changed your answer to the question?

6. What impact would each of the following have on the demand for economists?
   a. An increase in government research funds for the study of wage-price controls
   b. A reduction in government-financed scholarships and loans for students
   c. The establishment of a planning agency that must analyze and decide whether labor-management contracts are inflationary
   d. Reduced emphasis on government planning and an increase reliance on the market mechanism

PERSPECTIVES IN ECONOMICS

Baseball's $5 Million Man: Is He Worth It?
by Timothy Tregarthen

[Reprinted with permission from *The Margin*, Fall 1991, pp. 34–36, abridged.]

Boston Red Sox pitcher Roger Clemens became baseball's first $5 million man when he signed a $21.5 million, four-year contract early this year.

"We are all delighted to get this contract finished," said Red Sox general manager Lou Gorman after the signing. "He is not only one of the best pitchers in history, but the premier pitcher in baseball today."

Not everyone was as delighted as Mr. Gorman—or, presumably, Mr. Clemens. "It's another classic example of how ownership is tearing the heart out of baseball for no good reason," snapped Pittsburgh Pirates President Carl Berger.

Mr. Clemens is undoubtedly a great pitcher. He has twice won baseball's Cy Young award. Prior to the 1991 season he had won 69.5 percent of the games in which he pitched, while the Red Sox had won just 50.1 percent of the games in which Mr. Clemens had not pitched since he joined the club. But is he worth more than $5 million per season?

In one sense, the answer is obviously "yes." The Red Sox franchise chose to pay Mr. Clemens his huge wage; they must have thought he was worth $5 million.

"Clubs will typically do a calculation of what kind of additional revenue a player will generate," says Lou Guth, an economist and senior vice president of National Economic Research Association, a consulting firm in White Plains, New York. "It may well be that the greater attendance and better TV and radio contracts that having Roger Clemens on the roster could bring will prove to be worth it."

Apparently, many teams have high estimates of their players' ability to generate big revenues. Thirty-five players now earn $3 million or more. Mr. Clemens was joined in the $5 million club last spring by New York Mets pitcher Dwight Gooden, who signed a three-year pact for $15.45 million. The contract could be worth as much as $16.2 million, depending on Mr. Gooden's performance.

Economic theory suggests that firms will be willing to pay for a factor of production, whether it is an ace hurler or a ton of fertilizer, a price equal to its marginal revenue product—the additional revenue attributable to an additional unit of the factor.

Presumably, the Red Sox calculated Mr. Clemens' likely impact on team revenues. As long as his efforts bring fans to the stadium, viewers to the TV set and listeners to radio who will generate at least $5 million in revenue each year, Mr. Clemens will pay his way. It is the fans a player attracts that ultimately determine his worth.

In the words of Yankees owner George Steinbrenner,

"You measure the value of a ballplayer by the number of fannies he puts in the seats."

The notion that Mr. Clemens might account for $5 million in additional revenues is not implausible. The Red Sox drew 2,528,986 fans last year to Fenway Park and are thought to have grossed $40 million. "If you think about what might happen to their (the Red Sox) revenues if Mr. Clemens switched to another team, it's easy to see him being worth $5 million a year," Mr. Guth says.

Wins and Losses

Economists generally measure the marginal revenue product of a player using a method developed by Gerald W. Scully, an economist at the University of Texas at Dallas. Writing in the December 1974 issue of the *American Economic Review,* Mr. Scully proposed a two-step process to gauge a player's contribution to team revenues. First, Mr. Scully figured out what determines team revenue. Several factors are involved, including the population of the city in which the team plays, its average income level, and whether there are other professional sports teams in the city. A crucial factor is the team's win-loss record. Winners draw more fans than losers, all other things equal.

The second step was to identify the factors that determine how many games a team will win. Mr. Scully found that win-loss records are determined almost entirely by hitting and pitching ability.

Once these relationships were estimated, Mr. Scully could calculate the impact of a player with a given hitting or pitching record on his team's record and then compute the effect that would have on that team's revenues. Mr. Scully then subtracted costs associated with having a player on the roster, such as for training and transportation, to estimate the player's net marginal revenue product. Finally, he compared these figures to actual player salaries.

Startling Results

Mr. Scully's results were startling. He found that hitters and pitchers with average records earned salaries equal to only about 20 percent of their estimated net marginal revenue products. "Star" quality players earned just 15 percent of net marginal revenue products. Mr. Scully based his estimates on data for the 1968–69 season and compared salaries and net marginal revenue products over the likely course of a player's entire career.

The sharp disparity, Mr. Scully argued, resulted from a key provision then in effect under the Uniform Player's Contract. The provision, called the reserve clause, stipulated that players belonged to the teams that hired them. A team could sell or trade players to another team, but at no time could a player offer his services to other teams. If a player wanted a career in baseball, he had to agree to a system in which he would always be limited to negotiations with the team that owned his contract. Teams thus had monopsony power over their players' services.

A monopsony team faced an upward-sloping supply curve for players of a particular quality; getting more players of the same skill level requires paying higher salaries.

Hiring another player that good is likely to require a higher salary not only for that player but for the other players of that quality on the team's roster. The additional, or marginal, cost of the player will thus exceed his salary.

The accompanying graph illustrates the argument in the case of star pitchers. The net marginal revenue product curve (MRP) measures the contribution of additional star pitchers to a team's revenues, less their associated training, transportation and other costs. The supply curve (S) shows the number of players of that quality available at each wage. Because a team must offer a higher wage to obtain more star pitchers, its marginal factor cost curve (MFC) lies above this supply curve.

Theoretically, a profit-maximizing team will hire additional star pitchers up to the point at which the marginal factor cost equals net marginal revenue product. The wage—the player's salary—will then be determined by the supply curve. The monopsony model thus predicts that wages will fall short of net marginal revenue product, just as Mr. Scully observed.

An even sharper test of the theory was provided in the mid-1970s. Two players challenged the reserve clause, arguing it was an illegal restriction of their rights. An arbitrator agreed and ordered that baseball players be given status as "free agents"—able to seek offers from other teams—after six years of professional play.

At the close of the 1976 season, 25 players became free agents under the new stipulation. Paul M. Sommers, an economist at Middlebury College, and a student, Noel Quinton, analyzed the salaries won by the top 14 free agents.

Economic theory predicts that the shift to more competitive bidding should have moved player salaries closer to marginal revenue product. Using an approach similar to Mr. Scully's, the two researchers estimated each player's marginal revenue product in the 1977 season and compared that to the salary the player received that year.

Their results, reported in the Summer 1982 issue of the *Journal of Human Resources,* were consistent with the theory. The salaries of the hitters in the group rose to about half of marginal revenue product. The salaries of the pitchers were roughly equal to their marginal revenue product. The economists could not explain why pitcher salaries came so much closer to estimated marginal revenue product than hitter salaries.

Villanova University economist John Leonard reported in 1985 on a study of hitter salaries for the 1982 season. He found that they had risen to 75 percent of estimated marginal revenue product.

And today? "I think that salaries are, on average, about equal to the marginal revenue products of players," Mr. Leonard says. "Of course, it's difficult to predict just how well a player might perform, so some salaries end up being too high and some end up being too low. But on average, they're about right."

Mr. Guth notes that another factor that contributes to high player salaries is arbitration. Beginning in a player's third year, he can demand that his salary be set by an arbitrator. The arbitrator, whose rulings are binding, then de-

MONOPSONY EXPLOITATION OF STAR PITCHERS

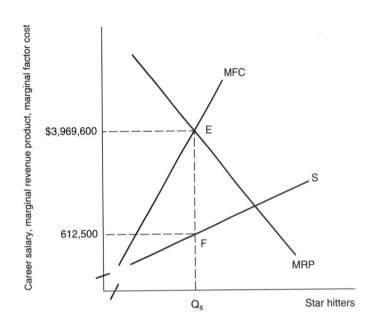

A monopsony firm hires additional units of an input up to the point that marginal factor cost and marginal revenue product are equal. It pays a wage determined by the supply curve. That results in a wage ($612,500) considerably below marginal revenue product ($3,969,600).

termines a salary that he or she thinks is justified, based on what other players of similar quality receive. Thus, according to Mr. Guth, the market affects a player's salary even before he can become a free agent.

The models economists use to analyze the player market assume that teams act as profit-maximizing entities. Is that a reasonable assumption?

"You hear a lot about owners being in it for the 'love of the sport' and things like that," Mr. Guth says. "And that might well be true. But profit considerations surely affect their choices. Every academic study I've seen suggests that

the owners make choices that are consistent with the assumption of profit-maximizing behavior."

Certainly the business has been profitable. Professional baseball reported a profit of $214 million in 1989, the most recent year for which figures have been released. Another gauge of expected profitability is the price new teams are willing to pay for the right to a franchise. Six ownership groups were vying last spring for two new major league expansion franchises. The teams chosen will have to pay a franchise fee of $95 million for the right to operate a major league team.

Discussion

1. The results cited in this article seem to be at odds with the general view that "professional athletes are over-paid, spoiled brats." What reasons can you think of that would explain this difference of opinion?
2. As Tregarthen admits, one of the weaknesses of this analysis is the manner in which marginal revenue product was measured. How would *you* go about measuring the marginal revenue product of an employee?
3. What about players who are hurt or who are in the minor leagues still improving their skills (human capital). If owners have to pay players whose marginal revenue products are zero, then shouldn't they be allowed to pay the other players less than their MRPs to even things out? Why or why not?

EARNINGS, PRODUCTIVITY, AND THE JOB MARKET

TRUE OR FALSE

T   F

☐ ☐   1. Immobility of labor is a major source of wage differentials.

☐ ☐   2. Higher productivity generally leads to higher wages.

☐ ☐   3. Firms seeking to maximize monetary profit will tend to hire very few minority workers.

☐ ☐   4. Owners of physical capital in the United States receive about 40 percent of national income.

☐ ☐   5. Automation always reduces production costs and employment within a firm.

☐ ☐   6. Automation *almost always* reduces the demand for labor in the economy.

☐ ☐   7. An expansion in production per worker is the primary source of high living standards.

☐ ☐   8. Minimum wage legislation helps low-wage workers, particularly teenagers, whereas the burden of the legislation is imposed almost exclusively on high-wage workers.

☐ ☐   9. The average wage rate in the United States is high in comparison with that of other countries largely because of the large amount of physical and human capital with which the average American works.

☐ ☐   10. Other things constant, the more dangerous a job, the higher the wage rate it will command.

☐ ☐   11. The wages of workers on jobs that require special skills or technical know-how will necessarily be high.

☐ ☐   12. The job opportunities of a minority group would be reduced if consumers discriminated against firms that hired minorities.

☐ ☐   13. The almost total exclusion of women from many high-paying professional occupations is consistent with the employment discrimination explanation of earnings differences according to gender.

PROBLEMS AND PROJECTS

EXHIBIT 1

Quantity demanded per month	Price	Quantity supplied per month
0	$600	6000
1000	500	5000
2000	400	4000
3000	300	3000
4000	200	2000
5000	100	1000
6000	0	0

1. Exhibit 1 is a hypothetical, demand-and-supply schedule for sophisticated pocket calculators in a competitive industry.
   a. What will be the equilibrium quantity and price in this market?
   b. Suppose that a new labor-saving technology is developed, resulting in an increase of 2000 in quantity supplied at every price. What will happen to the equilibrium quantity and price?
   c. The new technology reduces the quantity of labor used *per calculator* by 20 percent. What will happen to total employment in the industry? (Original employment was 120 workers.)
   d. Owing to the new technology, the computer industry substituted more machines for labor. Using the elasticity-of-demand argument, refute or support the following statement: "If we continue to allow machines to replace workers, we will run out of jobs. Automation is the major cause of unemployment."

2. The diagram in Exhibit 2 depicts the situation in the unskilled labor market with a minimum wage of $4.55 per hour:

EXHIBIT 2

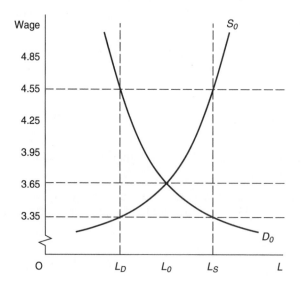

Suppose a proposal is made to replace the current minimum wage law with a wage subsidy. With the subsidy, employed unskilled workers would receive a $1.20 per hour subsidy in addition to their regular wage.

a. How many workers would be hired with the subsidy, L_O, L_S, L_D, or some different amount?

b. What is the total cost to the government of providing the subsidy?

c. Indicate whether the wage subsidy (compared to the $4.55 minimum wage) would raise (+), lower (–), leave unchanged (0), or change in an uncertain direction (?) the well-being of each of the following:

_____ i. Consumers of products that use unskilled labor

_____ ii. Currently employed unskilled workers

_____ iii. Currently unemployed unskilled workers

_____ iv. Skilled workers

_____ v. Taxpayers

d. How would you expect employers to adjust their cost minimizing combination of machinery and unskilled workers? Explain.

3. The text describes the following determinants of earnings differentials:

a. Nonhomogeneous labor
   Al: Worker productivity and specialized skills
   A2: Workers preferences
   A3: Race and gender

b. Nonhomogeneous jobs
   B1: Location of jobs
   B2: Nonpecuniary job characteristics

c. Immobility of labor
   C1: Temporary disequilibrium
   C2: Institutional restrictions

Indicate the main reason from the list above for each of the following wage differentials:

___ a. Urban wages are higher than rural wages.

___ b. Police officers in metropolitan areas with high violent crime rates earn higher wages than police officers elsewhere.

___ c. White basketball players receive about 20 percent higher salaries than equally talented black basketball players.

___ d. Primary care parents tend to choose jobs with flexible working conditions.

___ e. Taxicab drivers charge higher-than-average fares in cities with marketable taxi licenses.

___ f. Computer programmers earn higher salaries than computer operators.

4. Consider the following hypothetical information about productivity in Canada and Brazil:

Labor output per week

	Tons of steel	Bushels of wheat	Autos
Canada	10	5000	1
Brazil	5	500	1/5

a. If wages depend on productivity, how high would Canadian wages be compared to Brazilian wages if both countries produced
   ____ i. only steel? _____
   ____ ii. only wheat? _____
   ____ iii. only autos? _____

b. Suppose that the actual wage rate per week is $200 in Canada and $40 in Brazil. Assuming that other input costs are the same in both countries for each of these goods, indicate below which country is the low-cost producer of
   ____ i. steel_____
   ____ ii. wheat _____
   ____ iii. autos _____

c. Based on your answers to parts a and b, decide whether the following is true or false: "High-paid Canadian workers can't compete with cheap foreign labor." Explain.

LEARNING THE MECHANICS—MULTIPLE CHOICE

1. In 1992, the female-male earnings ratio indicated that the earnings of single women relative to the earnings of single men were
   a. much higher than the relative earnings of women in other marital status groupings.
   b. about the same as the relative earnings of women in other marital status groupings.
   c. much less than the relative earnings of women in other marital status groupings.
   d. not directly comparable to the relative earnings of women in other marital status groupings.

2. Real wages would be most likely to decrease over a period of time if
   a. the rate of inflation was higher than 3 percent.
   b. the demand for consumer goods decreased relative to the demand for capital goods.
   c. automation increased.
   d. output or productivity per labor-hour decreased.

3. If all persons were identical regarding preferences and productivity factors (ability, skill level, education, experience, etc.), the highest-paying jobs would be the most
   a. prestigious.
   b. convenient.
   c. pleasant.

    d. disagreeable.

4. If a minimum wage law was enacted and the demand for workers was inelastic
    a. employers would substitute machines for most of the present workers in the short run.
    b. the total income for workers would fall.
    c. the reduction in employment would be small.
    d. employers would hire more low-skill workers to keep the wage rate from rising even further.

5. Evidence suggests that education raises the earnings of the work force mainly by
    a. increasing the marginal productivity of labor.
    b. keeping young people out of the labor force, thereby reducing the supply of labor.
    c. teaching workers how to demand more pay.
    d. teaching people to read and write, although education beyond this point does not seem to increase worker productivity.

6. Increasing the minimum wage will probably result in
    a. lower profits and the same level of product prices.
    b. greater employment, since more people want to work at the new wage than at the previous equilibrium wage.
    c. reduced employment of the unskilled, as firms produce less output and substitute away from the more expensive unskilled labor.
    d. a decrease in the demand for workers in previously unionized high-wage firms.

7. Within an occupation, when a given job provides steadier work (fewer layoffs), the hourly wage tends to be
    a. lower than wage rates in jobs that are otherwise similar.
    b. higher than wage rates in jobs that are otherwise similar.
    c. no different from wage rates in jobs that are otherwise similar.
    d. determined by factors other than supply and demand.

8. Employment discrimination against members of a minority group invariably exists when the minority group members
    a. are paid less than other workers.
    b. are hired less frequently than other workers.
    c. are treated differently than other workers.
    d. are treated differently than other workers who are similarly qualified.

9. Indicate which of the following most accurately represents the capital formation rate of the United States relative to other countries.
    a. The United States invests a larger share of its GDP than most other industrial countries.
    b. The United States invests a smaller share of its GDP than most other industrial countries.
    c. The United States invests about the same share of its GDP as Japan and Germany.
    d. The United States invests about the same share of its GDP as most other industrial countries.

10. Automated production methods are attractive to a producer when
    a. they reduce cost.
    b. they replace workers.

c. output is increased.
d. wages are low.

Questions 11–14 refer to the following information:

Suppose that the labor force of an imaginary country is equally divided between men and women, who are equally skilled and productive, with similar preferences with respect to laboring. However, due to recent social upheavals, the labor market is rigidly segmented: The majority of occupations are reserved for men, the remainder for women. Important figures are given below.

Labor Market as a Whole			Segmented Markets			
Quantity supplied total	Quantity demanded total	Wage	Quantity supplied female	Quantity demanded female	Quantity supplied male	Quantity demanded male
60	140	$60	30	35	30	105
66	132	70	33	33	33	99
80	120	80	40	30	40	90
100	100	100	50	25	50	75
120	80	120	60	20	60	60
140	60	140	70	15	70	45

11. The best description of the current rigidly segmented labor market situation is that
    a. more men than women are hired, with men earning a higher wage.
    b. equal numbers of men and women are hired, with men earning a higher wage.
    c. equal numbers of men and women are hired, with women earning a higher wage.
    d. equal numbers of men and women are hired, with equal wages for both genders.

12. The impact of the market segmentation on employers is
    a. zero, since men and women are equally skilled.
    b. minor, since employers are paying only $10 more for men to do something that women could do equally well.
    c. major, since employers are paying more than 50% more for men to do something that women could do equally well.
    d. impossible to determine from the information given.

13. Suppose that the government decides to ensure that men and women earn the same wage. As a result, a law is passed mandating that the female wage be comparable in worth to the male wage that previously existed in the segmented male market. The market remains segmented. As a result,
    a. the total number of men working and their wages is unchanged.
    b. the total number of women working falls, but their wages rise.
    c. 40 women are unemployed (willing to work at the existing wage), but no men are unemployed.
    d. all of the above.

14. The Opposition floats a different proposal, which would outlaw segmentation. Gender differences would no longer be allowed to affect hiring. (Remember, the two groups are otherwise identical.) If this proposal could be perfectly enforced, the best description of the labor market would be that:
    a. more men than women would be hired, with men earning a higher wage.
    b. equal numbers of men and women would be hired, with men earning a higher wage.
    c. equal numbers of men and women would be hired, with equal wages of $100 for both genders.

d. equal numbers of men and women would be hired, with equal wages of $120 for both genders.

THE ECONOMIC WAY OF THINKING—MULTIPLE CHOICE

1. Use statements I and II to answer this question. **(I)** Differences in worker productivity are one major reason why individual earnings differ. **(II)** Even if all workers were identical, differences in the desirability of jobs would still cause earnings differentials.
   a. Both I and II are true.
   b. I is true, II is false.
   c. I is false, II is true.
   d. Both I and II are false.

2. When wage rates for a group of workers (teenagers, for example) are far above the equilibrium level, discrimination by employers on noneconomic grounds becomes
   a. more costly.
   b. more costly, but necessary.
   c. necessary and less costly.
   d. more costly and unnecessary.

3. One potential problem with Congress mandating that employers supply their employees with free child care services is that
   a. if employers can change wages, the wages of employees will be likely to eventually absorb the cost of the child care.
   b. if employers cannot change wages, the increased total compensation package will make employers likely to attempt to hire fewer employees, causing increased unemployment.
   c. total compensation will be greater for workers with children that can use child care than it will be for other workers.
   d. all of the above are potential problems.

4. Suppose that the government passed a law that required that all government employees be paid the average wage rate in the private sector. Which of the following would be true?
   a. Output would be maximized.
   b. Costs would be maximized.
   c. Those individuals with higher skills (and thus more options) could be expected to leave government employment for higher-paying alternatives.
   d. There would be no change in the allocation of resources.

5. Which one of the following would be *least* likely to occur if Congress passed legislation exempting teenagers from the minimum wage?
   a. The training opportunities available to teenagers would improve.
   b. The white-black unemployment differential would increase.
   c. The rate of unemployment for teenagers would decline.
   d. The rate of labor force participation for black teenagers would increase.

6. After correcting for differences in age, education, marital status, language, and regional characteristics, the earnings of women are not as great as those of men. This differential is due in part to
   a. discrimination against women in employment.
   b. work specialization within the family following traditional male-female patterns.

    c. both a and b.

    d. neither a nor b.

7. Which of the following most correctly states the relationship between machinery and the earnings of labor?

    a. Machines tend to reduce the demand for labor, thereby reducing the earnings rate of labor.

    b. Production of machinery creates jobs, thereby increasing the demand for (and wages of) labor.

    c. High productivity per worker-hour is a necessary ingredient for the attainment of high real earnings, and adoption of labor-saving machinery enhances the ability of labor to attain such high productivity.

    d. Output and real earnings can always be increased whenever a machine can be substituted for a function previously performed by labor.

8. A marketing representative for a firm selling equipment to automate car washes would probably be happy to see the minimum wage law

    a. abolished.

    b. changed to exempt teenagers from the law.

    c. extended to cover all car-wash establishments (including weekend operations run by service clubs).

    d. changed so that car-wash establishments would not be covered by the law (but other businesses would be).

9. Economic theory suggests that the standard of living for American workers would rise if

    a. the minimum wage was doubled.

    b. automation was outlawed.

    c. a new law required all wage rates to double.

    d. technological progress continued.

10. If large numbers of young Americans thought the life of a cowhand was great (despite the hardships), we would expect

    a. an increase in the wages of cowhands, to fit the image.

    b. a decrease in the wages of cowhands, since supply would be enlarged.

    c. no impact on wages, which are determined by supply and demand, not romantic notions.

    d. a decrease in the wages of cowhands, since demand would be reduced.

11. "One way to get higher labor productivity is to set higher wages. If bricklayers had to be paid $30 per hour next year, we could trust that virtually every bricklayer *working at that time* would be worth (have a marginal revenue product of) at least $30 per hour." This statement is

    a. true, and everyone would gain because of the higher productivity.

    b. true, although many of the current bricklayers would be unable to find employment at the $30 wage rate.

    c. false, since the marginal productivity of bricklayers could not rise so fast in one year.

    d. false, unless very rapid technological change occurred.

12. The effects of job discrimination in a given time period are

    a. not likely to carry over into the future.

    b. likely to carry over into the future, since human capital formation is often influenced.

    c. measured without consideration of past experience or discrimination.

    d. strictly dependent on employer actions at the time, not on what came earlier in the worker's career.

13. If customers are racist but employers are not, then employment discrimination will be

    a. less profitable than nondiscrimination.

    b. more profitable than nondiscrimination.

c. equally profitable as nondiscrimination.

d. easier to eliminate than if employers were racist but customers were not.

THE ECONOMIC WAY OF THINKING—DISCUSSION QUESTIONS

1. Suppose that a new invention halves the cost of making automobiles.
   a. What will happen to output in the auto industry?
   b. What will happen to auto industry employment if demand for automobiles is elastic? Inelastic?
   c. What will happen to output and employment elsewhere in the economy if the auto demand is elastic? Inelastic?
   d. Is it more likely for the new invention to make auto industry employment rise the short run and fall in the long run or fall in the short run and rise in the long run? Explain.

2. What are the major determinants of the elasticity of demand for a specific category (example, physicists, craftsmen) of labor? Explain. Be specific. How does time affect the elasticity of demand for labor?

3. Substantial differences, sometimes up to 150 percent, in wage rates for essentially the same kind of labor (for example, semiskilled labor) prevail between different industries even in the same locality.
   a. What are some of the causes of interindustry wage differentials? List an industry that illustrates each cause.
   b. Which kinds of industries are likely to be at the top of the wage scale? At the bottom?

4. Two components of U.S. antidiscrimination laws are (1) "equal pay for equal work" and (2) "equal opportunity."
   a. Which type of discrimination (wage rate or employment restriction) is addressed by each component? Explain.
   b. If employers practice racial discrimination, do you think "equal pay for equal work" alone would promote or discourage "equal opportunity" for employment?
   c. What are the pros and cons of actual hiring quotas as a method for eliminating employment discrimination?

5. If you owned a firm, how would you expect the wages and racial composition of your employees to compare with your competitors' employees if
   a. firms in general practice employment discrimination, but you don't.
   b. firms in general do not practice employment discrimination, but you do.
   Explain both answers.

6. A recent issue of importance has been that of illegal immigration from one country to another. Analyze the impact of such illegal immigration on (a) the immigrants, (b) the new employers of the immigrants, (c) workers who remained in the home country of the immigrants, and (d) workers in the country to which the immigrants came. Given this analysis, attempt to develop a solution for the issue of illegal immigration.

7. The following statement was made by John Kendrick of George Washington University:

I might point out that investment is a smaller portion of gross national product in the United States than in most other industrialized countries. And I believe this is one reason that we have a slower rate of advance in productivity than most other advanced nations.

Assuming that Kendrick's data are correct, do you agree with his conclusion? Why or why not?

CURRENT DEBATES IN ECONOMICS

Debate Number Two: Should We Adopt a Comparable Worth Program?

Yes, We Should Adopt a Comparable Worth Program:

Fair Pay
By Jodie T. Allen

[Reprinted with permission from *The Washington Post*, February 13, 1985.]

Quiz: Who wrote the following? "Comparable worth is an extension of women's demand for equal pay for equal work, an idea that is both reasonable and fair as a way of correcting the undeniable, historic wage discrimination against women."

Answer: the editors of *Business Week* magazine.

That's right. The quotation comes not from the annual report of the Radical Feminist League to Disrupt the American Economy, but from an editorial in a recent issue of a distinguished business journal. They recognize that "comparable worth"—the misnomer that generally refers to the idea that employers should not pay low wages for certain jobs just because they are typically held by women—is an idea that should not be dismissed by ridicule or misrepresentation.

Economists predict that, as skills of working women increase, the pay gap between men and women will narrow to "only" 25 percent by the end of the century. Part of the larger discrepancy is accounted for by differences in training, work experience, responsibility and, perhaps, such intangibles as "drive" and the distractions of family responsibilities. But there is no serious dispute that many employers pay less for jobs in which women are concentrated than those in which men predominate.

Women for centuries were crowded into a few occupations. It would have been remarkable if employers had *not* taken advantage of that fact by paying them less than their skills and responsibilities would have commanded in an open marketplace. Vestiges of this discrimination still exist. How else to explain the fact that New York City pays its police dispatchers (mostly black women) several thousand dollars less than it pays its predominantly white male fire dispatchers—to cite one current but far from isolated example?

Using similar examples, women have been pressing employers in wage negotiations (such as those recently concluded at Yale University) and in court suits alleging illegal discrimination (such as the successful suit brought against the State of Washington). The comparable pay practices being sought would not, as administration spokesmen and other pooh-poohers of the idea claim, require that ballet dancers be paid as much as football players, or nurses as much as lab technicians. Nor would the changes being asked of individual employers require the creation of another ghastly federal bureaucracy charged with assigning worth and wages to every worker.

In fact, as a recent report sponsored by 23 House Republicans pointed out, Title VII of the Civil Rights Act, as interpreted by the Supreme Court in the state of Washington case, already prohibits employers from adopting pay-setting schemes that discriminate between men and women in similar though not identical jobs. These Republican legislators did not find that the drive for comparable pay presaged the decline and fall of the free-enterprise system. Instead, they called on employers to eliminate bias from their pay practices and on federal agencies to speed up investigation of discriminatory practices.

Ending sex discrimination in wage-setting would not prohibit employers from setting pay scales that were different from those of other employers or from responding to skill shortages in male-dominated jobs. But fair pay would require that individual employers review their formal or informal job classification practices and ask themselves, for example, whether the differences in what they pay secretaries (who are in short supply) and truckdrivers (who are currently in great surplus) are really the result of impartial market forces.

In fact, most wages are not determined by the free interplay of supply and demand in a fluid market. Convention, monopoly power, unionization and employer preferences have had far more to do with the wages paid in many occupations. The relatively high pay for surgeons compared with other doctors for example, has been traced to the surgeons' dominance in fee setting arrangements when Blue Shield insurance was invented in the 1930s. The relatively low pay for nurses and secretaries has been charged to collusive practices among employers in some areas.

Like earlier legally enforced changes in the labor market—minimum wage, child-labor, health and safety, fair labor standards and equal-pay laws—reviewing comparable pay would be inconvenient and, in some cases, costly to employers. But forward-looking private and public employers—such as the editors of *Business Week* and the 23 House Republicans—are recognizing that inexplicable differences in pay for jobs requiring comparable skills are not only hard to justify but very likely to result in costly litigation.

By moving voluntarily to straighten out its pay practices, the state of Minnesota, for example, avoided both prolonged litigation and a costly settlement. By willfully ignoring repeated findings by independent job reviewers, the state of Washington ended up owing—deservedly—a costly back-pay award. Moreover, contrary to predictions of opponents, Minnesota's new pay practices seem to have encouraged women to move into traditionally male jobs—a trend that will ultimately help in narrowing the gap between male and female earnings.

The importance of pay equity is easy to exaggerate on both sides. While egregious pay discrimination because of gen-

Against 'Comparable Worth'
By Morris B. Abram

Both houses of Congress and a number of courts are grappling with the question of whether wages should be fixed on the basis of equal pay for work of comparable value to the employer—a proposed remedy for lower pay received by women. One can already see developing many complications and dangers built into the concept of "comparable worth."

These proposals would tie us up in a tangle of definitions that would reduce options for women and ultimately be a detriment to all of society. Comparable worth proposals do not attempt to equalize the wages of men and women doing the same job but to arbitrarily equate jobs that have entirely different market values.

What is the actual situation with regard to women's wages in this country? During the last Presidential campaign, Geraldine A. Ferraro frequently repeated that women are "paid 59 cents on the dollar for the same work as a man," implying a wage gap of 41 percent. This misleading statistic has been the basis for much well-meaning support of the proposals now before us.

But the 59 percent wage scale, with a 41 percent gap, comes from statistics for 1977; by 1983, that 41 percent gap had narrowed to 36 percent. This figure declines to 28 percent when the number of hours worked by women and men is taken into account, and then to 14 percent when other factors, including schooling and work experience, are considered.

The 14 percent gap, the real starting point for discussions of comparable worth, has not been adequately explained. Of course, part of it may be attributable to discrimination, but the Equal Pay Act of 1963 and the Civil Rights Act of 1964 already prohibit such practices. An alternative explanation could be that women may be willing to accept lower paying jobs that permit them to spend more time with their families.

More meaningful insights can be drawn from statistics of particular groups of employees. Among men and women between the ages of 20 and 24, for instance, the wage gap is only 10 percent. And for single men and women who have never been married, the gap is almost nonexistent—2.4 percent to 4 percent.

One of the dangers of comparable worth is that it would create a new claim by certain advocacy groups on the right to legislate economic equality. These groups would have us adopt a system of permanent wage and salary controls, first in Federal employment and inevitably in private business. Under their plan, wages and salaries would be decreed by "experts" and bureaucrats and deviations from their edicts would generate lawsuits in which the employer would bear the burden of proof that discrimination did not exist.

What's more, gender-based legislation is only the start. A bill introduced last July in the House brought race and ethnic qualifications into the wage formula as well. The latest proposals are likely to become a mechanism to give leverage to any subgroup of employees seeking a raise.

How would women fare in the proposed brave new world of comparable worth? Women would suffer a decline in the standard of living as does everyone in society when wages are inflated artificially. To maintain their previous standard, more women than at present would find work a necessity rather than an option. Even women in occupations targeted for wage raises would not benefit. For example, if secretarial wages were mandated to rise to a certain level, one could expect more businesses to opt for automation. The result would be fewer jobs for women and further narrowing of their options.

The attempt to write comparable worth into Federal laws marks a reversal of the civil rights revolution. Comparable worth moves from the assertion of civil and political equality, which we all support, to economic and social equality, which many of us do not support.

Guaranteed economic and social equality have never been part of the heritage of a free country because they ultimately impinge on freedom, by making government the arbiter of the rewards of human effort. This raises the old question of whether government should be dependent on the people or people on government.

Holding a Debate

Many students will enjoy participating in a debate on this topic either in class or in an informal study group. After completing both readings and possibly doing some additional research (for example, in your textbook), get three to four volunteers for each side of the debate, choose a moderator if your instructor is not available, and devote about a half an hour to opening statements, rebuttals, and summaries.

Discussion

1. What exactly *is* comparable worth? Pick two occupations you know fairly well and describe how a comparable worth program would work in those occupations. Is it possible to be in favor of equal pay for equal work and still be against a comparable worth program? How?

2. Having read the Allen article, note that one of the hardest problems to solve when implementing a comparable worth program is choosing the jobs that have equivalent "worth." In particular, some jobs that are similar in terms of skills required have differences in terms of working conditions (such as more flexible hours). Are such jobs comparable or not? Explain.

3. Having read the Abram article, note that there is an unexplained gap of at least 14 percent between the earnings of male and female workers. How then could he be against legislation that would get rid of this discriminatory difference?

CHAPTER FOURTEEN

CAPITAL, INTEREST, AND PROFIT

TRUE OR FALSE

T   F

☐ ☐   1. We must divert resources from the production of current consumption in order to expand the availability of capital goods.

☐ ☐   2. The net present value of a payment to be received one year from now can be expressed as the ratio of the amount of money to be received divided by the interest rate.

☐ ☐   3. Suppose that an investor hears that the supply of loanable funds has just increased but that inflation (and expected inflation) has not. This news might encourage her to borrow to buy a machine that she previously had thought was too expensive.

☐ ☐   4. Agricultural price support programs don't always work perfectly, but they are unquestionably effective at increasing farmers' incomes.

☐ ☐   5. The net present value of a payment to be received a year in the future can be expressed as the receipts one year from now divided by one plus the interest rate.

☐ ☐   6. A higher rate of time preference implies a higher interest rate.

☐ ☐   7. If a governmental price control and acreage allotment program increases the price of raw tobacco above the market equilibrium level, the price of land with an acreage allotment to grow tobacco will rise.

☐ ☐   8. The real rate of interest rises when the rate of inflation accelerates.

☐ ☐   9. Risk usually influences the interest rate agreed to by business decision-makers.

☐ ☐   10. The interest rate charged by a lender has three components: the inflationary premium, the risk premium, and the pure nominal interest rate component.

☐ ☐   11. Changes in a corporation's stock price happen too slowly to give corporate officers much feedback on how market investors evaluate their investment decisions.

☐ ☐   12. Entrepreneurial decision-making usually involves choosing under conditions of uncertainty.

PROBLEMS AND PROJECTS

You will need to use the net present values in Exhibit 3 of the text to work various problems in this chapter.

1. Suppose that you have $1000. Broker A offers an opportunity that should pay $2000 after six years. After considering the expected rate of inflation and the risk involved, you determine that a 12 percent discount rate is appropriate. Broker B offers a different opportunity that will pay $1000 in five years and another $1000 in ten years. Since it is safer, an 8 percent discount rate is appropriate.
   a. What is the net present value to you, today, of broker A's option? Broker B's option?
   b. Suppose you learn that broker B's option is a bit more risky, and it, too should be evaluated with a 12 percent discount rate. Now what is it worth today?
   c. Having evaluated both options at 12 percent, you are advised that an extra 2 percent should be allowed as an annual inflation factor. If 12 percent was the initial appropriate rate (and the money payoff and timing remain the same), what interest rate is appropriate now that the expected rate of inflation has risen by 2 percent?

2. The owner of a small forest in Florida is raising trees as a cash crop. A forester friend mentions that certain silvicultural practices, costing $334 now, will yield an extra 10,000 board feet of timber when the forest is harvested in 30 years. Harvesting and other costs will not change significantly. What price of timber per board foot would be required for the silvicultural practices to be worthwhile if the appropriate discount rate is 12 percent?

3. Reconstruct Exhibit 4 of the text by using $14,000 per year as the expected income, and 12 percent as the discount rate. What is the net present value? (*Hint:* Be sure to round the discounted value to three digits, as the text does, for your answers to check exactly.)

4. It was noted in the text that the present value of an equal payment received or paid each year forever is:

   Present value = payment / interest rate.

   In fact, this formula can be used to approximate present value whenever the payments last for a fairly long time. Try the following examples to see how well this simple formula works as an approximation.
   a. Recently, Life Cereal held a "Life Cereal Lifetime Allowance Sweepstakes." Each grand prize winner was promised $1000 per year for life. At an interest rate of 8 percent, what would be the approximate present value of the grand prize? (If you expect to live for another 50 years, the true present value is $12,234.)
   b. A few years ago households across the country received a letter from Ed McMahon (of the Johnny Carson show) urging them to enter the American Family Publishers sweepstakes which offered America's "first TEN MILLION DOLLAR prize!" The winner of the prize was promised $333,333 per year for 30 years. At 7 percent interest, what is the approximate present value of this stream of receipts? (The true present value is $4,136,329.)
   c. Suppose you or your parents borrow $150,000 to buy a new home. If the interest rate is 10 percent, what is the approximate size of the mortgage payments each year? (*Hint:* Rearrange the terms of the formula. Assuming annual payments, the actual payment size for a 30-year mortgage would be $15,912 per year.)

5. You have an opportunity to attend a six-month course in computer programming. The course meets every afternoon and would require that you work at your present job only half-time, in the mornings. Your employer has agreed to your half-time absence, but you must accept only half-time pay for the duration of the course, which would reduce your take-home pay by $1250 per month. You have personal savings which would comfortably cover the $6000 cost of the course itself. In discussions with your present employer, you have decided that if you acquire the skills offered by the course it will raise your take-home pay by $2000 per year for the next ten years until you retire. If the appropriate discount rate is 8 percent, should you make this investment in your "human capital"?

6. The table in Exhibit 1 is available to help you answer the questions below. The middle column is similar to Exhibit 14-3 of the text. The right-hand column gives the total present value of $100 received each year rather than at one time.

EXHIBIT 1

Interest rate: 10 percent

Present value of $100 received

Year (t)	at the end of year t	each year for t year(s)
1	$90.91	$ 90.91
2	82.64	173.55
3	75.13	248.68
4	68.30	316.98
5	62.09	379.08
6	56.45	435.53
7	51.32	486.84
8	46.65	533.49
9	42.41	575.90
10	38.55	614.46

a. According to the figures in the middle column, what is the total present value of $100 received at the end of one year, another $100 received after two years, and a final $100 received after three years? How does this compare to the value listed in the right-hand column for $t = 3$?

b. Suppose you decide to rent an apartment for 7 years. Further suppose that the owner offers to let you use an old refrigerator for free and promises to keep the refrigerator repaired for all 7 years. You also have the option of buying a new energy efficient refrigerator (with a 7-year free maintenance agreement) for $700. The new refrigerator will reduce your electric bill by $150 per year and will have a market value of $100 after 7 years. With an interest rate of 10 percent, which option should you choose?

LEARNING THE MECHANICS—MULTIPLE CHOICE

1. The development and construction of machines that enhance our ability to produce goods and services in the future require
   a. the owners of these capital assets to borrow.
   b. the owners of these capital assets to reduce the growth rate of their consumption.
   c. that current consumption be sacrificed.
   d. that future consumption be sacrificed.

2. If the rate of time preference increased, we would expect
   a. the interest rate to fall.
   b. more capital investment.
   c. less capital investment.
   d. more *future* consumption.

3. A higher rate of inflation mainly tends to
   a. raise the real rate of interest.
   b. reduce the real rate of interest.
   c. raise the money rate of interest.
   d. lower the money rate of interest.

4. The net present value of $100, delivered one year from now, would
   a. rise, if inflation rose.
   b. fall, if the money rate of interest fell.
   c. rise, if the money rate of interest rose.
   d. fall, if the money rate of interest rose.

5. If the interest rate were 6 percent, the net present value of $100 to be received one year from now would be
   a. $94.34.
   b. $93.04.
   c. $100.00.
   d. $106.00.

6. The pure interest yield, a component of the cost of an investment project
   a. is positively related to the risk of undertaking the project.
   b. is negatively related to the risk of undertaking the project.
   c. is unaffected by the riskiness of the project.
   d. is irrelevant to whether the project will be undertaken.

7. The net present value of $100 received one year from now will
   a. increase with the interest rate.
   b. be greater than $100 as long as the interest rate is positive.
   c. be greater than the net present value of $100 to be received two years from now.
   d. be unaffected by the money rate of interest.

8. Use statements I and II to answer this question. (I) Discounting procedures apply to decisions to invest in physical capital, but are not relevant to human capital investment decisions. (II) Nonmonetary considerations are usually more important in human capital investment decisions than in nonhuman capital investment decisions.
   a. I is true, II is false.
   b. I is false, II is true.
   c. Both I and II are true.
   d. Both I and II are false.

9. Pure interest is the payment to
   a. an investor bearing little or no risk.
   b. business entrepreneurs.
   c. owners of capital items.
   d. people who clip coupons, but contribute nothing to production.

Questions 10–12 refer to the following information:

You manage a local widget factory and have to decide whether or not to buy a new improved widget machine. The machine will last for one year and then turn to dust. The machine will produce 100 widgets. The factory currently earns economic profit at a rate of 12%, the real interest rate is 4%, the inflation rate (and expected inflation rate) is 3% and the riskiness of the investment is evaluated at 2%. Your expectation is that each widget produced will sell for $100.00. (For simplicity, assume you sell all of them at the end of the year.)

10. The nominal rate of interest on a totally secure loan would be
    a. 9%.
    b. 7%.
    c. 6%.
    d. 4%.

11. The most you would be willing to pay for the machine is
    a. $9345.
    b. $9174.
    c. $8928.
    d. $5263.

12. Now assume that the nominal rate of interest is 10% and that the price of the machine is $9,000. In order for you to invest in the machine you would have to expect that the price of widgets would be at least
    a. $100.80.
    b. $100.00.
    c. $99.00.
    d. $97.20.

THE ECONOMIC WAY OF THINKING—MULTIPLE CHOICE

1. If an era of new inventions began next year, with many and new promising investment opportunities suddenly appearing, we would expect
   a. a lower interest rate as many people saved more.
   b. a higher interest rate as the demand for loanable funds increased, along with investment.
   c. more investment, but no change in the interest rate.
   d. a higher interest rate with no change in investment.

2. In an economy without money, an interest rate
   a. would be meaningless.
   b. could not exist.
   c. would simply be the price of earlier availability.
   d. would always be zero.

3. For an individual, the rate of time preference
   a. indicates irrational decisions.
   b. is greater whenever inflation is greater.
   c. is a subjective valuation.
   d. could never be negative, whatever the circumstances.

4. Economic analysis indicates that if usury laws held the interest rate below the equilibrium level
   a. saving would increase.
   b. borrowers would demand less from the loanable funds market.
   c. anyone who wanted to borrow would be happy with the lower interest rate.
   d. funds must be rationed to borrowers by some means other than price (the interest rate).

5. If inflation increased during a year, the dollar price of existing corporate bonds would
   a. rise because during times of inflation it takes more dollars to buy an asset.
   b. rise because the bond is really a loan, and loans rise in value with inflation.
   c. fall because each bond promises a fixed return, which falls in value as the price level rises.
   d. fall because the risk element (the likelihood of not receiving payment) is roughly proportional to inflation.

6. In the West, many people dream of being cattle ranchers, even if it means a low income. On the other hand, few if any people seem to dream of raising hogs or sheep. Thus, if we examined the financial records of ranchers raising cattle, we would expect to find that (relative to hog and sheep ranches)
   a. cattle ranches would show a higher rate of return.
   b. cattle ranches would show a lower rate of return.
   c. there would be no difference in the rates of return.
   d. the preference for cattle ranching would have no effect on the financial rate of return.

7. We would expect most risky investment ventures to be financed by owners rather than by bankers lending money because
   a. bankers are always cautious.
   b. bankers want interest payments, not profits.
   c. with a bank loan, the bank might lose all it puts in, but can never get more than the agreed-upon principal and interest.
   d. most entrepreneurs think bank interest rates are too high.

8. Theresa spends $1000 on General Motors stock and $1000 on General Motors bonds. However, inflation develops unexpectedly, and prices rise steadily at a rate 5 percent faster than what was previously anticipated. GM product prices rise with inflation, and its sales are unaffected. Theresa will probably find that the
   a. real value of her bonds rises, whereas the real value of her stocks falls.
   b. real values of her bonds and stocks fall equally.
   c. real values of her bonds and stocks rise equally.
   d. real value of her bonds falls *relative* to the real value of her stocks.

9. A company that mines coal on federally owned land is about to be told by the federal government that, beginning in five years, it must abandon the mine it expected to operate for another 20 years. This will mean a reduction in accounting profits beginning in five years. If the announcement of this ruling was made tomorrow, the price of the firm's stock would
   a. fall in about five years, just before the reduction in accounting profits was to begin.
   b. fall gradually, as the reduction in the firm's accounting profit drew near.
   c. fall immediately by the full amount of the discounted value of the decrease in future profit.
   d. fall immediately, since some investors would panic irrationally, whereas smart investors would put the same value on the stock as before, up to the time of the decline in accounting profit.

10. Use statements I and II when answering this question. (I) When the government restricts the number of acres that farmers can utilize to raise a crop such as wheat, the supply of the product will decline, making it possible for farmers to receive a higher price for the product. (II) If a price support and acre restriction program increases the price of a farm product, persons purchasing farm land with an acreage allotment for that product will be able to make a higher rate of return on their investment than would be true in the absence of the government program.
    a. I is true, II is false.
    b. I is false, II is true.
    c. Both I and II are true.
    d. Both I and II are false.

11. Which of these are the major sources of economic profit?
    a. Uncertainty, entrepreneurial alertness, and barriers to entry
    b. Competition, perfect information, and elasticity of market demand
    c. Size of firm, economies of scale, and freedom from unionism
    d. Externalities, inflation, and size of firm

12. The value of farmland is approximately equal to the present value of the expected future receipts from farming the land, net of other expenses. Which of the following would most likely raise the price of farmland?
    a. Higher interest rates
    b. Higher government price supports for farm products
    c. Higher fertilizer prices
    d. Higher value of the dollar compared to foreign currencies

13. Which of the following would reduce the net present value of your college education?
    a. Higher interest rates
    b. Earlier retirement age
    c. Higher wages for high school graduates
    d. All of the above

THE ECONOMIC WAY OF THINKING—DISCUSSION QUESTIONS

1. Assume that Congress is debating two plans to increase the profitability of wildcat oil-drilling firms. Those in Congress agree that more profits in drilling would lead to more drilling. Plan A would give a tax break on current drilling activities, so that profits on current drilling operations would rise by $10 billion—providing that much extra capital for future investment. Plan B would give tax breaks on *future* discoveries. The tax breaks derived from plan B would be worth $3.4 billion per year for the next three years to the same wildcat drillers. Which plan is likely to generate more oil production? (*Hint:* Remember the effects of marginal price changes and the discount rate.)

2. U.S. government bonds are considered risk-free in the sense that there is a negligible chance of default.
    a. What uncertainty is still involved in purchasing government bonds?
    b. How can you earn a profit from the purchase and resale of government bonds? How can you suffer a loss?

3. a. What are the components of the money interest rate? The real interest rate?
    b. Are risk premiums efficient since the result is that different borrowers pay different interest rates? Explain.
    c. From the self-interested viewpoint of a future generation responsible for interest payments, it is beneficial to use a positive, market-clearing interest rate for rationing loanable funds among competing investment opportunities? Why or why not?

4. If you were going to lend someone money, would the following events cause you to increase, decrease, or leave unchanged the nominal interest rate you were thinking of asking for?
    a. You hear a news report that causes you to increase the inflation rate you expect to exist over the life of the loan.
    b. You discover documents that cause you to think that there is a reasonable chance that the loan might not be completely repaid. (Assume that you still want to loan the money.)
    c. You read in the newspaper that most major banks have lowered the interest rate they charge their prime customers.

5. "When a firm's total costs are less than its sales, the firm has increased the value of the resources it has used. Such firms will be rewarded with profits. In contrast, losses indicate that the resources used to produce a good were more valuable than the good that was produced. Profits are evidence of the wise utilization of resources, whereas losses are indicative of waste and inefficiency." Is this statement always true, never true, or sometimes true? Explain your answer.

PERSPECTIVES IN ECONOMICS

State's Lottery 'Millionaires' Will be Somewhat Less Than
by Lee Dembart

[From the *Los Angeles Times*, August 16, 1985. Reprinted with permission.]

When the California lottery gets into full swing this fall, it will offer jackpots of $1 million, $2 million and $3 million. The lucky winners, therefore, will be "millionaires," according to common parlance.

Not so fast. There's a rub. "All million-dollar prizes will be awarded as annuities over a 20-year period," said an article in The Times. In other words, if you win, say, a million dollars, the Lottery Commission won't hand you a check for a million. It will pay you $50,000 now and promise to pay another $50,000 a year for 19 more years, for a total of $1 million.

Now, $50,000 a year for 20 years is not worth a million dollars by a long shot. In fact, according to Bill Seaton, spokesman for the Lottery Commission, if you win "a million dollars" in the lottery, what they actually will give you is not a million dollars but an annuity worth $400,000 today.

A $400,000 annuity winds up being worth $1 million over 20 years because of the miracle of compound interest. Think about it. Money that is put aside today earns interest and is worth more in the future. The longer the future is, the more it grows.

So if the state promises to pay you $50,000 19 years from now—the time of the last payment—how much does it have to put aside in order to have the $50,000 then? It depends, obviously, on the interest rate. The higher the interest rate, the less that has to be set aside initially. If it earns 8%, $11,585.60 will yield $50,000 in 19 years. At a 10% rate, $8,175.40 will grow to $50,000 in 19 years. And at 12%, it would take just $5,805.34 today to produce $50,000 in 2004.

This a well-known bit of straight-forward mathematics, which is called the present-value or present-worth calculation. It involves running the formula for compound interest backward, and it answers the question, "What is the present value of a future sum of money?" Everybody understands that if a person invested $1,000 today at 10% interest it would earn $100 in a year and be worth $1,100. The question can be asked the other way: If you wind up with $1,100 in a year at 10% interest, how much did you start with? The answer is $1,000, and that is called the present value of $1,100 in a year at 10% interest.

Occasionally, when athletes sign multiyear, multimillion-dollar contracts, someone points out an owner who promises to pay $2 million 30 years from now can do it with much less than $2 million today.

How does the lottery figure the present value of $1 million doled out in 20-year installments of $50,000 a year? The same calculation is done for year 19—the last year—can also be done for years 18, 17, 16 and so on to determine the amount of money that must be set aside today to pay the $50,000 in each of the subsequent years. Then those present values can be added to yield the total present value of the state's "million dollar lottery." The following is a table showing the present values of 20 once-a-year payments of $50,000 each, assuming earnings of 12.8%:

Year	Payment	Present value
0	$50,000	$50,000.00
1	50,000	44,326.24
2	50,000	39,296.31
3	50,000	34,837.16
4	50,000	30,884.00
5	50,000	27,379.44
6	50,000	24,272.55
7	50,000	21,518.22
8	50,000	19,076.43
9	50,000	16,911.73
10	50,000	14,992.67
11	50,000	13,291.38
12	50,000	11,783.13
13	50,000	10,446.04
14	50,000	9,260.67
15	50,000	8,209.82
16	50,000	7,278.21
17	50,000	6,452.31
18	50,000	5,720.13
19	50,000	5,071.04

The total present value of $1 million handed out in $50,000 chunks over 20 years is $401,007.48.

So it is at least misleading to call $50,000 a year for 20 years "a million dollars." (This analysis ignores income tax, inflation, life expectancy and all other factors related to the question of which is a better deal, $400,000 today or $50,000 a year for 20 years.)

The Lottery Commission says further that, based on the same calculation, a winner of a $2-million jackpot will receive an $800,000 annuity. In addition, the commission says, the odds against winning a $2-million pot are 25 million to 1.

So a person who buys a $1 ticket will have a 25 million-to-1 shot at winning a "$2-million prize." That sounds like bad odds to begin with. The odds are made worse by the fact that the $2-million prize is really only $800,000.

Discussion

1. After reading the article, a friend says, "It seems to me that a million dollars is a million dollars. As long as you get the money eventually, it's still worth the same amount!" How would you convince your friend that it matters quite a bit when you get the money? Be specific.

2. The present values in the article were calculated assuming earnings of 12.8%, but this might seem a bit high. Use Exhibit 14-3 of the text to calculate the present value of $50,000 a year for twenty years if the interest rate (earnings) were only 6 percent a year. Does the total go up or down? Why?

3. How ethical is it of the State of California to advertise a $2 million dollar prize when it knows the actual value is less than half of that? What could be done to change the lottery (or at least its advertising) to make the truth obvious? Is making such changes worth the trouble? (After all, gambling is illegal in California anyway!)

MICROCROSS

By Cindy Kelly and Debbie Shay

[Reprinted with permission from *The Margin*, Fall 1991, p. 82.]

Across

1. Tax imposed on importation of a good.
6. A good for which demand increases if income increases, other things constant.
7. Results when quantity supplied is greater than quantity demanded.
8. Costs that do not vary with output.
9. The additional cost of one more unit of output.
12. The exchange value of a commodity.
13. Ratio of the change in total revenue to the change in quantity.
14. Monopoly profit per unit in Figure 1.
16. Type of good for which consumption is nonrival and exclusion prohibitively difficult.
19. Market with only two sellers.
20. One sector in the circular flow.
21. What 20 across seeks to maximize.
22. Workers organization.
23. What chicken is to beef.

Down

2. Return to a good or service with a vertical supply curve.
3. Machines, tools, and factories are examples of this.
4. What one more worker contributes to a firm's total revenue.
5. Schedule that relates quantity of a good producers are willing to provide to the price of the good.
7. The fundamental problem in economics.
10. What tires are to cars.
11. If price falls below P in Figure 2 the firm will _____.
15. What economists assume decision-makers do.
17. Goods and services purchased from foreign countries.
18. Competition with many sellers and buyers, homogeneous product, full information and no barriers to entry and exit.

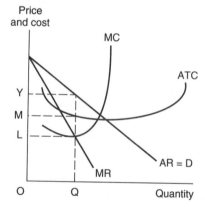

Figure 14–1

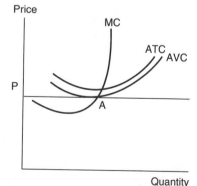

Figure 14–2

CHAPTER FIFTEEN

LABOR UNIONS
AND COLLECTIVE BARGAINING

TRUE OR FALSE

T F

☐ ☐ 1. Union membership as a percentage of the labor force has steadily increased since 1960.

☐ ☐ 2. The share of national income going to labor has increased steadily as more and more workers have joined unions.

☐ ☐ 3. A union shop labor contract requires all workers to join a union after a specified length of employment.

☐ ☐ 4. Right-to-work laws require all union-management contracts to contain a union shop provision.

☐ ☐ 5. Unions have played a central role in the development of contractual or formal rules and procedures that govern promotions, raises, layoffs, terminations, and other aspects of the relationship between employers and employees.

☐ ☐ 6. Failure to organize all of the firms in an industry does not greatly limit the ability of a union to attain large wage gains from the individual firms of the industry that are unionized.

☐ ☐ 7. The amount of work time lost because of strikes has steadily increased since World War II.

☐ ☐ 8. Strikes involving public employees and community services often result in inconvenience and reductions in output in other sectors of the economy.

☐ ☐ 9. The greater the ability of management to substitute machines and nonunion labor for union labor, the weaker the bargaining power of a union.

☐ ☐ 10. A monopsony is to a monopoly as a seller is to a buyer.

☐ ☐ 11. The evidence from other countries indicates that unions raise the wages of workers, including nonunion workers.

PROBLEMS AND PROJECTS

EXHIBIT 1

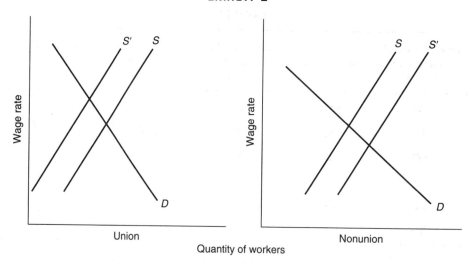

1. "The problem with unions is that they bring higher wage rates for workers and thus force all employers to raise wages in order to compete in the labor market." Refute this statement by explaining the phenomenon described by the supply-and-demand conditions in Exhibit 1.

EXHIBIT 2

Quantity of labor demanded	Wage rate	Quantity of labor supplied
100	$10	1000
300	9	900
500	8	800
700	7	700
900	6	600

2. Exhibit 2 is a demand-and-supply schedule for the competitive engineering labor market. Suppose that you are the president of the American Machines Corporation, and you must hire a group of engineers for your firm.
   a. What wage rate will you offer the hired engineers?
   b. Assume the UEU, the United Engineers Union, is formed, reducing the quantity supplied of engineers at every wage rate by 300 because of increased qualifications in this discipline. What will be the new wage rate?
   c. What effect will the union have on employment and total incomes of the unionized engineers?
   d. Calculate the elasticity of demand for engineers between these two equilibrium points.

3. International Manufacturing, Incorporated (IMI) is a monopsonistic employer of labor. Exhibit 3 shows the quantity of labor IMI demands at each wage and the supply curve that IMI faces in its hiring of labor.

EXHIBIT 3

Labor demanded (hundreds of hours)	Hourly wage (dollars)	Labor supplied (hundreds of hours)	Total labor cost (dollars)	Marginal labor cost (dollars)
450	$16	100	$1600	$20
400	18	200	3600	_____
350	20	300	_____	_____
300	22	400	_____	_____
250	24	500	_____	_____
200	26	600	_____	

a. Fill in the missing information in the table.
b. On a piece of graph paper plot IMI's labor demand curve, labor supply curve, and marginal labor cost curve. (Be sure to plot values for marginal labor cost at the appropriate *midpoints* of the quantities.)
c. What quantity of labor will IMI hire? What wage will it pay?
d. Suppose that IMI workers form a union and establish a wage floor of $22 per hour. Will this new (and higher) wage result in more or less employment at IMI? Exactly how many hours of labor will IMI employ at this minimum wage?

4. It is difficult to know exactly what income goal unions try to achieve. Suppose a hotel clerks' union faces the following demand and supply situation in Exhibit 4:

EXHIBIT 4

The market is initially in a competitive equilibrium.

For each of the following union goals, determine the wage level the union will bargain for and the resulting number of workers hired. Record your answers in the table that follows the list of goals:

Goals

a. Maximize employment.
b. Get the highest wage that at least half of the membership will approve. (Workers with the greatest seniority will retain their jobs.)
c. Maximize the total wage bill paid by hotel owners.
d. Maximize union members' "profits" (the excess of total wages over worker opportunity cost).

Goal	Wage	Number of workers hired (thousands)
a.	_____	_____
b.	_____	_____
c.	_____	_____
d.	_____	_____

5. According to the text, unions can raise wages three ways:
   (1) supply restrictions
   (2) bargaining power (resulting in a wage floor above the equilibrium level)
   (3) increase in the demand for union workers

For each of the following union strategies, list the number given above for the type of effect the strategy illustrates, and indicate whether employment in the unionized industry rises (+) or falls (−) as a result. The first case is completed as an example.

Type of effect	Change in employment	Union strategy
3	+	a. In a practice called featherbedding, railroad unions require that all trains carry firemen, even though modern locomotives pose little fire danger.
___	___	b. The American Medical Association restricts accreditation of medical schools.
___	___	c. Garment workers run an ad campaign with the jingle, "Look for the union label."
___	___	d. Unions commonly bargain for wage increases indexed to inflation plus a negotiated premium.
___	___	e. Auto workers lobby for domestic content legislation stipulating that at least 90 percent of each car sold in the U.S. be constructed from U.S.-made parts.
___	___	f. To become Certified Public Accountants, candidates must pass an industry-administered exam that over three-fourths of all applicants fail.

LEARNING THE MECHANICS—MULTIPLE CHOICE

1. Which of the following factors will substantially *improve* the ability of a union to raise the wages of its workers?
   a. A tax increase on firms that employ the union labor
   b. An inelastic demand for the product produced by union labor
   c. A reduction in tariffs on the type of products the union workers produce
   d. Passage of a right-to-work law in the state where the union operates

2. Wages of unionized workers are usually estimated to be how much higher than they would have been under nonunion conditions?
   a. 90–110 percent
   b. 50–70 percent
   c. 12–16 percent
   d. 40–45 percent

3. A monopsony is
   a. another word for monopoly.
   b. the existence of a single buyer in a market.
   c. the existence of several sellers in a market.
   d. the existence of a single seller in a market.

4. If a craft union was able to reduce the supply of workers into the craft, it would most likely *not*
   a. increase wages.
   b. reduce employment.
   c. increase the wages of all workers in the economy.
   d. increase wages without the need for hard bargaining.

5. Unions are not likely to obtain large wage increases for their workers when
   a. the demand for the product is inelastic.
   b. the supply of substitute inputs is highly inelastic.
   c. the demand for the product the workers produce is elastic, and machines can easily be substituted for labor.
   d. the demand for the product is rapidly increasing.

6. "Marginal factor cost is to a monopsonist as marginal revenue is to a monopolist." Which of the following is true?
   a. The quotation is inherently incorrect.
   b. The quotation is basically correct.
   c. The quotation is partially correct, but the comparison should be to marginal revenue for a perfectly competitive firm.
   d. The quotation is partially correct, but the comparison should be to average revenue for a monopolist.

7. Use statements I and II to answer this question. (I) During the past 20 years, the number of worker-hours of work time lost as a result of strikes has been less than three-tenths of 1 percent of the total—far less than the work time lost due to absenteeism. (II) A strike often imposes substantial costs on secondary parties (wholesalers, consumers, and other manufacturers, for example) who are not involved in the labor-management collective bargaining.
   a. I is true, II is false.
   b. I is false, II is true.
   c. Both I and II are true.
   d. Both I and II are false.

8. A union shop provision means that a worker
   a. cannot be employed until he has joined the union.
   b. must agree when he is hired never to join a union.
   c. must join the union within a specified length of time after he is hired.
   d. has the freedom to join the union at any time, should he wish to do so.

9. The data on the distribution of income among individuals and families in the United States
   a. indicate that the power of labor unions is the major determinant of income inequality.
   b. indicate that unions have no impact on the incomes of members.
   c. indicate that substantial inequality in annual income emanates from differences in education, age, hours worked, and family size.
   d. indicate that differences in annual income emanating from ownership of capital assets are the major source of economic inequality.

10. In winning concessions from employers, a labor union has as its most important tool
    a. the strike.
    b. the lockout.
    c. monopsony power.
    d. the injunction.

Questions 11–13 are based on the following material:

"Rap Rapture," a small cloth manufacturer, can sell all the cloth it can produce at $1.00 per yard on the national cloth market. In the local market for cloth laborers (their only factor of production), they are a monopsonist. Their production and cost schedules for various numbers of workers hired are:

Number of workers	Wage ($/hour)	Total cloth produced (yards/hour)
1	3.00	10
2	3.50	20
3	4.00	29
4	4.50	37
5	5.00	44
6	5.50	50
7	6.00	55

11. Given the above information, Rap Rapture will hire
    a. 2 workers.
    b. 3 workers.
    c. 5 workers.
    d. 6 workers.

12. The firm's profits (per hour) are
    a. $44.00.
    b. $25.00.
    c. $19.00.
    d. $17.00.

13. The cloth workers organize, and the company accepts a minimum wage of $6.00 per hour. As a result, the firm now hires
    a. 3 workers.
    b. 4 workers.
    c. 6 workers.
    d. 7 workers.

THE ECONOMIC WAY OF THINKING—MULTIPLE CHOICE

1. As the baseball season approaches, the likelihood of a player strike would
   a. give neither party much incentive to bargain seriously.
   b. give only management incentive to bargain seriously.
   c. give only players incentive to bargain seriously.
   d. give both players and management incentive to bargain seriously.

2. Suppose that during a ten-year period the number of coal miners declined from 400,000 to 300,000. The hourly wages of the mine workers doubled during this same period because of the strength of the United Mine Workers. Which of the following set of economic factors is most consistent with the wage and employment data of the mining industry?
   a. The supply of miners was highly inelastic, and therefore a small reduction in the demand for mining labor led to a small reduction in employment.
   b. Even though the demand for mining labor was inelastic, as wages increased, the number of miners employed declined significantly.
   c. While the supply of miners was increasing, the demand was increasing more rapidly, leading to higher wages.
   d. The demand for mining labor was elastic, and the supply of miners was reduced, leading to higher wages.

3. Over the last four decades, the share of national income going to labor, including self-employed workers, has
   a. remained nearly constant at slightly more than 80 percent of national income.
   b. fluctuated between 50 and 75 percent of total national income.
   c. increased, as union members became a larger percent of the total work force.
   d. decreased from nearly 75 percent to its current level, approximately 50 percent of national income.

4. The empirical evidence strongly suggests that unions have increased
   a. wages of industrial workers more than those of craft employees.
   b. the share of national income going to labor by 25 percent.
   c. the average wage of union members, but have had little impact on the share of income going to labor.
   d. the wages of most union members by at least 35 percent.

5. Regarding union strength, the "importance of being unimportant" refers to
   a. a lack of political clout on the part of the union.
   b. the union's having organized only a small share of workers in its trade.
   c. the union's wage bill being small, compared to the costs the management would incur if operations were shut down because of a strike.
   d. the union leadership's desire to avoid headlines.

6. As a result of union strength, nonunion workers might suffer if
   a. inflation were an indirect result of the attempts of macro planners to offset cutbacks in employment caused by union wage increases.
   b. supply restrictions in unionized areas increased the supply of workers in nonunion markets, causing nonunion wage rates to decline.
   c. union wage increases in competitive industries were passed on to consumers in the form of higher prices.
   d. All of the above are likely to harm nonunion workers.

7. In which case below are both union strategies listed likely to have similar effects on wages and employment?
   a. Supply restriction and demand increase
   b. Bargaining power in a monopsony situation and supply restriction
   c. Bargaining power in a monopsony situation and demand increase
   d. None of the above

8. Because the demand for broadly defined product line (automobiles, for example) is less elastic than the demand for a more narrow product category (Fords, for example), a union will be better able to raise wages without large unemployment effects when
   a. it has organized an entire industry, rather than only one firm.
   b. it organizes only a few firms in each industry.
   c. it bargains with all firms in a narrow product line, but ignores the rest of the industry.
   d. only a small part of the industry that makes the broadly defined product is unionized.

9. By raising wages, unions typically have
   a. increased total productivity, which must rise proportionally with the wage rate.
   b. encouraged employers to find a substitute for the union labor.
   c. raised the wages of nonunion workers.
   d. caused much of the inflation experience in the United States.

10. Some advocates of unions argue that higher union wages induce greater work effort, so both employees *and* employers end up better off. Which of the following indicates an inconsistency with this line of reasoning?
    a. Employers would not pay higher wages even if higher wages increased work effort and labor productivity.
    b. Employers would not resist higher wages if they were more than offset by productivity increases.
    c. Unions are unable to raise the wages of their members.
    d. Nonunion workers have higher productivity than union workers.

11. The addition of a player's union to the originally monopsonistic baseball industry is likely to
    a. decrease the number of players hired.
    b. increase the average wage of the players.
    c. decrease the average wage of the players but allow more players to be hired.
    d. have little impact on the average wage of the players but allow more players to be hired.

12. According to recent figures, the percentage of nonfarm-working time lost due to strikes is the lowest it has been in the last forty years. This decrease can be attributed in part to the fact that
    a. union membership as a proportion of nonfarm employment has been increasing at only approximately 1% a year.
    b. unions have increased the wages of all workers, both union and nonunion, higher than they would have been otherwise, so strikes are less necessary.
    c. both a and b.
    d. neither a nor b.

THE ECONOMIC WAY OF THINKING — DISCUSSION QUESTIONS

1. Consider the following contrasting opinions about strikes:

   Opinion 1: "The right to strike is a basic right of all workers. Without strikes, unions would be powerless against industrial interests when bargaining for the employee."

   Opinion 2: "The threat of a strike is a form of economic blackmail. The right to strike grants unions the power to collect bribes for not interfering with what is actually a perfectly legitimate economic function—the productive process."

   a. Are workers "powerless against industrial interests" without strikes? Why or why not?
   b. Are strikes "economic blackmail"? Are they more painful for employers than employees? Why or why not?
   c. On balance, which opinion do you find more persuasive? Explain.

2. "The wages of union workers are higher than the wages of nonunion workers." Which of the following can we conclude from this observation? Explain your decision in each case.
   a. Unions raise the wage rates of union members.
   b. Unions are effective in organizing low-wage workers.
   c. Higher union wages put upward pressure on the wages of all employees.

3. For each pair of situations below, decide which condition is more conducive to the ability of unions to raise the wages of their members. Explain your reasoning in each case.
   a. A union shop versus an open shop.
   b. A union in an oligopoly industry versus a union in a competitive industry.
   c. An industry in which each firm has its own union versus an industry with a single union for all the industry employees.
   d. A union whose workers produce an internationally traded good versus a union whose workers produce a good protected from international competition.
   e. A union in the public sector versus a union in the private sector.

4. Business decision-makers can sometimes argue that they cannot make a profit because of the excessive wage demands of unions. Suppose that a strong union in a highly competitive industry obtains for its members a 15 percent increase in wages.
   a. Will the higher wage rates reduce the industry's rate of profit in the short run? In the long run?
   b. Who will actually shoulder the burden of the higher wage rates?

5. "Every union knows that an airline is more vulnerable to strikes than most other businesses. Airlines have high fixed costs regardless of whether their planes are flying. They can neither stockpile seats during a strike nor sell from inventory afterward. Strike losses cannot be recovered. The strong impulse is to avoid a strike, even if that means settling on an unsatisfactory basis." [From an airline newsletter.]

   a. Do you think the airline industry is particularly vulnerable to union demands? Why or why not?

   b. If the airlines are vulnerable, who would pay for an "unsatisfactory" labor settlement in the short run? In the long run? Explain.

   c. Many economists have concluded that, in the absence of regulation, barriers to entry are pretty low in the airline industry. How does this affect your answer to part a?

   d. Do you think unions would favor or oppose a return to government regulation of airlines? Why or why not?

CHAPTER SIXTEEN

INEQUALITY, INCOME MOBILITY, AND THE BATTLE AGAINST POVERTY

TRUE OR FALSE

T F

□ □ 1. Differences in hours worked are an important source of income inequality among households in the United States.

□ □ 2. Official poverty figures indicate that more than 11 percent of U.S. families lived in poverty in 1992.

□ □ 3. The wealthiest 5 percent of all income recipients in the United States receive approximately 40 percent of all income.

□ □ 4. Income is distributed more unequally in the United States than in most other countries in the world.

□ □ 5. In general, income is distributed more equally in Sweden than in the United States.

□ □ 6. One way to help the social security system solve its future financial problems would be to decrease the normal eligibility age from 65 to 62.

□ □ 7. Households headed by females are overrepresented among the poor.

□ □ 8. Of all children born to parents in the top fifth of the income distribution, more than three-fourths maintain that high-income status.

□ □ 9. U.S. income inequality remained relatively unchanged from 1950 through 1970 but income inequality increased somewhat during the 1970s and 1980s.

□ □ 10. Official poverty figures fail to recognize transfers in kind.

PROBLEMS AND PROJECTS

1. Susan Smith is an orthodontist. Jane Jones is a part-time clerk in a small store, where she earns $3.50 per hour. Jane would like Dr. Smith to straighten the teeth of Brenda Jones, Jane's daughter. Jane is willing to work an extra part-time job (at the same pay) to meet this expense, even though it is not a medical necessity. Dr. Smith would be willing to take on this extra work if she were paid $700.

   a. In the absence of taxes, how many hours does Jane have to work in order to pay for her daughter's treatment?

   b. If Dr. Smith was in the 50 percent tax bracket, and Jane received transfer payments (for example, food stamps, housing subsidies, AFDC) that put her in the 65 percent *implicit* tax bracket, how many hours must Jane work to enable Dr. Smith to earn the same $700 in exchange for the treatment? (*Hint:* Hours × $3.50 × 0.35 × 0.5 = $700.)

   c. If Dr. Smith paid no taxes, but Jane was in the 65 percent implicit tax bracket, how many hours must Jane work to earn the $700?

   d. If Dr. Smith paid 70 percent of her income in taxes, and Jane paid none at all, how many hours would Jane have to work for Dr. Smith to take home $700?

   e. Considering your answer to part d, would you say that high taxes on productive, highly paid people hurt low-income people?

   f. Considering your answer to part c, would you say that taxes on productive lower-paid people hurt higher-income recipients?

   g. Would Jane (and Brenda) Jones be better off without the transfer program that puts Jane in the implicit 65 percent tax bracket? Why?

2. Suppose that the government passed a negative income tax that involved a $4000 government subsidy to a family of four if zero income was earned. Assume a 50 percent marginal tax rate on earned income; that is, for every $1000 earned, the subsidy is reduced by 50 percent of the $1000. Using this NIT plan, fill in the columns labeled government subsidy and total income in Exhibit 1. Do you think this is a good plan for achieving a more equal income distribution? Why or why not?

EXHIBIT 1

Earned income	Government subsidy	Total income
$ 0	$4000	_____
2000	_____	_____
3000	_____	_____
4000	_____	_____
5000	_____	_____
6000	_____	_____
7000	_____	_____
8000	_____	_____

3. Robert Reckman is currently unemployed and qualifies for unemployment compensation of $138.00 per week. He has been offered a new job paying $200.00 per week, subject to income taxes of 33 percent and social security taxes of 7 percent.
   a. From society's point of view, is it desirable that Reckman accept the job? Why?
   b. Is it to Reckman's financial advantage to accept the job? Why?
   c. Calculate Reckman's marginal tax rate (including both explicit and implicit taxes) if he accepted the job.
   d. If Reckman's unemployment benefits had been subject to an income tax of 20 percent, would it have been in his financial interest to accept the job? Why?

4. The more income mobility there is, the less serious the poverty problem.
   a. The income mobility information from Exhibit 16-5 of the text is summarized below:

	Family Income Position, 1984		
Family Income Position, 1980	*Top 20%*	*Middle 60%*	*Bottom 20%*
Top 20%	62%	36%	2%
Middle 60%	12%	77%	11%
Bottom 20%	1%	34%	65%

   Which occurs more frequently, falling from the top, or rising from the bottom?
   b. Consider the country of Static discussed in the text. Complete the table below to reflect the complete absence of income mobility in Static:

	Family Income Position, 1984		
Family Income Position, 1980	*Top 20%*	*Middle 60%*	*Bottom 20%*
Top 20%	_____	_____	_____
Middle 60%	_____	_____	_____
Bottom 20%	_____	_____	_____

   c. Now consider the country of Dynamic discussed in the text. Complete the table below to reflect perfect income mobility:

	Family Income Position, 1984		
Family Income Position, 1980	*Top 20%*	*Middle 60%*	*Bottom 20%*
Top 20%	_____	_____	_____
Middle 60%	_____	_____	_____
Bottom 20%	_____	_____	_____

5. A handy way to compare income distributions is to rank each country's households from poor to rich (usually by quintile), and compute a running total of the percentage of the country's households and their percentage share of total household income. The following information can be used for these comparisons.

a. Before we can use the information, we must convert it slightly. To do so, fill in the missing information below (the first two cases are completed as examples):

	Percentage Share of Household Income Received by:		
Country Line 1: Line 2:	Lowest 20% Lowest 20%	Middle 60% Lower 80%	Top 20% All 100%
(1) Perfect Equality	20.0% 20.0%	60.0% 80.0%	20.0% 100.0%
(2) Brazil	2.4 2.4	35.0 36.4	62.6 100.0
(3) Japan	8.7	53.8	37.5
(4) United States	4.6	50.8	44.6
(5) Sweden	7.4	50.9	41.7

b. The diagram in Exhibit 2 plots the cumulative household and household income information from the table above. The result is called a Lorenz Curve. The Lorenz Curve for Brazil has already been plotted. Plot the Lorenz Curves for Perfect Equality, Japan, and the United States.

EXHIBIT 2

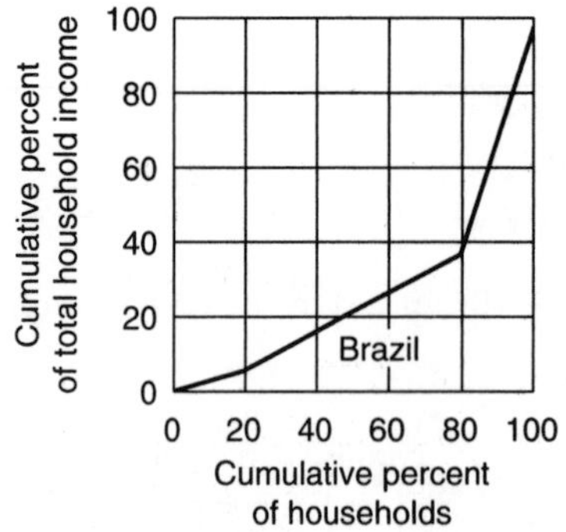

c. Plot the Lorenz Curve for Sweden. Is Sweden's income distribution more or less equal than Brazil's? Than Japan's? Why is it difficult to compare the income distributions of Sweden and the United States?

LEARNING THE MECHANICS—MULTIPLE CHOICE

1. As of 1992, the poorest 20 percent of all U.S. families received what percentage of the total income?
   a. Approximately 2 percent
   b. Approximately 4 percent
   c. Between 11 and 12 percent
   d. Between 18 and 20 percent

2. The distribution of income in which of the following countries is more equal than that of the United States?
   a. Malaysia
   b. Japan
   c. Brazil
   d. Mexico

3. Under the negative income tax concept, an additional dollar of earnings would cause the disposable income of
   a. a high-income taxpayer to increase by an additional dollar.
   b. a low-income recipient to increase by more than a dollar.
   c. a low-income recipient to increase, but by less than a dollar.
   d. a high-income taxpayer to decrease by some positive tax, and that of a low-income recipient to remain unchanged.

4. From 1976 to 1989, the percentage of poor families that were headed by an elderly person
   a. fell steadily.
   b. rose steadily.
   c. remained virtually unchanged.
   d. fell steadily until President Reagan took office.

5. In the last 20 years or so, it appears that family incomes have
   a. become less equal.
   b. become more equal.
   c. maintained the same level of inequality.
   d. declined substantially.

6. Compared to high-income families, low-income families tend to have
   a. fewer workers.
   b. more workers.
   c. fewer youthful or retired members.
   d. about the same level of education.

7. Which of the following is false about data on the inequality of annual family (or household) incomes?
   a. The degree of inequality is reduced when transfers and taxes are considered.
   b. The inequality in annual income data actually understates the degree of inequality in lifetime income.
   c. Differences in age and family characteristics contribute to the degree of inequality.
   d. The difference between the after-tax and transfer income per hour worked between high- and low-income recipients is much smaller than the difference in annual income.

8. The official definition of poverty in the United States does not account for
   a. social security income.
   b. cash income transfers.
   c. income earned by workers other than the head of a household.
   d. in-kind transfers.

9. The negative income tax, a scheme that would have the Internal Revenue Service pay money directly to individuals with low incomes, is closely identified with
   a. Milton Friedman.
   b. Adam Smith.
   c. Arthur Okun.
   d. Alan Blinder.

10. By the year 2025, when some of you may be retiring, it is estimated that the number of workers per social security beneficiary will be
    a. ten.
    b. five.
    c. four.
    d. two.

11. Which of the following contributed to the increase in income inequality in the U.S. over the last two decades?
    a. Poor people have become more and more lazy.
    b. The proportion of dual-parent, single-earner families has increased during the last two decades.
    c. As marginal tax rates were reduced during the 1980s, the observed incomes of high-income Americans increased sharply.
    d. Earnings differentials between skilled and less-skilled workers have decreased during the last two decades.

THE ECONOMIC WAY OF THINKING—MULTIPLE CHOICE

1. In a market system, each individual chooses how to employ his or her own resources. One who chooses not to employ his or her resources is held responsible by
   a. the high prices of goods.
   b. laws against vagrancy.
   c. welfare case workers.
   d. the opportunity cost of leisure.

2. (I) High implicit marginal tax rates reduce the incentive of the poor to earn. (II) The transfer program unwittingly encourages activities that lead to poverty.
   a. Both I and II are true.
   b. Both I and II are false.
   c. I is true, II is false.
   d. II is true, I is false.

3. With a few exceptions, it is generally true in most countries that the share of income going to the wealthiest people is greater in
   a. more developed countries.
   b. less developed countries.
   c. countries with a homogeneous population.
   d. industrialized countries.

4. Even if lifetime incomes were equal, there still might be substantial inequality in annual income data because
   a. wage rates might differ substantially.
   b. some might have inherited their wealth.
   c. some might have retired, while others are prime-age earners.
   d. educational levels might differ substantially.

5. The poverty threshold income level is calculated and adjusted in such a way that, for a given family, it would rise 10 percent in one year if
   a. the family's income rose 10 percent.
   b. the family's income fell 10 percent.
   c. the price of all consumer items rose 10 percent.
   d. national income rose 10 percent.

6. Of all poverty families, approximately one-half are headed by
   a. a female.
   b. a female who does not work.
   c. a male who does not work.
   d. a male working full time.

7. Placing a dollar value on in-kind transfers to the poor is problematic because
   a. no market price is available for many of the items.
   b. the taxpayer cost of the items is usually unrelated to their market price.
   c. the market price of many of the items is a poor measure of actual production cost.
   d. the value of the items to the poor is often less than the market price of the items.

8. The advantages of a negative income tax system include which of the following?
   a. Some of the degradation and despair associated with our current transfer system would be avoided.
   b. The costs of our redistribution system would almost surely fall.
   c. An individual would never have an implicit marginal tax rate greater than 100%.
   d. All of the above.

9. (I) In 1989, almost 70 percent of all poor people were white. (II) In 1989, blacks were overrepresented in the poverty population.
   a. Both I and II are true.
   b. I is true, II is false.
   c. I is false, II is true.
   d. Both I and II are false.

10. (I) Our tax transfer system frequently adds thousands of dollars to the income of the poor families, in the form of cash as well as in-kind transfers. (II) A poor family receiving welfare payments and in-kind benefits will generally be able to take home a larger share of a $1000-per-year increase in its earnings than would a family earning $20,000 per year and receiving no transfers.
   a. I and II are true.
   b. I is true, II is false.
   c. I is false, II is true.
   d. I and II are false.

11. Imagine two cities, Engelgrad and Legreeville, that have identical average annual incomes. In the city of Engelgrad, the poorest families one year almost always end up as the richest families the next year and become middle-income families the year after that. In the city of Legreeville, however, poor remain poor and rich remain rich. Which of the following is true about the two cities?
    a. The distribution of income in any given year is more equitable in Engelgrad than it is in Legreeville.
    b. The distribution of income in any given year is more equitable in Legreeville than it is in Engelgrad.
    c. The dynamic distribution of income over time is more equitable in Engelgrad than it is in Legreeville.
    d. The dynamic distribution of income over time is more equitable in Legreeville than it is in Engelgrad.

THE ECONOMIC WAY OF THINKING—DISCUSSION QUESTIONS

1. What happened to income inequality in the United States from the 1950s to the 1990s? What happened to the amount of poverty in the United States from the 1950s to the 1990s? How, if at all, could the level of poverty change without the amount of income inequality changing at the same time?

2. What are some of the problems with annual income data at a given time as a measure of one's economic well-being? Do you think that, across individuals, lifetime earnings are more or less unequal than annual earnings? Explain.

3. What are some of the social costs of having nearly 13 percent of the U.S. population living in poverty? Could the United States eliminate its poverty? If so, how? What would be some of the social costs of your anti-poverty proposal?

4. a. Do you think a free-market economy results in a socially optimal distribution of income? Why or why not?
   b. Economist Milton Friedman has argued that a perfectly equal income distribution would thoroughly undermine our incentives to be productive. Do you agree or disagree?
   c. Friedman was also one of the first advocates of a negative income tax. Do you favor a negative income tax? If so, why? If not, why not? What would you recommend, if anything, to make the income distribution of a free-market economy fairer?

5. Many economists, including Marxists, suggest that people born into low-income families in market economies have little chance to escape their low-income positions, whereas those born to rich parents will remain wealthy. What does the empirical evidence indicate concerning the amount of income mobility that actually exists? Do you think the evidence supports the view that there is in fact little income mobility?

6. How does income distribution in the United States compare with that of other developed nations? Of less developed nations?

7. Do you think the official poverty statistics in the United States are misleading? If so, in what ways? How would you change the way poverty is measured?

8. "All this worry about marginal tax rates is silly. Anyone who thinks a poor person will remain poor just to collect welfare payments has never had to live on those meager payments." Comment.

9. Recent welfare reform (the Family Support Act of 1988) changed welfare regulations with respect to child-support payments, medicaid and child-care benefits, eligibility for AFDC, and work and training requirements. Which of these four changes do you think will do the most good in our battle against poverty? Why? Explain why some economists think at least one of these categories might potentially hurt the people it was intended to help. Why do you think Congress passed this provision?

PERSPECTIVES IN ECONOMICS

Why the "Income Distribution" Is So Misleading
by Mark Lilla

[Reprinted with permission from *The Public Interest*, Fall 1984, pp. 62–67, abridged.]

Among social scientists, the yearly distribution of money income is one of the most frequently used measures of economic and social well-being. Whether expressed graphically (as a bell-shaped curve), in terms of averages (a certain percentage of the population receives less than half of the median income), or in percentiles (people in the top X percent receive over Y percent of national income), this distribution is assumed to tell us a great deal about our social and economic reality.

But what is this reality? Frequently, the income distribution is taken to reflect something about the extent of "relative poverty." Even though, in the United States at least, we have rather complicated needs indices that are official poverty measures, many social scientists (and others) believe that one's relative position in the income distribution will make one feel and act poor, quite apart from objective needs. The income distribution is also taken to be our best indicator of the degree of economic inequality, which may be measured in a rough manner or with more sophisticated calculations such as the "Gini coefficient." Some go so far as to make this straightforward tautology: Economic inequality simply is an unequal distribution of income. Finally, inequality is the belief that income distribution is a matter of basic social justice, which may be measured, or at least approximated, with statistics. Even philosophy professors have come to address the original philosophical question—"What is justice?"—in terms of the social sciences, asking, "What is a just distribution of income?" and, "Is the distribution of income in the U.S.—or the West, or the world—becoming more or less just?"

Yet social scientists who make it their business to study the workings of the economy have understood for some time that the *idea* of "the income distribution" presupposed by these debates is somewhat problematic. To begin, all income that enhances economic well-being is not captured in the official income statistics. Net income, which would factor in government taxes and benefits (both money and in-kind), is undoubtedly a better measure, but is not always easy to calculate. Also missing is the implicit, "nonpecuniary" income produced within the family household; for example, a housewife's work in the home is not included, but if she works outside the home it is—even if she then must hire someone to fill her former jobs of housekeeper or babysitter. (In Third World countries much income is of this implicit kind, rendering official income statistics virtually worthless.) Studies that attempt to determine the value of this implicit income and then compute *real* net income are highly speculative, though they probably do give a "truer" measure of income.

A stickier problem is measuring life-cycle earnings. Since an individual's lifetime earnings typically follow an up-and-down pattern—low while a young adult, highest just before retirement, and then a leveling or reduction—there always will be a "natural level" of income inequality at any one time, if only because of the age distribution. Ideally, one would want to compute each individual's earnings in each year—discounted and adjusted for inflation—and then over an entire lifetime before comparing. Such a research project would be very expensive and difficult, so social scientists either have had to use special samples that make generalization difficult, or they have had to rely on the questionable econometric technique of "controlling" a cross-sectional income distribution for age and assuming that this corrected distribution represents the life-cycle distribution over a very long period. (In truth, no one knows.)

Researchers who specialize in the study of income and poverty fully understand these shortcomings of ordinary income distribution statistics, and usually compute "corrected" figures before studying these issues seriously. Ordinarily, however, these results can only be understood by the econometrically literate and bear an uncertain relation to ordinary conceptions of poverty, equality, and economic justice. The simple, official income distribution is easier to use than the "corrected" measures, so this is what nonspecialists—other social scientists—generally do use. When social research enters the public realm, it is an axiom that, between a simple but misleading statistic and a complicated precise one, the simple one will always survive.

Income Dynamics: The Missing Link But even if we were able to produce a simple, problem-free, fully corrected measure of the distribution of American income, would it tell us what we think it should about the nature of poverty, equality, or justice? The simple answer is no, because the income *distribution* can never reflect anything about income *dynamics.* By dynamics I mean the processes by which individuals and families change their economic fortunes, processes that tell us something different about what their economic positions are at any one time.

To illustrate this distinction, imagine two economies with the same relative distribution of (net, fully corrected) income. Each year, economists studying the two economies take cross-sections of the populations and announce that the distributions are unchanged and identical. But in the first economy, let us say, everyone remains in the same position each year: If someone was in the ninetieth percentile last year, he will be there this year; if he was below the poverty line, there he will remain; and so on. In the second economy, however, everyone changes places each year. Indeed, every three years there is complete turnover in this economy, every family spending one year each in the upper, middle, or lower class; no one is rich for more than one year at a time, and no one is poor for more than one year at a time. Ordinary common sense tells us that our two hypothetical economies have very different poverty problems, have different levels or kinds of inequality, are not equally just. *But in terms of their annual income distributions, they are indistinguishable.*

This seems very strange. But even a moment's reflection on such a simple example makes clear that dynamics of income can be as or more important than its distribution—yet the former is an economic phenomenon about which social scientists know surprisingly little. There are, of course, countless studies of economic and social mobility, most relying on limited or specialized samples—for example, twins reared apart—to understand this fundamental economic process. Together they do not give a clear picture of this process, nor can they offer an economic theory of income dynamics. Real income dynamics among real families are difficult and expensive to measure, and the standard statistical methods for testing the data do not seem to apply. Consequently, the complicated questions of poverty, equality, and economic justice have remained on the Procrustean bed of income distribution.

Dynamic Poverty Take poverty, for example. Even though poverty is clearly more than a question of income, every official or academic definition of poverty in current use depends (explicitly or implicitly) on a fixed notion of the income distribution. Those families of a certain size that fall below a certain income level for a whole year are said, by definition, to be in poverty. Long-term and short-term poverty are to be distinguished as different social problems, but in any particular year they are said to be the same condition. There are ongoing debates inside and outside government over the level at which poverty is to be defined, and different federal and state agencies compute different family budget standards using the local costs of food, housing, clothing, and the like. Defining poverty in this way has notorious problems, among them accounting at the federal level for local price differences, valuing work in the home, including the value of different welfare benefits, and allowing for differences in "life-style."

Still, there are good, practical reasons for using such a fixed poverty standard. It allows government to decide easily how many people deserve benefits and how many people have been served each year; for program advocates, it provides a comprehensible—and, more important, a relatively stable—measure of the job still to be done. But can a fixed standard really tell us what we want to know about what poverty is and how public policy might cope with it? Most research on poverty has clearly shown that the long-term poor and short-term poor face dissimilar problems and opportunities, and that different sorts of programs and incentives may be required for these two subgroups. A simple income distribution cannot tell us the relative sizes of these groups. If a significant proportion of the people poor in 1984 were not poor in 1983, and will not be poor in 1985, then the character of American poverty is radically different from what it would be if there was no turnover in this population. This is not to say that the problem would necessarily be more or less severe; it is simply to recognize that the problem and the programs meant to cope with it would have to be conceived in quite different terms.

Discussion

1. Do you agree with Lilla that an important measure of the fairness of the distribution of income in a society is income mobility as well as the income statistics at any given time? Why or why not?
2. Exhibit 5 in your textbook presents a measure of income mobility from a study of a group of families. Would you say that this group did or did not experience reasonable income mobility? Explain your answer.
3. Philosopher John Rawls makes the case that income inequalities are only justified if they make the worst-off the best off they can be. To best measure Rawls's version of economic justice, should we use a static income distribution or a dynamic income distribution? Do you think Rawls would agree with your opinion?

CHAPTER SEVENTEEN

NATURAL RESOURCE

AND ENVIRONMENTAL ECONOMICS

TRUE OR FALSE

T F

1. The economic way of thinking indicates that, for certain vital resources such as energy, the demand curve will be vertical.

2. According to the economic way of thinking, consumers will adjust more completely to a rise in the price of energy products when more time is allowed for the adjustment.

3. In a study of eight socialist nations, Mikhail Bernstam found that energy efficiency fell as energy costs rose during the 1980s, exactly the opposite of what happened in market economies.

4. The relevant cost to consider when making a decision involving energy or natural resources is opportunity cost, not historical or purchase cost.

5. The fact that some natural resource decisions are irreversible (for example, building a dam and flooding the Grand Canyon) proves that projects involving such resources should be postponed in order to preserve our future options.

6. The energy crisis reflects the fact that the energy needs of consumers are greater than the absolute reserves of crude oil.

7. Proved reserves of petroleum are less than absolute reserves.

8. Private ownership of many environmentally threatened areas is the major threat that we face in attempting to protect the environment.

9. One benefit of private property rights is that they provide incentives for maximizing the long-term value of a resource, even for owners whose personal outlook is short-term.

10. In 1914, the U.S. Bureau of Mines announced that the total supply of crude oil in the United States was about 6 billion barrels, although we now produce that much every 20 months.

PROBLEMS AND PROJECTS

EXHIBIT 1: HYPOTHETICAL CONDITION
OF U.S. GASOLINE MARKET

Price (dollars/ gallon)	Quantity demanded (millions of gallons/day)	Quantity supplied (millions of gallons/day)
1.57	85	112
1.47	90	110
1.38	95	105
1.30	100	100
1.22	105	95
1.15	110	90

1. Assume that Exhibit 1 accurately describes the conditions of the U.S. gasoline market.
   a. What is the market-clearing price?
   b. Considering your answers to the above question, what would be the impact of a 16-cent additional tax per gallon imposed on this market? What would be the new price? The new quantity sold per day?
   c. Is the demand schedule above more likely to be a short-run or a long-run demand schedule, given the demand elasticities for gasoline reported in the text?
   d. Using positive economics, how could you argue that a tax is the most efficient way to bring about a given reduction in quantity demanded? Explain also why such a tax introduces some inefficiency into the market, and show the gains from trade that are eliminated by the tax.

2. For each of the following, decide whether the event described will promote conservation (C) or depletion (D) of petroleum supplies in the United States and in the rest of the world (ROW). The first event is completed as an example:

   U.S.   ROW

   __D__ __C__   a. OPEC raises its petroleum prices to $40 per barrel.
   _____ _____ b. The United States raises gasoline taxes to $.50 per gallon.
   _____ _____ c. The United States imposes a $10 per barrel oil import fee.
   _____ _____ d. Concerns about acid rain result in greater restrictions on coal-burning power plants.
   _____ _____ e. In response to the Exxon Valdez oil spill, stricter safeguards are imposed on the transport of Alaskan crude oil.

3. With some difficulty (and with decreasing success) OPEC has managed during the 1970s and 1980s to coordinate and control the supply decisions of OPEC producers of crude oil. Controlling the supply decisions of its members allowed OPEC to significantly influence the world price of oil. One thing that OPEC could not control, however, was the long-run supply decisions of *non*-OPEC producers of crude petroleum whose products, of course, compete with OPEC's. Producers in countries like the United States, Mexico, and the Soviet Union (among others) were free to adjust their supplies in response to OPEC's pricing policies, and the long-run response of these countries was much greater than the short-run. Though hypothetical, Exhibit 2 is designed to represent these circumstances. It assumes that the quantity of crude oil supplied by non-OPEC producers is determined in the long and short run by the non-OPEC producers according to the supply schedules given in the exhibit. It further assumes that when OPEC sets the price of

crude oil, it sells an amount of oil equal to the difference between the world quantity demanded at that price and the quantity supplied by non-OPEC producers. Finally, we will assume that OPEC can produce oil at a constant cost of $10 per barrel.

EXHIBIT 2

Price (dollars/ barrel)	World quantity demanded	Non-OPEC quantity supplied		OPEC quantity supplied	
		Short run	Long run	Short run	Long run
		(billions of barrels)			
$40	60	60	120	0	0
35	70	55	105	15	0
30	80	50	90	30	0
25	90	45	75	_____	15
20	100	40	60	_____	_____
15	110	35	45	_____	_____
10	120	30	30	_____	_____
5	130	25	15	_____	_____

a. Fill in the missing information for OPEC's quantity supplied in the short run.
b. Suppose that initially the world price of oil is $10 per barrel. What will OPEC's total profits be at this price?
c. Now suppose that OPEC raises the price of oil from $10 to $25 per barrel. In the short run, what will happen to OPEC's profits? What is the short-run elasticity of supply of non-OPEC producers between those two prices? (Use the arc formula to calculate the short-run elasticity.)
d. Now fill in the missing information for OPEC's long-run quantity supplied.
e. In the long run, what will OPEC's profits be at the price of $25 per barrel? How does this compare to their short-run profits at this price? What is the long-run elasticity of supply of non-OPEC producers? Why might it be greater in the long run than in the short run?

4. In Exhibit 3, the left-hand panel depicts a hypothetical demand and supply situation facing OPEC members, and the right-hand panel shows the cost curves for a potential domestic offshore supply of oil. The potential offshore producer is a price taker in the petroleum market.
   a. Suppose OPEC members initially behave as perfect competitors. What will be the price of oil? The quantity supplied by OPEC members? Will the potential offshore supplier enter the market? If so, how much will the offshore supplier produce?
   b. Now suppose OPEC members jointly monopolize the market for petroleum. What will be the price of oil? The quantity supplied by OPEC members? Will the potential offshore supplier enter the market? If so, how much will the offshore supplier produce?
   c. Finally, suppose the OPEC cartel breaks down, and the members again behave as perfect competitors. What will be the price of oil? The quantity supplied by OPEC members? Will the domestic offshore supplier shut down in the short run by "capping its wells"? If not, how much will the offshore supplier produce?

EXHIBIT 3

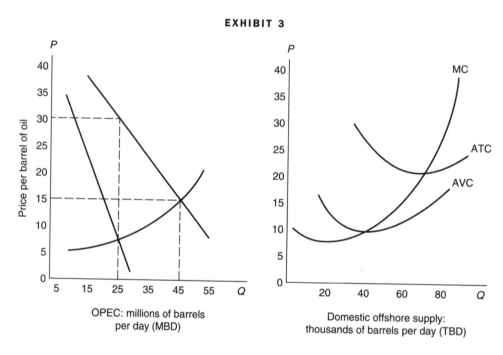

OPEC: millions of barrels per day (MBD)

Domestic offshore supply: thousands of barrels per day (TBD)

LEARNING THE MECHANICS—MULTIPLE CHOICE

1. The mythical view that energy prices do not matter implies that
   a. both supply and demand are horizontal curves.
   b. both supply and demand are vertical curves.
   c. energy supplies will expand more with time.
   d. energy demands will adjust more thoroughly with time.

2. As we move from the short run to the long run in the energy market,
   a. supply tends to become more elastic while demand tends to become more inelastic.
   b. supply tends to become more inelastic while demand tends to become more elastic.
   c. supply and demand both tend to become more elastic.
   d. supply and demand both tend to become more inelastic.

3. Which of the following approaches to values and costs should be used when dealing with natural resources?
   a. Opportunity costs
   b. Marginal values
   c. Both a and b
   d. Neither a nor b

4. Use statements I and II to answer this question. **(I)** The demand for energy products is considerably less elastic in the short run than is true for the long run. **(II)** As the result of the lengthy time period between exploratory activities and the refining of a petroleum product, the supply of petroleum is generally more elastic in the short run than in the long run.
   a. Both I and II are true.
   b. Both I and II are false.
   c. I is true, II is false.
   d. I is false, II is true.

5. Between 1950 and 1980, proved inventories of copper, iron, lead, and aluminum
   a. increased substantially, because new ores had been discovered and the cost of processing lower-grade ores had fallen.
   b. increased slightly, because conservation efforts cut down our use of these ores.
   c. decreased slightly, because new discoveries were swamped by increased usage of these ores.
   d. decreased substantially, because no amount of discoveries or conservation will keep us from running out of nonrenewable resources like these ores.

6. Proved reserves of petroleum are
   a. the only reserves likely to be available in the future.
   b. refined products waiting to be shipped to market.
   c. the oil industry's equivalent to raw material inventories.
   d. the same thing as absolute reserves.

7. Over the last twenty-five years, the amount of metal required per beverage can has
   a. increased slightly.
   b. decreased slightly.
   c. decreased to only one-half of the former amount.
   d. decreased to only one-fifth of the former amount.

8. When the demand for whale oil increased sharply during the mid-1800s, the price of whale oil rose sharply. As a result
   a. many people were unable to afford to light their homes until electricity was developed.
   b. the supply of whale oil increased rapidly, as entrepreneurs developed a new technique for breeding whales.
   c. consumers turned to substitute energy sources, which eventually provided much cheaper heating and lighting than could be supplied with whale oil.
   d. the government imposed rigid price controls and rationed whale oil in order to mitigate the energy crisis.

9. "Doomsday" predictions about the imminent depletion of one or more of our vital natural resources usually are
   a. correct but are not reflected by relative price changes within our market economy.
   b. incorrect because of arithmetic calculation mistakes.
   c. incorrect because they disregard human responses to relative price changes.
   d. incorrect because they disregard the ever-decreasing availability of substitutes for such natural resources.

10. The classic study of Barnett and Morse found that
    a. resource costs have been rising at a rate that implies that within 50 years, we will have impossibly high prices for natural resources.
    b. the ever-increasing availability of substitutes has outrun our ability to use up scarce natural resources.
    c. resource costs have been rising for a long period, but predictions of a coming "doomsday" are unlikely to be correct.
    d. the currently proven reserves of most minerals are becoming perilously low.

11. The demand for energy products is
    a. perfectly inelastic, since energy is needed to produce everything we consume.
    b. quite inelastic in the short run, but considerably more elastic in the long run.
    c. quite elastic in the short run, but considerably more inelastic in the long run.
    d. highly elastic in both the short and long runs.

12. Proved reserves are
    a. the total reserve supply of a resource that will be available for future consumption.
    b. the total reserve supply of a resource that is recoverable, assuming that energy prices and technology continue to increase at current rates.
    c. the total amount of reserves in existence.
    d. the current holdings of verified reserves that we can expect to recover at current energy prices and technology.

THE ECONOMIC WAY OF THINKING—MULTIPLE CHOICE

1. "Our timberlands are being depleted by short-sighted profiteers who are clear-cutting whole forests without planting replacements or even worrying about erosion." The situation described in this statement is a good example of the problems that occur when owners of forestland
   a. maximize profits without regard to environmental impact.
   b. do not maximize long-run profits or are not held accountable for some of the costs of their actions.
   c. worry too much about the environmental impact of their decisions.
   d. use benefit-cost analysis to make decisions.

2. One flaw in the argument that the environment can be helped by private ownership of land and other non-renewable resources is that
   a. since short-run profits are the goal of the private owners, they will ignore the long-run implications of their decisions.
   b. even if long-run profits are the goal of the private owners, they still will ignore the social costs of their decisions.
   c. private owners will only look at superficial business issues when making decisions and have no incentive to investigate future pollution costs or similar problems.
   d. the private owner may attempt to conceal any pollution caused in order to avoid the loss of profits.

3. Opportunity cost is used in determining the most valued use of a resource like land or capital; when deciding how to use natural resources, opportunity cost is
   a. not applicable because natural resources are not replaceable.
   b. just as applicable.
   c. only as applicable in cases where wildlife is not involved.
   d. only applicable in cases where cost-benefit analysis is involved.

4. Cost-benefit analysis sometimes does a poor job of separating the efficient from the inefficient because
   a. assigning a dollar amount to the costs and benefits of a project can be difficult.
   b. an inappropriate rate of interest may be used when calculating the present value of the benefits and costs.
   c. political decision-makers often listen to special interest groups.
   d. all of the above.

Questions 5–8 refer to the following material:

The Chicago Board of Trade recently proposed the opening of the first national market in air-pollution allotments for sulfur dioxide, the prime component of acid rain. Under mechanisms created by the 1990 amendment to the federal Clean Air Act, polluters will be prohibited from emitting sulfur dioxide beyond certain specific allotments (based on their current needs and EPA clean-air goals). Polluters will be free to choose between polluting up to their allotment or investing in cleaner technology and thus have allotments available for sale.

5. This new program probably
   a. won't work because some rich polluters will be able to buy up allotments and keep polluting.
   b. won't work because the EPA is sending a signal that profits are more important than the environment.
   c. will work because some firms will be able to pay for the purchase of sulfur-dioxide reducing technologies through the sale of allotments.
   d. will work because the allotment payments will provide income that the EPA can use to do a better job of enforcing sulfur-dioxide regulations.

6. For the new program to be most effective, the allotment prices should be
   a. set as low as possible, so as to encourage trading.
   b. set as high as possible so as to discourage pollution.
   c. set by the EPA, the agency that best understands the costs involved with sulfur-dioxide pollution.
   d. set by supply and demand, working through the Board of Trade market.

7. As we learned in the text, many economists and other market-oriented environmentalists think that a greater reliance on property rights will help improve the environment. How are these pro-property-rights individuals likely to react to the proposed Board of Trade allotment program?
   a. They are likely to approve, since the allotment proposal is a variant of the property rights proposal.
   b. They are likely to approve, but only because the allotment proposal is better than the current regulations and therefore is "the lesser of two evils."
   c. They are likely to disapprove, because the allotment proposal establishes no property rights.
   d. They are likely to disapprove, because the allotment proposal is likely to encourage firms to act exactly opposite the way they would act under a property rights mechanism.

8. If the Chicago Board of Trade allows the price of sulfur-dioxide pollution allotments to move freely in an open market, we'd expect the price per ton eventually (perhaps after a few years) to
   a. be approximately equal (on average) to the cost of society of one ton of sulfur-dioxide pollution.
   b. be approximately equal (on average) to the expected cost of avoiding one ton of sulfur-dioxide pollution.
   c. be approximately equal (on average) to the expected cost of cleaning up the acid rain caused by one ton of sulfur-dioxide pollution.
   d. randomly fluctuate up and down, having no meaningful average approximate value.

9. Given the past relationship between conservation in the capitalist nations and conservation in socialist nations, the recent move toward market economies of the former Soviet Union and other previously communist nations seems likely to
   a. improve conservation in the newly market-oriented economies immediately.
   b. worsen conservation in the newly market-oriented economies immediately.
   c. improve conservation in the newly market-oriented economies in the long run.
   d. worsen conservation in the newly market-oriented economies in the long run.

10. The irreversibility effect makes decision-making about natural resource preservation especially difficult because
    a. a natural resource, once ruined, is ruined irreversibly.
    b. a delay in taking advantage of an economically sound use of a natural resource can postpone benefits in a way that loses a portion of them irreversibly.
    c. both of the above.
    d. neither of the above.

11. Formerly, the U.S. Army Corps of Engineers used a discount rate of zero when conducting benefit-cost analyses of proposed waterway transportation projects. Since costs tend to precede benefits in these projects, the zero discount rate tended to result in
    a. excessive approval rates for proposed waterway projects.
    b. excessive denial rates of proposed waterway projects.
    c. no impact on the approval rates of proposed waterway projects.
    d. an uncertain impact on the approval rates for proposed waterway projects.

THE ECONOMIC WAY OF THINKING—DISCUSSION QUESTIONS

1. What are some of the instances of price responsiveness cited in the text? Why do you think they might surprise many people? Why should they be less surprising to students of microeconomics? Can you think of some other cases of price responsiveness in resource markets?

2. Diesel fuel can be rationed by price, by waiting in line, or by government allocation. Rank these three rationing methods according to the amount of each of the following activities they generate by diesel fuel users such as trucking firms and farmers: (a) conservation efforts, (b) rent-seeking efforts, and (c) time diverted from output activities. Rank the three rationing methods with regard to their impact on the future supply of diesel fuel.

3. Suppose that the government installed in your family car a monitor that measured the pollutants in the car's exhaust. Further suppose that you received a monthly bill of $1.00 for every pound your car polluted the air. How fair would this be? Would you change the amount of your driving because of it? If you were charged only for those pollutants that were emitted during smog alerts, would you change the times of your driving?

4. What was the whale oil crisis of the early 1800s? What lessons, if any, does it have for us now?

5. What are the social costs of massive substitution of nuclear power for fossil fuel power? What are the social benefits? How should society go about choosing between these alternatives?

6. Suppose that an African nation unfriendly to the United States has a huge oil strike, and sells to anyone except the United States. How will this affect oil supplies reaching the United States? How much could the United States gain by making political concessions to the oil-rich country in order to buy the oil? Use a supply-demand diagram for the world oil market in writing an explanation of why the United States might gain nothing from such concessions, so long as a worldwide market for oil exists.

PERSPECTIVES IN ECONOMICS

Disposable vs. Cloth Diapers
"Which Are Best for the Environment?"
By The Consumers Union

Disposable diapers have come to symbolize all things one throws away heedlessly. Like other disposable products, they take up space in landfills at a time when many landfills are just about full and others are getting there fast.

Far from cutting back on waste, Americans are putting out more—four pounds per person per day, up from less than three pounds 20 years ago, says the U.S. Environmental Protection Agency. As old landfills have closed, few have replaced them, because of rising land costs, stricter standards, and people's reluctance to have a landfill as a neighbor.

The disposable diaper is often seen as the pariah of America's dumps. Myriad books on environmental themes have recommended cloth diapers, and legislators in at least 20 states are considering proposals to tax or ban disposables or otherwise restrict their use.

Actually, though, disposable diapers make up only 1.7 percent, by weight, of the solid waste that is landfilled or burned. (By volume, according to the EPA, they make up about 3.3 percent.) That's the same share that paper bags have. Plenty of materials account for a greater portion: Paper as a whole heads the list, with a 40 to 50 percent share; plastics, metals, and yard waste each account for a sizable part. Still, 1.7 percent is high for a single product used by a relatively small fraction of the populace.

Cloth would be the clear choice for parents concerned about the environment if overstuffed landfills were the planet's only problem. But they're not. When you look at cloth and disposable diapers at every stage of their existence, in what's called a life-cycle analysis, you'll see that each has a variety of environmental drawbacks.

In the beginning, when the cotton for cloth diapers is grown, for example, pesticides are used, water is consumed, and soil can erode. When disposables are made, trees are cut and the wood is turned into pulp through a process that can result in air and water pollution. The plastic parts of the diaper come from petroleum, whose extraction and refining also pollute air and water.

Energy is used in manufacturing both cloth and disposable diapers, and the trucks and cars that transport them to stores and homes use fuel and pollute the air.

At home, when you load the washing machine and dryer to launder cloth diapers, you're using a lot of water and energy. Human wastes from cloth diapers leave the house in wastewater, along with plenty of detergent and bleach. With disposable diapers, wastes usually go to a landfill.

At the end of the line, it's obvious that disposables contribute much more than cloth diapers to solid-waste problems. A child will wear 6000 or so disposable diapers before being toilet-trained, whereas a child wearing cloth will go through about 50 diapers.

Several organizations have already performed this kind of "cradle-to-grave" study on diapers. What have they concluded about environmental effects? That depends on which analysis you look at. In March 1990, Arthur D. Little Inc. released the results of a study commissioned by Proctor & Gamble, which makes disposable diapers. Not surprisingly, the report concluded that disposables were no worse than cloth diapers, environmentally speaking.

Four months later, Franklin Associates Ltd. unveiled a report sponsored by the American Paper Institute. It came to much the same conclusion as the Arthur D. Little study: It didn't flatly recommend either type of diaper.

Last January, the National Association of Diaper Services released a study it had assigned to consultants Lehrburger, Mullen, and Jones. No surprises there, either. It favored cloth.

Comparing these analyses is a bit like comparing strained apples and orange juice. There is no standard method for conducting life-cycle analyses, so each study was free to make its own—often divergent—assumptions. For instance, for the number of diapers a baby uses each day, the Arthur D. Little study assumed 6.4 disposables or 12.1 cloth; Franklin Associates assumed 5.4 disposables or 9.7 cloth; Lehrburger et al. omitted this factor and simply compared the environmental impacts per 1000 changed.

All three studies also oversimplified complex comparisons. How is a consumer to compare a ton of solid waste produced by throwing away disposables with, say, a million gallons of wastewater produced by washing cloth diapers? Which is worse: 10 pounds of nitrogen oxides or 1500 parts per million of hydrocarbons?

The life-cycle analyses are far better at raising questions than they are at providing answers, but one thing is clear: Consumers won't make a big contribution to the health of the environment by choosing one type of diaper over another. They may, however, make a small contribution to the well-being of their region. If you live in an area where the solid-waste problem has become acute, as it has in many parts of the Northeast and Midwest, consider using cloth diapers. If water is at a premium in your town or city, as it is in California and much of the Southwest, disposables might be the better choice for the environment.

Discussion

1. Everyone knows that using disposable diapers causes pollution. How does Consumers Union visualize a circumstance in which disposable diapers are best for the environment?

2. Think about the landfill, energy, and water situations where you live. Given the life-cycle analysis in the article, do you think that disposable diapers or cloth diapers are best for your area? Why?

3. To what other kinds of environmental decisions might life-cycle analysis be applied? Explain how you might go about applying life-cycle analysis to one of those decisions. What information would you need? What value judgements, if any, would you have to make?

CHAPTER EIGHTEEN

PROBLEM AREAS FOR THE MARKET

TRUE OR FALSE

T F

1. Voluntary exchange is proof of expected mutual gain.

2. Private interest and ideal economic efficiency sometimes conflict, even for a smoothly functioning, competitive price system.

3. Poor information on the part of buyers is very seldom a factor in real-world markets.

4. Spillover, or neighborhood, effects are the same thing as externalities.

5. When externalities are present, some parties must be trying to harm others.

6. Social costs include those accruing to consenting *and* secondary parties.

7. Getting accurate information is often difficult for consumers, but sellers offering good values have incentives to provide this information.

8. When external costs are low, markets are unlikely to handle externalities in a socially desirable manner.

9. When large numbers of people are involved, external costs are usually low.

10. Poorly defined property rights increase external costs.

11. Taxing polluters according to the damage they do is administratively simple, but makes no sense economically.

12. When externalities are present, secondary effects are always negative, not positive.

13. Public goods are a special case of spillover benefits to secondary parties.

14. The free-rider problem occurs when an activity benefits people who are not forced to pay for their benefits.

15. An advantage of the zero-price solution to the public goods problem is that extra information is made available about consumer valuation of the goods.

PROBLEMS AND PROJECTS

EXHIBIT 1

Output (per month)	Supply: producer's marginal cost	Demand: consumer's valuation	External cost (for alternative levels of supply)	Marginal social cost
70	65¢	110¢	0¢	65¢
80	70	95	5	75
90	75	85	10	85
100	80	80	15	95
110	90	75	20	_____
120	100	70	30	_____

1. Exhibit 1 presents data on the producer's cost and consumer's valuation of paper pulp, a competitively produced product. Since production of the pulp generates an undesirable odor, the market supply curve does not accurately reflect the marginal social cost. The estimated external costs at alternative output levels are presented in Exhibit 1.

   a. At what price and output would the quantity supplied equal the quantity demanded?

   b. Fill in the marginal social cost data for alternative output levels. How does the marginal social cost compare with the consumer's valuation of paper pulp at the competitive equilibrium price?

   c. What would be the ideal output level, considering the costs that are external to the producer? (*Hint:* Use marginal social cost to determine equilibrium instead of just the producer's marginal cost.)

2. You have just been hired to be on the staff of a member of the U.S. House of Representatives from a coastal state. An electric utility is trying to build a power plant near the mouth of a river in the state and wants the right to use water from the river in its cooling towers. Agricultural interests own the water rights, however, and law forbids their transfer to industrial users. The utility points out that water rights among farmers trade for about $10 per unit, whereas the utility would pay $80. You are told to spend the night writing a short paper briefing the representative on (a) whether or not the private property rights system is working efficiently in this case, (b) the true value of the water in dispute, and (c) the distribution of benefits (who would thank the representative) and costs (who would complain to the representative) if Congress overruled state law and gave the utility the right to bid for the water in this specific case. As you write this short, clear paper, remember the basic principles of economics concerning marginal valuation and the opportunity cost. (Would you analysis differ if the power plant location were 200 miles inland, where much of each farm's irrigation water returned to the river and was reused?)

3. Exhibit 2 shows the actual estimated costs of pollution reduction (measured in percentages) for a beet sugar refining firm and a petroleum refining firm, both of which initially emit identical amounts of pollution.

EXHIBIT 2

Amount of pollution reduction (percent)	Marginal cost of reduction	
	Beet refining	*Petroleum refining*
	(cents/pound)	
10	0.5	3.0
20	0.5	3.0
30	0.5	3.5
40	0.5	4.0
50	1.0	5.0
60	2.0	6.0
70	3.0	14.0
80	4.5	15.0
90	6.0	21.0

Source: Based on data in Allen V. Kneese and Charles Schultze, *Pollution, Prices and Public Policy,* (Washington, D.C.: Brookings Institution, 1975).

a. Suppose the government instituted a maximum emission standard that required each firm to reduce its pollution by 60 percent. What would be the marginal cost of reduction for the beet refiner? For the petroleum refiner?

b. If instead government instituted a pollution tax of 4.5 cents per pound of pollution emitted, by what percent would the beet refiner reduce pollution? The petroleum refiner?

c. Explain briefly why the second approach is more economical (efficient) than the first.

4. Dan Vencill is a likable fellow who hates yardwork, partly because he dislikes the activity and partly because he doesn't mind a somewhat unkempt yard. however, his neighbors all love to work on their yards and are extremely fastidious about them. Exhibit 3 shows Vencill's estimate of his marginal cost of yardwork (per hour) along with his estimate of the marginal value (to him) of his yardwork (per hour). Also shown is Vencill's neighbors' estimate of the value to them of Vencill's work on his yard, a benefit which has nothing to do with Vencill's private decision about how much time to spend working on his yard.

EXHIBIT 3

Quantity of Vencill's yardwork (hours/week)	Vencill's marginal cost of yardwork (dollars/hour)	Vencill's marginal value of yardwork (dollars/hour)	Vencill's neighbors' marginal value of Vencill's yardwork (dollars/hour)	Social marginal value of Vencill's yardwork (dollars/hour)
1	1.00	3.00	18.00	21.00
2	2.00	2.00	16.00	18.00
3	3.00	1.00	13.00	_____
4	4.00	0	10.00	_____
5	5.00	0	8.00	_____
6	6.00	0	6.00	_____
7	7.00	0	4.00	_____

a. Fill in the missing information in the table.
b. Considering only Vencill's benefits and costs of yardwork, how many hours per week will he spend working on his yard?
c. Calculate the *total net* benefit (to Vencill alone) of this many hours per week. How much do Vencill's neighbors benefit from this amount of work?
d. Considering all costs and benefits of Vencill's yardwork, what is the socially ideal (efficient) number of hours for Vencill to work on his yard? How much would Vencill's neighbors benefit if he spent this much time working? What is the total *social* net benefit of this many hours?
e. Suppose Vencill's neighbors told him that if he spent 6 hours per week working on his yard, they would pay him $30.00. Based solely on the information in the exhibit, would Vencill accept this offer? Is the offer an economically sensible one from the neighbors' point of view? Explain.
f. Suggest some reasons why the solution above would probably not work as a general solution to this sort of problem. (*Hint:* Remember the free-rider problem.)

5. In the diagrams in Exhibit 4, the two left-hand panels depict the water pollution attributable to two industries, paper producers and beer producers. The right-hand panel depicts the total water pollution of the two industries and the marginal external damage cost of the water pollution:

EXHIBIT 4

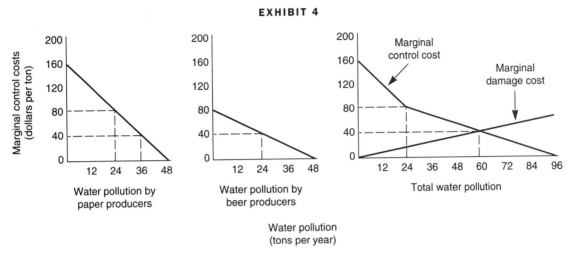

Water pollution by paper producers

Water pollution by beer producers

Total water pollution

Water pollution (tons per year)

a. In the absence of any policy to control water pollution, what is the amount of
   i. water pollution by paper producers? _____
   ii. water pollution by beer producers? _____
   iii. total water pollution? _____
b. What is the socially efficient amount of water pollution? Why isn't a pollution level of zero preferable?
c. Suppose the government mandates that both industries reduce their water pollution 30 tons per year. At the new levels of pollution, what is the marginal pollution control cost for
   i. paper producers? _____
   ii. beer producers? _____
   Why is this inefficient?
d. Suppose instead the government achieves the same pollution reduction by levying an effluent charge. How large should the effluent charge be?
e. With the effluent charge policy, what is the amount of water pollution by
   i. paper producers? _____
   ii. beer producers? _____
f. Comparing the effluent charge to the reduction in part c,
   i. does paper producer pollution rise or fall? _____
   ii. does beer producer pollution rise or fall? _____
   iii. does social efficiency rise or fall? (Why?) _____

LEARNING THE MECHANICS — MULTIPLE CHOICE

1. Production and distribution of which of the following is more likely to impose significant externalities in the absence of government intervention?
   a. Ice cream
   b. Household maid service
   c. Paper pulp
   d. Soap

2. If there are no spillover effects, voluntary exchange results in
   a. expected net gain for each participant.
   b. expected social benefits that exceed the expected social costs.
   c. both a and b.
   d. neither a nor b.

3. The absence of well-defined and enforceable private property rights often
   a. causes people to work together for the common good.
   b. improves society because it avoids the selfish actions of property owners in a capitalist society.
   c. causes difficulties for society due to external costs and public good problems.
   d. brings about efficiency in production by rewarding producers for getting the most highly valued production from the bundle of resources they use and for minimizing the cost of those resource inputs.

4. Which of the following activities is most likely to result in substantial costs that are external to the decision-maker?
   a. Consumption of an ice cream cone
   b. Production of a handcrafted billfold
   c. Consumption of a supersonic air flight from New York to Los Angeles
   d. A firing of a high-powered rifle in the desert lands of Nevada

5. The major distinction between pure private and pure public goods is that
   a. private goods generate external effects, whereas public goods do not.
   b. the government can produce public goods, but not private goods.
   c. public goods must be consumed jointly, since supplying goods to one person simultaneously makes them available to others.
   d. public goods are free, whereas private goods have a cost.

6. When costs are incurred that are external to the decision-maker, a firm is likely to be producing more of a good than is socially desirable
   a. because it is not required to fully consider external costs when its price and output decisions are made.
   b. because the firm will not pay attention to buyers' wishes in such a case.
   c. because the firm is a free rider.
   d. because communal property rights are absent.

7. Producers are more likely to be concerned with customer satisfaction when
   a. they are largely dependent on repeat customers.
   b. it is difficult for the customer to evaluate product quality accurately.
   c. they are dependent on tourism for their sales.
   d. the demand for the products of the producer is inelastic.

8. Even if one assumes a purely competitive market, the pricing mechanism can be (and is) criticized because it
   a. encourages firms to seek profits by neglecting the preferences of consumers.
   b. fails to register fully the benefits and costs resulting from externalities.
   c. encourages workers to unionize because of the low wages that will prevail in a market economy.
   d. fails to provide an incentive for firms to minimize their per unit dollar costs of production.

9. Emission charges increase the cost of
   a. catering to the preferences of repeat customers more than to tourists.
   b. producing pollution-intensive goods.
   c. using production methods that result in less pollution.
   d. using pollution control devices.

10. The Montagnais Indians were
    a. not willing to use any type of private property rights.
    b. successful at using private property rights to preserve buffalo populations.
    c. successful at using private property rights to preserve beaver populations.
    d. a tribe that was nearly responsible for the extinction of the plains buffalo.

11. When property rights to a farm are held by an individual, the individual
    a. has an incentive to see that the resource is put to the use of its highest valuation.
    b. has no incentive to use the resource such that others can benefit.
    c. has no choice but to use the resource wisely.
    d. cannot benefit *personally* when the resource is not used such that society benefits.

12. Which of the following is the least costly way to achieve the efficient output of an easily monitored pollutant?
    a. Ban the pollutant.
    b. Issue marketable discharge permits for the pollutants.
    c. Issue nonmarketable discharge permits for the pollutant.
    d. Rely on unrestricted private markets.

THE ECONOMIC WAY OF THINKING—MULTIPLE CHOICE

1. Fish in the sea are "owned" communally. No individual, group of individuals, or firm has the right to buy, sell, and/or trade the fish of the sea. A leading consequence of this lack of ownership is
    a. monopoly power in commercial fishing because of the ease of restricting entry.
    b. that individual fishermen have almost no incentive to practice conservation.
    c. full economies of scale cannot be attained with respect to the size of individual fishing boats.
    d. that fishermen inevitably earn lower wages than persons in other activities.

2. Even when the market is working with ideal efficiency, some observers object to the income distribution that results (from the free market) because they feel that
    a. the economy is still not producing enough output to keep everyone above the poverty level.
    b. income is not distributed to those who most deserve it.
    c. governmental restrictions, taxes, and subsidies are needed to improve economic efficiency.
    d. most economic arguments for government intervention are based on the idea that the marketplace cannot provide public goods or handle externalities.

3. Courts have consistently held that people ("receptors") have a right to clean air (a property right); therefore, if a polluter begins to foul the air and cause problems for receptors, the receptors can collect all damages proved to be caused by the polluter. Yet, the market system recognizably fails to handle the pollution problem adequately. This is because
    a. receptors have no property rights regarding pollution.
    b. no one knows whether damage truly results from air pollution ("proof" does not exist).
    c. polluters are monopolists.
    d. receptors have property rights, but since it is difficult to *prove* damages, causation, and a specific culprit, *enforcement* of the rights is often very costly.

4. A pure market economy is unlikely to provide a sufficient amount of public good like national defense because
    a. the consumers are poorly informed as to the value of national defense.
    b. it is generally impossible to withhold national defense from a nonpaying customer.
    c. national defense does not yield a benefit to individuals.
    d. private firms will be less efficient than public firms when producing a public good such as national defense.

5. Control of air and water pollution is likely to be an important economic issue in the foreseeable future. Using economic efficiency as our criterion, which of the following general approaches to pollution control would be best?
   a. Reduce the role of economic growth, which is the major cause of pollution.
   b. Prohibit all economic activities that cause pollution.
   c. Use our existing resources to eliminate all damage to our environment that results from pollution.
   d. Eliminate a pollution-causing activity only when the marginal damage costs of the action exceed the marginal social benefits associated with the use of the resource in a manner that leads to pollution.

6. Which of the following activities is most likely to generate a positive externality—an external benefit—that will result in a free-market output level that is less than the socially desirable amount?
   a. The production of crude oil and its by-product, natural gas
   b. Research on a new diet and exercise program that will reduce the likelihood of cancer
   c. The delivery of orange juice by milkmen, reducing the net cost to the consumer
   d. The development and patent of a new automatic clutch designed to improve the efficiency of the automobile.

7. Suppose that on the outskirts of Orlando, Florida, a city of about 100,000 people, an orange grove were bought by the city and turned into Orange Grove Park, where the care, upkeep, and orange consumption will be handled by all city individuals on a volunteer basis, "not for the benefit of one greedy individual." The result of this institutional change, the elimination of *private* property rights, would most likely include
   a. more resources devoted to the orchard's upkeep, since roughly 100,000 people would have a stake in the orchard's production.
   b. many oranges to be picked before optimal ripeness, since for any individual, waiting for those particular oranges to ripen completely might mean only one chance in 100,000 that he or she would be the one to benefit from waiting.
   c. less wasting of oranges from the grove, since every picker would realize the social value of oranges.
   d. more fertilizer being purchased by volunteer individuals and applied at appropriate times.

8. In many countries, cigarettes are sold by a government monopoly. If cigarette smoking generates external costs, then having a monopoly carry out cigarette sales
   a. reduces cigarette consumption below the efficient level.
   b. increases cigarette consumption above the efficient level.
   c. results in the efficient level of cigarette consumption.
   d. could result in too much, too little, or just the right amount of cigarette consumption.

9. Compared to the maximum emission standard method of control, the emission charge method will produce a given reduction in pollution with
   a. a larger impact on the product's social cost, since the polluter pays money in addition to control costs.
   b. a higher social cost, since many firms will continue to pollute.
   c. a lower social cost, since the most economical reductions in pollution will be made first.
   d. a lower social cost, since virtually all pollution will cease if it really costs firms money to pollute.

10. New products provide a classic case of the consumer information problem. However, in some cases consumers partially solve the problem by trusting the "brand name" of the producer of the new product. Since firms spend millions of dollars advertising and maintaining their brand names, the likelihood of a "brand name" firm's intentionally selling a dangerous or shoddy new product is
   a. high, because big firms are always after a quick dollar.
   b. high, because their brand name is a communal property right.
   c. low, because big firms do not make mistakes.
   d. low, because the firm with a brand name has a lot to lose if word spreads about bad consumer experiences.

Questions 11–14 relate to the following material:

Fishermen who use nets to catch tuna also sometimes net dolphins, which, because they are mammals, drown before they can be released. Currently the price and quantity of tuna determined by the market does not take into account the cost to society of killing the dolphins (marginal external cost). Listed below are market demand and supply schedules for tuna as well as the marginal external social costs associated with dolphins killed in the process of catching the tuna. All costs and valuations are listed in terms of dollars per pound of tuna.

Quantity of tuna (thousands)	Consumers' valuation (of tuna)	Marginal private costs (of tuna)	Marginal external costs (of dolphins)
1,000	$3.50	$1.70	$0.90
2,000	3.00	1.80	1.20
3,000	2.50	1.90	1.50
4,000	2.00	2.00	1.80
5,000	1.50	2.10	2.10
6,000	1.00	2.20	2.40
7,000	0.50	2.30	2.70

11. The current price per pound of tuna is
    a. $2.00.
    b. $2.10.
    c. $3.00.
    d. undefined, but somewhere between $1.50 and $2.00.

12. The socially optimal quantity of tuna (in thousands of pounds) is
    a. 2,000.
    b. 3,000.
    c. 4,000.
    d. 5,000.

13. In order to attain the socially optimal equilibrium, the government would have to impose a per-pound tax on suppliers of
    a. $1.00.
    b. $1.20
    c. $1.80
    d. $3.00

14. Of this tax, consumers would end up paying, per pound,
    a. $0.20
    b. $0.65
    c. $1.00
    d. $1.20

THE ECONOMIC WAY OF THINKING—DISCUSSION QUESTIONS

1. The previous group of multiple-choice questions (and some of the Problems and Projects in this chapter) give you hypothetical figures for social costs and social benefits and ask you to make decisions that produce socially optimal results. In the real world, how easy would it be to come up with these social costs and benefits? Where would you start if you were going to try to estimate such numbers?

2. Jones gets a real bargain on 100 acres of land because it is near an airport. He decides to use the land to breed his prize-winning race horses. One year after buying the land, Jones sues the airport because his horses, disrupted by the noise of jet planes, are not breeding.
   a. If you were the judge, how would you decide Jones's case? Why?
   b. Would you have decided any differently if Jones had owned the land before anyone considered building an airport nearby? Why?

3. With a system of emissions charges, some polluters would find it cheaper to pay some emissions charges than to stop polluting entirely, even when the pollution is damaging to the public's health. Does this mean that emissions charges are useless policies? Why or why not?

4. What do you consider to be the main advantages and disadvantages of each of the following anti-pollution policies?
   a. effluent charges
   b. marketable discharge permits
   c. maximum emission standards

   Could any of these policies result in too little pollution, from a social point of view?

5. For each of the following pairs of firms, decide which, if either, has the greater incentive to provide customer satisfaction regarding price and quality control:
   a. A large franchised hamburger stand versus a single stand operation, both located at a busy interstate freeway exit.
   b. A major brand-name whiskey distiller versus a regional distiller with no plans to expand nationwide.

6. "The unregulated private economy will always provide consumers with what they want at the lowest possible cost to society. As long as consumers are willing to pay the cost of an item, the free market will provide it for them." Evaluate this statement. Do you agree? Do you disagree? Explain your reasoning.

7. In general, we have argued that private sector markets will allocate too few resources to public goods like national defense. Do you think the public sector allocates too few, too many, or just the right amount of resources to such goods? What is your evidence? How should we go about determining the socially optimal amount of public goods to produce?

8. A good topic for a group discussion is the economics of pollution. Be sure to discuss
   a. why air and water pollution are problems.
   b. the ideal amount of pollution from society's point of view.
   c. who gains (and loses) from failure to force polluters to pay for the use of valuable resources, such as clean air and water.
   d. alternative strategies for pollution control.

9. Do you think charity is a public good? A pure public good? Why might individuals be more willing to contribute $25 to the local community charity drive if they could be assured that others would do so? How does the raising of money for charitable purposes illustrate the free-rider problem?

CHAPTER NINETEEN

PUBLIC CHOICE: UNDERSTANDING GOVERNMENT AND GOVERNMENT FAILURE

TRUE OR FALSE

T F

1. Market failure enhances the argument for, and likelihood of, government intervention in overcoming particular shortcomings of the market.

2. A politician can be viewed as a political entrepreneur or supplier.

3. Voting, like other decisions, is carried out with imperfect information.

4. Most voters are chiefly concerned with just a few of the many issues decided legislatively.

5. With collective action, an individual can usually be sure that she will not pay for something she does not want.

6. The efficiency of the political process would be enhanced if the primary beneficiaries of government activities were a clearly identified small group of voters.

7. The "public good" quality of antipoverty efforts will, according to economic analysis, encourage collective action for redistribution of income.

8. Government failure strengthens the case for use of the market system.

9. An individual voter has a strong economic incentive to fight special interest legislation with his or her own time and money, because such legislation is costly to all members of society.

10. Passage of special interest legislation is not always inefficient.

11. Voters are more likely to be short-sighted on a complex issue than a simple one.

12. Public sector decision-makers have a strong incentive to be efficient, since most of the people they deal with are their employers.

13. When exercising their voting rights, voters usually must choose among complex bundles of goods, services, and costs.

PROBLEMS AND PROJECTS

EXHIBIT 1

	Actual net dollar benefits (+) or costs (−) for the voter			Political entrepreneur's estimate of the voter's perceived net dollar benefits (+) or costs (−)		
Voter	Proposal A	Proposal B	Proposal C	Proposal A	Proposal B	Proposal C
1	$5	$10	$10	$5	$10	$10
2	5	4	−4	5	4	−4
3	5	3	−2	5	3	−2
4	3	1	−1	3	0	0
5	3	1	−1	3	0	0
6	3	1	−1	3	0	0
7	1	−8	−1	1	−8	0
8	1	−4	−1	1	−4	0
9	−2	−3	−1	−2	−3	0
10	−2	−3	−1	−2	−3	0

1. Exhibit 1 presents data on the actual and perceived benefits of voters resulting from the passage of three different legislative proposals.
   a. Calculate the actual benefit/cost ratio for each of the three proposals.
   b. Which of the three proposals do you think will be favored (opposed) by the political entrepreneur? Why?
   c. Given that proposal B exerts only a small impact on voters 4, 5, and 6, why might it be sensible for them to ignore proposal B?

2. Assume that price supports for dairy products are in the interests of U.S. dairy product producers but not in the interests of U.S. dairy product consumers.
   a. Use the concepts and analysis of this chapter to indicate why dairy farmers might be successful in organizing to persuade Congress to adopt price supports.
   b. Conduct a similar analysis to show why consumers might be unsuccessful in attempting to organize to persuade Congress not to adopt price supports.

3. Match the letters on the right with the numbers on the left.

   ___ (1) Special interest groups

   ___ (2) Externalities

   ___ (3) The free-rider problem

   ___ (4) The rational ignorance effect

   ___ (5) The short-sightedness effect

   a. It explains why the market has trouble allocating public goods efficiently.
   b. It results because information is costly, and voters do not expect their vote to be decisive.
   c. They are a good potential source of campaign contributions for political entrepreneurs.
   d. They strengthen the case for government intervention.
   e. It explains why macropolicy is likely to be excessively expansionary 12–18 months before a major election.

4. Some activities, such as prostitution and the marketing of certain recreational drugs, involve voluntary transactions between buyers and sellers and have therefore been classified as victimless crimes. However, the activities appear to generate external costs by morally offending many nonparticipants. Consider the example of a recreational drug presented in Exhibit 2. (Quantities are in millions of grams, and values are in dollars per gram.):

   a. Complete the last two columns of the table.

EXHIBIT 2

	Users		Nonusers		Society	
Quantity of drug use	Marginal benefit	Marginal cost	Marginal benefit	Marginal cost	Marginal benefit	Marginal cost
10	150	30	0	20	150	50
20	120	30	0	40	_____	_____
30	90	30	0	60	_____	_____
40	60	30	0	80	_____	_____
50	30	30	0	100	_____	_____
60	0	30	0	120	_____	_____

   Suppose that 5 percent of the total adult U.S. population would be users of this drug in an unrestricted market. These several million potential users are widely dispersed and unable to effectively organize for political purposes.

   b. Determine the quantity of drug use that would
      i.   be socially efficient: _____
      ii. occur in an unrestricted private market: _____
      iii. tend to result from the political process: _____
   c. Your text covered what might be called the "tyranny of special interests." Explain why the problem here illustrates a possible "tyranny of the majority."

5. Consider each of the following quotes:

   Following the example set by the ending of Prohibition, we should legalize marijuana, cocaine, and certain other drugs we have failed to control. Excise taxes and punishments could hold drug use to tolerable levels and discourage their use prior to engaging in activities that might harm others. (Gary Becker, economist)

   Drug use is out of control in our society. Making it legal would only reinforce the erroneous perception that drugs such as marijuana and cocaine can be used without consequences. (Lee I. Dogoloff, Executive Director, American Council for Drug Education)

   Assume that you are the vice-president of the United States and have to cast a vote to break a tie in the Senate on the issue of legalization of marijuana and cocaine. In a single paragraph, state your decision, and carefully and clearly support your position. Be sure to address both points of view expressed above.

LEARNING THE MECHANICS—MULTIPLE CHOICE

1. Ideal public sector action can potentially improve economic efficiency
   a. because goods can be provided free by the public sector.
   b. when market inefficiency results because of spillover effects.
   c. if prices can be fixed below the equilibrium level, thereby limiting the power of greedy businesses.
   d. because political decision-makers generally place the public interest above the pursuit of personal gain.

2. With economic efficiency as the criterion, which of the following is the best justification for the government's providing some economic goods and services, rather than relying on the market?
   a. Government provision of goods eliminates misallocation that results from the power of special interest groups.
   b. It is important that political goods and services be provided free of charge.
   c. There is often no way to sell public goods in a private market, because the benefits cannot be limited to persons who pay for them.
   d. It would be unethical and unreasonable to allow private individuals to make a profit by providing education, police protection, and similar services.

3. The political roles of legislators and voters
   a. are analogous to those of producers and consumers in the market.
   b. have no relation to the actions of market participants.
   c. can serve to express collective preferences, but not individual preferences.
   d. are effective for expressing preferences only by voting.

4. In explaining public sector choices, economic theory
   a. is perfectly appropriate, since money prices are used in the public sector in the same way as in the private sector.
   b. is inappropriate, since individuals act in the public interest, not out of self-interest, when doing the public's business.
   c. is useful because individuals, including those who participate in the political process, will respond in a predictable way to changes in personal costs and benefits.
   d. is useful only if political entrepreneurs are highly selfish.

5. In general, voters are concerned
   a. with most issues, since information on most issues is cost free.
   b. with most issues, since each issue will have some impact, however slight, on each citizen.
   c. with the views of a particular political candidate on all issues.
   d. with a few specific issues—those that directly affect them in a substantial way.

6. Which of the following groups is likely to have the greatest influence on legislative collective decision making? (*Hint:* Remember special interest issues.)
   a. Nonunion employees
   b. Consumers
   c. Taxpayers
   d. Business interests and labor unions

7. A characteristic of the public sector is that individuals, in selecting their legislative representatives
   a. have no influence over political decision-makers.
   b. can normally use their voting power on an issue-by-issue basis.
   c. cannot effectively vote for politicians on an issue-by-issue basis, but must accept all the views of a candidate as a package.
   d. can usually find a representative who reflects the individual's views on all significant issues.

8. Governmental allocation will more likely be preferred to market allocation when
   a. consumers are well informed.
   b. the shortsightedness effect dominates.
   c. the rational ignorance effect dominates.
   d. high external costs are associated with market decision-making.

9. Economic theory suggests that it is often rational for a vote-maximizing politician to support special interest groups at the expense of other unorganized, widely dispersed groups (for example, taxpayers or consumers)
   a. when the gains that accrue to the special interest groups are much smaller than the costs imposed on others.
   b. when the non-special interest voter is unconcerned or uninformed, and campaign funds are readily available from the special interest.
   c. if, and only if, government action is socially efficient.
   d. if the government action would reduce the monopoly power of business or labor.

10. General agreement exists that the legitimate economic functions of government include
    a. protection against invasions from a foreign power.
    b. provision of goods that cannot easily be provided through markets.
    c. the maintenance of a framework of rules within which people can interact peacefully with one another.
    d. all of the above.

11. Operational efficiency in the public sector tends to be low because the individual government employee
    a. is usually able, in a dishonest manner, to take home money that would be called profit in the private sector.
    b. is unable to profit directly from the extra care and effort efficiency requires.
    c. is usually not as competent as the private sector employee.
    d. usually is a victim of rent seeking.

THE ECONOMIC WAY OF THINKING—MULTIPLE CHOICE

1. (I) In the public sector, unlike the private sector, personal gain is usually not the stated goal of entrepreneurial decision-makers. (II) In the public sector, as in the private sector, we can expect individuals, including political entrepreneurs to be motivated by self-interest most of the time.
   a. Both I and II are true.
   b. I is true, II is false.
   c. I is false, II is true.
   d. Both I and II are false.

2. Economic theory leads us to expect that the typical voter will be uninformed on many issues because
   a. most issues are so complex that voters will be unable to understand them.
   b. even though information is free, most voters do not care what politicians are doing.
   c. information is costly, and the individual voter casting a well-informed vote can expect negligible personal benefit.
   d. citizen apathy about political matters is inevitable, except when decisions are made by referendum.

3. In a market system, individuals normally pay for what they get. With public sector operation
   a. the individual consumer often does not pay, although someone else must.
   b. the individual often does not pay, nor does anyone else, since production is not for profit.
   c. an individual's tax bill will approximate the value to him or her of government's service.
   d. payment is avoided since costs are irrelevant in the public sector.

4. Economic theory suggests that laws against crimes such as murder, arson, and robbery are
   a. the result of our moral code, even though they promote economic efficiency.
   b. examples of government actions that improve resource allocation by discouraging activities that generate external costs and violate our moral code.
   c. impossible to understand from a strictly economic viewpoint.
   d. examples of government action that stem from the power of special interest groups.

5. Public choice theory suggests that political entrepreneurs will be most likely to favor redistribution of income from
   a. the rich to the poor.
   b. disorganized individuals to well-organized special interest groups.
   c. middle-income taxpayers to both rich and the poor.
   d. well-organized business and labor groups to consumers.

6. According to economic theory, each voter supports the candidate
   a. who offers the greatest number of programs.
   b. who offers to make the greatest aggregate decrease in taxes, other things constant.
   c. who offers the greatest personal gain, with no consideration of effects on others.
   d. who offers the greatest *net* benefits, including utility that might be derived as the result of improvement in the economic welfare of others.

7. "The ideal public policy, from the viewpoint of the political entrepreneur, is one that provides widespread benefits to the voting populace, even if it means that a small number of voters will *individually* bear substantial cost." This statement is probably
   a. correct, because voters will be well informed when they are the beneficiaries of a political action.
   b. incorrect, because most of the beneficiaries are likely to be rationally uninformed, whereas the special interest group that bears the cost will tend to oppose strenuously politicians who follow such a course.
   c. correct, since the political process dilutes the influence of special interests because each has only one vote.
   d. incorrect, because the well-informed voter will oppose policies that conflict with the views of small groups of people.

8. "Special interests will no longer have special influence, once we throw the rascals out of office and elect people who are basically honest." The facts of life bias representative government against this view because
   a. special interest group members are richer and can buy more votes than other people.
   b. all politicians are basically honest.
   c. even perfect and costless information for voters could not reduce special interest groups' influence by much.
   d. even honest politicians have a strong incentive to support special interest positions.

9. Suppose that macroeconomic policy increases output and employment between 6 and 18 months before it causes an acceleration in the rate of inflation. According to the short-sightedness effect, expansionary macroeconomic policy would be
   a. highly attractive to political entrepreneurs before each election.
   b. highly attractive to political entrepreneurs after an election.
   c. attractive to political entrepreneurs only if such a policy would help stabilize the economy.
   d. unattractive to political entrepreneurs because of the future inflation it might cause.

10. Which of the following political positions does the special interest effect make more attractive to a vote-maximizing political entrepreneur?
    a. Abolition of the present tax credit for industry X
    b. Abolition of tenure for college professors
    c. 15 percent increase in social security benefits
    d. 50 percent reduction in import taxes on foreign-produced automobiles

11. Garbage-removal services are provided in different cities by different kinds of organizations. If a newly developed truck has just come on the market, and managers in all garbage-removal organizations are analyzing the net benefits of buying the new type of truck, which of the following should be expected to undertake the most serious, painstaking examinations?
    a. Managers of city-owned garbage agencies
    b. Managers of large, profitable corporations in little danger of sinking below the normal level of profits
    c. Owner-managers of medium-sized private firms
    d. Big-city mayors

12. When a federal agency requests funds to build a dam to subsidize irrigation of farmland used to grow potatoes near a river in Idaho, we would expect the *least* active support from
    a. farmers with land near the proposed dam.
    b. the construction unions whose members would work on the project.
    c. the chamber of commerce in a city located near the project.
    d. consumers of potatoes nationally.

13. Several economists have argued that when the government imposes import quotas, the import permits should be auctioned off to the highest bidder rather than given away. Auctioning off the permits would
    a. reduce the economic rents earned by importing firms.
    b. make it easier to see the economic costs of the quotas.
    c. reduce the government budget deficit.
    d. have all of the above effects.

14. One problem contributing to government failure is the short-sightedness of politicians. Stockholders of business firms are
    a. also likely to be short-sighted since they won't own their stock forever.
    b. less likely to be short-sighted because a dollar in the future is worth more than a dollar today.
    c. less likely to be short-sighted because short-sighted policies reduce the resale value of stocks.
    d. also short-sighted since they generally hire business executives to make day-to-day decisions, and the business executives eventually retire.

15. Assume that you're a member of the U.S. House of Representatives from your home state and district. Which of the following best explains why you have a strong incentive to force the Federal Government to finance pork barrel projects in your district?
    a. Most of the benefits of pork barrel projects within your district will accrue to your constituents, while most of the costs will be imposed on voters from other districts.
    b. Most of the costs of pork barrel projects within your district will be imposed on your constituents, while most of the benefits will accrue to voters from other districts.
    c. Pork producers are a powerful political lobby that will influence the actions of legislators in all districts.
    d. This is a trick question; in a representative democracy, there is little incentive for legislators to support pork barrel projects.

THE ECONOMIC WAY OF THINKING—DISCUSSION QUESTIONS

1. Do you think real-world politicians consider how their positions on issues will affect their election prospects? For each of the following pairs of states and constituents, what type of special-interest legislation can you think of that was almost certainly favored by the politicians in the indicated state?

State	Constituents
a. Michigan	autoworkers
b. Florida	retirees
c. Texas	oil producers
d. Name-a-state	defense contractors

2. "We may always have death and taxes, but we will never see a government agency go bankrupt."
   a. Under what circumstances should a government agency discontinue a current function?
   b. Is the absence of the bankruptcy criterion a strength or a weakness of the public sector?

3. Which of the following do you think are special interest issues?
   a. Tariffs on imports of television sets
   b. Tax-free interest income from municipal bonds
   c. Tenure for college professors
   d. Below-cost tuition for college students
   e. Rent controls for your local community
   f. Interest-free educational loans for college students

   Are you in favor of some special interest issues? Which ones?

4. "Government bureaucrats are only as important as the size of their departments, so they will always spend their entire budget allocation so as to avoid having their budgets cut in the next year."
   a. Do you agree with this quote? Why or why not?
   b. If bureaucrats act this way, are they profit maximizers? Are they cost minimizers?
   c. If they aren't maximizing profit, what are they maximizing?

5. What are the major factors that contribute to market failure? What are the major factors that contribute to government failure? Which type of failure do you think is more common? More costly?

6. Explain how the theory of public choice, laid out by James Buchanan, Anthony Downs, Gordon Tullock, and others, accounts for
   a. rational ignorance.
   b. low voter turnouts.
   c. the disproportionate strength of special interest groups.
   d. the prevalence of biased and misleading information.
   e. a cynical attitude toward politicians.

7. Would you favor or oppose each of the following?
   a. A ban on lobbying and campaign contributions.
   b. A federal law requiring that state and local governments auction off their restrictive occupational licenses instead of giving them away.
   c. A requirement that legislators set a budget constraint.

   Support your position in each case.

CURRENT DEBATES IN ECONOMICS

Debate Number Three: Should We Have a Capitalist/Market Economy?

Yes, We Should Have a Capitalist/Market Economy:

Return of the Invisible Hand
By Geoffrey Sampson

[Adapted, with permission, from the August 1985 issue of *Reason* magazine. Copyright ©1985 by the Reason Foundation, 2716 Ocean Park Blvd., Suite 1062, Santa Monica, CA 90405.]

In any human society there must be *some* means—perhaps efficient or perhaps inefficient, perhaps morally admirable or perhaps abominable—by which the activities of its members are coordinated. By this means, the various choices that individuals might be disposed to make in isolation are resolved into a set of decisions that are compatible taken as a whole, so that nobody is processing or consuming anything that does not exist because it has not been produced.

There are two contrasting principles by which this coordination can be achieved. The principle that, arguably, seems most natural is the principle of *planning and command.* The task of finding an efficient and fair solution to the coordination problem is an immensely complex task, so a competently staffed organ of state is charged to work out a satisfactory solution, and the state delegates to this body the authority to impose its solution on individuals in their roles as producers and consumers.

The opposite principle is that of the *market.* Under this principle, the state claims no authority to dispose of the various resources within society, each of which is controlled instead by some particular individual or voluntarily established institution. No overall plan of coordination is formulated and instead a pattern of coordination emerges spontaneously as individuals attempt to satisfy their wants as consumers by engaging with others in voluntary exchanges of the resources under their respective control (including their labor).

Surely, if the problem of coordinating millions or tens of millions of individuals' lives is as difficult as I have suggested, the natural thing is to suppose that a satisfactory solution requires a great deal of careful and well-informed thought. Perhaps plans can never be better than just sitting back and leaving everything to the accidents of billions of decisions made by millions of independent individuals, few of whom know, or care, very much about the implications of their decisions for society in general. Any wise man tries to plan his own affairs, rather than just drifting at the mercy of every momentary gust and current in life. Surely we owe it to ourselves and to one another to arrange for society's affairs to be organized at least as carefully as we organize our own?

Not until 200 years ago was the remarkable idea first propounded that the market system is actually better than the command system at achieving the very goals—the bene-

ficial coordination of individuals' decisions—that motivates the command system's idealistic supporters. The classic statement of the virtues of the market was Adam Smith's *Wealth of Nations,* published in 1776. As Smith put it, in a market system based on private property, each participant "neither intends to promote the public interest, nor knows how much he is promoting it . . . he intends only his own gain, and he is in this . . . led by an invisible hand to promote an end which was no part of his intention. . . . By pursuing his own interest he frequently promotes that of the society more effectually than when he really intends to promote it."

Smith's "invisible hand" is for liberals a key concept in understanding the functioning of society. Any attempt to invoke state power to modify society's workings, liberals argue, is likely to lead to results that are the opposite of those intended. Society is a delicately balanced self-regulating machine, and if we find that things are going amiss in some areas of society, the liberal's reaction is to look for a cause in terms of unnecessary state regulation of some activity or failure to parcel out some collectively held resource into a set of private property rights.

When decisions about how to allocate resources are made politically, public life becomes a sea of individuals and groups all constantly asking, with various degrees of urbanity or shrillness, for more resources. Only a finite quantity of resources is available, so decisions get made almost accidentally, in terms of which pressure group can best publicize its case, who knows how to get access to the relevant decision makers, which minister is felt to deserve a success, and the like—all of which has very little connection with satisfying people's real needs.

Running an economy is a job so massively complex that, as Adam Smith put it in *The Wealth of Nations,* "no human wisdom or knowledge could ever be sufficient." We need to leave it to the market because its system of transmitting information and motivation via prices is subtler than any human alternative.

One virtue of the market is that, since individual consumers exert control over production decisions, resources are diverted to those users where they can yield most real benefit. Another virtue is that it maximizes the *quantity* of benefit derived from each resource and minimizes waste. By treating each resource as the private property of some individual, it gives that individual a motive to husband the resource so that it yields the most good.

The point can be illustrated by a trivial example. In my university department, two electric typewriters are housed in neighboring rooms. One is in the department secretary's office; legally she is not its owner, but in practice it is controlled by her, and no one else touches it without her permission. The machine next door is available for any member of the teaching staff to use. The secretary's typewriter is beautifully looked after; it has given many years of good service, and if any problem arises its "owner" has it seen to without delay. The "public" machine, by contrast, is mistreated badly. Users rarely replace the dustcover and sometimes even leave the motor running overnight; the typeheads fill with dirt, faults are left to cure themselves, the work done on the machine deteriorates and fairly soon it will be a write-off.

Taking good care of an electric typewriter requires a certain amount of effort—it is quicker not to bother to replace the dustcover after use, for instance. To the secretary, it is worth making this effort because it is repaid in terms of easier and more satisfying work with the machine in the future. But many of the individual users of the "public" machine no doubt calculate, consciously or unconsciously, that it is pointless for them to do their share of looking after the machine, since they cannot force other users to be equally careful; so the machine is neglected.

This example is on a very small scale, but what is true on a small scale is true in the large. Consider, for instance, how stocks of some species of fish have been virtually eliminated by overfishing in the North Sea and elsewhere. Fish in the sea are a public resource, so no one fishing enterprise has a motive to restrain its catches. It cannot prevent others from taking the fish that it does not, so for each enterprise it is rational to take as much as it can while stocks last. If it were technically feasible, a liberal would prefer the world's oceans to be divided up into privately owned sectors separated by underwater fences impermeable to fish; then it would be in the interests of each owner to take each year only as many fish as enabled the stock to keep up its numbers.

Replacement of the market by the command system of social organization is objectionable because it robs consumers of their power to influence producers and because it leads to wasteful, destructive uses of a society's resources. Perhaps worst of all, though, it creates a class of people with a direct interest in further increasing state power and in misusing the resources that come under the control of the state: namely, state employees.

What is distinctive about a "welfare" state is that it provides the citizen with goods and services whose production and distribution can without difficulty be controlled by private market interactions. But what about the core of state activities that are necessarily performed by the state because the market is inherently incapable of providing them? The two obvious examples are defense of the realm and a judicial system that enforces private contracts and punishes force and fraud. More generally, there is a range of what economists call "public goods" (some economists prefer the term "collective goods").

A "public good," to an economist, is something that, if provided at all, cannot be provided exclusively to those who choose to pay for it—which makes it difficult or impossible to provide it through the mechanism of the market. The example commonly cited is the lighthouse: there is no way to stop sailors who have not subscribed to a private-enterprise lighthouse service from seeing its beams and acting on their warning, so it would seem to be impossible to run private-enterprise lighthouses profitably. (As it

happens, the example is less straightforward than it seems; private enterprise did play an important role in the development of British lighthouses.) Defense might be regarded as a particularly central example of a public good.

Liberals accept that states are needed to produce public goods and also to limit the production of "public bads" such as air pollution. But liberals would add that the categories of public good and bad must be defined narrowly, since the extension of state power needed to produce extra public goods or control extra public bads is itself a major public bad—as Milton Friedman puts it, "Every government measure bears, as it were, a smokestack on its back."

Defense, the judiciary, and the financing of public goods were for Adam Smith the three proper fields of state activity. Friedman, and other contemporary liberals, would add to Adam Smith's agenda the duty of guarding the interests of individuals who cannot provide for themselves, such as children and lunatics. Most children are provided for by their parents; but if a child has unusually cruel or feckless parents, or is an orphan, he cannot fend for himself, and Friedman would argue that the state should look after him rather than leaving this task to private charity.

Again, however, any liberal would want to draw a tight boundary around the class of people who are regarded as nonparticipants in the market system because of youth or infirmity. One of the liberal's objections to the welfare state is that it effectively broadens this category to include masses of ordinary able-bodied adults in command of their mental facilities.

Since state activities in a liberal society are few, taxation is low, so that questions about the precise system of taxation lose their urgency. But it is worth examining why liberals reject the idea of redistribution from richer to poorer, since, obviously, this concept lies at the heart of welfare-state ideology.

In the first place, even if morality were thought to require either equality of incomes or at least some closer approximation to equality than the market yields, there is no way that state action could achieve that result. If decisions are made politically rather than in the market, individuals do not stop striving to better their lot; they simply redirect their efforts toward the new source of benefits. If increased money incomes are robbed of their value to the individual by steeply progressive taxation, then people will strive to secure other kinds of benefit—money is only a device for getting real goods, after all.

Our state provides extensive subsidies for the arts—picture galleries, opera, and so forth. These are not in the economist's sense "public goods" (there is no *technical* difficulty in charging for admission), and it seems implausible that most of the poor people on whose behalf the welfare state is supposed to spend perceive a strong need for these things; but the upper-middle-class types who know how to influence the state like them, so the state gives them the opportunity of visits to the opera subsidized heavily by ordinary blokes out in the sticks who prefer relaxing in front of video recorders that they have had to buy themselves out of after-tax income.

Inequality is inevitable, whether in a market or a command system. The difference is that, in a market system, the individual's urge to a better life is harnessed to the satisfaction of others' wants; in a command system, one person's success is bought at others' expense. To put the point very personally: the welfare state, looked at objectively rather than through rose-tinted ideological spectacles, is largely an enormously costly device for subsidizing people like me, with our "civilized," middle-class tastes. I cannot believe that people like me are the proper object of public charity.

Liberals go further and argue that there is no moral justification for redistribution. In a free market, if one individual's contributions to society are 10 times as lucrative as another's, then the first individual has given 10 times as much value and is entitled to 10 times the return. The state has no resources of its own; it can make the poor less poor only by making the rich less rich. For liberals, then, progressive taxation is not merely inexpedient (because, for instance, it reduces the incentive for possessors of highly valuable skills to work long hours) but actually immoral: it is a device by which society exploits its more prosperous members by taking their productive contributions and then depriving them of their fair return.

Particularly objectionable from a liberal point of view are taxes on capital, such as capital-gains tax or death duties, since these are blatantly unrelated to any notion of payment in exchange for services rendered. Collectivists often justify capital taxes by suggesting that even a self-made man cannot be seen as having created his wealth independently: we are all dependent in all aspects of our lives on the society we inhabit, so our society has every right to decide how to dispose ultimately of the accumulation of wealth that rich men are allowed to use temporarily.

What is likely is that the patterns of activity that emerged in a liberal society would differ quite a lot from the patterns of activity promoted by a command system. Command systems always tend to favor what is orthodox, what is seen as morally uplifting or in accordance with traditional values, rather than what is experimental or offbeat. Partly, no doubt, this is because people who attain positions of responsibility in a political structure tend to be . . . men with traditional tastes, and partly it is because traditional values are perceived as supporting state power while "underground" movements may threaten it.

The consequence is that, although the world of business is often seen as hostile to iconoclastic, experimental styles of living, in reality just the reverse is the case. Probably many men in the record industry find the various waves of modern music as unpleasant as I do, but if it is what the kids want, then to a businessman his personal tastes are irrelevant—he produces the records, because there is a market for them. In a thoroughgoing command economy such as those of Eastern Europe, on the other hand, pop music is scarcely obtainable. The state asserts by implication that its tastes are the real, "proper" tastes, and conflicting tastes (however real for those who hold them) are somehow improper and not to be taken into account.

It is ironic that so many partisans of this or that brand of "alternative society" believe that in some vague way socialism is on their side. The reality is that thoroughgoing socialism would be likely to kill stone dead almost all of their various attempts to create the good life. However, as Samuel Brittan, assistant editor of the *Financial Times* and a leading British advocate of classical liberalism, pointed out in his 1973 book, *Capitalism and the Permissive Society*:

> *The values of competitive capitalism have a great deal in common with . . . contemporary radical attitudes. Above all they share a similar stress on allowing people to do . . . what they feel inclined to do rather than conform to the wishes of the authority, custom, or convention. Under a competitive system, the businessman will make money by catering to whatever it is that people wish to do—by providing pop records, or nude shows, or candy floss. He will not make anything by providing what the establishment thinks is good for them.*

Brittan noted, however, that when it comes to the test of practical application, the market has at least as many opponents among businessmen as among trade unionists. As it was in Adam Smith's day: businessmen and the propertied classes are no more natural supporters of genuinely free society than any other group. Markets force them to cater to others' free choice, often much against their own instincts.

No, We Should Not Have a Capitalist/Market Economy:

Is Capitalism Efficient, Fair and Democratic?
By Samuel Bowles and Richard Edwards

[Reprinted with permission from Chapter 15 of *Understanding Capitalism*, (New York: Harper and Row Publishers, 1985.) Abridged and edited.]

How efficient, fair or democratic is U.S. capitalism? An economy is *efficient* if it requires as little of the time and energy we spend in producing things as is necessary and if it does as little damage as necessary to our surroundings. An economy is *fair* if burdens and benefits of work are shared in an equitable manner. An economy is *democratic* if important economic choices—what is to be produced, where, how, when, by whom, and for whom—are subject to deliberation and control by the people affected by these choices.

Efficiency The argument from neoclassical economics that capitalism is efficient is extremely simple. The price of an input, according to this argument, measures how scarce it is. Since profit-maximizing capitalists will try to achieve the lowest possible costs, they will use as little as possible of those inputs that have the highest prices (and are most scarce). Competition will drive capitalists to provide society with the maximum amount of goods and services possible, given the available inputs.

But economists have pointed out many serious problems with this argument; three of the most important involve unemployment, the environment, and the intensity of work.

Competition among workers and capitalists does not eliminate unemployment, primarily because the power of employers over workers and the threat of firing is effective only if each worker would have difficulty finding another job. Indeed, if there were no unemployment, profits would fall, workers would be laid off, and unemployment would reappear. A clearing labor market could not and would not persist—and the government, responding to employers' need to restore their power over workers, often also adopts policies that result in such unemployment.

Such unemployment means that there is an input—labor time—that is being wasted. Other inputs—the capital goods that make up our industrial capacity, for example—are also often idled by recessions. Today's lost production is lost forever; no matter how hard we work now, we can never recover the potential production lost in the Great Depression. And the continuing inefficient non-use of resources is substantial: the amount of wasted potential output from 1979 through 1983 amounted to a sum sufficient to pay every family more than the average family makes working from January to September.

How capitalism uses our natural environment is a second source of inefficiency. Capitalists will minimize the use of scarce inputs into production only if those inputs have a price; if they are scarce but free, capitalists will have no incentive not to use as much as they like. An example of such an input is clean river water. If used freely for waste disposal by chemical plants, paper mills, and other factories, the result would be polluted rivers and lakes and a loss of recreational, fishing, or other productive uses of the water. Another example is air, which is used by capitalists as if it were free because to them it *is* free—it has no price. But clean air is also scarce. Polluting it imposes costs on others, who cannot charge capitalists for either their pains (discomfort, annoyance, and illness) or the costs of avoiding these (air conditioners and the expense of travel in order to enjoy outdoor recreation).

Thus one major flaw in the argument that capitalism is efficient is that it assumes that all inputs and outputs are commodities—are produced to be exchanged for a profit and therefore have a price. Whenever any major inputs or outputs of a labor process are not themselves a commodity, capitalism is likely to be inefficient. The clean river water used in a production process was not produced in order to make a profit—it is not a commodity. Our natural environment, other than land, is usually not a commodity. For this reason capitalism does not deal sensibly with our natural environment.

Capitalism not only wastes labor time through nonuse (unemployment) it wastes labor through misuse, a third important inefficiency. Both our *time* and our *effort* are scarce, and they are not the same thing. Our time, when sold as labor hours, has a price. Capitalists attempt to use as little as possible in production. Our effort—our sweat, creativity, and intelligence—when it takes the form of actual work done, has no price. Actual work done, has no price. Actual work done, like the environment, is not a commodity. And like the natural environment, it needs to be used wastefully in a capitalist society.

Capitalists have no interest in minimizing the intensity of work—how much effort workers put out per hour on the job—unless this lowers the price of labor time. Capitalists' interests are in fact to maximize the amount of effort expended for each hour of labor time purchased. In order to do this, capitalists hire large numbers of people who produce nothing at all; they simply control the labor of others. If capitalists pay for labor time but not for work itself, there is no more reason to expect that they will make sensible use of work effort than there is to think that they will make sensible use of clean air or water.

A new technology that uses surveillance cameras to make people work faster may lower costs but it is not necessarily more efficient: working harder (and being forced through the use of an extra input, surveillance) may not be working better. Discrimination, if it disorganizes workers and keeps their overall wages low, may be profitable to the employer but it is inefficient (and unfair) for everyone else; workers won't go to the jobs that best use their capacities and the children of discriminated groups sometimes grow up poor and unprepared for productive futures.

As a result of the problems of unemployment, the environment, and work intensity, capitalism departs from the standard of efficiency.

Fairness Both capitalism and democratic government have notions of fair processes, but they are different. Sometimes it is said that in a capitalist economy we vote with our dollars. Our demands—our wants backed up by dollars—are what ultimately direct the economy, according to this view. But how many "dollars votes" we can cast in the capitalist economy depends on how many dollars we have to spend.

Thus the fact that capitalism (at least ideally) treats dollars equally does not make it fair. We must ask why some have more dollars than others. Is the process determining the distribution of income fair? And is the resulting distribution of income fair? Only then will the results of "voting with dollars" be fair.

How might we judge the process that determines the distribution of income as either fair or unfair? Two principles seem essential. First, it is not fair for some people to start out life—from birth—with a head start or with a penalty. Being born a member of the duPont family confers millions of dollars of inherited wealth on a person, giving that person the resources and the freedom to live a life closed to most others. On the other hand, being born female or black is to inherit an economic situation that on the average will be characterized by lower incomes and obstacles to getting ahead in certain desirable occupations. When people are rich or poor as a result of inherited wealth or because of racial, sexual, or other discrimination, the results of voting with dollars are not fair.

Second, the time people spend at work should be treated more or less equally and rewarded more or less equally (of course, if some jobs are more unpleasant or difficult or dangerous than others, it may be fair to reward them more highly). There are really two idea here: work time should be the basis of economic reward (except for those unable to work), and work time should be rewarded roughly equally. Thus it is not fair that most capitalists receive the bulk of their income not in return for time they have spent at work, but simply as a result of their ownership of the capital goods used in production. Moreover, it is not fair that managers of major corporations pay themselves salaries that amount to over $500 per hour when the average hourly wage is about one-fiftieth of the amount.

These are basic aspects of capitalism: profits as a return on ownership of capital goods rather than as a reward for work; the private ownership and hence inheritance of capital goods used in production; substantial wage and salary difference among those who do work; and various forms of discrimination. These elements are not the *imperfections* of an otherwise fair system. They are its *basic structure*. In this case, capitalism departs from the standard of fairness.

Democracy Democracy provides a third ideal standard against which to evaluate the performance of U.S. capitalism.

The fundamental idea of democracy is that basic decisions affecting the lives of substantial numbers of people should be considered and voted upon by those who are affected. Of course, people may vote directly on major decisions—as in referenda—or they may elect representatives with whom they agree or in whom they have confidence. But the basic idea is that those affected by decisions have the right to control, directly or indirectly, these decisions.

Does capitalism as an economic system support and reinforce democracy in government? Does capitalism promote democratic decision making in the economy and in other social relationships?

Democratic government and the capitalist economy are organized by entirely different sets of rules. In the economy, important decisions, affecting the life and death of whole communities, the health and safety of workers and consumers, and the livelihood of millions of families are taken by owners and managers of firms. The chief executive officers and major owners of the largest 500 corporations in the United States may well have considerably more power over peoples' lives and over the destiny of the nation than do the 535 members of the U.S. Senate and House of Representatives. Corporate leaders are a select group. They wield their power not by democratic election of those affected by corporate decisions but by being selected by people who own the capital goods (with owners casting votes in proportion to how much they own). And their decisions—to build big cars rather than small cars, to build nuclear power plants rather than solar collectors, to spend millions of dollar manipulating public opinion or pressur-ing elected representatives, to move their plants to Haiti or South Korea—are made behind closed doors, far beyond the reaches of public and open discussion by those immediately affected by their decisions.

Whatever desirable characteristics may be claimed for an economic system in which so few people make decisions affecting the lives of so many, democracy is not among them.

Few economists would disagree. Indeed, the standard definition of the capitalist enterprise—the firm—is that it is a command economy in which decisions are made and resources allocated according to some form of top-down authority. In this sense the firm is sharply contrasted with competitive markets, in which voluntary exchange—not command—is the rule.

In defense of this admittedly undemocratic system of command, it is often said that the economy—and specifically the capitalist enterprise—is private, not public, and democratic rule should only apply to public decisions. This reasoning is often based on the idea that the economy is made up of small businesses and self-employed people. But today's corporations each command the labor of thousands of people and wield power over the lives of many more. It is difficult to deny that these are public institutions, making decisions of general concern to all.

Capitalist organization departs substantially, then from the standard of democracy. Historically capitalism has provided a context in which prodemocratic movements could successfully achieve greater democracy in government, but capitalism has been a powerful force opposing greater democratic control over the economy.

In conclusion, we see that U.S. capitalism (and capitalism in general) departs substantially from all three of the ideal standards of efficiency, fairness, and democracy. These failures to be efficient, fair and democratic are not inadvertent lapses or the results of misguided policies or simply imperfections in the system. Rather, they are the consequences of capitalism's most central and basic institutions and the results of the way capitalism as a system is organized.

Holding a Debate

Many students will enjoy participating in a debate on this topic either in class or in an informal study group. After completing both readings and possibly doing some additional research (for example, see your textbook), get three to four volunteers for each side of the debate, choose a moderator if your instructor is not available, and devote about a half an hour to opening statements, rebuttals, and summaries.

Discussion

1. If you read both of these fairly long articles, what did you conclude? Could we improve efficiency, fairness, and democracy by moving away from capitalism? Could we do a better job of coordinating our country's activities if we moved more towards the market? Is it possible that *both* articles could be right? Explain your answers.

2. If you read the Sampson article, was the author discussing our current economy or an economy that was idealistically "liberal" (the 18th century equivalent of what we call "conservative" in the United States)? Do you think he would have argued any differently had he been discussing our economy directly? Explain your answer.

3. One additional interesting point made by Bowles and Edwards is that a fair process does not necessarily produce a fair outcome. They cite as an example a random lottery that is used to determine which single individual in a society will win title to all the property in that society. Is this a fair process? Is this a fair outcome?

CHAPTER TWENTY

GAINING FROM INTERNATIONAL TRADE

TRUE OR FALSE

T F

1. Economic theory suggests that *both* partners gain from free trade. Voluntary exchange does *not* generate gain for one nation at the expense of the other.

2. Our analysis shows that every individual consumer gains from international free trade whenever it takes place.

3. The joint output of countries would be maximized if each country specialized in production of those commodities for which it is the low opportunity-cost producer, exchanging them for other commodities for which it is a high opportunity-cost producer.

4. In a sense, tariffs are like transportation costs—they are obstacles that prevent trading partners from fully realizing the potential gains from trade.

5. A secondary effect of policies that restrict imports is the additional demand generated for the nation's export products.

6. An import quota places a ceiling on the amount of a product that can be imported during a specific time period.

7. A country that is rich in resources and an efficient producer will gain if it refuses to trade, although this action hurts the rest of the world.

8. One problem with the removal of all tariffs would probably be increased unemployment in domestic import-competing industries in the short run.

9. If all tariffs were removed in the United States, fewer jobs would be available to U.S. workers, since wage rates are high in the United States.

10. Regarding the removal of an import quota on automobiles: We would expect the chairman of the board of General Motors and the president of the United Auto Workers' union to disagree on the merit of quota removal.

11. The primary economic motive behind exports is the accumulation of foreign currency; imports are best regarded as a necessary evil, required at some level to keep the goodwill of the selling nations.

12. U.S. tariffs, in general, are much lower now than they were in 1930.

13. Typically, the larger the country, the larger the share of GDP involved in international trade.

PROBLEMS AND PROJECTS

1. Use Exhibit 1 when answering the following:

EXHIBIT 1
THE PRODUCTION POSSIBILITIES OF RHINELAND AND NEPAL

	Rhineland			Nepal	
	Food	*Clothing*		*Food*	*Clothing*
A	0	900	A	0	500
B	100	750	B	100	450
C	200	600	C	200	400
D	300	400	D	300	300
E	400	200	E	400	150
F	500	0	F	500	0

a. What is the per unit opportunity cost of expanding food production from 200 to 300 in Rhineland? In Nepal?

b. In the absence of trade, the people of Rhineland will choose to produce at point D. The people of Nepal will choose point B. Given their preferences for food and clothing, could the nations gain from trade? How can you tell? How would trade flow between the two countries?

c. Suppose that both countries produced at point C and that Rhineland traded 100 units of its domestically produced clothing for 100 units of food produced in Nepal. Compared to the no-trade point B alternative, how would this transaction affect the goods available to the people of Nepal? What would happen to the joint output of the two countries?

d. Suppose that Rhineland produced at point B and Nepal at point D. If Rhineland traded 225 units of clothing for 200 units of Nepal's food, how much would each country gain, relative to the no-trade chosen combination of part b? What would happen to their joint output, relative to their mutual production at point C?

e. If Rhineland expanded its clothing production still farther, to 900, what would be its per unit opportunity cost of producing clothing in this range? What would be Nepal's per unit opportunity cost of producing clothing in this range? What would be Nepal's per unit opportunity cost of the first 300 units of clothing domestically? Once Rhineland is producing at point B and Nepal at point D, can joint output be expanded by additional specialization? Are *additional* mutual gains from the trade possible? Explain.

2. The country of Arcadia produces and consumes unique computers. Exhibit 2 shows Arcadia's demand and supply curves for their computers along with the demand for Arcadian computers from the rest of the world (ROW).

EXHIBIT 2

Price (dollars/ unit)	Arcadia's quantity supplied	Arcadia's quantity demanded	ROW's quantity demanded	Total quantity demanded
$2400	1200	750	280	1030
2200	1100	800	300	_____
2000	1000	850	320	_____
1800	900	900	340	_____
1600	800	950	360	_____
1400	700	1000	380	_____
1200	600	1050	400	_____
1000	500	1100	420	_____

a. Fill in the missing information in the table.
b. If Arcadia has no trade with the rest of the world, what will be the equilibrium price of computers in Arcadia? What will be the equilibrium quantity demanded and supplied?
c. What will be the equilibrium price of computers if Arcadia trades with the ROW? Compare this price to the equilibrium price of part b. Why is it higher?
d. With trade, what is Arcadia's equilibrium quantity of computers supplied? Compare this with the quantity without trade. What must have happened to Arcadia's productions of other goods and services as a result of international trade?
e. With trade, what is Arcadia's quantity of computers demanded? Compare the quantity of computers demanded in Arcadia without trade. In what way can this difference be of benefit generally to Arcadia consumers?
f. What quantity of computers is exported by Arcadia? Do Arcadia's computer producers clearly benefit by unrestricted international trade in computers?
g. As a result of Arcadia's exports, what do you suppose has happened to the price of computers in the ROW? How would you feel about this if you were an ROW computer "producer," either worker or entrepreneur? And if you were an ROW buyer, how would you react?

3. Suppose that the United States can purchase motorcycles from abroad for $3,000 each, and that this price does not vary with the quantity the U.S. purchases. Alternatively, the United States can produce its own motorcycles according to a supply schedule given in Exhibit 3, which also shows the United States's demand for motorcycles.

EXHIBIT 3

Price (dollars/unit)	Domestic quantity supplied	Domestic quantity demanded
	(thousands/year)	
$4500	1000	700
4000	900	900
3500	800	1100
3000	700	1300
2500	600	1500
2000	500	1700

a. In the absence of international trade what would be the price of motorcycles in the United States? What quantities would be demanded and supplied?

b. Suppose that motorcycles can be imported into the United States without restriction. What will be the price of motorcycles in the United States? What will be the quantities demanded and produced domestically? What will be the quantity of imports? By how much will domestic production decline relative to the no-trade amount?

c. Suppose that workers and management lobby Congress for a tariff on imports on the grounds that they need temporary protection from imports in order to maintain domestic markets while they "retool" to incorporate the latest and most efficient techniques of motorcycle production (a version of the "infant" industry argument). If government grants domestic producers a tariff on imports of $500 per cycle, what will be the domestic price of motorcycles? By how much will domestic production increase? (This is called the "protective effect" of a tariff.) By how much will U.S. purchases of motorcycles fall? By how much will imports fall?

d. Suppose that *instead* of the tariff of part c, government imposed a quota on imports of 300 motorcycles per year. In this case, what would happen to the price of motorcycles as compared to the unrestricted ("free") trade price? (*Hint:* Locate a price at which the domestic quantity supplied plus 300 equals the domestic quantity demanded at the price.) What will be the protective effect (increase in domestic quantity produced) of the quota?

e. Judging from your answers to c and d above, what is the basic difference between a tariff and a quota?

4. Consider the following hypothetical information about the United States and South Korea:

	Output per worker per day	
	United States	South Korea
Tons of steel	8	4
Bushels of wheat	80	8

a. Which country has the
   absolute advantage in steel production? _____
   absolute advantage in wheat production? _____
   comparative advantage in steel production? _____
   comparative advantage in wheat production? _____
b. If these countries trade steel and wheat with each other, which country will export steel and import wheat?
c. Suppose that the United States and South Korea agree to a daily trade of 10 tons of steel for 50 bushels of wheat. One worker in the United States then switches from steel production to wheat production. Complete the following table to show that both countries end up with more steel and more wheat then they had initially:

United States	Tons of steel	Bushels of wheat
Change in production:	−8	+80
Trade:	_____	_____
Change in consumption:	_____	_____
South Korea	Tons of steel	Bushels of wheat
Change in production:	_____	_____
Trade:	_____	_____
Change in consumption:	_____	_____

5. The diagram in Exhibit 4 reflects the approximate impact on the domestic heavyweight motorcycle market of the motorcycle tariffs recently imposed by the United States (Pf denotes the free trade price, and Pt denotes the price with the tariff):

EXHIBIT 4

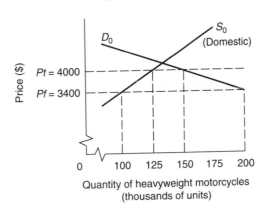

a. Use the figures from the diagram to compute the following values:
   Consumers' cost of the tariff _____
   Domestic producers' gain from the tariff: _____
   Tariff revenue: _____
   Net social cost of the tariff: _____
b. It has been estimated that the tariff on heavyweight motorcycles created 700 jobs in the domestic motorcycle industry. How much did each of these jobs "cost" U.S. consumers?
c. What size quota on heavyweight motorcycles would have achieved the same impact as the indicated tariff?

LEARNING THE MECHANICS—MULTIPLE CHOICE

1. Which of the following best describes the implications of the law of comparative advantage? Each trading nation can gain by
   a. selling services for which it is a high opportunity-cost producer and buying goods that it produces at a low cost.
   b. selling those services that it enjoys, while buying goods for which it is a low opportunity-cost producer.
   c. selling services for which it is a low opportunity-cost producer and buying those things for which it is a high opportunity-cost producer.
   d. selling those services that it dislikes while buying those that it finds most enjoyable to produce.

2. A trade policy that limits the entry of foreign goods to the U.S. market will
   a. benefit consumers at the expense of producers.
   b. increase the nation's real income by protecting domestic jobs from foreign competition.
   c. reduce the demand for U.S. export goods, since foreigners will be less able to purchase our goods if they cannot sell to us.
   d. enhance economic efficiency by permitting domestic resources to be fully utilized.

3. The national defense argument for high tariffs on a commodity
   a. is stronger if large supplies of the commodity can be stored cheaply.
   b. is stronger if storage of the commodity is costly.
   c. is based on the economic principle of comparative advantage.
   d. is based on the economic principle of absolute advantage.

4. A higher tariff on foreign-produced steel would be most likely to benefit
   a. domestic consumers of products that contain steel.
   b. producers in export industries.
   c. producers and workers in the steel industry.
   d. producers and workers in all industries except steel.

5. A nation will benefit from international trade when it
   a. imports more than it exports.
   b. exports more than it imports.
   c. imports goods for which it is a high opportunity-cost producer, while exporting goods for which it is a low opportunity-cost producer.
   d. exports goods for which it is a high opportunity-cost producer, while importing those goods for which it is a low opportunity-cost producer.

Use the following information to answer the next *three* questions. Exhibit 5 outlines the production possibilities of Italia and Slavia for food and clothing.

EXHIBIT 5

Italia		Slavia	
Food	*Clothing*	*Food*	*Clothing*
0	8	0	20
4	6	2	15
8	4	4	10
12	2	6	5
16	0	8	0

6. What is the opportunity cost of producing one unit of food in Italia?
    a. One-quarter of a unit of clothing
    b. One-half of a unit of clothing
    c. Two units of clothing
    d. Five units of clothing

7. Which of the following is true?
    a. Slavia has a comparative advantage in the production of both goods.
    b. Italia has a comparative advantage in the production of food.
    c. Slavia is the low opportunity-cost producer of food.
    d. None of the above.

8. The law of comparative advantage suggests that
    a. neither country would gain from trade even if the transportation costs for the products were zero.
    b. Slavia would not gain from trade because it has an absolute advantage in the production of both goods.
    c. both countries could gain if Italia traded food for Slavia clothing.
    d. both countries could gain if Slavia traded food for Italia clothing.

9. The law of comparative advantage
    a. is applicable to both domestic and international production and trade.
    b. applies only in domestic situations, such as occur when doctors who are good typists hire secretaries to do medical typing.
    c. applies only when one nation is absolutely more efficient in the production of the first good and another nations is absolutely more efficient at the production of the second.
    d. is only theoretical; it does not work in the real world.

10. The infant-industry argument about tariffs states that
    a. it is unfair to place tariffs on items for use by infants.
    b. tariffs should be placed on items produced by new domestic industries only in the short run.
    c. tariffs should be placed on items intended by new domestic industries in the short or long run.
    d. tariffs should be placed on items produced by new domestic industries in the short or long run.

11. Which of the following is a true statement about trade liberalization?
    a. Trade liberalization reduces efficiency since it reduces competition in industries affected by the trade.
    b. Trade liberalization tends to increase the rate of inflation since it pushes the prices of exports upward.
    c. Trade liberalization improves consumer welfare by increasing product variety.
    d. All of the above are results of trade liberalization.

12. Exhibit 6 compares the production possibilities of the country of Brenton for wine and bread before specialization and trade (point O) with a number of post-trade consumption possibilities. International trade (based on comparative advantage), which resulted in the export of wine and the import of bread, will move Brenton from point O to point
   a. A
   b. B
   c. C
   d. D

EXHIBIT 6

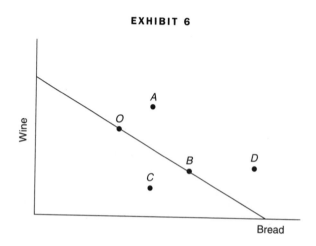

THE ECONOMIC WAY OF THINKING — MULTIPLE CHOICE

1. Suppose that the United States eliminated its tariff on automobiles, granting foreign-produced automobiles free entry into the U.S. market. Which of the following would be most likely to occur?
   a. The price of automobiles to U.S. consumers would decline, and the demand for U.S. export products would increase.
   b. The price of automobiles to U.S. consumers would increase, and the demand for U.S. export products would decline.
   c. The price of automobiles to U.S. consumers would decline, and the demand for U.S. export products would decline.
   d. The price of automobiles to U.S. consumers would increase, and the demand for U.S. export products would increase.

2. Economic incentives suggest that the union leaders of workers in a protected "infant industry" will support tariff protection for the industry
   a. if, and only if, they believe that the industry is still immature.
   b. unless they believe that the tariff is harming the consumers of the industry's product.
   c. if management is opposed to the protection.
   d. regardless of how mature the industry may be at the time.

3. If a country had a comparative disadvantage in the production of watches, a tariff on imported watches set just high enough to offset this disadvantage in the retail market
   a. would help the entire economy by increasing employment.
   b. would help watch consumers as a group, by giving them a real choice between foreign and domestic brands.
   c. would help workers in the watch industry by increasing the demand for their services.
   d. would help watch producers at the expense of the workers in the domestic watch industry.

The following quotation from a U.S. textile industry executive applies to the next *two* questions.

> What bothers our manufacturers is that it is not really a matter of Japanese competitiveness, but a maze of impenetrable supports and subsidies. Our people feel that whatever they do, the Japanese will just lower their prices.

Assume that the Japanese government does, in fact, continually subsidize their textile industry so that they can undersell other exporters.

4. A textile-importing nation would best take advantage of the Japanese subsidization policy by
   a. setting a tariff high enough to keep cheap foreign competitors out of its own potential textile industry.
   b. setting a declining quota on the import of Japanese textiles such that its own textile industry could continue growing at the same rate as the rest of the economy.
   c. gladly accepting the subsidy of the Japanese government to textile users, making whatever adjustment assistance seems appropriate to the temporarily displaced resources in the domestic textile industry.
   d. setting a tariff just to equalize Japanese and domestic textile prices to the consumer.

5. We would expect that domestic textile industry executives and textile union leaders would
   a. gladly accept the reduced burden of having to produce ever-increasing amounts of textile goods domestically.
   b. fight for tariffs and quotas on imported Japanese textiles "to protect the American economy."
   c. argue that comparative advantage should prevail, so that domestic producers would be forced to meet the price of textiles that prevails in the world market if they were to survive.
   d. disagree among themselves, with the industry executives demanding protection, whereas union leaders would favor a tariff reduction that would benefit the worker-consumers.

6. Relative to a no-trade situation, what effect will importing a good from foreign nations have on the domestic market for the good?
   a. Equilibrium price will rise and total domestic output will fall.
   b. Equilibrium price will rise and total domestic output will rise.
   c. Equilibrium price will fall and total domestic output will fall.
   d. Equilibrium price will fall and total domestic output will rise.

7. Economic theory suggests that the popularity of tariffs among politicians is
   a. surprising, since tariffs generally lower a nation's level of real income.
   b. not surprising, since tariff protection for an industry is generally a special interest issue.
   c. surprising, since numerous consumers are generally harmed in order to help a few industrial and labor interests.
   d. not surprising, since tariffs generally help domestic investors, workers, and consumers at the expense of foreigners who cannot vote.

8. Economics suggests that some of the political popularity of tariffs stems from the fact that "jobs lost" due to an expansion of imports are easily identified
   a. whereas "jobs created" by an increase in foreign spending on domestic exports can seldom be traced back to the reduction in tariffs.
   b. whereas the gains associated with holding larger amounts of foreign currencies are elusive, even though they are real gains.
   c. and they cannot be replaced by an expansion in other industries.
   d. and they cannot be replaced without a trade policy to restrict competition with cheap foreign labor.

9. If all tariffs (and quotas) between countries on the North American continent were eliminated
   a. small Central American countries would be hurt, since they would be unable to compete with larger nations,
   b. the United States would gain at the expense of the less-developed North American countries.
   c. the combined wealth of the countries would increase, since elimination of trade restrictions would permit greater gains from specialization.
   d. wage rates in the United States would decline to the average for the North American continent.

10. Relative to a no-trade situation, what effect will exporting a good to foreign nations have on the domestic market for the product?
    a. Equilibrium price will rise and total domestic output will fall
    b. Equilibrium price will rise and total domestic output will rise
    c. Equilibrium price will fall and total domestic output will fall
    d. Equilibrium price will fall and total domestic output will rise

Questions 11–14 refer to Exhibit 7, which contains hypothetical data on the market for shoes (per month) in the United States and in the entire world (including the United States).

EXHIBIT 7

Price per pair	World Market (including the United States)		Domestic market (United States only)	
	Q supplied	Q demanded	Q supplied	Q demanded
$10	5900	6100	250	400
$20	6000	6000	275	375
$30	6100	5900	300	350
$40	6200	5800	325	325
$50	6300	5700	350	300
$60	6400	5600	375	275
$70	6500	5500	400	250

11. Under a regime of free international trade, the United States would
    a. import 50 pairs of shoes per month.
    b. import 100 pairs of shoes per month.
    c. export 100 pairs of shoes per month.
    d. purchase a total of 325 pairs of shoes per month.

12. Suppose that the domestic shoe industry is in long-run equilibrium under international free trade but that then the United States imposes a $10/pair tariff on shoes. What would be the most likely result?
    a. The price of shoes in the United States would increase by $10 per pair.
    b. The price of shoes in the United States would increase, but by less than $10 per pair.
    c. The U.S. supply curve of shoes would shift to the right (increase) in the short run.
    d. The U.S. demand curve for shoes would shift to the left.

13. Given the tariff described in question #12 above,
    a. the tariff revenues of $500 outweigh U.S. social deadweight loss, so overall producer plus consumer surplus increases.
    b. tariff revenues of something less than $500 outweigh U.S. social deadweight loss, so overall producer plus consumer surplus increases.
    c. tariff revenues do not compensate for U.S. social deadweight loss, so overall producer plus consumer surplus decreases.
    d. there is a redistribution of surplus between producers and consumers, but the overall magnitude of the producer plus consumer surplus is constant.

14. The same U.S. price and quantity of shoes purchased under the tariff described in question #12 above could have resulted from the imposition of a quota of
    a. 50 pairs of shoes per month.
    b. between 50 and 100 pairs of shoes per month.
    c. 100 pairs of shoes per month.
    d. more than 100 pairs of shoes per month.

THE ECONOMIC WAY OF THINKING—DISCUSSION QUESTIONS

1. "We are not opposed to competition when it does not destroy jobs. But last year, while many American auto workers were idle, we exported a million jobs to foreigners by importing automobiles that could have been produced by domestic workers. An increase in the tariff on automobiles would strengthen our economy, provide jobs, and improve our standard of living." [Auto Workers' Union official]
    a. Do you agree that higher automobile tariffs would "provide jobs"? Why or why not?
    b. Do you agree that higher automobile tariffs would "improve our standard of living"? Why or why not?
    c. Prior to the 1970s, the United Auto Workers was an advocate of free trade. What do you think accounts for the reversal in their position?

2. Why would you expect the management of U.S. Steel and the president of the United Steel Workers' Union to fight strongly together for tariffs on imported steel "for the good of the nation," when they disagree on so many other matters of public concern? Would you expect both to oppose lower tariffs on copper, aluminum, or other steel substitutes? Why or why not?

3. Nations have become increasingly interdependent since the Second World War.
    a. What are the advantages of self-sufficiency? The disadvantages?
    b. From a political perspective, do you think nations should endeavor to become more or less interdependent?
    c. Why do you think international trade as a percentage of GDP is 54 percent for the Netherlands but only 9 percent for the United States?

4. a. Montana encourages a local liquor-bottling industry by taxing bulk imports into the state at lower rates than bottled liquors. Does this make economic sense? Why or why not?

   b. Should Connecticut ban imports of bananas to promote a local banana industry? Explain.

   c. Should state governments adopt trade restrictions to target specific industries for promotions? If not, why not? If so, why, and under what circumstances?

5. In the United States, the price of labor is relatively high and the price of capital is relatively low. In developing countries, the reverse is true.

   a. Based on these resource market conditions, what types of products would you expect the United States to import from developing countries? To export to them?

   b. Most U.S. trade is with other industrial high-wage nations. In light of the law of comparative advantage, is this surprising? If not, why not? If so, why, and how can you account for this aspect of U.S. trade?

6. Suppose that Brazil, the world's leading coffee producer, decides to levy an export tax on coffee.

   a. Use a demand and supply curve for Brazilian coffee to determine whether each of the following will rise, fall, or change in an uncertain direction: (i) the world price of coffee; (ii) world expenditures on Brazilian coffee; and (iii) the receipts of Brazilian coffee growers.

   b. Decide whether you think each of the following would favor or oppose the export tax: (i) Brazilian coffee growers; (ii) U.S. coffee drinkers; (iii) U.S. tea drinkers; and (iv) Colombian coffee growers.

CURRENT DEBATES IN ECONOMICS

Debate Number Four: Should We Adopt Free International Trade?

Yes, We Should Adopt Free International Trade:

The Economic Case for Free Trade
By Milton and Rose Friedman

[Reprinted with permission from Chapter 2 of *Free to Choose* (New York: Harcourt Brace Jovanovich, 1980.) Abridged.]

Today, as always, there is much support for tariffs—euphemistically labeled "protection," a good label for a bad cause. Producers of steel and steelworkers' unions press for restrictions on steel imports from Japan. Producers of TV sets and their workers lobby for "voluntary agreements" to limit imports of TV sets or components from Japan, Taiwan, or Hong Kong. Producers of textiles, shoes, cattle, sugar—they and myriad others complain about "unfair" competition from abroad and demand that government do something to "protect" them. Of course, no group makes its claim on the basis of naked self-interest. Every group speaks of the "general interest," of the need to preserve jobs or to promote national security.

One voice that is hardly ever raised is the consumer's. The individual consumer's voice is drowned out in the cacophony of the "interested sophistry of merchants and manufacturers" and their employees. The result is a serious distortion of the issue. For example, the supporters of tariffs treat it as self-evident that the creation of jobs is a desirable end, in and of itself, regardless of what the persons employed do. That is clearly wrong. If all we want are jobs, we can create any number—for example, have people dig holes and then fill them up again, or perform other useless tasks. Work is sometimes its own reward. Mostly, however, it is the price we pay to get the things we want. Our real objective is not just jobs but productive jobs—jobs that will mean more goods and services to consume.

Another fallacy seldom contradicted is that exports are good, imports bad. The truth is very different. We cannot eat, wear, or enjoy the goods we send abroad. We eat bananas from Central America, wear Italian shoes, drive German automobiles, and enjoy programs we see on our Japanese TV sets. Our gain from foreign trade is what we import. Exports are the price we pay to get imports. As Adam Smith saw so clearly, the citizens of a nation benefit from getting as large a volume of imports as possible in return for its exports, or equivalently, from exporting as little as possible to pay for its imports.

The misleading terminology we use reflects these erroneous ideas. "Protection" really means exploiting the consumer. A "favorable balance of trade" really means exporting more than we import, sending abroad goods of greater total value than the goods we get from abroad. In your private household, you would surely prefer to pay less for more rather than the other way around, yet that would be termed an "unfavorable balance of payments" in foreign trade.

The argument in favor of tariffs that has the greatest emotional appeal to the public at large is the alleged need to protect the high standard of living of American workers from the "unfair" competition of workers in Japan or Korea or Hong Kong who are willing to work for a much lower wage. What is wrong with this argument? Don't we want to protect the high standard of living of our people?

The fallacy in this argument is the loose use of the terms "high" wage and "low" wage. What do high and low wages mean? American workers are paid in dollars; Japanese workers are paid in yen. How do we compare wages in dollars with wages in yen? How many yen equal a dollar? What determines that exchange rate?

It is simply not true that high-wage American workers are, as a group, threatened by "unfair" competition from low-wage foreign workers. Of course, particular workers may be harmed if a new or improved product is developed abroad, or if foreign producers become able to produce such products more cheaply. But that is no different from the effect on a particular group of workers of other American firms' developing new or improved products or discovering how to produce at lower costs. That is simply market competition in practice, the major source of the high standard of life of the American worker. If we want to benefit from a vital, dynamic, innovative economic system, we must accept the need for mobility and adjustment. It may be desirable to ease these adjustments, and we have adopted many arrangements, such as unemployment insurance, to do so, but we should try to achieve that objective without destroying the flexibility of the system—that would be to kill the goose that has been laying the golden eggs. In any event, whatever we do should be evenhanded with respect to foreign and domestic trade.

What determines the items it pays us to import and to export? An American worker is currently more productive than a Japanese worker. It is hard to determine just how much more productive—estimates differ. But suppose he is one and a half times as productive. Then, on average, the American's wages would buy about one and half times as much as a Japanese worker's wages. It is wasteful to use American workers to do anything at which they are less than one and a half times as efficient as their Japanese counterparts. In the economic jargon coined more than 150 years ago, that is *principle of comparative advantage.* Even if we were more efficient than the Japanese at producing everything, it would not pay us to produce everything. We should concentrate on doing those things we do best, those things where our superiority is the greatest.

Another source of "unfair competition" is said to be subsidies by foreign governments to their producers that enable them to sell in the United States below cost. Suppose a foreign government gives such subsidies, as no doubt some do. Who is hurt and who benefits? To pay for the subsidies the foreign government must tax its citizens. They are the ones who pay for the subsidies. U.S. consumers benefit. They get cheap TV sets or automobiles or whatever it is that is subsidized. Should we complain about such a program of reverse foreign aid? Was it noble of the United States to send goods and services as gifts to other countries in the form of Marshall Plan aid or, later, foreign aid, but ignoble for foreign countries to send us gifts in the indirect form of goods and services sold to us below cost? The citizens of the foreign government might well complain. They must suffer a lower standard of living for the benefit of American consumers and of some of their fellow citizens who own or work in the industries that are subsidized. No doubt, if such subsidies are introduced suddenly or erratically, that will adversely affect owners and workers in U.S. industries producing the same products. However, that is one of the ordinary risks of doing business. Enterprises never complain about unusual or accidental events that confer windfall gains. The free enterprise system is a *profit* and *loss* system, As already noted, any measures to ease the adjustment to sudden changes should be applied evenhandedly to domestic and foreign trade.

We are a great nation, the leader of the free world. It ill behooves us to require Hong Kong and Taiwan to impose export quotas on textiles to "protect" our textile industry at the expense of U.S. consumers and of Chinese workers in Hong Kong and Taiwan. We speak glowingly of the virtues of free trade, while we use our political and economic power to induce Japan to restrict exports of steel and TV sets. We should move unilaterally to free trade, not instantaneously, but over a period of, say, five years, at a pace announced in advance.

Few measures that we could take would do more to promote the cause of freedom at home and abroad than complete free trade. Instead of making grants to foreign governments in the name of economic aid—thereby promoting socialism—while at the same time imposing restrictions on the products they produce—thereby hindering free enterprise—we could assume a consistent and principled stance. We could say to the ret of the world: we believe in freedom and intend to practice it. We cannot force you to be free. But we can offer full cooperation on equal terms to all. Our market is open to you without tariffs

or other restrictions. Sell here what you can and wish to. Buy whatever you can and wish to. In that way cooperation among

individuals can be worldwide and free.

No, We Should Not Adopt Free International Trade:

"Free Trade" Is Impoverishing the West
By John M. Culbertson

[Reprinted from *The New York Times,* July 28, 1985.
©1985 by The New York Times Company.
Reprinted by permission.]

For most of this century, United States trade policy has been based on the belief that unregulated international trade, or "free trade," fits a theoretical pattern that automatically makes it beneficial to the nations involved. Thus, "barriers to trade" and "protectionism" are harmful. The difficulty with this elegantly simple theory is that it bears little relation to reality.

The evidence shows that not all trade is the same—different patterns of foreign trade exist, and they have different effects. Some are very damaging. The pattern of foreign trade that has caused the extraordinary shift of industries from the United States in recent years is of the destructive kind.

The stereotype within which economists have viewed international trade was developed by Adam Smith, in the 18th century. It depicts each nation as specializing in products to which it is peculiarly suited, in which it has low relative costs or a *comparative advantage.* Thus, a nation rich in iron ore might trade with a nation that produces steel efficiently. Both would gain by the trade.

In this "comparative-advantage rule," the gain in efficiency from international specialization benefits both nations. Further, the trade is assumed to be in balance, so there is no general shift of industries from one nation to another—with the chain of serious consequences it can bring.

The error in the theory gained new importance in the modern era, when changes in technology, transportation and communications began to break down the conventional barriers between countries. Today, most United States trade is not based on comparative advantage and is not efficient. There is no gain in efficiency from shifting factories that are producing goods for the domestic market from the United States to Asia or Latin America. There is little comparative advantage in today's manufacturing industries, since they produce the same goods the same ways in all parts of the world. Why, then, is industry after industry moving out of the United States?

These industry shifts are based on the transfer of industries and jobs to countries with low standards of living and low wage rates. American factories are closed because foreign-made goods are cheaper. These goods are cheaper because the workers who make them earn wages one-half, one-fifth and even one-tenth as high as those of American workers. This trade is not comparative-advantage trade, but "wage-cutting trade."

Wage-cutting trade does not offer the benefits arising from comparative-advantage trade. It does not increase economic efficiency; often it reduces efficiency by adding transportation costs. Thus, it cannot possibly make both nations, and the world, better off. If wage-cutting trade benefits one nation, it does so by damaging the other one. In an immediate sense, such trade commonly benefits the low-wage nation that is gaining industries and jobs and damages the high-wage nation that is losing them. In the long run, it may be damaging all around, dragging all nations down to a low standard of living. There are signs that even Japan is becoming concerned with this trend.

The debilitating, long-run effects of wage-cutting trade derive from its out-of-balance character. The high-wage nation cannot go on forever losing industries and jobs, importing more than it exports and running up its foreign debt. It is forced by rising unemployment and burgeoning foreign debt to "become competitive," which it must do by

accepting declining wage rates—as the United States has begun to do.

How much does the high-income nation's standard of living have to decline to make it "competitive" under "free trade?" That depends entirely on the circumstances of the case. With cheap transportation, instant communications, multinational corporations to shift technology and management around the world, low-wage and unemployed people now numbering in the billions and population rising very rapidly in some already populous nations, the economic decline suffered by the United States and Europe under "free trade" could be a shattering one.

More broadly, "free trade" in an increasingly overpopulated world would cause wage-cutting trade to pull all nations down to a lowest-common-denominator level. It would put all nations into a shared "population trap" in which no accomplishment would permit a nation to improve its lot. Thus, a nation that perfected a particular industrial process would not be enriched. It would simply lose its industry to a lower-wage nation. In this respect, "free trade" has the same effects as "free migration."

The implications for the United States of comparative-advantage trade and of wage-cutting trade are as different as day and night. When the facts are considered, it is impossible to deny that recent economic developments in the United States have been dominated by wage-cutting trade. To argue for a policy of "free trade"—and to terminate the import quota on Japanese automobiles, and seek further reductions in tariffs and quotas—on the basis of comparative advantage is not just erroneous but dangerously misleading.

Past economic progress has occurred through an evolutionary process in which one nation finds a way to put together a more effective economy. Other nations advance by copying the success. This pattern requires that nations have the economic independence to experiment, to create constructive patterns—rather than being helpless within a worldwide commune forced by "free trade."

A reasonable trade policy in today's world, then, must encourage mutually beneficial, comparative-advantage trade by curbing destructive wage-cutting trade and other destructive patterns of foreign trade. The starting point for a realistic interpretation of trade is the recognition that different patterns have different effects, and some are destructive.

To curb wage-cutting trade requires balancing arrangements. Balance in trade prevents excessive imports from low-wage nations from undercutting the standard of living of high-wage nations. Balanced trade thus provides the framework within which mutually beneficial trade between nations can develop. Actions to limit a nation's imports, and mutual agreements between nations to prevent damaging trade developments, have been common. We need to use such policies more coherently and cooperatively, with a new understanding of the patterns of trade that are to be encouraged or curbed.

The recent trade policy of the United States has encouraged the wage-cutting foreign trade that has been draining away the nation's industries and jobs and created an enormous trade deficit. Given this starting point, the economic state of the nation can be radically improved simply by adopting realistic policies that limit imports so as to bring the nation's foreign trade into balance.

Holding a Debate

Many students will enjoy participating in a debate on this topic in class or in an informal study group. After completing both readings and possibly doing some additional research (for example, see your textbook), get three to four volunteers for each side of the debate, choose a moderator if your instructor is not available, and devote about a half an hour to opening statements, rebuttals, and summaries.

Discussion

1. If you read both articles, what did you conclude? When a Senator speaks out in favor of protectionism against imports, how do you react? Is this debate a question of economic theory against political reality, or are there political and economic arguments on both sides? Explain.

2. As you read the Friedman article, you were probably impressed with the superb logic and internal consistency with which the Friedmans write. If you were going to attempt to refute their arguments, where would you start? Are there any major assumptions you could question? Are there secondary effects that they neglect to analyze? Explain.

3. If you read the Culbertson article, how did you react to his statement that "'free trade' has the same effects as 'free migration'"? Under what circumstances would Culbertson be right? Can you think of a situation in which free trade would be substantially different in impact from free migration? Explain your answer.

INTERNATIONAL FINANCE AND THE FOREIGN EXCHANGE MARKET

TRUE OR FALSE

T F

1. Foreign exchange markets enable an individual to exchange the currency of one nation for units of currency of another nation.

2. A nation's exports generate a demand for the currency of the exporting nation on the foreign exchange market.

3. Under a system of fixed exchange rates, a balance-of-trade equilibrium is automatic.

4. Under a system of flexible exchange rates, the government must use monetary policy to ensure balance-of-payments equilibrium.

5. The economic analysis of foreign trade is unique in that supply-and-demand relationships do not usually determine equilibrium.

6. One problem with a system of flexible exchange rates is that black markets in foreign currencies are more likely to develop than with controlled rates of exchange.

7. A country's balance of trade has no effect on its balance of payments on current account.

8. The United States would invariably import more than it exports if foreigners were willing to accumulate ever larger amounts of dollars.

9. If imports consistently exceeded exports, U.S. consumers would be hurt as a result of an unfavorable balance of trade implied by such a situation.

10. If Israel sold U.S. dollars to France, the U.S. balance of payments would be unaffected.

11. A rapid U.S. monetary expansion would tend to make the price of German marks rise, in dollar terms, other things constant.

12. Domestic macropolicy-makers can effectively disregard the foreign exchange markets when making a choice between alternative policies.

PROBLEMS AND PROJECTS

1. Match the letters on the right with the numbers on the left.

   _____ (1) balance-of-payments deficit-fixed exchange rates

   _____ (2) will cause the domestic currency to appreciate

   _____ (3) will cause the domestic currency to depreciate

   _____ (4) flexible exchange rates

   _____ (5) fixed exchange rates

   _____ (6) currency inconvertibility

   a. an increase in the nation's exports
   b. will cause a depreciation of the nation's currency when it is experiencing a balance-of-payments deficit
   c. a major obstacle to trade
   d. excess supply of the nation's currency on the exchange market
   e. higher interest rates abroad
   f. reduce the flexibility of macropolicy

2. Each of the diagrams below represents the U.S. demand for and supply of foreign exchange (English pounds). For each of the events described below, diagram how the demand and/or supply of pounds changes (use +, –, or 0 to show no change); and then fill in the blanks to the right of the diagram, indicating in the last blank whether the dollar has appreciated, depreciated, or undergone an indeterminate change as a result of the event(s). (The first question has been answered as an example.) (*Hint:* P = dollars per pound.)

Events	Diagrams	D	S	Change

a. As a result of recovering from a depression, U.S. incomes rise significantly.

+   0   depreciated

b. The United Kingdom experiences a serious recession causing a decline in income.

_____ _____ _____

c. Restrictive monetary policy in the United States causes U.S. interest rates to rise relative to United Kingdom rates.

_____ _____ _____

d. The Chairman of the Fed is quoted as saying, "If the high value of the dollar is not soon corrected by market forces, the Fed will take corrective action."

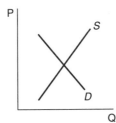

_____ _____ _____

e. While the U.S. experiences stable prices, prices in the United Kingdom rise by 15 percent.

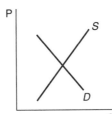

_____ _____ _____

f. In an effort to stimulate the economy, the United States embarks on an expansionary fiscal policy.

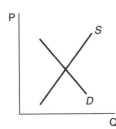

_____ _____ _____

g. Both the United States and the United Kingdom experience inflation rates of 20 percent.

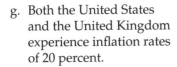

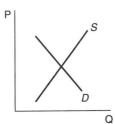

_____ _____ _____

3. Exhibit 1 presents balance-of-payment data for the United States for 1980.

EXHIBIT 1

Debit		Credit	
	(billions of dollars)		
Current account			
Merchandise imports	249.3	Merchandise exports	224.0
Service imports	84.6	Service exports	120.7
Net unilateral transfers	7.1		
Capital account			
U.S. investment abroad	18.5	Foreign investment in the United States	10.9
Loans to foreigners	58.1	Loans from foreigners	70.2

a. Use the data in Exhibit 1 to calculate the balance on (1) merchandise trade account, (2) services account, (3) current account, (4) capital account, and (5) current-and-capital account.

b. Compare these balances to the ones for 1992 in Exhibit 6 in the text. What happened to U.S. international balances between those years? Why do you think this occurred?

LEARNING THE MECHANICS—MULTIPLE CHOICE

1. Since each nation has its own currency
   a. transactions across national borders normally require the conversion of one currency into another.
   b. gold must be used as the international medium of exchange.
   c. direct exchange of goods, through brokers, is the normal means of exchange.
   d. one dominant currency (currently the English pound) is used in more than 95 percent of all international transactions.

2. An appreciation in the value of the U.S. dollar would
   a. encourage foreigners to make more investments in the United States.
   b. encourage U.S. consumers to purchase more foreign-produced goods.
   c. increase the number of dollars that could be purchased with the Mexican peso.
   d. discourage U.S. consumers from traveling abroad.

3. The balance of payments is an annual accounting statement of a nation's
   a. exports and imports.
   b. balance due on imports and exports.
   c. holdings of gold and foreign currencies.
   d. international trade and financial transactions.

4. A nation that has a balance-of-payments surplus is
   a. importing more goods and services than it is exporting.
   b. selling more goods, services, financial assets abroad than it is purchasing from foreigners.
   c. exporting more tangible goods than it is importing from foreigners.
   d. exporting more tangible goods than intangible services and financial assets.

5. Which of the following would *not* be likely to cause a nation's currency to depreciate?
   a. Europeans demand many more U.S. products
   b. More rapid domestic rate of inflation than that of the nation's trading partners
   c. Lower domestic interest rates
   d. Higher foreign interest rates

6. Under a system of flexible exchange rates, transactions that supply the nation's currency to the foreign-exchange market will cause the nation's
   a. currency to depreciate in value.
   b. balance-of-payments surplus to increase.
   c. balance-of-payments deficit to fall.
   d. products to increase in price in terms of foreign currencies.

7. Currency convertibility is crucial to a country's ability to maximize gains from trade. To accomplish convertibility without risking huge fluctuations in the exchange rates, however, some small countries tie the exchange rate value of their domestic currency to a widely accepted foreign currency like the U.S. dollar. This strategy has the disadvantage of
   a. having all domestic transactions undertaken in foreign currency rather than domestic currency.
   b. foregoing domestic fiscal policy independence.
   c. foregoing domestic monetary policy independence.
   d. foregoing domestic trade policy independence.

8. If, to correct a balance-of-payments deficit, U.S. authorities increased import tariffs in order to cut imports, we should also expect
   a. foreign demand for U.S. exports to increase.
   b. U.S. consumers to benefit.
   c. decreased exports as well as decreased imports.
   d. strong opposition from U.S. industries now forced to supply goods formerly imported.

9. With fixed exchange rates, a balance-of-payments surplus would probably be lessened by
   a. restrictive monetary policy, keeping prices down and real interest rates up.
   b. expansionary monetary policy, pushing prices up and real interest rates down.
   c. a decrease in foreign-aid payments.
   d. an increase in income from abroad.

10. Which of the following is *not* a debit item in the U.S. balance of trade?
    a. A U.S. purchase of a German car
    b. A U.S. purchase of insurance from Lloyds of London
    c. A trip to Japan by an American student
    d. A short-term loan to a U.S. resident from South America

11. With time, a depreciation in the value of a nation's currency in the foreign market will cause the nation's
    a. imports to increase and exports to decline.
    b. exports to increase and imports to decline.
    c. both imports and exports to decline.
    d. both imports and exports to rise.

12. The tendency of a nation's current account deficit to react to a depreciation by worsening in the short run and improving in the long run is called
    a. a double change in the 10-currency index.
    b. a hyper-reactive deficit.
    c. the J-curve.
    d. a capital account outflow problem.

13. All of the following are likely impacts on the United States of an unanticipated expansion in the U.S. monetary policy except:
    a. a depreciation in the exchange rate.
    b. a decline in the real interest rate.
    c. an outflow of capital.
    d. an increase in the size of a current account deficit.

THE ECONOMIC WAY OF THINKING—MULTIPLE CHOICE

1. "Wine experts are discovering that California wines of several varieties and vintages are comparable to many of the best French wines. The result is an increased demand, here and abroad, for California wines." With regard to the U.S. balance on current account, this trend will
    a. increase the U.S. deficit, because of the rise in the price of California wine.
    b. decrease the U.S. deficit, because of increased shipments of California wines abroad.
    c. decrease the demand for U.S. dollars.
    d. increase the U.S. demand for French francs.

2. In a world of fixed exchange rates, if a country cut its foreign-aid grants by 50 percent, and if the aid had been "tied" so that 75 percent of the grant had to be spent in the granting country for exports to the recipient, we would expect the change to
    a. increase any existing balance-of-payments deficit existing in the granting nation, since its exports would fall.
    b. decrease any existing balance-of-payments deficit existing in the granting nation by the amount of the cut in foreign aid.
    c. decrease any existing balance-of-payments deficit by less than the cut in foreign aid.
    d. have no impact on the granting nation's balance-of-payments.

3. If the United States could, with fixed exchange rates, run a perpetual balance-of-trade deficit so that other countries held ever-increasing stocks of dollars, Americans would, compared to a no-trade deficit situation, be
    a. better off, since consumption could be perpetually higher.
    b. worse off, since the balance of payments would always be unfavorable.
    c. better off, since exports would have to be higher.
    d. worse off, since imports would have to be lower.

4. A fad that made a particular brand of cross-country skis, imported from Norway, extremely popular in the United States would tend to
    a. increase any existing balance-of-trade surplus for the United States.
    b. decrease any existing balance-of-trade deficit in the United States.
    c. decrease any existing U.S. balance-of-trade surplus.
    d. affect the U.S. balance of payments, but not the balance of trade.

5. The major impact of a restrictive monetary policy on the domestic exchange rate would be (assuming that domestic real interest rates rise in the short run)
    a. an increase in the foreign exchange value of the domestic currency.
    b. a decrease in in the foreign exchange value of the domestic currency.
    c. no change in the foreign exchange value of the domestic currency.
    d. It is impossible to predict the impact on the foreign exchange value of the domestic currency.

6. Which of the following transactions would increase the supply of dollars on the foreign exchange market?
   a. Sale of wheat to the Russians
   b. The spending of a French trade delegation touring the United States
   c. The purchase of a Mexican copper mine by a U.S. business
   d. The earnings of a California business on a Canadian investment

7. Under a system of flexible exchange rates, which of the following will cause the nation's currency to depreciate in the exchange market?
   a. An increase in foreign incomes
   b. A domestic inflation rate of 10 percent while the nation's trading partners are experiencing stable prices
   c. An increase in domestic interest rates
   d. A reduction in interest rates abroad

8. According to the text, which of the following combinations of national economic policies are mutually exclusive?
   a. Currency convertibility, independent monetary policy, flexible exchange rates
   b. Currency convertibility, independent monetary policy, fixed exchange rates
   c. Currency convertibility, restricted monetary policy, flexible exchange rates
   d. Currency convertibility, restricted monetary policy, fixed exchange rates

9. A major difference between devaluation and depreciation is that
   a. a depreciation does not involve a change in the price of gold, in domestic terms.
   b. a devaluation can be a depreciation, but a depreciation can never be a devaluation.
   c. a devaluation is an official government act under fixed exchange rates.
   d. All of the above are correct.

10. The dollar is said to have depreciated if
    a. it once was exchanged for 10 pesos, but now it is exchanged for 12.
    b. foreign goods are now more expensive to Americans even though the prices of the goods in the foreign country remained constant.
    c. under fixed exchange rates the number of dollars supplied exceeds the number of dollars demanded.
    d. the United States has a balance-of-trade deficit under flexible exchange rates.

11. If a nation imports more goods and services than it exports to foreigners, then it must be
    a. borrowing more from foreigners or loaning less to foreigners.
    b. borrowing less from foreigners or loaning more to foreigners.
    c. experiencing a deficit on its current account transactions.
    d. trading under a system of fixed exchange rates, because it would be impossible for imports to exceed exports under a system of flexible exchange rates.

12. A depreciation in the value of a nation's currency on the foreign exchange market will not immediately induce additional exports relative to imports if
    a. the short-run demand of foreigners for the nation's imports is inelastic, whereas the demand of the nation's consumers for foreign goods is also inelastic.
    b. the short-run demand of foreigners for the nations imports is elastic, whereas the demand of the nation's consumers is also elastic.
    c. the long-run demand of foreigners for the nation's imports is elastic, whereas the long-run demand of the nation's consumers for foreign goods is inelastic.
    d. the long-run demand of foreigners for the nation's imports is inelastic, whereas the long-run demand of the nation's consumers for foreign goods is elastic.

13. Expansionary fiscal policy exerts upward pressure on prices, output, and interest rates. As a result, expansionary fiscal policy tends to cause
    a. an appreciation of the exchange rate and a deficit in the current account.
    b. a depreciation of the exchange rate and a surplus in the current account.
    c. an uncertain effect on the exchange rate and a deficit in the current account.
    d. uncertain effects on both the exchange rate and the current account.

14. Suppose a country with fixed exchange rates has a $50 billion current account surplus and a $70 billion net capital outflow. The country
    a. has a balance of payments surplus and should consider revaluing its currency.
    b. has a balance of payments surplus and should consider devaluing its currency.
    c. has a balance of payments deficit and should consider revaluing its currency.
    d. has a balance of payments deficit and should consider devaluing its currency.

15. If our country's real interest rate is lower than the real interest rate of its trading partners, what will tend to happen to the foreign exchange value of our country's currency and our country's balance on current account?

	Currency will:	*Current account will:*
a.	appreciate	move toward a deficit
b.	depreciate	move toward a deficit
c.	appreciate	move toward a surplus
d.	depreciate	move toward a surplus

THE ECONOMIC WAY OF THINKING—DISCUSSION QUESTIONS

1. "Exports pay for a nation's imports. Other countries will not continue shipping us their goods if they lose interest in the goods, services, and financial assets we export to them in exchange." Do you agree? Explain.

2. "No patriotic American wants the value of the dollar to fall on the foreign exchange market." Whether or not this quote is true, it is fair to say that Americans seem to like a strong dollar and a trade surplus.
    a. What are the advantages of a strong dollar? The disadvantages?
    b. What are the advantages of a trade surplus? The disadvantages?
    c. Why is it difficult to have both a strong dollar and a trade surplus at the same time?

3. In today's world of flexible exchange rates and mobile financial assets, a country's domestic macroeconomic policies and its foreign sector are closely interrelated. Economists focus especially on the interaction between domestic policies, interest rates, exchange rates, and international capital flows.
    a. How can a budget deficit contribute to capital inflows and an offsetting current account deficit?
    b. With flexible exchange rates, why does trade protection tend to be ineffective as a cure for a current account deficit?
    c. Some economists have recommended that a tax be imposed on international capital flows to reduce their volume. Would you favor such a tax? Why or why not?

4. "A nation's balance of payments must always be in balance." In what sense is this true? What is a "balance-of-payments deficit"? Under a flexible exchange system, will a balance-of-payments deficit automatically be corrected? Explain.

5. "A system of flexible exchange rates is advantageous because it enables a nation to stabilize domestic employment and prices without regard to the foreign sector and insulates a country from the effects of foreign macroeconomic policies." Do you agree or not? Explain.

6. Discuss the role of time in balance-of-payments adjustments. Why might the current account of a country with a depreciating currency deteriorate in the short run and improve in the long run? Why would the opposite scenario for the current account be surprising?

PERSPECTIVES IN ECONOMICS

Don't Worry About the Trade Deficit
By Herbert Stein

[From *The Wall Street Journal*, May 16, 1989. Reprinted with permission from The Wall Street Journal ©Dow Jones & Co., Inc. All Rights Reserved.]

There seems to be a conspiracy against telling even the simplest truth.

This somber thought was brought home to me by an experience on a recent Tuesday afternoon. I'm goofing off, staying at home and watching daytime TV. I have a choice of 16 channels. On 15 of them beautiful women and handsome men are working out the complications of their love-lives, mostly in hospital rooms. I know that at my age I cannot expect any of these complications to be resolved during my lifetime, so I settle for C-SPAN and the U.S. Senate at "work."

I'm hearing a senator carrying on about how terrible it is that other countries insist on selling us more stuff than they buy from us. He demands that we let these countries know in no uncertain terms that we are not going to put up with that kind of thing any longer.

Excuses for Economists At first I am shocked. Is there no limit to what can be put over the air, even in the daytime when children may be listening? But then I get over it and become more philosophical. I know that this senator has an undergraduate degree from one of our leading liberal arts colleges and another degree from one of our most eminent law schools. He is, however, a senator and may be forgiven for committing nonsense on the public airwaves.

But what about the trained staffs of international financial institutions who write serious reports about the need to correct "imbalances"—which is polite language for eliminating or reducing the U.S. trade deficit? What about the finance ministers from the industrial countries who meet every six months or so to cook up plans for correcting these "imbalances"—again meaning the U.S. trade deficit? An what about my sophisticated economist friends who talk about the need to eliminate the trade deficit? What are they all talking about?

I say to my economist friends that the trade deficit is not hurting the U.S., but, on the contrary, is helping us, and I ask them why we should be concerned about reducing the trade deficit. The more candid among them answer as follows: "We know that the trade deficit is not hurting us. But there are a lot of people out there—including presidents, senators, and congressmen—who think that the trade deficit is a bad thing and as long as it persists they will feel driven to protectionist measures, which would be very bad. In order to restrain the protectionist movement the trade deficit must be reduced."

What this comes down to is an argument for reducing the budget deficit as a way to reduce the trade deficit and thereby head off protectionism, even though we all know that the trade deficit is not hurting us and does not constitute a valid reason for protectionism.

Readers of this page may know that I am more willing than most people to pay more taxes and give up some of my Social Security and Medicare benefits in order to balance the federal budget and run a surplus. There are good reasons for wanting to do that. But I would hate to pay anything in the hope of thereby heading off protectionism.

Some people have good reason to be protectionist; they have immediate interests at stake. No economist, however much devoted to free trade, ever denied that. These "knowing" protectionists will not be dissuaded by seeing the trade deficit disappear. But most people have no good reason to be protectionist. They support or tolerate protectionism out of ignorance. There should be a more efficient way to convert them to the virtues of free trade than by eliminating the trade deficit. Or, to put the case more modestly, it is worth trying to convert them by telling the truth. That is what economists are for. If some more "devious" ways of avoiding protectionism have to be found, let some one else do it.

Let's remember a few simple propositions.

1. The U.S. has a trade deficit because people in the rest of the world invest their savings here. This inflow of capital is voluntary on both sides—foreigners are seeking the best place to put their money and American governments and companies are seeking the best place to obtain money. Foreigners seeking to invest here have to obtain dollars. Their demand for dollars keep the exchange rate of the dollar at a level where U.S. imports exceed U.S. exports.

2. As a result of the capital inflow—and the accompanying trade deficit—over the past eight years, the stock of productive capital in the U.S. is now about $700 billion higher than it would otherwise have been. This fact is commonly misunderstood because people think the capital inflow is financing the budget deficit. It is true that foreigners have bought a large amount of U.S. Treasury securities. But if foreigners had not bought them they would have had to be bought by Americans, who would have had less of their own savings to invest in productive assets.

3. This inflow if capital has been mainly of benefit to American workers, who as a result of it, work with a larger capital stock and have higher productivity and real incomes. It has also increased the U.S. tax base.

4. Large and persistent trade deficits have not prevented an unusually long recovery and the achievement of an unusually high level of total output.

5. Continuation of the capital inflow-trade deficit combination will increase the amount of interest and dividends that American governments and corporations have to pay to foreigners. But it will also increase the amount of capital in this country that would not otherwise be here, and that additional capital will generate the income to pay for foreigners. That income will not come out of income that Americans would otherwise have earned.

6. The inflow of capital and ownership of assets in the U.S. by foreigners is not a cause of dangerous dependence that is a political or security danger to us. What may be politically dangerous is the effort of governments to manipulate this relationship—an effort to which we are the leaders, unfortunately.

7. The inflow of goods and capital may not go on forever, but it is unlikely to stop so abruptly as to create difficulties for us. The two-sided inflow is an adaptation to basic conditions—propensities to save and investment opportunities at home and abroad—that will change only gradually. The most serious qualification is that government efforts to manage exchange rates may cause such great uncertainties about the future of those rates that international capital flows dry up for a time.

Exchange Rates Everything

8. Protectionist measures imposed by government, ours and others, impair efficiency but do not cause the trade deficit. Trying to eliminate these measures would be worthwhile whether we have a deficit or a surplus, but success would not change the deficit.

9. Having a trade deficit is not a sign of low productivity or economy weakness. Poor, weak countries—like Brazil—can have trade surpluses. Rich, strong countries like us can have trade deficits. Everything depends on prices and exchange rates.

10. Let's forget about the trade deficit. We have plenty of real deficits to worry about—including the education deficit, the defense deficit, the poverty deficit and the investment deficit.

Discussion

1. Do you agree with Stein? Should we worry about the trade deficit? Why or why not?

2. If Stein is right that "rich, strong countries like us can have trade deficits," then why are Congress, the media, and many economists so concerned with avoiding the current U.S. trade deficit? Is it possible so many highly qualified people are wrong?

3. If the trade deficit isn't hurting the U.S. but policy-makers think it is and are considering protectionist policies that *will* hurt the country, which would be easier, fixing the trade deficit or educating the policy-makers? Explain your reasoning.

CHAPTER TWENTY-TWO

ECONOMIC DEVELOPMENT
AND THE GROWTH OF INCOME

TRUE OR FALSE

T F

1. The most obvious characteristic of a less-developed nation is low per capita income.

2. Low incomes and widespread poverty are still the norm in most countries.

3. The exchange-rate conversion method of comparing GDPs is a good indicator of differences in the purchasing power of currencies for goods and services that are not exchanged on international markets.

4. Comparison of per-capita GDP between nations is made more difficult if nations fix their exchange rates at levels that differ substantially from the equilibrium rates.

5. Monetary instability discourages investment and therefore hurts economic growth.

6. The evidence since the Second World War suggests that one policy option for governments that want to promote prosperity is to follow macroeconomic policies consistent with relatively stable prices.

7. Technological advance, defined as the invention of—but not adoption of—new techniques, enables workers to produce additional output with the same amount of resources.

8. The exchange-rate conversion method and the purchasing-power parity method of comparing the per-capita GDPs of nations provide substantially different results.

9. There is an enormous gulf between the economic well-being of developed and less-developed nations.

10. Capital market restrictions such as interest rate controls tend to keep interest rates low enough to stimulate investment and therefore help economic growth.

11. The annual per capita growth rate of real GDP for Taiwan, Hong Kong, and South Korea exceeds the growth rate of most industrial nations, including the United States.

PROBLEMS AND PROJECTS

1. The text specifies four key sources of economic growth:
   (1) Investment in human and physical capital
   (2) Technological progress
   (3) Efficient allocation of resources
   (4) Investment in infrastructure

   Each item below is an impediment to one of the key conditions for economic development listed above. Match each impediment with the relevant development condition.

   ___ a. Much of the labor-saving research and development that occurs in advanced countries is not very useful to developing countries where labor is abundant and capital is scarce.

   ___ b. Instead of exploiting their comparative advantage, many developing countries have tried to become self-sufficient through import-substitution policies.

   ___ c. Because of the debt crisis, foreign loans and direct investments in most developing countries have dropped sharply since 1982.

   ___ d. In response to the debt crisis, many governments in developing countries have curtailed spending on transportation and communication systems in order to reduce their budget deficits.

2. Exhibit 1 is a compound interest table in which each entry shows the amount to which $1.00 will accumulate at various rates of interest after n years. For example, if $10.00 were to grow at 2% interest for 5 years, it would grow to a value of $11.04 = $10.00 × 1.104.

EXHIBIT 1

			Rate of interest or growth			
Years	2%	3%	4%	5%	6%	7%
5	1.104	1.159	1.217	1.276	1.338	1.403
10	1.219	1.344	1.480	1.629	1.791	1.967
15	1.346	1.558	1.801	2.079	2.397	2.759
20	1.486	1.806	2.191	2.653	3.207	3.870
25	1.641	2.094	2.666	3.386	4.292	5.427
30	1.811	2.427	3.243	4.330	5.743	7.612
35	2.000	2.814	3.946	5.516	7.686	10.677
40	2.208	3.262	4.801	7.040	10.286	14.974
45	2.438	3.781	5.841	8.985	13.765	21.002

   a. Suppose the mythical economy of Gromangro has in 1950 a real GDP of &20 billion and a population of 100 million. (& is the symbol for "mango," the national currency of Gromangro.) What is the real GDP per capita of Gromangro in 1950?

   b. In 1950, the U.S.'s real GDP per capita was $6,330. If in 1950 the exchange rate between the dollar and the mango was &1 = $2, what was Gromangro's 1950 GDP per capita in dollars? What was the difference in dollars between the per capita GDPs of the two?

   c. Suppose that Gromangro's GDP grows at 7% from 1950 to 1990 while her population grows at 3%. Use Exhibit 1 to calculate the value (in mangos) of Gromangro's GDP and her population in 1990. What is Gromangro's per capita GDP in 1990?

   d. Suppose the U.S.'s per capita GDP grows at 2% from 1950 to 1990. What is its value in 1990?

   e. If the dollar/mango exchange rate remains the same as in part b, what is Gromangro's 1990 per capita GDP in dollars? What is the dollar difference between the two countries' per capita GDPs in 1990?

f. Gromangro's grew at a faster *rate* than the United States. What happened to the *absolute* difference in per capita income?

3. One way of analyzing economic growth is through simple equilibrium GDP models. Consider a hypothetical economy in which

$$Y = C + I + G$$
$$C = 200 + 0.9Y_D$$
$$Y_D = Y - T$$

investment is constant at 50, government expenditure is 300, and taxation is 250. Verify that equilibrium GDP is 3250. One problem with this economic model is that it is for a closed economy. How could you change it to incorporate international trade? (*Hint:* Remember that our definition of GDP also includes net exports.) How could an economy incapable of borrowing from abroad or from the public increase equilibrium GDP? Try a few alternatives to see what could be done; as you will quickly realize, without capital of some sort, it is very difficult to generate sustained economic growth.

4. One handy device to help get a good feel for what various growth rates mean is the "Simple 70" rule. The rule is just a formula for closely approximating how long it takes a growing value to double in size:

Doubling time = 70 / percentage growth rate

a. The Simple 70 rule works quite well. Try it with the following hypothetical GDP growth rates:

Annual growth rate of GDP	Years required for GDP to double:	
	Actual	*Simple 70 rule estimate*
2.0	35.0	_____
3.5	20.1	_____
7.0	10.2	_____

b. Use the Simple 70 rule to contrast the estimated per capita GDP doubling times in each of the following countries:

	Annual growth of GDP per capita 1965–1986	*Years required for GDP per capita to double*
India	1.8	_____
Brazil	4.3	_____
China	5.1	_____
South Korea	6.7	_____
Japan	4.3	_____
United States	1.6	_____

c. Many observers are concerned about the impact of population growth on development prospects, since per capita GDP growth % is approximately equal to GDP growth minus population growth %. For countries in Exhibit 2, compute the current per capita GDP doubling times and then compute the per capita GDP doubling times if population growth could be reduced to 1.0 percent, the current rate in the United States.

EXHIBIT 2

Annual growth rate, 1965–1986	India	China	Brazil
GDP:	4.1	7.0	6.6
Population:	2.3	1.9	2.3
GDP per capita:	1.8	5.1	4.3
GDP per capita with 1.0% pop. growth:	___	___	___
Years required for GDP per capita to double:			
Presently:	___	___	___
With 1% pop. growth:	___	___	___

LEARNING THE MECHANICS—MULTIPLE CHOICE

1. The *simplest* method for comparing income levels between nations is the
   a. exchange-rate conversion method.
   b. dependency ratio method.
   c. purchasing-power parity method.
   d. price distortion comparison method.

2. "This method calculates the purchasing power of each nation's currency in terms of the typical bundle of goods and services that is included in GDP. Once the purchasing power of each nation's currency is determined, this information is used to convert the GDP of each country to a common monetary unit such as the U.S. dollar." This statement describes the
   a. purchasing power parity method of converting GDP to a common monetary unit.
   b. exchange rate conversion method of converting GDP to a common monetary unit.
   c. vicious cycle of poverty of less-developed nations.
   d. trickle-down theory of measuring economic development.

3. The most *accurate* method for comparing income levels between nations is the
   a. exchange-rate conversion method.
   b. dependency ratio method.
   c. purchasing-power parity method.
   d. trickle-down method.

4. Which of the following most accurately states the importance of technological advancements as a source of economic growth for less-developed countries?
   a. Restraints imposed by the slow advancements in modern technology have severely constrained the growth of less-developed countries.
   b. If modern technology were the only requirement for economic growth, less-developed countries would be growing rapidly.
   c. Most less-developed nations have the necessary complementary factors of production to make good use of modern technology if they could just afford the complex machines.
   d. The rate of return on the adoption of modern technology is high in less-developed countries, but nonetheless capital investors are unwilling to channel investment funds to these countries.

5. The exchange-rate conversion method is
   a. a method of converting per capita income from one nation into another nation's currency through exchange rates.
   b. a method of converting exchange rates between countries to allow for differences between levels of per capita income.
   c. a method of converting exchange rates to allow for purchasing-power parity.
   d. a method of converting per capita income from one nation into another nation's currency through purchasing-power parity.

6. How do high tariffs and other restraints on international trade affect the prosperity of a nation?
   a. They increase employment and thereby promote the growth of real GDP.
   b. They prevent the nation from realizing fully the potential gains from specialization, exchange, and competition.
   c. They protect domestic producers and thereby promote economic growth.
   d. Both a and c are correct.

7. If the political leaders of a country wanted to promote economic growth, which of the following policy alternatives would be most effective?
   a. Price controls on agricultural products in order to keep the price of food low
   b. Expansionary monetary policies designed to keep interest rates low
   c. Regulations prohibiting foreigners from owning domestic business and withdrawing profits from domestic investments
   d. Elimination of price controls and trade restraints and establishment of a monetary policy consistent with long-run price stability (or a low rate of inflation)

8. A highly negative real interest rate would seem to encourage borrowing, investing, and (therefore) high economic growth rates
   a. but it doesn't, because negative real interest rates are impossible.
   b. but it doesn't, mainly because a highly negative real interest rate guarantees rampant hyperinflation, which tends to discourage investing.
   c. but it doesn't, mainly because the highly negative real interest rate stimulates a large capital outflow.
   d. and it does.

9. A 3 percent growth rate in GDP will bring about a doubling of GDP in about how many years?
   a. 3
   b. 12
   c. 24
   d. 48

10. If the results of a recent study are to be believed, a high level of marginal tax rates appear to be associated with low growth rates of per capita income in developing countries. One possible reason for this observation is that
    a. countries that are growing slowly have greater fiscal needs than countries that are growing quickly, and so tax rates are higher.
    b. high tax rates can potentially discourage productive activity.
    c. both a and b.
    d. neither a nor b.

THE ECONOMIC WAY OF THINKING — MULTIPLE CHOICE

When answering the next two questions, use the information in Exhibit 3:

EXHIBIT 3

	Per capita GDP (dollars)	GDP growth rate (percent)	Rate of population growth (percent)
Egypt	710	5.3	2.7
Cameroun	910	5.2	1.0
United States	18,430	3.0	1.0

1. In which country is the level of economic development (not growth) the highest?
    a. Egypt
    b. Cameroun
    c. United States
    d. It is impossible to tell because of the problems of comparing GDPs from different countries and the lack of information about items other than per capita GDP.

2. In which country is the *growth rate* of per capita GDP the highest?
    a. Egypt
    b. Cameroun
    c. United States
    d. It is impossible to tell because adequate information is not given.

3. Which of the following best characterizes the relationship between the developed nations and the less-developed nations?
    a. The developed nations are growing and the less-developed nations are stagnating.
    b. The less-developed nations are growing, but the developed nations are growing even faster.
    c. Population is growing faster in developed nations.
    d. It is an oversimplification to divide the world into the growing, developed nations and the stagnating, less-developed nations.

4. Which of the following is *not* a good reason for using indices other than per capita GDP to measure economic development?
    a. Per capita GDP does not take income distribution into account.
    b. Per capita GDP is overly influenced by changes in population.
    c. Per capita GDP does not take nonmarket transactions into account.
    d. Per capita GDP does not take externalities, such as pollution, into account.

5. Which of the following "absurd" suggestions is the best government policy in terms of improving economic growth?
   a. Cut all tax rates to zero, since it has been shown that low taxes encourage rapid growth.
   b. Cut all tariff rates to zero, since it has been shown that high tariffs discourage rapid growth.
   c. Cut all real interest rates to zero, since it has been shown that high interest rates hurt rapid growth.
   d. Cut government expenditures to zero, since it has been shown that state ownership of enterprises hinders rapid growth.

6. If annual per capita GDP in the United States is $16,000 and in Great Britain is £6,000, then under which of the following exchange rates would Great Britain have a larger GDP than the United States?
   a. £1 = $2
   b. £1 = $3
   c. £3 = $1
   d. £2 = $1

EXHIBIT 4

	Mexico		United States	
	1975	*1985*	*1975*	*1985*
Gross domestic product (billions of units of domestic currency):	1,100.1	45,588.5	1,697.5	3,957.0
Population (millions):	60.1	78.5	216.0	239.3
Pesos per dollar:	12.5	256.9	—	—

The next two questions can be answered using the information in Exhibit 4.

7. In 1985, GDP per capita in Mexico was
   a. about 14 percent as large as GDP per capita in the United States.
   b. about 4 percent as large as GDP per capita in the United States.
   c. about 19 percent as large as GDP per capita in the United States.
   d. about 5 percent as large as GDP per capita in the United States.

8. Comparing the changes between 1975 and 1985 in GDP and GDP per capita in Mexico as proportions of GDP and GDP per capita in the United States,
   a. both proportions rose.
   b. GDP in Mexico rose relative to GDP in the United States, but GDP per capita fell relative to GDP per capita in the United States.
   c. GDP in Mexico fell relative to GDP in the United States, but GDP per capita rose relative to GDP per capita in the United States.
   d. both proportions fell.

9. Which of the following would be most likely to improve the rate of growth of a less-developed nation?
   a. Development of strong labor unions
   b. An increase in foreign investment attracted by the expectation of economic and political stability
   c. An increase in the dependency ratio
   d. Foreign aid to construct a steel plant

10. According to Alvin Rabushka, a country with low marginal tax rates (or high thresholds for medium- and high-rate tax schedules) is likely to:
   a. grow rapidly, because the low rates will give businesses and entrepreneurs an incentive to expand economic activity.
   b. grow rapidly, because the low rates will allow the government to afford to improve the educational system, eventually improving economic growth.
   c. grow slowly, because the low rates will make it difficult for the government to improve the infra- structure.
   d. grow slowly, because the low rates will encourage the rich to move elsewhere.

THE ECONOMIC WAY OF THINKING—DISCUSSION QUESTIONS

1. What are the major conditions for economic growth? The major obstacles? Can you think of a country that has experienced rapid economic growth without a strong natural resource base? Without a slowing in the rate of population growth? Without a high rate of investment? Without substantial upgrading of literacy?

2. Why do you think the purchasing power parity method of comparing living standards yields smaller gaps across countries than the exchange rate conversion method? Which method do you think is more accurate? Which is easier to compute? Explain.

3. How do you think the less-developed countries can best help themselves attain more rapid growth rates? How do you think the developed countries can best help them?

4. In this chapter, it is implicitly assumed that most countries *want* to become developed. What arguments can you think of that might lead a country to want to stall its development?

5. Some argue that most households below the poverty line in the United States are not poor when compared to typical households of less-developed countries. Do you think such a comparison is valid? Why or why not? Who should we help most, the poor at home or those abroad who are even poorer?

6. A huge percentage of the world's population lives in countries where average annual per capita GDP is less than $100 a month. Plan a budget and try to figure out how you might get through a month with less than $100. (*Hint:* Assume that prices are similar in both places.) Does it matter that a large percentage of production in some countries is produced in the household and therefore not measured in GDP? How?

PERSPECTIVES IN ECONOMICS

Third World Facts and Fictions
by Charles Wolf Jr.

[Reprinted with permission of Charles Wolf Jr. from the *Los Angeles Times*, January 27, 1981.]

Secretary of State Alexander Haig Jr. has observed that the Third World ("A misleading term if ever there was one") is a myth.

"Recent American foreign policy," Haig said, "has suffered from the misperception which lumps together nations as diverse as Brazil and Libya, Indonesia and South Yemen, Cuba and Kuwait . . . (The) failure to tailor policy to the individual circumstances of developing nations has frequently aggravated the very internal stresses which Western policy should seek instead to diminish."

Following Haig's lead, it may be timely to try to separate myths from realities, because the conventional wisdom about the so-called Third World is more conventional than wise.

Myth: The "Third World," consisting of some 130 less-developed nations, is a reasonably cohesive entity, unified by similar interests and ideologies that enable its members to act effectively and in concert.

Reality: The nations of the Third World are, in fact, divided in many more ways and by many more conflicting interests than those that unify them.

Of course, it is a fact that certain attitudes—intense nationalism, hypersensitivity to foreign condescension, a liking, perhaps waning, for socialist ideology, to name only a few—are shared by many developing nations. But more objective circumstances tend to divide them.

For example, the Third World includes oil importers (Brazil, India, Pakistan) and oil exporters (Saudi Arabia, Libya, Iraq, Mexico, Venezuela); rapidly growing economies (Korea, Brazil, Singapore) and slowly growing or stagnating ones (most of the remaining nations); centrally planned economies as well as market economies; major international debtors (Brazil, Mexico, Turkey) and major international creditors (Saudi Arabia, Libya, Kuwait); communist nations, procommunist nations and vigorously anticommunist (as well as many in between), and nations ruled by military governments and nations that profess the primacy of civil over military control.

The rhetoric of Third World unity is more spurious than real. The reality of the Third World is cultural, political and economic diversity.

Thus, almost any action by the Reagan administration is likely to evoke support from some Third World nations, opposition from others and indifference from many. Our policy-makers would be well advised to think about the "Third World" as a plural, not a singular, entity.

Myth: Achieving significant and sustained economic development in the Third World is an overwhelming and intractable problem, made even more difficult by the rigidity and discrimination of the present international economic order.

Reality: Achieving rapid and sustained development, with the present international economic order, is a much less formidable problem than is usually supposed. The means and methods for realizing economic development are well known, have been widely demonstrated and are generally acknowledged even if they are not widely adopted. By and large, these recipes have been amply demonstrated by the impressive development of the small number of Third World nations (Brazil, Korea, Taiwan and Singapore) that have maintained average rates of real economic growth of 9 percent annually during the 1970s.

These nations have made economic progress possible by achieving political stability, including infrequent changes in government. In addition, such nations have provided a hospitable economic climate for market forces and market prices, have encouraged infusions of foreign capital and the selective import of foreign technology, and have avoided hyperinflation.

Orientation toward the market, while typical of these relatively successful Third World nations, does not necessarily imply private ownership, or an inactive role for government. Where government interventions occur, they usually are selective and limited in number.

As to the rigidity and adverse effects of the present economic international order, and the sometimes shrill call for a "new international economic order," again the reality departs sharply from the myth. In fact, the "old" order has been remarkably flexible, rather than rigid, and hospitable rather than resistant to development in the Third World.

For example, the drastic shift from a regime of fixed exchange rates to fluctuating ones, the recycling of several hundred billion petrodollars over the last half dozen years, and the transfer of technology are all indications of the adaptability of the present international economic setup to changing needs and forces.

Myth: Economic development is essential for political stability and democratization in the Third World.

Reality: There is no significant relationship between economic development and either political stability or democratization. Nations such as South Korea have developed dramatically without significant progress toward democracy. Nations such as India have maintained relatively democratic and stable institutions without notable success in economic development. In some nations—for example, Iran—rapid economic development has brought with it political instability. And in other nations, such as Turkey, adverse economic conditions have provided an environment in which terrorism has flourished and emerging democratic institutions have been set back.

Perhaps there is a weak relationship between economic progress and political stability. If an economy stagnates and if unemployment is high, it is probably easier for the opposition to be kindled, simply because idle hands are more likely to be mischievous ones.

Myth: The primary objective of Third World nations is to modernize their economies as rapidly as they can.

Reality: On the contrary, most Third World leaders have other goals and objectives. These include achieving greater national recognition and prestige in the international community; acquiring modern and advanced military equipment; pursuing ideological preferences; and agitating for international redistribution of income, rather than domestic economic growth.

If one looks at behavior rather than rhetoric, development is among the goals and priorities of most of the nations of the Third World, but not at the top of the list.

There is a paradox in all this: If development is accorded primary emphasis among national objectives, success seems to depend on imposing limits on the scope and character of government intervention. Few Third World leaders are willing to let go of the reins of control and unleash the market forces that can help their economies grow.

Discussion

1. Do you agree with Wolf's perceptions of reality in all four cases? About which are you skeptical? Why?

2. What sort of changes in policies toward Third World nations do these new "realities" imply? How easy would it be to bring these policy changes about?

3. Can you think of other "Third World facts and fictions"? If so, what are they?

CHAPTER TWENTY-THREE

ECONOMIES IN TRANSITION

TRUE OR FALSE

T F

1. In many of the formerly communist countries, the production bundle produced under central planning was way out of line with what would have been chosen by consumers.

2. Ownership of physical capital differs between socialist and market systems, but the mechanism for allocating resources is the same.

3. One of the keys to a successful transition from a command economy to a market economy is the protection of domestic industries from foreign competition.

4. In the Czech Republic, the proportion of retail sales that came from the private sector increased by almost 150% from 1991 to 1993.

5. In reality, all modern economies are a combination of capitalist and socialist economic organization.

6. The concept of opportunity cost does not apply to a centrally planned system.

7. In the first stages of the transition to a market economy, major improvements in customer satisfaction can be accomplished with only minor changes in operating style. For example, Kmart's initial advertising campaign (after they took over 13 stores in the former Czechoslovakia) emphasized that you could enter Kmart without the previously required basket or cart.

8. In general, the GDP data indicate that some transitional economies have had increases in output and that of the rest, only Russia has had a sharp decline in output.

9. The transition from socialism to market system has proven to be substantially more difficult than many people, including a good number of economists, thought would be the case.

10. The "transitional trap" involves budget deficits that lead to money creation, which leads to inflation.

11. For all intents and purposes, the countries of Eastern Europe and the former Soviet Union confront similar problems and have followed similar transition strategies.

12. If the experiment in China is any guide, it would appear that the agricultural sector is easier to divide up and privatize than the industrial sector.

PROBLEMS AND PROJECTS

1. Match up items in each column by placing a number from the right into each of the blanks on the left.

   ___ a. A characteristic of a socialist economy

   ___ b. A characteristic of a capitalist economy

   ___ c. The price of housing in Russia

   ___ d. A key element to a successful transition plan

   ___ e. A reason that transition is so difficult

   ___ f. A reason for the failure of socialism

   ___ g. The transitional trap

1. Nonhuman resources are owned by individuals
2. Below equilibrium and below cost
3. The priorities of a central plan reflect the preferences of those with political power
4. Physical resources are owned by the state
5. Budget deficits, money creation, and inflation
6. Dismantling the collective farms
7. Monetary overhang makes price decontrol difficult
8. Privatization

2. Read over the Thumbnail Sketch in the text and then, using the same economic characteristics, devise a similar exhibit to demonstrate the differences between the methods that the economies of Russia and the Czech Republic are using in their transitions from socialism to capitalism.

3. Match the countries below with an identifying characteristic by placing a number from the right into each of the blanks on the left.

   ___ a. Poland

   ___ b. China

   ___ c. Russia

   ___ d. Czech Republic

   ___ e. Romania

   ___ f. Latvia

1. Like Poland, it had a large private sector in 1989
2. Largest combined 1992–93 percent declines in GDP among transition nations
3. Used tight macropolicy and privatization to avoid hyperinflation
4. Only transitional economy to grow in 1993
5. Prices rose by 250 percent in one day (January 3, 1992)
6. Started a slow transition by dismantling collective farms
7. Private sector in 1989 was little more than one percent of GDP

LEARNING THE MECHANICS—MULTIPLE CHOICE

1. The business firms in a socialist economy
   a. are guided by boards of directors that perform functions similar to those of boards of directors of market economies.
   b. typically confront a strong labor union.
   c. are guided by central planners who use a reward–penalty system to affect the decisions of plant managers and workers.
   d. operate outside of the central planning apparatus.

2. At least four basic economic concepts apply to all economic systems. These four include all of the following except
   a. the law of demand.
   b. comparative advantage and efficiency.
   c. opportunity cost.
   d. private property rights.

3. Monetary overhang
   a. simplifies the transition of a socialist nation into a capitalist nation because the overhang provides ready funds for new ventures and investment.
   b. is the building up of financial hard-currency reserves in socialist central banks.
   c. is the building up of monetary reserves in socialist nations because incomes are greater than the amounts that can be spent.
   d. is quite dangerous to pedestrians who walk under it.

4. Which of the following, is *not* a characteristic of a socialist economy?
   a. Detailed central planning
   b. Government ownership of physical capital
   c. Government ownership of human capital
   d. Wages and prices that are fixed by government edict

5. Of the following which is *not* key to a successful transition plan in a market economy?
   a. Decontrol of prices
   b. Monetary stability
   c. Privatization
   d. Decreasing the rate of unemployment

6. Under communism, shopping could be a real ordeal. Often, lines were long, customer service was poor, and the quality and selection of products was inconsistent. Today, the retail sector in Eastern Europe has changed dramatically; for example,
   a. in Poland, 80 percent of the products offered by stores in the Hit supermarket chain are from outside Poland, thus improving quality.
   b. in the Czech Republic, Kmart workers have been trained to be helpful, friendly, and courteous, thus improving service.
   c. in the Slovak Republic, the inter-company debt of state enterprises rose by a factor of one million in only seven months, thus providing the funds to improve selection.
   d. all of the above.

7. The official 1993 figures for Russia indicate that the GDP was about 50 percent lower than the comparable figure for 1989. This reduction probably is at least partially the result of
   a. severe deflation in the economy, causing nominal GDP to fall even though real output didn't change by much.
   b. a shift in resources from consumption to defense, leaving very little for the consumer retail sector.
   c. the monetary overhang allowing individuals to buy goods and services without having to actually work for them.
   d. incorrect data; the official figures overstate the actual reductions in output for a number of reasons.

8. Which of the following is *not* a reason that the transition from command economies to market economies has been more difficult than most people expected?
   a. It turned out to be quite difficult to reduce subsidies to existing enterprises.
   b. There was no legal framework for the protection of private property and the enforcement of contracts.
   c. The monetary overhang made price decontrol more difficult.
   d. The central-planning process left behind an aftermath of inefficient, "too-small" enterprises.

9. Suppose that a centrally planned country changes the way it specifies goals for bread production from the number of loaves of bread produced to the number of pounds of bread produced. All else equal, we'd expect the average size of a loaf of bread in this country to
   a. decrease.
   b. increase.
   c. remain unchanged.
   d. increase, decrease, or remain unchanged, depending on the most efficient size of a loaf of bread.

10. Socialist central planning failed for which of the following reasons?
    a. Under socialism, there is an incentive for enterprises to produce high-quality products that are valued by consumers.
    b. Central planners are often unable to get the vast amount of information required to develop a sensible plan.
    c. Under central planning, the incentive for continuing the status quo is quite weak.
    d. The priorities of the central plan will reflect the selfish preferences of many individuals rather than the more altruistic desires of those in political power.

11. During privatization in Russia, more than three-fourths of the enterprises opted for allowing the employees to purchase 51 percent of the shares in that enterprise. It seems likely that this will result in
    a. increased wages and dividends.
    b. decreased wages and dividends.
    c. increased wages, but decreased dividends.
    d. decreased wages, but increased dividends.

THE ECONOMIC WAY OF THINKING—MULTIPLE CHOICE

1. Which of the following is *not* a characteristic of socialist economic organization?
    a. Centralized economic planning
    b. Workers are employed by government or by government-controlled cooperatives
    c. The rate of return on human capital is determined by market forces
    d. Investment in nonhuman capital is determined by political factors

2. If central planners wanted to allocate resources efficiently, they would
    a. attempt to have each product produced by the low-opportunity-cost producer.
    b. expand the use of a resource as long as its marginal product were positive.
    c. expand the production of a good as long as consumers received some positive marginal utility from it.
    d. not need to utilize such capitalist concepts as opportunity cost and comparative advantage.

3. Improving competition among suppliers is considered a key to a successful transition plan (to a market economy). What would you do first if you were in charge of creating a more competitive environment among suppliers?
    a. Allow and encourage new firms to enter markets
    b. Require existing firms to expand into new markets
    c. Force suppliers to lower prices, thus improving competition
    d. Encourage exports to foreign nations by creating export subsidies and/or tax breaks for exports

4. If the black market price of a good is higher than the price of that good as determined by a centrally planned government,
    a. consumers probably want more of that good than is currently being produced.
    b. consumers probably want less of that good than is currently being produced.
    c. consumers probably are unhappy with the quality of the good being offered on the black market.
    d. consumers must be happy with the quality of the good being offered on the black market.

5. The communist retail sector, with its long lines, indifferent service, and poor product selection, made it difficult to achieve an efficient and equitable distribution of goods and services in part because
    a. of the opportunity cost of the aggregate amount of time wasted standing in line.
    b. consumers often were unable to purchase what they needed, even if they had the money.
    c. both of the above.
    d. none of the above.

6. If a centrally planned economy fixes the quantity of blue jeans produced and also fixes the price of blue jeans below the equilibrium price for that quantity of jeans,
   a. blue jeans shortages will develop and lines will form.
   b. the black market price of blue jeans will be higher than the fixed price.
   c. tourists will have an incentive to bring an extra pair of blue jeans into the country to trade for local goods.
   d. all of the above.

7. Although each country reacted differently, which of the following statements best *summarizes* changes in the rate of unemployment during the first years of transition from communism to capitalism in Eastern Europe?
   a. The unemployment rate didn't change much in nations that had accomplished rapid transitions, but it rose by quite a bit in nations that had accomplished little in terms of transition.
   b. The unemployment rate rose by quite a bit in nations that had accomplished rapid transitions, but changed only slightly in nations that had accomplished little in terms of transition.
   c. The unemployment rate didn't change much for nations that had accomplished rapid transitions *or* for nations that had accomplished little, if any, transition.
   d. The unemployment rate rose by quite a bit for nations that had accomplished rapid transitions *and* for nations that had accomplished little, if any, transition.

8. Assume that a transition economy is changing from fixed prices to completely flexible prices and that a substantial monetary overhang exists. It's likely that the monetary overhang will combine with price decontrol to
   a. cause sharp price increases in both the short and long run.
   b. cause sharp short-run price increases, but the rate of these price increases will moderate in the long run.
   c. cause only minor short-run price changes but cause sharp long-run price increases instead.
   d. have no impact on prices in the short or long run because the monetary overhang will provide the funds needed for investment, allowing aggregate output to grow as rapidly as aggregate demand.

9. The transitional (or reform) trap of budget deficits, money creation, and inflation can best be avoided if
   a. the transition government cuts subsidies to state enterprises and therefore cuts government expenditures.
   b. the transition government devalues the currency and borrows abroad and therefore limits domestic hyperinflation.
   c. the transition government uses expansionary macroeconomic policy to stimulate the economy and therefore increases tax revenues.
   d. a miracle happens. In all honesty, the transitional trap is unavoidable.

10. The centerpiece of Czech privatization strategy was
    a. price decontrol of 85 percent of goods very early in the transition period.
    b. expansionary fiscal policy that increased aggregate output enough for the government to be able to restore 30,000 state enterprises to their rightful owners.
    c. sales at public auctions of 20,000 restaurants, stores, and companies providing services.
    d. the use of a voucher plan to transfer ownership of medium- and large-scale enterprises to the market sector.

11. Perhaps the biggest transition made by the Russians during the early 1990s was to
    a. dramatically restructure state enterprises, including laying off a significant number of workers.
    b. hold the money supply constant even though prices were increasing and the demand for money for transactions purposes was rising rapidly.
    c. decontrol 90 percent of prices in the face of high inflation, a huge monetary overhang, and continuing subsidies to state enterprises.
    d. allow the creation of company credit vouchers for health care, education, and housing.

THE ECONOMIC WAY OF THINKING—DISCUSSION QUESTIONS

1. How do you think that capitalist (market) economies compare to socialist (centrally planned) economies with regard to
   a. variety of products available?
   b. quality of products available?
   c. innovative behavior?
   d. equality in the distribution of income?
   e. share of income allocated to investment?
   f. amount of cyclical unemployment?
   g. efficiency in the allocation of resources?

2. The text lists four reasons that explain why centrally planned socialist economies failed. Review those reasons. With which of these reasons do you agree? Why? Can you think of other reasons that might be just as important? (*Hint:* Consider political reasons as well as economic ones.) Explain your answer.

3. Suppose that a country wants to make a fairly slow transition from communism to capitalism. Which of the four keys to a successful transition plan (listed in the text) would you install first? Which seems least important in the short run? Which ideas would only work if the others were also in place? Why?

4. What is a black market? Why do black markets exist? Do you think that the existence of a black market helps or hurts the performance of a socialist or centrally planned economy? Why? What does the existence of a black market in a transition economy imply? Explain.

5. Consider the following statement: "When the subsidies to firms selling at prices below cost exceed the revenues derived from goods sold at prices above cost, the income payments to the resource suppliers will be greater than the amount required to purchase the available goods at the prices fixed by the planners." In what circumstances could the situation described in this statement occur? What is the likely consequence of such a situation? What policy changes would be necessary to change the situation?

6. Compare and contrast the transition policies of the Czech Republic and Russia. How did the two countries handle price decontrol? privatization? international trade? fiscal and monetary policy?

7. The differences in privatization mentioned in question #6 resulted in Russia having quite a bit of insider control over previous state enterprises and the Czech Republic having quite a bit of outsider control over large and medium-sized previous state enterprises. How would this difference in control be likely to affect the internal operations of the enterprises with respect to incentives, innovativeness, layoffs, and the determination of wages, dividends, and working conditions?

PERSPECTIVES IN ECONOMICS

The Swedish Disease
by Paul Klebnikov

[Reprinted with permission from *Forbes.* May 24, 1993, p. 78.]

For decades Sweden was held up as a model of how to combine a vigorous capitalist industrial sector with a lavish social welfare system—market socialism at its best. By channeling 70% of the country's gross domestic product into the state's coffers, the government was able to pay 90% or even 100% of Swedes' working incomes to the unemployed, the sick, or those who simply wanted to quit work and take care of their children. Even now, many East bloc leaders speak of adopting the Swedish model for their newly liberated economies. The Clinton Administration's liberals who are pushing for more taxes, a bigger welfare state, bigger labor unions, currency devaluation and an industrial policy, should take note: The Swedish model is doing abysmally.

Sweden's industrial production has plunged 15% since 1989. The jobless rate is 12% and rising. The budget deficit accounts for a third of the central government's spending and 13% of the country's GDP (compared with 5% in the U.S.). The currency is sinking even faster than the dollar.

What's Sweden's problem? "The Swedish model is Sweden's problem," says Ian Wachtmeister, a former aluminum company executive who heads the recently formed, market-oriented New Democracy Party, and was elected to parliament in 1991. "People are sick of the Big Brother-type of state. It's all connected with what's happening in Eastern Europe, because they had 100% socialism and we had 70%."

Sweden's welfare state has all but destroyed the country's work ethic. The absentee rate in Swedish industry reached an astounding 25% several years ago before recent welfare cutbacks encouraged people to work more. Many companies used to overstaff themselves by 25% just to make sure that they had enough workers on the production line.

In an interview with FORBES in his Stockholm office last month, Sweden's Prime Minister, Carl Bildt, a conservative whose coalition government has been trying to cut spending since coming to office in 1991, blames the high absentee rate on the generous workers' insurance schemes.

"A few years ago this used to be the sickest society on earth, according to the statistics," he says. "When we had the ice hockey world championship on television, for instance, people tended to be very sick."

Bildt's Finance Minister, Anne Wibble, underscores another hangover from her country's socialist binge: By becoming every Swede's rich grandfather, the state has destroyed most people's incentive to save. "Most households in our country do not have any private savings," says Wibble, "and that means they are not independent of either employers or politicians."

Meanwhile, some of the world's highest taxes on capital and income have driven Swedish entrepreneurs to less hostile environments in continental Europe and America.

That Sweden has managed to muddle along without social upheaval for the past two decades is testament mainly to the depth of capital accumulated during the 100 years between 1870 and 1970, when the country was committed to open markets and produced some of the best multinational corporations in the world. As recently as 1970 Sweden's GDP per capita was higher than that of any other country except Switzerland and the United States.

The Social Democrats, who came to power in 1932, began to construct a rudimentary welfare state, but were careful not to kill or seriously maim the capitalist goose laying all those nice golden eggs. Taxes in particular were kept in line with the European and American norms.

But in 1969 Olof Palme and a group of left-wingers took over the Social Democrats. Under Palme, the government decided to "help" industry with planning guidelines, with subsidies, and even by nationalizing many companies. Taxes were raised to exorbitant levels; the top marginal income rate soon reached 85%.

Before he was assassinated in 1986, Palme tried to make Sweden into a workers' Garden of Eden. Labor was given subsidized housing and an iron-clad full-employment policy. The labor unions (which accounted for over 80% of the work force) also took control of billions of dollars of unemployment insurance funds. In 1984 the socialist government slapped a surtax on corporate earnings and funneled the money into special union-run equity funds, which were used to increase the unions' control over their employers. Before the funds were finally liquidated by the conservative coalition in 1991, they grew to over $3 billion and

bought important stakes in many companies, including 5% of Volvo.

Still, the 1980s were so prosperous—and the government's willingness to devalue the krona so great—that even Sweden seemed to proper. But because Sweden's private sector had shrunk, and since Swedish capital was effectively prohibited from going abroad, corporate profits were channeled through the banks into Swedish real estate. Real estate prices rose tenfold. And the public sector continued to grow.

Finally, three years ago, the bubble burst. The golden-egg-laying goose keeled over as real estate prices dropped by 50% in two years, banks collapsed and the government's budget deficit exploded.

In 1991 Carl Bildt's conservative coalition was elected to clean up the socialists' mess. Like some ancient hero of Norse legend, Carl Bildt has been swinging a mighty ax to clear away the tangles of the welfare state. Government expenditure has been cut by $11 billion (80 billion kronor, equal to 6% of GDP). Welfare payments have been cut. Inflation has been tamed to an underlying rate of 2%. A voucher system has been introduced in the public school system. Capital gains taxes are 30%. The top marginal tax rates on income are still 50%—high, but that's a big improvement over the 85% of the recent past.

Yet for all of Prime Minister Bildt's efforts, Sweden's public sector has been reduced only slightly, from 70% of GDP in 1990 to around 67% last year. And the government's ambitious privatization program is stalled because of a sagging stock market and entrenched opposition from the Social Democrats.

Can Bildt prevail? Stig Ramel, the distinguished former director of the Nobel Foundation, which distributes the Nobel Prize, argues that meaningful cutbacks in the public sector can occur only through a revolution or a war. Notes he: "Germany and Japan became very successful after the Second World War because they could start from scratch as far as the public sector was concerned."

Ramel does point to a third alternative: a financial crisis culminating in pressure from outside lenders. "Sweden is deeply integrated into the world market," says Ramel. "When the international financiers who are financing our enormous deficit conclude that we are not creditworthy, then we will be forced to make the changes."

Sweden, a second Mexico? In fact, the process of putting the bloated economy on a crash diet has already begun. Much of the cost-cutting of the Bildt coalition over the past year was part of Sweden's effort to maintain its link to the European Currency Unit. With the Swedish krona losing about a quarter of its value against the ECU since last November, and with credit agencies like Moody's and S&P having recently downgraded Swedish government debt, international pressure on Bildt's government to do whatever is necessary to stabilize the krona is mounting.

Sweden may or may not recover fully from its socialistic experimentation. But this isn't just a story about Sweden. It's about any country where politicians believe in the infinite ability of the private sector to fund an ambitious social agenda, be it through taxes, mandates, regulation or other forms of state intervention.

The New Democracy Party's Wachtmeister worries that Sweden's experience with market socialism has been lost on many of the liberals in the Clinton Administration. The key lesson, as Sweden is now finding, is that once in place this kind of socialism is very hard to dislodge.

"Right now I'd rather be in Sweden than in the U.S., because we have seen the problems and are moving away from the welfare state, " says Wachtmeister. "On your side, you are moving right into it, and you risk destroying your country."

Discussion

1. How is Sweden's transition from socialism to capitalism similar to the other countries described in the chapter? How is it different?

2. Go back to the text and review the four keys to a successful transition plan. Which of these is Sweden doing? Which did Sweden already have in place? Does this information change your answer to 1 above? How?

3. The author implies that the United States is heading in the same direction that Sweden once was. Do you agree? Why or why not? Is there any reason to be concerned about such a trend?

ANSWER KEY

CHAPTER 1

TRUE OR FALSE

The following are true: 1, 3, 5, 7, 8, 11, 13.

PROBLEMS AND PROJECTS

1. a. No
   b. Yes
   c. Yes
   d. Remaining workload
   e. No
   f. Lower
   g. Both
   h. Yes
2. b. Positively related
   c. 15 miles; 1/15
3. b. 8/1; 4/1
4. b. Positive
   c. $239 billion; $227 billion; 227/239 = 0.95
   d. 0.90; no.

5. (Guideposts are listed by number)
   a. 5
   b. 6
   c. 1
   d. 2
   e. 3
   f. 7
   g. 4
6. c. Negatively related.
   d. Increase by 160 thousand tons.
7. a. (3)
   b. (2)
   c. (1)

LEARNING THE MECHANICS—MULTIPLE CHOICE

1. c. Economists define scarcity in this specific way.
2. c. This is the exact definition.
3. c. See the definition.
4. d. There's more to economizing behavior than just running a business efficiently or making money.
5. a. The statement concerns what the government "ought" to do.
6. d. The first three are guideposts, but the last confuses scarcity with poverty.
7. c. You would move along the production possibility curve.
8. b. Humans may provide freely but cannot acquire or produce freely.
9. a. It stresses the interdependence of economic effects.
10. d. Each can be used to produce economic goods.
11. d. This is an example of thinking at the margin.

12. a. Plotting the functions will show this.
13. d. P increases by 10 while Q increases by 5.
14. b. Both Y and Z have P = 50 when Q = 25.

THE ECONOMIC WAY OF THINKING — MULTIPLE CHOICE

1. c. All other answers are characteristics of *both* micro and macro.
2. b. All other answers involve costs with no gains.
3. d. In the other answers, individuals act contrary to their self-interest.
4. c. "Should" implies normative economic reasoning.
5. b. Both positive and normative economics deal with costs, benefits, and theory.
6. d. In each answer benefits and costs of action must be weighed.
7. a. Even Presidents think about personal costs and benefits.
8. b. Not necessarily; both could be caused by some other factor.
9. b. The others would shift the PPC in.
10. a. The behavior of large groups often can be predicted.
11. d. Persons often desire nonmaterial items and sometimes their actions are ill-formed or appear to be irrational to others.
12. a. Smith opposed *b* but had some sympathy for *c* and *d*.
13. a. The $3 billion is an unrecoverable cost; if the remaining cost does not exceed value of $25 billion, the project is worthwhile.
14. b. Computing and comparing costs is an objective process.

CHAPTER 2

TRUE OR FALSE

The following are true: 3, 4, 7, 8, 9, 11.

PROBLEMS AND PROJECTS

1. a. 2; 1
   b. no; Sam makes 10 chairs, Larry makes 4 tables.
2. a. no
   b. yes; 400 bushels of wheat, 150 bushels of oranges
   c. yes; he would gain 50 bushels of oranges; total output increases by 100 bushels of oranges
   d. yes
3. a. The U.S.'s opportunity cost for coffee = 1/3; Brazil's = 1/2. The U.S.'s opportunity cost for tobacco = 3; Brazil's = 2
   b. The U.S. has a comparative advantage in coffee. Brazil has a comparative advantage in tobacco.
   c. U.S.
   d. Brazil
4. a. yes; yes; no.
   b. 900 million bushels; 200 million bushels.
   c. 100 million bushels; 1 bushel of wheat.
   d. 2 bushels of wheat.

5. a. $13,000
   b. $19,600
   c. The U.S. birthrate would fall.
6. a. (3)
   b. (1)
   c. (5)
   d. (4)
   e. (2)
7. a. (1) C = 3; I = 5 (2) C = 5; I = 3 (3) Any of the points on the curve between C = 3, I = 5 to C = 5, I = 3.
   b. The answer to all three parts of *a* would be C = 3, I = 3.

LEARNING THE MECHANICS—MULTIPLE CHOICE

1. c. See the definition.
2. c. The opportunity cost of time spent not working is the wage forgone.
3. c. Opportunity cost always refers to values of *alternatives*.
4. a. Comparative advantage ensures efficiency which raises available output.
5. a. Since *each* trader can gain, exchange will arise voluntarily.
6. c. See the discussion.
7. b. If misuse of property is not enforced, there is no incentive to consider the wishes of others.
8. d. Two units of food must be sacrificed for eight units of clothing; 2/8 = 1/4.
9. d. Italia's opportunity cost of food = 1; Slavia's = 4.
10. c. Gains arise when countries export their low opportunity cost goods.
11. c. Curve represents output possibilities when resources are fully utilized.
12. d. See the definition.
13. c. See the definition.
14. b. "Middlemen" specialize in providing information and arranging trades so you will not have to.
15. c. See the definition.

THE ECONOMIC WAY OF THINKING—MULTIPLE CHOICE

1. b. Failure to realize specialization gains means inefficient resource use.
2. b. Crusoe's opportunity cost of good $y = x$; Friday's is $y = 1/2 \, x$.
3. b. See Exhibit 2.
4. b. Going to school means sacrificing the alternative of working and earning income.
5. a. Specialization raises efficiency and reduces costs (time) of production.
6. b. The alternative to the date is to have $10 and play tennis.
7. b. Higher investment means greater production possibilities in the future.
8. d. The extra money cost of driving is $(3 \times \$80) - \$50 = \$190$.
9. b. Because production according to comparative advantage concentrates on minimizing opportunity cost.
10. a. Most (not all) wealth was built through voluntary (non-exploitative) trade.
11. d. Considering the wishes of others will help maximize income.
12. c. This is a part of the "worker alienation" that can accompany specialization.
13. a. The last soybean produced (at A) causes rice production to decrease by much more than the first (at D).
14. a. The production possibilities frontier shifts in.
15. c. Productivity improves for soybeans but not rice.

CHAPTER 3

TRUE OR FALSE

The following are true: 1, 2, 3, 5, 7, 8, 9.

PROBLEMS AND PROJECTS

1. b. $12
   d. $15
2. a. $4; 10
   b. $7; 12
   c. Higher soybean prices will shift the demand for wheat to the right.
3. a. Decrease, increase
   b. decreased demand for steel, increased demand for áluminum
   c. increase
   d. increased unemployment
   e. increase
   f. increase, increase
   g. increase
   h. increase
   i. increase
   j. decrease
   k. remain the same
   l. increase
4. b. $0, -, +, -$
   c. $-, 0, -, -$
   d. $+, +, ?, +$
   e. $-, +, -, ?$
5. b. increase
   d. The below equilibrium rental price reduces the incentive of sellers to expand the future supply of rental housing.
   e. no; landlords will favor friends and discriminate against groups they don't like
6. a. $P = \$2.20; Q = 3.3$
   b. $Q_s = 3.7; Q_d = 3.1; Q$ stockpiled $= 0.6$
   c. Receipts = $9.25 billion; Consumer spending = $7.75 billion; Taxpayer cost = $1.5 billion
   d. Market price = $1.60. Deficiency payment = $.90
   e. i. remain the same; ii. rise. Target price option is better because overall cost is the same but corn consumption is higher.
7. Correct: "risk of driving many dairy farm families out of business." Incorrect: "higher milk prices."

LEARNING THE MECHANICS—MULTIPLE CHOICE

1. d. A below-equilibrium price results in an excess of quantity demanded relative to quantity supplied.
2. b. If soybean prices rise, demand for wheat rises (demand curve shifts right).
3. c. The demand curve shows how quantity responds to *changes* in price.
4. a. When cigar prices rise, smokers will substitute cigarettes for cigars.

5. d. Sellers will want to supply more and buyers will demand less, resulting in a surplus.
6. a. Assuming Bud is a substitute for Miller.
7. a. This reflects the law of demand; see the definition.
8. a. Travelers will substitute bus, train and air travel for auto travel.
9. a. The price mechanism rations goods to their most highly valued use.
10. b. This is necessary to eliminate excess supply; see Exhibit 4.
11. b. Demand for U.S. cars (a substitute) increases; higher price raises quantity supplied.
12. b. This is "abstract" as opposed to "historical" time.
13. d. See the definition.
14. d. While markets are not always (necessarily) in harmony with the general welfare, they are generally so.

THE ECONOMIC WAY OF THINKING—MULTIPLE CHOICE

1. b. Increased price raises quantity supplied and reduces quantity demanded.
2. c. The tax raises price causing *quantity demanded* (not demand) to fall.
3. a. Driving smaller cars is one way of economizing on higher priced gas.
4. b. With lower prices, landlords attempt to maintain profits by cutting costs.
5. c. A price ceiling above equilibrium has no effect.
6. d. The drought reduced supply; the millers' expectations of higher future prices raised current demand.
7. a. Florida's demand is not affected; if California's supply rises, price falls.
8. c. All other answers involve "interferences" with the price mechanism.
9. b. This lowers auto *demand*, which changes *quantity supplied*, not supply.
10. c. Response *a* would lower price; *b* lowers quantity; *d* sharply raises quantity.
11. c. Supply of nannies will shift left and up.
12. d. All others shift the demand for nannies.
13. d. Demand for day care will shift right and up.
14. b. At $120, quantity demanded exceeds quantity supplied.

CHAPTER 4

TRUE OR FALSE

The following are true: 1, 2, 4, 5, 6, 7, 8, 11.

PROBLEMS AND PROJECTS

1. a. B
   b. B
   c. PG
   d. P
   e. B
   f. P
   g. P
   h. B
   i. PG
   j. B
2. a. (2)
   b. (3)
   c. (1)
   d. (3)

3. a. $10, 100 billion
   b. $1000 billion
   c. $15; $1200 billion
   d. Consumer valuation of the last barrel is $15, which is greater than the producer valuation of $5, so this is inefficient.
4. a. P = $120, Q = 4,000 tons/year
   b. P = $130, Q = 3,000 tons/year (*Hint:* Add $20 to each price and graph the new supply curve. Find the new equilibrium point.)
5. a. P = 50; Q = 26
   b. 32
   c. A subsidy.
   d. The supply and demand for public sector action.

LEARNING THE MECHANICS—MULTIPLE CHOICE

1. d. Lower quantity supplied leaves some mutual gains unrealized; see Exhibit 1.
2. a. Answers *c* and *d* assume no "spillover effects" (externalities).
3. c. The other responses may lead government to *reduce* efficiency.
4. c. Such exchange reduces efficiency and may or may not lead to political action.
5. b. Public goods are characterized by non-rivalry in consumption.
6. c. External costs are not included in private production decisions; see Exhibit 3.
7. b. Inefficiency may result from the special interest or shortsightedness effects.
8. b. Element of compulsion may prevent public use of price mechanism.
9. a. Defining the ideal income distribution is a perplexing matter.
10. d. The personal benefits of casting an informed vote may be less than the costs of being informed.
11. d. This reflects the "no free lunch" guide to economic thinking.
12. d. Response *a* confers external benefits; *b* external costs; *c* external benefits.
13. b. Rent-seeking is an action aimed at restructuring public policy to redistribute income to a group or industry.

THE ECONOMIC WAY OF THINKING—MULTIPLE CHOICE

1. a. Spillover effects are unconsidered impacts of your actions on others.
2. c. Public goods break the individual consumption-payment link.
3. d. With no individual consumption-payment link, there may be insufficient private demand.
4. a. If either is violated, some mutual gains will be unrealized; see Exhibit 1.
5. c. The *individual* consumption-payment link may be absent.
6. d. If individual costs are small it is rational for others to be ignorant.
7. c. Costs of organizing "influence" are justified by large potential gains.
8. b. Each of the others has *some* public good aspect, but clean air has more.
9. c. One may *favor* an action (altruistically) without personally gaining.
10. a. Those who do not gain from voluntary exchange do not participate.
11. d. Gains to special interest groups justify the costs to them of influencing politicians.
12. a. This appears to be an effective way of getting votes.
13. a. Both buyers and sellers overlook the external costs.

CHAPTER 5

TRUE OR FALSE

The following are true: 1, 2, 3, 6, 9, 12.

PROBLEMS AND PROJECTS

1. a. 0.10 ($20,000) + 0.20 ($10,000) = $4,000
   b. $11,000
   c. progressive
   d. Add 10% to each income level, keeping tax rates the same.
2. a. 14.7%, 29.6%; progressive
   b. 19.6%, 44.0%; greater than
   c. no; yes; bracket creep
3. a. $150, $180, $200, $210, $210, $200
   b. Laffer curve
4. a. canned peas; cigarettes
   b. cigarettes; equilibrium quantity falls less.
   c. Cigarette smoking imposes external costs.
5. a. 67%   22%   15%
      22%   22%   20%
      13%   22%   25%
   b. Option 1: regressive; option 2: proportional; Option 3: progressive

LEARNING THE MECHANICS—MULTIPLE CHOICE

1. c. See Exhibit 10.
2. a. See Exhibit 10.
3. b. See the definition.
4. b. See Exhibit 7.
5. b. See the definition.
6. d. Divide the increase in taxes ($200) by the increase in income ($1000).
7. b. The rate of taxation on real income would be constant.
8. a. See Exhibit 6.
9. d. See Exhibit 2.
10. b. See Exhibit 10.
11. d. By taking the same *number* of dollars, a low-income individual will pay a larger percentage of her income than will a high-income recipient.
12. c. With equal consumption, all will pay equal taxes, so tax bill as a share of income falls as income rises.

THE ECONOMIC WAY OF THINKING—MULTIPLE CHOICE

1. a. The average tax rate would be greater for high-income families.
2. c. The current method is not appropriately indexed.
3. c. The revenues that businesses use to pay taxes come from consumers, stockholders, or employees.

4. d. Such a special-interest group would oppose tax revision most of all.
5. d. Price would rise by 2 cents only if demand were completely vertical.
6. c. An increase in rates will tend to shrink the tax base, thus the tax revenues increase less than proportionally.
7. d. See the definition.
8. d. One's *constant purchasing power* tax liability would remain the same.
9. a. The marginal rate determines after-tax value of *additional* income.
10. b. Either case means equilibrium price rises by full amount of tax.
11. c. Laffer popularized, but did not discover, the principle involved.
12. c. The tax equals "S + tax" minus S; at Q = 80, this can be seen to be $0.50.
13. b. 80 times $0.50 equals $40.00.
14. b. See Exhibit 7.

CHAPTER 6

TRUE OR FALSE

The following are true: 1, 3, 4, 8, 9, 12, 14, 15.

PROBLEMS AND PROJECTS

1. Gasoline and air travel are substitutes; gasoline and auto tires, and gasoline and Yellowstone tourism are complements.
2. a. 1500, 1400, 1650; elastic, inelastic
   b. Price elasticity between $1 and $2 = (800/1100)/(1/1.5) = (−) 1.09
      Price elasticity between $2 and $3 = (150/625)/(1/2.5) = (−) 0.60
3. a.   Food: 30,   25,   20,   15,   10,   5
       Clothing: 10,   7,   5,   4,   2,   1
       Housing: 35,   30,   20,   15,   10,   8
   b. 3/2; 1; 35/30; food
   c. 3 food, 1 clothing, 2 housing
   d. 2 units of food are purchased when P = $30; 4 units of food are purchased when P = $15.
   e. Food consumption would increase from 3 to 5 units, clothing from 1 to 3 units, and housing from 2 to 4 units.
4. a. 4 cups
   b. $1.75 + 0.75 + 0.25 = $2.75
   c. $2.75 + (−0.15) + (−0.20) + (−0.25) = $2.15; it is less
   d. 5 cups; $3.35; $3.20; it is less
5. down; up; none; up; 1.0; up

6.

a.	b.	c.	d.
D	S	S	D
+	+	+	+
+	−	−	+
+	+	+	+
D	S	S	S
+	+	+	+
+	−	−	−
+	−	−	−
D	S	D	D
−	+	+	+
−	−	+	+
−	0	+	+
D	D	D	D
−	−	+	+
−	−	+	+
−	−	+	+

7. a.

Q_d	TE	Elasticity
27	486	
36	540	1.57
45	540	1.00
54	486	0.64

   b. falls
   c. inelastic; elastic; unit elastic
   d. P = 12; Q = 45

LEARNING THE MECHANICS — MULTIPLE CHOICE

1. b. Demand is *elastic* (elasticity = 30%/15% = 2); when P rises, spending falls.
2. c. This causes a *movement along* the demand curve for green peas. (Thumbnail Sketch)
3. c. This reflects the basic postulate of economizing behavior.
4. b. See the definition.
5. d. When income rises, purchases fall (negative change); see the definition.
6. a. Consumers substitute oranges for grapefruit at any given price of oranges.
7. d. "Demand" refers to the entire demand curve which shifts to the right. (Thumbnail Sketch)
8. a. For inferior goods, changes in income and demand are inversely related.
9. c. Each alternative answer suggests a change in the *quantity* of milk *demanded*. (Thumbnail Sketch)
10. d. The large quantity of rock music caused a low *marginal* utility.
11. c. If beef is normal; also, other answers suggest a decrease in demand for beef.
12. a. A change in price of pork chops results in a movement along the demand curve. (Thumbnail Sketch)
13. d. Demand is inelastic (elasticity = 10%/50% = .2); when P rises, spending rises.

THE ECONOMIC WAY OF THINKING — MULTIPLE CHOICE

1. d. The new information shifted (decreased) the demand for cigarettes.
2. c. A decrease in quantity sold is expected to raise both price and spending.
3. c. Equilibrium is at Q = 30, so price = G.

4. c. Surplus will almost surely increase, but not because ACG is greater than JKF.
5. d. Choices *a* and *b* increase demand; *c* decreases *quantity demanded*.
6. c. "Snob" goods do not conform to the usual law of demand.
7. c. Reduced quantity and spending with an increased price implies elastic demand.
8. c. Elastic implies that lower price increases revenues; costs are constant.
9. c. Color set demand will decrease; elasticity of demand for B&W sets is unknown.
10. a. Both (I) and (II) are basic assumptions of consumer choice theory.
11. a. See Exhibit 6–7.
12. d. The owners expect an increase in price to lower quantity but raise revenues.
13. b. Revenue moved in the same direction as price (both rose).
14. c. If quantity demanded rises, consumer surplus will rise by more than $2.00; change in spending depends on the price elasticity of demand.

CHAPTER 7

TRUE OR FALSE

The following are true: 1, 2, 3, 4, 5, 7, 8, 9, 10, 12.

PROBLEMS AND PROJECTS

1. a. $9,000
   b. Owner's labor services and interest income forgone on Joe's equity capital.
   c. $48,000 + 0.10 (30,000) + 10,000 = $61,000
   d. $4,000 loss
2. a. TVC: 50, 90, 127, 166, 215, 274, 349, 446 (TFC = 50 at all output)
      ATC: 100, 70, 59, 54, 53, 54, 57, 62
      AVC: 50, 45, 42.3, 41.5, 43, 45.7, 49.9, 55.75
      MC: 100, 40, 37, 39, 49, 59, 75, 97
   b. 5
   c. Beyond 3
3. a. Auto A = 32 cents per mile; Auto B = 31 cents per mile; Auto B is cheaper.
   b. Auto A = 25 cents per mile; Auto B = 25.5 cents per mile; Auto A is cheaper.
   c. They decline primarily because average fixed cost is falling as the miles driven increases from 10,000 to 20,000.
4. a. Marginal product: 20, 15, 10, 5
      Marginal cost: 2.50, 3.33, 5.00, 10.00
      Total cost: 250, 300, 350, 400, 450
   b. Yes

5. | 360 | 210 | 150 | 60 |
   |-----|-----|-----|-----|
   | 600 | 450 | 150 | 100 |

6. a. 0; 0; –
   b. Economies of scale; ATC falls as Q rises.
   c. $70,000; yes, since extra revenue exceeds extra cost.

LEARNING THE MECHANICS—MULTIPLE CHOICE

1. c.
2. d. Use of variable inputs expands relative to fixed inputs so productivity falls.
3. a. It involves no actual money payments; it is income sacrificed.
4. c. Demand informs firms; resources are scarce because they have alternative uses.
5. c. Usually the case since labor is normally variable in the short run.
6. b. See the definition.
7. b. One of the major reasons for the popularity of this legal structure.
8. c. As output rises, average fixed cost declines. (see Exhibit 7–6)
9. a. A shift in demand will not cause the cost curves to shift.
10. d. When MC > ATC, ATC must rise and vice-versa; see Exhibit 7–6.
11. d. Implicit costs are included in economic, but not in accounting, profits.
12. a. Carefully study the definition.
13. a. AFC = ATC − AVC, or 12 minus 8 = 4.
14. d. Total fixed costs remain constant.
15. a. Marginal cost (returns) rises from Q = 6 on.

THE ECONOMIC WAY OF THINKING—MULTIPLE CHOICE

1. a. Answer *d* would mean higher price; answers *b* and *c* are nonsense.
2. d. Usually plant is fixed in the short run; the other inputs are variable.
3. d. Relaxing these physical constraints offsets short-run diminishing returns.
4. a. Efficient (ideal) plant size is an output where long-run unit cost is minimized.
5. d. The car will last more than one year; implicit interest is an opportunity cost.
6. b. The $300 mortgage payment is a sunk cost; local service charges are avoidable.
7. c. All marginal concepts relate to *changes* such as additions.
8. c. Sacrificed rental value is an implicit cost included in economic profit.
9. c. Both product spoilage and change in market conditions are valid reasons.
10. c. Increased output would significantly reduce *average* fixed cost and ATC.
11. d. Higher demand for orange-growing inputs raises their prices and hence, the price of grapefruit.
12. c. Harvester productivity is raised, lowering harvester cost per unit produced.
13. b. Including normal return on investment as a cost unambiguously reduces economic profits.
14. c. At any Q, area under MC equals TVC, as does Q × AVC.

CHAPTER 8

TRUE OR FALSE

The following are true: 1, 3, 4, 5, 6, 9, 10, 11.

PROBLEMS AND PROJECTS

1. a. ATC and AVC: 25, 25, 23, 21, 20, 19.8. 20, 21
   MC: 25, 25, 19, 15, 16, 19, 21, 28
   b. 6; $1 per month
   c. 7; $35 per month

2. a. FC: 40000
   VC: 0, 20000, 40000, 60000, 80000, 102000, 128000, 158000, 192000, 230000, 275000
   ATC: –, 60000, 40000, 33333, 30000, 28400, 28000, 28286, 29000, 30000, 31500
   AFC: –, 40000, 20000, 13333, 10000, 8000, 6667, 5714, 5000, 4444, 4000
   AVC: –, 20000, 20000, 20000, 20000, 20400, 21333, 22571, 24000, 25556, 27500
   MC: –, 20000, 20000, 20000, 20000, 22000, 26000, 30000, 34000, 38000, 45000
   b. 6; $9,000 per month
   c. 7; $26,000 per month
   d. 5; $17,000 per month loss; 4; $36,000 per month loss; yes, in the short run, but not in the long run.
3. a. Q_s: 400, 500, 600, 700, 800, 900, 1000
   Price: 20000, 22000, 26000, 30000, 34000, 38000, 45000
   b. $29,000
   c. Each firm is making profits of $6,000 per month; yes.
   d. It will fall as new profit-seeking firms enter the market.
4. a. 1000; 8000; 8; 0
   b. Yes
   c. No change
   d. Go out of business—but the firm's expectation that market conditions will remain the same is probably incorrect because the market price will rise as some of the firms in the industry go out of business.
5. c. Yes; no
6. a. 80
   b. 20
   c. 60
   d. 70
7. a. 30 +; 20 –; 25 0; 0 –
   b. Average profits over all four seasons must be non-negative.

LEARNING THE MECHANICS — MULTIPLE CHOICE

1. c. All of the firm's inputs are variable in the long run, hence all costs are too.
2. d. They will seek better profit opportunities in alternative industries.
3. b. If P > ATC, firms earn economic (excess) profits which attract new entrants.
4. a. *b* should read "average *total* cost"; *c* "total *variable* cost"; *d* "average *variable* cost."
5. c. Costs (hence prices) would be lower; other answers raise demand (hence price).
6. d. Firms exit alternative industries where profit opportunities are less attractive.
7. b. Entry and expansion require that all resources be variable (the long run).
8. c. The *market* refers to the aggregate supply decisions of all suppliers.
9. c. See the discussion in the text.
10. c. AFC = (Fixed Cost/Output) must decline as output rises.
11. b. Some inputs are fixed, hence output responds less to changes in price.
12. d. See "Applications in Economics."
13. c. At P = OF, ATC is at a minimum.
14. d. The firm will make a profit until supply shifts out, lowering the equilibrium price to OF.

THE ECONOMIC WAY OF THINKING — MULTIPLE CHOICE

1. d. During long-run adjustment some firms would exit and price would rise.
2. a. Price nearly tripled suggesting increased demand and inelastic supply.

3. d. The cost of the inputs, grains, rose for each of these outputs.
4. a. Price will initially exceed ATC causing entry and expansion in the wheat market.
5. c. Both supply and demand would increase (curves shift to the right).
6. b. Firms want more than zero profits, but free entry prevents this outcome.
7. b. Short-run supply is less elastic than long-run supply.
8. d. Peak-period quantity demanded would be reduced.
9. b. At prices below average variable cost, the firm would shut down.
10. b. The producer should sell out since she expects only losses in the long run.
11. c. Knowing "how to do well" (maximizing profit) implies the ability to compete.
12. b. One more unit would *add* more to cost (MC) than it would to revenue (MR).
13. b. From Q_0 to Q_1, MR exceeds MC, so profits rise.
14. d. Profits equal zero at A and C and exceed zero at B.
15. b. Most firms can react in the long run but not in the short run.

CHAPTER 9

TRUE OR FALSE

The following are true: 1, 2, 5, 7, 9, 10, 11, 12, 14.

PROBLEMS AND PROJECTS

1. a. TR: 60, 110, 150, 180, 200, 210
      MR: 60, 50, 40, 30, 20, 10
      TC: 90, 110, 136, 166, 206, 256
   b. Reduce the price to $45
   c. $14
2. a. Since the LRATC curve decreases over the range of quantities that are demanded, a single firm would be the lowest-cost producer.
   e. Probably not; new competitors would have very high production costs if they started out small and would be unable to make high profits (if any).
3. a. TR: 6400, 7000, 7800, 8400, 8800, 9000, 9000
      MR: –, 600, 800, 600, 400, 200, 0
      MC: –, 400, 400, 500, 700, 1000, 1200
   b. $1.20
   c. Yes; $1,100 per month
   d. $1.00
   e. Approximately $13,200 or the present value of the expected economic profit; the university would then reap the monopoly benefits.
4. a. P_4
   b. P_2
   c. P_3; profit
5. a. 1
   b. 1
   c. 2
   d. 2

6. a.	8	4	32	32	0	32	0
b.	4	8	32	16	16	8	8
c.	6	6	36	24	12	18	2

7. a. c. (table):

1.10	1.10	1.00	1.00
2.00	.90	1.90	.90
2.70	.70	2.70	.80
3.20	.50	3.40	.70
3.50	.30	4.00	.60
3.60	.10	4.50	.50
3.50	−.10	5.00	.50
3.20	−.30	5.50	.50

  b. P = $.80; Q = 4; Profit = $1.20
  d. Q = 7 (or 6); Profit = $1.50
  e. Yes; profits are higher.

LEARNING THE MECHANICS—MULTIPLE CHOICE

1. a. See the definition.
2. a. Usually in monopoly P > MC, leading to allocative inefficiency.
3. a. The profit-maximizing behavior is restriction of output to raise price. (Exhibit 9–6)
4. a. MR should = MC for maximum profit, which may not occur if (II) is achieved.
5. b. Each firm would operate at an inefficient small level of output.
6. d. Output should always be raised if MR > MC and lowered if MR < MC.
7. d. This may be a *result* of monopoly, but it is not a source of monopoly.
8. d. A competitive firm produces an output at which P = MC.
9. b. A monopolized firm produces an output at which P > MC.
10. d. Each serves to restrain price increases by the monopolist.
11. a. These barriers are probably as old as government itself.
12. c. Product development may depend on statically inefficient monopoly profits.

THE ECONOMIC WAY OF THINKING—MULTIPLE CHOICE

1. d. This is a potential outcome of the special interest effect.
2. a. Total revenue will rise and total cost will fall.
3. a. The profit-maximizing behavior is to raise profits at the expense of consumers.
4. a. For inelastic demand, higher prices reduce sales, raise total revenues, and lower total costs. (Exhibit 9–2)
5. d. See the discussion in the text.
6. c. The benefits of efficiency are widely dispersed over the consumers of the product.
7. c. The others compete with producers of several (if not many) close substitutes.
8. c. Firm will set MR = MC to maximize profit; you want MR = 0 to maximize total revenue.
9. d. DuPont's control over price depends on how closely other wraps can be substituted.
10. c. ATC is somewhere between $6 and $0.
11. d. The monopolist will produce at MC = MR.
12. b. AT Q = 48, MC will shift from $6 to $8, but MR = MC at less than $8 but more than $6.
13. b. MR = MC at P = $8.
14. c. At P = $9, MC intersects the demand curve.

CHAPTER 10

TRUE OR FALSE

The following are true: 1, 2, 5, 6, 7, 10, 12.

PROBLEMS AND PROJECTS

1. a. TR (market): 750,000; 1,000,000; 1,350,000; 1,600,000; 2,400,000; 3,000,000; 3,200,000; 3,500,000; 3,600,000; 3,500,000; 3,200,000
   TR (firm): 187,500; 250,000; 337,500; 400,000; 600,000; 750,000; 800,000; 875,000; 900,000; 875,000, 800,000
   b. $150; 24,000; 6,000
   c. $400; $300; $250
   d. $250
   e. A certain amount of collusion is likely since there are only four firms with equal cost conditions and equal output.
2. a. His plan will work if demand for the firm's tricycles is elastic and if other firms don't follow his move.
   b. By 5000 units to a total of 25,000 tricycles.
   [TR – TC = profits → $9 (Q) – (120,000 + $4 (Q)) = 5000 → Q = 25,000]
   c. Price elasticity = [(5000/22500)/(1/9.5)] = 2.11
3. a. Demand when industry price varies:
   TR: 270, 280, 250, 180, 70, 0, 0
   MR: 50, 10, –30, –70, –110, –70, 0
   Demand when only SC's price varies:
   TR: 240, 280, 300, 300, 280, 240, 180, 100
   MR: 60, 40, 20, 0, –20, –40, –60, –80
   b. $70; $240
   c. 5; $60; $250; profit has increased
   d. No
4. No; after-tax profits as a percentage of corporate sales or stockholder equity
5. a. 51
   b. Loose oligopoly; 12.5 percent
6. a. –
   b. +
   c. +
   d. +
   e. –; If the firms were colluding, they would raise prices to increase total revenue.
   f. +; Entry induced by above normal profit increases supply and lowers prices.

LEARNING THE MECHANICS—MULTIPLE CHOICE

1. a. Entry increases competition, which drives down market price and eliminates profits.
2. c. Better products at the same price from competitors limits price increases.
3. a. P > MC due to product differentiation; P = AC due to low entry barriers.
4. d. Stable, fairly certain information makes agreement easier to reach and enforce.
5. a. Oligopolies control competition to some extent, but less than monopolists can.

6. c. Both *a* and *b* are false.
7. c. See Exhibit 10–8.
8. b. Firms would pay Amy premium wages up to the value of her extra efficiency.
9. a. The more producers, the more difficult it is to collude.
10. b. The ratio gives us an indication of industry structure but not firm behavior.
11. c. Long-run normal profits are a result of low entry barriers.
12. c. Since entry barriers are low, economic profits will attract new entrants.
13. a. Evidence shows no strong relation between concentration and profit.
14. c. If there are hundreds of small competitors, at least 60%; if only 1–4, 100%.

THE ECONOMIC WAY OF THINKING—MULTIPLE CHOICE

1. d. A better product at the same price is equivalent to a price cut (competition).
2. b. Reduction in supply as some firms exit raises price and restores normal profits.
3. d. Buyers are willing to pay a premium for such stocks; the "early bird . . . ."
4. a. This is a basic similarity between pure and monopolistic competition.
5. a. Since profits are higher, it would pay more to protect them.
6. c. This would limit entry allowing higher prices and some economic profits.
7. d. The innovative spirit might be dulled but certainly not eliminated.
8. c. Return to zero-profit equilibrium causes price to rise as much as costs.
9. d. Successful collusion + little entry = successful price control.
10. b. Price competition might be used in an attempt to restore sales.
11. c. Competition equates long-run profits to zero in both cities.
12. d. The license fee is a sunk cost.
13. d. This also helps to explain the success of McDonald's.

CHAPTER 11

TRUE OR FALSE

The following are true: 1, 3, 8, 11.

PROBLEMS AND PROJECTS

1. a.

Q	AFC	ATC
50	.20	.26
60	.17	.23
70	.14	.20

b. At each output level, there is a $10 million loss (the total fixed cost), after rounding.
c. At each output level, there is no profit and no loss; total revenue = total cost.
d. See the discussion of the regulation of natural monopoly.

2. (Second item listed is the actual winner of the given case):
   a. Sherman Section 2; United States
   b. Clayton Section 7; United States
   c. Sherman Section 1; Major League Baseball
   d. Sherman Section 2; United States
   e. Clayton Section 3; United States

3. a.   +   +
          −   +
   b. Yes; no

LEARNING THE MECHANICS—MULTIPLE CHOICE

1. c. Price below competitor or below ATC can make economic sense, but price below MC does not.
2. c. See the definition.
3. d. Such tax improvements do not enhance economic productivity.
4. c. See the discussion in the text.
5. d. See the Thumbnail Sketch.
6. d. Each of the others inhibits competition by raising the cost of entry. (Thumbnail Sketch)
7. c. (I) political machines work slowly; (II) a result of special interest effects.
8. c. Apparently the income elasticity of demand for these services is high.
9. c. This tends to promote rather than restrict competition.
10. a. See the definition.
11. b. Rivalry to promote divisional interests; cooperation to promote GM's interest.
12. c. Social regulations can be seen as taxes on productive activity; see Exhibit 11–3.

THE ECONOMIC WAY OF THINKING—MULTIPLE CHOICE

1. a. As it is a license to earn excess profits, it is worth some effort to acquire.
2. a. Cost minimization is an aspect of profit maximization.
3. b. Efficiency requires reliance on lowest (opportunity) cost sources of output.
4. b. Other proposals promote entry which tends to defeat the aim of the proposal.
5. c. The political mechanism does not always yield consistent public policies.
6. b. This increases the number of relevant competitors for the industry in question.
7. b. Such regulation has much the same impact as a production tax; see Exhibit 11–5.
8. b. Income fell from $40,000 to $28,000.
9. c. 80 births at $100 each.
10. b. Drawing a diagram will help get the answer.
11. d. The analysis in #11 omitted the 20 births now handled by doctors.

CHAPTER 12

TRUE OR FALSE

The following are true: 1, 2, 3, 5, 8, 9, 10, 11, 13, 14.

PROBLEMS AND PROJECTS

1. a. MPP: 5, 4, 3, 2, 1
      TR: 500, 900, 1200, 1400, 1500
      MRP: 500, 400, 300, 200, 100
   b. 4
   c. 3
   d. Employment level = 4; TR = $2100; profit = $900 less capital costs
   e. Yes
2. a. MPP: –, 5, 7, 6, 3.5, 2.5, 1
      TR: 0, 500, 1200, 1800, 2150, 2400, 2500
      MRP: –, 500, 700, 600, 350, 250, 100
   b. Quantity demanded: 1, 2, 3, 4, 5, 6
      Wage (per week): 500, 700, 600, 350, 250, 100
   c. 5
   d. 4
3. a. 0, –, +, –
   b. +, 0, +, +
   c. 0, +, –, +
   d. –, 0, –, –
   e. +, –, +, ?
4. a. No, MP of Vitacorn/P of Vitacorn = 200/800 < 400/1200 = MP of Cornpower/P of Cornpower.
   b. The farmer could produce the same output for $400 less.
   c. Yes, the decrease in the MP of Cornpower as its usage increases will cause the ratio of the MP of Corn-power to its price to decrease, eventually fulfilling the condition for cost minimization: MP of Vita-corn/P of Vitacorn = MP of Cornpower/P of Cornpower.
5. a. Short-run: (10/190)/(5/35) = 0.37; long-run: (50/150)/(5/35) = 2.33
6. a.

500	500
912	412
1242	330
1496	254
1680	184
1800	120
1911	111
1976	65
1998	22
1980	–18

   b. L = 7; Q = 49; profit = 1111; ATC = 16.33
   c. 4 × 39 = 156; no, because the relevant figure for compensation is MRP, not MP.

LEARNING THE MECHANICS—MULTIPLE CHOICE

1. c. There will be many workers with these skills (many close substitutes).
2. b. The demand for resources is *derived from* the demand for the product.
3. a. The "marginal revenue product" is the value of the labor services to the firm.
4. c. A small change in resource price raises product cost and reduces sales greatly.
5. b. Additional employment would *add* more to revenue than it would *add* to cost.
6. a. The greater the demand for the product, the greater the demand for the resources.

7. a. Products that use the resource intensively will become more expensive.
8. b. It takes time to develop substitutes for the skills of carpenters.
9. b. Since P = MR, marginal revenue product = value of marginal product.
10. d. It would use the cheaper resource intensively, driving down its marginal product.
11. a. If, e.g., $MPP_L/P_L > MPP_K/P_K$, diverting \$1 from buying K to buying L raises output.
12. d. This causes a *movement along* the demand curve (change in quantity demanded).
13. b. The increased demand for law services will raise the clerks' MRP.
14. b. Wages will fall because of the lack of competition. [This question anticipates the topic of monopsony.]
15. b. Capital is more productive and costs less.

THE ECONOMIC WAY OF THINKING — MULTIPLE CHOICE

1. a. The other three have more easily available substitutes.
2. c. Price and quantity usually decrease when demand decreases.
3. b. The large short-run wage increase will encourage acquisition of engineering skills.
4. c. This requires few acquired skills, hence there are many substitutes.
5. d. The aid would attract more students, increasing supply.
6. b. Economists are choosing alternative employments.
7. d. Both would tend to offset the decrease in quantity demanded caused by higher prices.
8. c. In most "capitalist" countries, but trading physical capital is illegal in some countries.
9. b. Lower cost resources would be substituted; less intensive use raises marginal product.
10. a. Aluminum bats and canoes are artificially underpriced.
11. c. If machines have human sensibilities we are unaware of them.
12. c. This would make supply very inelastic in the (one year) short run.
13. b. Employers will not be willing to pay more for workers with college degrees; competition will equalize wages.

CHAPTER 13

TRUE OR FALSE

The following are true: 1, 2, 7, 9, 10, 12, 13.

PROBLEMS AND PROJECTS

1. a. Q = 3,000; P = \$300
   b. Q = 4,000; P = \$200
   c. Employment rises from 120 to 128.
   d. See "Myths of Economics."
2. a. L_S
   b. $L_S \times 1.20$
   c. +; 0; +; ?; −
   d. Employers would substitute unskilled workers for machinery.

3. a. B1
   b. B2
   c. A3
   d. A2
   e. C2
   f. A1
4. a. 2 times as high; 10 times as high; 5 times as high.
   b. Brazil; Canada; neither
   c. False; Canadian workers can still compete because of their greater productivity.

LEARNING THE MECHANICS — MULTIPLE CHOICE

1. a. A result of traditional work specialization patterns within the family.
2. d. Real wages are principally determined by productivity.
3. d. By assumption the question eliminates other reasons for earnings differentials. (Thumbnail Sketch)
4. c. Elasticity measures responsiveness between wage changes and employment changes.
5. a. Believe it or not, your marginal productivity is rising as you read these words.
6. c. When required to pay more, firms will reduce employment of the least skilled.
7. a. Security of income attracts more workers (increases supply) and lowers wages.
8. d. See the definition.
9. b. See The Economic Way of Thinking—Discussion Questions, problem 7.
10. a. Profit-minded producers are usually interested in keeping costs low. (See the definition)
11. a. 60 men are hired at $120, while only 33 women are hired at $70.
12. c. Employers are paying men $120 to do what a woman could do for only slightly more than $70.
13. d. The wage will be $120 for both males and females.
14. c. The wage would fall to $100.

THE ECONOMIC WAY OF THINKING — MULTIPLE CHOICE

1. a. Services of more productive workers are worth more; undesirable jobs would pay more.
2. c. There would be excess supply of these workers' services.
3. d. These are some of the problems with mandated benefits.
4. c. They could earn more than the average wage by working in the private sector.
5. b. The exemption would increase employment of black teenagers.
6. c. See the discussion in the text.
7. c. True, although automation can harm *specific* individuals or groups.
8. c. The extension would encourage automation in the car wash industry.
9. d. Technological progress raises labor productivity which raises real wages.
10. b. Is that a "discouraging word?"
11. b. Only the most productive bricklayers would find employment at the high wage. (The increase in wages might also make people work harder.)
12. b. Training (human capital formation) is often acquired on the job.
13. b. Customers will be willing to pay higher prices to the discriminating firm.

CHAPTER 14

TRUE OR FALSE

The following are true: 1, 3, 5, 6, 7, 9, 12.

PROBLEMS AND PROJECTS

1. a. $2000(0.5066) = $1013.20 = value of broker A option
      $1000(0.6806) + $1000(0.4632) = $1143.80 = value of broker B option
   b. $1000(0.5674) + $1000(0.3220) = $889.40
   c. 14% = 12% + 2% inflationary premium
2. Price would have to exceed $1 per board foot. [$334/0.0334 = $10,000, so $334 now = $10,000 in 30 years = $1 per board foot for 10,000 board feet]
3. $12,502 + $11,158 + $9,968 + $8,904 = $42,532
4. a. $12,500
   b. $4,761,900
   c. $15,000
5. The present value of the cost of the course is $6,000 + 6($1,250) = $13,500. The present value of the income stream of $2,000 a year at an interest rate of 8% is $13,420 (from Exhibit 14–3 in the text), so you should *not* make this investment in your "human capital" for income reasons alone. If the course (or the skills it provides you with) is worth $81 or more in personal enjoyment, then you should take it.
6. a. 248.68; same
   b. Buy the new refrigerator; the present value of the electricity savings (486.84 × 1.5 = $730.26) plus the resale value ($51.32) = $781.58; this exceeds the $700 cost of the refrigerator.

LEARNING THE MECHANICS — MULTIPLE CHOICE

1. c. Constructing capital equipment uses resources that could produce consumption goods.
2. c. More resources would be used for present consumption leaving less for investment.
3. c. To offset the decline in the real value of a given nominal amount invested.
4. d. Net Present Value = $100/(1 + i)$.
5. a. Net Present Value = $100/(1.06) = $94.34.
6. c. "Pure" interest is yielded regardless of the risk premium.
7. c. NPV after 1 year = $100/(1 + i)$; NPV after two years = $100/(1 + i)^2$.
8. b. Discounting applies to *any* investment decision; do machines have feelings?
9. a. See the definition.
10. b. 4% plus 3%. (Exhibit 14–2)
11. b. With risk, the interest rate should be 9%, and $10,000/(1.09) = $9,174.
12. c. $9,900/(1.10) = $9,000.

THE ECONOMIC WAY OF THINKING — MULTIPLE CHOICE

1. b. A change in profit expectations will *shift* the demand for loanable funds out.
2. c. Interest could be paid in corn or fish or any other item of value.

3. c. Grasshoppers have high time preference; ants have low (remember the fable?).
4. d. A below-equilibrium interest rate means excess demand for loanable funds.
5. c. Dollar price falls so fixed dollar return yields a higher nominal *rate* of return.
6. b. Heavy investment raises the supply of cattle, reducing return to cattle ranching.
7. c. The owner could benefit from high risk premiums.
8. d. Bond prices fall so their fixed returns may yield higher nominal rates of return.
9. c. Current value of investments reflects current expectations of future profits.
10. a. See the discussion.
11. a. Luck, efficiency, and protection from competition can yield economic profit.
12. b. Guaranteed higher prices raise the value of crops produced on the farmland.
13. d. Higher interest rates mean heavier discounting; earlier retirement means shorter benefit period; higher high school graduate wage means smaller wage premium for college degree.

MICROCROSS

CHAPTER 15

TRUE OR FALSE

The following are true: 3, 5, 8, 9.

PROBLEMS AND PROJECTS

2. a. $7
   b. $8
   c. Employment will decrease by 200 and total income will fall by $900 from $4,900 to $4,000 per hour.
   d. $(200/1)/(15/200) = (-) 2.5$
3. a. Total labor cost: 6000, 8800, 12000, 15600
      Marginal labor cost: 24, 28, 32, 36
   c. 250; $19
   d. More, 300
4. a.   8   12
   b. 14   6
   c. 10   10
   d. 12   8
5. b.   1   −
   c.   3   +
   d.   2   −
   e.   3   +
   f.   1   −

LEARNING THE MECHANICS—MULTIPLE CHOICE

1. b. Making the demand for union labor relatively inelastic increasing union strength.
2. c. See the data in the text.
3. b. See the definition.
4. c. To the contrary, increased supplies in other areas might reduce other wages.
5. c. Higher product prices would cause layoffs; machines would replace lost jobs.
6. b. Just as MFC > resource price, so MR < product price.
7. c. See Exhibit 15–3.
8. c. See the definition.
9. c. These factors largely determine income. (A preview from the next chapter!)
10. a. Strikes can be extremely costly to employers.
11. c. The fifth worker produces and costs an extra $7.00/hour.
12. c. $44 minus $25 equals $19.
13. c. The seventh worker produces only an extra $5 and will not be hired.

THE ECONOMIC WAY OF THINKING—MULTIPLE CHOICE

1. d. A strike would be extremely costly to both.
2. b. Arc elasticity of demand = $(100,000/700,000)/1.00 = 0.14$

3. a. See the "Myth."
4. c. See the data in the text.
5. c. Management would be more likely to grant wage increases.
6. d. All would reduce the real wages of nonunion workers.
7. c. Both can raise both wage level and quantity employed.
8. a. The more inelastic the product demand, the more powerful the union.
9. b. A specific result of the general phenomenon of "economizing behavior."
10. b. Employers would favor higher wages that raise profits.
11. b. Monopoly power may successfully bargain with monopsony power.
12. d. Union membership has been declining; there is no evidence that unions raise the wages of all workers. (Exhibit 15–1)

CHAPTER 16

TRUE OR FALSE

The following are true: 1, 5, 7, 9, 10.

PROBLEMS AND PROJECTS

1. a. 200 hours
    b. 1143 hours
    c. 571 hours
    d. 667 hours
    g. Probably not; presumably, Jane could drop out of the transfer program if she wished.
2. Government subsidy: 3000, 2500, 2000, 1500, 1000, 500, 0
    Total income: 4000, 5000, 5500, 6000, 6500, 7000, 7500, 8000
3. a. Yes; society's tax burden is reduced by $58 each week that Reckman works.
    b. No, he will lose $18 a week by taking the job.
    c. Marginal tax rate = 109%
    d. Yes, his net income from the job would be greater than his net unemployment compensation.
4. a. Falling from the top
    b. 100   0   0
        0   100   0
        0   0   100
    c. 20   60   20
        20   60   20
        20   60   20
5. a. (3)8.7 62.5   100.0
        (4)4.6 55.4   100.0
        (5)7.4 58.3   100.0
    c. More; less; Lorenz Curves cross

LEARNING THE MECHANICS — MULTIPLE CHOICE

1. b. See Exhibit 16–1.
2. b. See Exhibit 16–4.

3. c. Some of the recipient's transfer income would be reduced.
4. a. See Exhibit 16–8.
5. a. See Exhibit 16–1.
6. a. See Exhibit 16–2.
7. b. Lifetime income inequality is overstated by annual income data.
8. d. See the discussion.
9. a. That's right, a "conservative."
10. d. See Applications in Economics.
11. c. Tax rate cuts did help high-income Americans.

THE ECONOMIC WAY OF THINKING—MULTIPLE CHOICE

1. d. Which equals the return the individual would have earned on employed resources.
2. a. We have created a system that actually makes it more difficult to escape poverty.
3. b. See Exhibit 16–4.
4. c. Annual incomes for the retired are less than their lifetime average; vice versa for prime-age earners.
5. c. The threshold income level is measured in "real" (inflation adjusted) terms.
6. a. See the discussion.
7. d. People generally prefer money to specific goods.
8. d. All three have been suggested as reasons for a negative income tax system.
9. a. See Exhibit 16–8.
10. b. Increased earnings usually mean decreased welfare benefits, often equally.
11. c. Income mobility and time are important in determining income inequality.

CHAPTER 17

TRUE OR FALSE

The following are true: 2, 3, 4, 7, 9, 10.

PROBLEMS AND PROJECTS

1. a. $1.30
   b. $1.38; 95 million gallons per day
   c. Long run
2. b. C   C
   c. D   C
   d. D   D
   e. C   D
3. a. 45, 60, 75, 90, 105
   b. Zero
   c. Profits will increase to $675; 0.47
   d. 40, 65, 90, 115
   e. $225; profits are lower in the long run; 1.00
4. a. $15; 45 MBD; no
   b. $30; 25 MBD; yes; 70 TBD
   c. $15; 45 MBD; no; 50 TBD
      (answers approximate)

LEARNING THE MECHANICS—MULTIPLE CHOICE

1. b. Changes in energy prices would not affect either quantity demanded or supplied.
2. c. In the long run, changes can be made more easily.
3. a. Marginal values are used, but opportunity costs *should* be used.
4. c. It takes time to adjust consumption; lengthy time period means inelastic short run.
5. a. See the data in the text.
6. c. See the definition and discussion in the text.
7. d. See Exhibit 17–2.
8. c. An economic response based on the principle of economizing behavior. (See Myths of Economics.)
9. c. As items become scarce, we use more alternatives.
10. b. See Myths of Economics.
11. b. The development of substitutes (energy saving technology) requires time.
12. d. See the definition.

THE ECONOMIC WAY OF THINKING—MULTIPLE CHOICE

1. b. Such profiteers may maximize short-run profits, but they are ignoring the long-run situation.
2. b. Social costs are very difficult to evaluate and incorporate into profit-maximizing behavior.
3. b. Natural resources should be used in their most valued use.
4. d. See the discussion.
5. c. The goal of the program is to reduce pollution efficiently, not to eliminate all pollution.
6. d. An EPA official stated that determining prices for the allotments "can best be done in the private sector."
7. a. The underlying principles are similar.
8. b. Polluters should decline to pay a higher allotment price.
9. c. There should be long-run gains, although short-run losses are certainly possible.
10. c. See the discussion.
11. a. Not discounting future benefits raises apparent net benefits.

CHAPTER 18

TRUE OR FALSE

The following are true: 1, 2, 4, 6, 7, 10, 13, 14

PROBLEMS AND PROJECTS

1. a. 80 cents, 100 per month
   b. 110, 130 (marginal social cost = producer's marginal cost + external cost)
   c. 90 per month
3. a. 2.0 cents per pound for the beet refiner and 6.0 cents per pound for the petroleum refiner.
   b. beet refiner: 80%; petroleum refiner: 45%
   c. See the discussion.

4. a. 14.00, 10.00, 8.00, 6.00, 4.00
    b. 2
    c. $5.00 – $3.00 = $2.00; $34.00
    d. 6; $71.00; $56.00
    e. yes; yes
    f. People have a strong incentive to become free-riders and enjoy external benefits (like a nice looking neighborhood) without paying part of the costs.
5. a. 48; 48; 96
    b. 60; at zero pollution, control costs exceed damage costs.
    c. 60; 30
    d. $40 per ton
    e. 36; 24
    f. rise; fall; rise

LEARNING THE MECHANICS—MULTIPLE CHOICE

1. c. There are significant external costs of production; both air and water pollution.
2. c. No net gains means no participation; sum of individual net gains = net social gain.
3. c. Property rights give owners incentives not otherwise likely.
4. c. This generates both noise and air pollution, which are external costs.
5. c. See the discussion.
6. a. External costs are external to (not included in) private price and output decisions.
7. a. Unsatisfied customers may not return.
8. b. Externalities are not part of the decisions of competitive decision makers.
9. b. Since they add significantly to the costs of producing pollution-intensive goods.
10. c. See the discussion.
11. a. The socially highest-valued use is also of the highest value to the individual.
12. b. A ban or no policy won't reach the target; discharge permits can reach the target but are more efficient if marketable.

THE ECONOMIC WAY OF THINKING—MULTIPLE CHOICE

1. b. What one individual does not catch (conserve), another most likely will.
2. b. The income distribution that results from the free market is not necessarily optimal.
3. d. Courts have given receptors property rights, but enforcement costs can be high.
4. b. This is an instance of the "free rider" problem.
5. d. Economizing behavior means acting only when benefits exceed costs at the margin.
6. b. Such information is easily available and subject to the free rider problem.
7. b. Overutilization is one of the problems associated with common property rights.
8. d. Monopolies restrict output, which can raise efficiency of the good has external costs, but the result depends on how much output falls. (Ch. 20 or *Economics* Ch. 34)
9. c. Only reductions costing less than the emission charge will be undertaken.
10. d. The firm may lose sales of *all* its various products, not just the new one.
11. a. At Q = 4000.
12. a. P = $3.00 includes private and external costs.
13. b. $1.20 plus the $1.80 marginal cost.
14. c. $3.00 minus $2.00

CHAPTER 19

TRUE OR FALSE

The following are true: 1, 2, 3, 4, 7, 8, 10, 11, 13.

PROBLEMS AND PROJECTS

1. a. 26/4, 20/18, 10/13.
   b. Proposal A will be attractive to the political entrepreneur. B will be unattractive. Proposal C will be attractive since the perceived benefit/cost ratio is $10/6 = 1.67$, and the voters would favor it.
   c. The costs of obtaining information about Proposal B might be higher than the benefits of the proposal for these voters.
3. (1) c; (2) e; (3) a; (4) b; (5) f; (6) d.
4. a. 120   70
        90   90
        60   110
        30   130
         0   150
   b. 30; 50; 0

LEARNING THE MECHANICS—MULTIPLE CHOICE

1. b. Public sector action may correct the inefficiency of the market.
2. c. If some persons benefit without paying, private demand is inefficiently low.
3. a. Legislators and voters are self-interested as well as socially-interested.
4. c. These persons are guided by self-interest as well as public interest.
5. d. Information costs may be worthwhile only if there are direct personal benefits.
6. d. These groups are less costly to organize and gain substantially from lobbying.
7. c. The collective process only imprecisely reflects individual preferences.
8. d. Government allocation can efficiently correct this market failure.
9. b. This minimizes vote loss and maximizes vote gain for the politician.
10. d. All three are generally agreed on.
11. b. In fact, savings due to extra efficiency may *reduce* the agency's budget.

THE ECONOMIC WAY OF THINKING—MULTIPLE CHOICE

1. a. Pursuit of gain is a strong motivator in both sectors, regardless of whether decision-makers admit it.
2. c. This is the rational ignorance effect.
3. a. There's no free lunch for society, but individuals may take a "free ride." (Ch. 4)
4. b. Private market demand for this enforcement is low due to free rider effects.
5. b. This is likely to maximize political entrepreneurs' votes.
6. d. This is consistent with maximum self-interest for the voter.
7. b. This is consistent with maximum self-interest for the voters.
8. d. This is consistent with vote maximization for the politician.
9. a. Voters perceive only benefits before election, maximizing politicians' chances.

10. c. Low organization costs would produce strong opposition from the other groups.
11. c. They stand to benefit directly from cost reductions; the others do not.
12. d. Each consumer benefits little while the others reap substantial individual benefits.
13. d. Auctioning permits removes rents, makes costs explicit and raises government revenue.
14. c. The present value of the expected benefits from smart moves is captured in stock prices.
15. a. See the discussion.

CHAPTER 20

TRUE OR FALSE

The following are true: 1, 3, 4, 6, 8, 12.

PROBLEMS AND PROJECTS

1. a. 2 units of clothing; 1 unit of clothing
   b. Mutual gains would result if Rhineland traded clothing for Nepal's food.
   c. 100 *additional* units are available to Rhineland; 50 *additional* units of clothing are available to Nepal; joint output has increased.
   d. 125 *additional* units of clothing are available to Rhineland; 75 *additional* units of clothing are available to Nepal; joint output has increased.
   e. 2/3 of a unit of food; 2/3 of a unit of food; no; no; additional gains are not possible because the opportunity costs of production have been equalized in the two countries.
2. a. 1110, 1170, 1240, 1310, 1380, 1450, 1520.
   b. $1800; 900
   c. $2200
   d. 1100
   e. 800
   f. 300
   g. price has decreased; I would be unhappy about receiving a lower price for my product; I would increase my quantity demanded.
3. a. $4000; 900
   b. $3000; 1300; 700; 600; 200
   c. $3500; 100; 200; 300
   d. rise to $3500; 100
   e. The only difference is that with a tariff the government gets the $500 per motorcycle, and with the quota the motorcycle importers receive the $500 difference (per imported motorcycle) between the import price of $3000 and the domestic motorcycle price of $3500.
4. a. US; US; SK; US
   b. South Korea
   c. +10   −50
      + 2   +30
      +16   −32
      −10   +50
      + 6   +18
5. a. $105 million; $67.5 million; $15 million; $22.5 million
   b. $105,000
   c. 25,000

LEARNING THE MECHANICS—MULTIPLE CHOICE

1. c. Having comparative advantage means being a low-opportunity-cost producer.
2. c. Foreign exports (our imports) provide foreign buying power for our exports.
3. b. Otherwise we should buy and store cheap imports.
4. c. Such a tariff protects them from foreign competition.
5. c. Buy goods abroad when they are cheaper than alternative domestic products.
6. b. 2 units of clothing must be sacrificed to obtain 4 units of food; 2/4 = 1/2.
7. b. Slavia's opportunity cost of food = 5/3 clothing > 1/2 = Italia's opportunity cost.
8. c. Each country should export its low-opportunity-cost product.
9. a. Iowa exports corn both to the other states and to the rest of the world.
10. b. To help them "mature" (become efficient) in the long run.
11. c. Both *a* and *b* are opposite the correct statements.
12. d. Total consumption increases and less wine is consumed in order to trade it for more bread.

THE ECONOMIC WAY OF THINKING—MULTIPLE CHOICE

1. a. Increased competition lowers price; increased foreign sales raise their incomes.
2. d. Reduced foreign competition from the tariff benefits workers in the industry.
3. c. Increased price of foreign watches causes increased demand for domestic watches.
4. c. Consumers gain through low prices; producers at worst do not lose.
5. b. Arguments for restrictions usually appeal (wrongly?) to the "national interest."
6. c. Foreign competition lowers price which lowers domestic quantity supplied.
7. b. Special interest groups have a disproportionate influence on politicians.
8. a. Try, for example, to trace increased farm employment to reduced auto tariffs.
9. c. This is the *basic* lesson of comparative advantage.
10. b. Foreign demand raises price which increases domestic quantity supplied.
11. b. World equilibrium is at P = $20.
12. b. The U.S. tariff will have a small but measurable effect on the world market. (Exhibit 10)
13. c. The tariff creates deadweight loss. (See Exhibit 10)
14. b. The amount needed to get the same result as #12 above.

CHAPTER 21

TRUE OR FALSE

The following are true: 1, 2, 8, 10, 11.

PROBLEMS AND PROJECTS

1. (1). d; (2) a; (3) e; (4) b; (5) f; (6) c.
2. b. 0, –, depreciate
   c. –, +, appreciate
   d. +, –, depreciate
   e. –, +, appreciate
   f. +, +, indeterminate
   g. 0, 0, no change

3. a. (1) –25.3; (2) 36.1; (3) 3.7; (4) 4.5; (5) 8.2
   b. See the discussion.

LEARNING THE MECHANICS—MULTIPLE CHOICE

1. a. Residents usually want payment in their own national currency.
2. b. Cheaper foreign currency means cheaper foreign goods and services.
3. d. The statement includes *all* the international economic transactions.
4. b. Excess sales mean excess receipts (a surplus) of payments.
5. a. More exports mean greater demand for a nation's currency causing *appreciation*.
6. a. An increase in supply (of *anything*) tends to decrease price (cause depreciation).
7. c. With fixed exchange rates, domestic monetary policies would be swamped by the larger country's policies.
8. c. Foreign ability to buy from us depends (partly) on the amount we buy from them.
9. b. High prices promote imports; low interest rates promote financial asset exports.
10. d. This creates a foreign (South American) demand for U.S. currency (to be loaned).
11. b. Depreciation makes foreign goods more expensive and domestic goods cheaper.
12. c. See the definition.
13. d. The exchange rate depreciation more than offsets the effect on imports of any increase in GDP.

THE ECONOMIC WAY OF THINKING—MULTIPLE CHOICE

1. b. Increased sales increase U.S. receipts and reduce the deficit.
2. c. Unilateral transfers abroad decrease; exports decrease but by a lesser amount.
3. a. U.S. receives more goods to consume and gives up only pieces of paper.
4. c. Increased imports mean increased payments to foreigners.
5. a. Higher real interest rates promote financial asset exports.
6. c. Dollars are spent to acquire the pesos to buy the mine.
7. b. Higher prices raise demand for foreign exchange (imports) and lower supply (exports).
8. b. With fixed exchanges rates and currency convertibility, domestic monetary policy is swamped.
9. c. See the definitions.
10. b. It raises dollar price of foreign currency, raising dollar price of foreign goods.
11. c. It is making excess payments on current account transactions.
12. a. Inelastic means *quantities* imported and exported respond little to price changes.
13. c. Higher prices and output cause depreciation, while higher interest rates cause appreciation, but all induce a deficit in the current account.
14. d. The deficit in the capital account exceeds the surplus in the current account, thereby draining official reserves.
15. d. The lower rate will cause a capital outflow, depreciating the currency and causing a current account surplus.

CHAPTER 22

TRUE OR FALSE

The following are true: 1, 2, 4, 5, 6, 8, 9, 11.

PROBLEMS AND PROJECTS

1. a. (2)
    b. (3)
    c. (1)
    d. (4)
2. a. &200
    b. $400; difference = $5930
    c. &299.5 billion; 326.2 million; &918.15.
    d. $13,976.64.
    e. $1,836.30; $12,140.34; even though Gromangro grew at a faster rate than the U.S., the amount that its per capita GDP was lagging behind that of the U.S. more than doubled.
4. a. 35; 20; 10
    b. 38.9; 16.3; 13.7; 10.4; 16.3; 48.8
    c.
3.1	6.0	5.6
38.9	13.7	16.3
22.6	11.7	12.5

LEARNING THE MECHANICS—MULTIPLE CHOICE

1. a. It uses readily available data.
2. a. This is the definition of the purchasing power parity method.
3. c. It attempts to measure the actual consumption bundles available.
4. b. Technology is important, but other factors are even more vital.
5. a. See the definition in the text.
6. b. High tariffs usually hurt specialization and exchange.
7. d. Improving price stability and trade seems to work well.
8. c. The negative interest rate causes capital flight.
9. c. See Problems and Projects, Exhibit 1.
10. c. See the discussion in the text.

THE ECONOMIC WAY OF THINKING—MULTIPLE CHOICE

1. c. U.S. per capita GDP is 26 times the per capita GDP of Egypt.
2. b. % per capita GDP growth = % GDP growth – % population growth.
3. d. There is a wide variety of growth experiences *within* each of these groups.
4. b. The influence of population change is precisely what is meant by *per capita*.
5. b. All the others are much more "absurd."
6. b. 6000 pounds × $3 per pound = $18,000 > $16,000.
7. a. $[(45,588.5/256.9)/78.5]/(3957.0/239.3) = 2,261/16,536 = 13.7\%$
8. d. GDP in Mexico has fallen from 5 to 4.5 percent of U.S. GDP; GDP per capita in Mexico has fallen from 19 percent to 14 percent of U.S. GDP per capita.
9. b. Low investment caused by such instability is a main obstacle to growth.
10. a. Rabushka feels that the improved incentives will outweigh any reduced spending.

CHAPTER 23

TRUE OR FALSE

The following are true: 1, 4, 5, 7, 9, 10, 12

PROBLEMS AND PROJECTS

1. a-4, b-1, c-2, d-8, e-7, f-3, g-5
3. a-4, b-6, c-5, d-3, e-1, f-2

LEARNING THE MECHANICS — MULTIPLE CHOICE

1. c. Central planning is the key to socialist business decisions.
2. d. Private property rights do not have to exist in a socialist or communist state.
3. c. See the definition in the text.
4. c. Under socialism, workers own the rights to the fruits of their labor.
5. d. It would be quite difficult for any transition to decrease the already-low rate of unemployment in a socialist nation.
6. b. See the boxed feature.
7. d. All of the other answers have obvious flaws in them.
8. d. Central planning left behind many "too-large" enterprises.
9. b. Only if the optimization of pounds of bread optimization also optimizes loaves of bread would we expect the average size to remain unchanged.
10. b. Proper central planning requires huge amounts of information.
11. c. Workers would be likely to vote to increase their own wages at the expense of dividends.

THE ECONOMIC WAY OF THINKING — MULTIPLE CHOICE

1. c. Market forces are unimportant in a socialist labor market.
2. a. Answers *b* and *c* omit issues of marginal cost, etc.
3. a. Allowing entry is a fairly quick way to foster competition.
4. a. The high black market price signals a shortage at the government price but says little about quality.
5. c. Both *a* and *b* are true.
6. d. The shortage will cause all three of these effects.
7. c. See the section on unemployment in transitional economies.
8. b. The main impact of the overhang is in the short run.
9. a. As tempting as a miracle is, cutting subsidies is key.
10. d. See the section in the text on the Czech transition.
11. c. The creation of the credit vouchers had some value.